Good Housekeeping

STEP-BY-STEP
COOK BOOK

OVER 650 EASY-TO-FOLLOW TECHNIQUES
AND 400 TRIPLE-TESTED RECIPES

Good Housekeeping

STEP-BY-STEP COOK BOOK

OVER 650 EASY-TO-FOLLOW TECHNIQUES AND 400 TRIPLE-TESTED RECIPES

First published in the United Kingdom in 2007
This edition first published in the United Kingdom in 2012 by
Collins & Brown
10 Southcombe Street
London W14 0RA

An imprint of Anova Books Company Ltd

The Good Housekeeping website is
www.allaboutyou.com/goodhousekeeping

ISBN 978-1-90844-932-0

A catalogue record for this book is available from the
British Library.

Reproduction by by Dot Gradations Ltd, UK
Printed and bound by Everbest Printing Ltd, China

This book can be ordered direct from the publisher. Contact the
marketing department, but try your bookshop first.

www.anovabooks.com

DIETARY GUIDELINES

- Note that certain recipes contain raw or lightly
  cooked eggs. The young, elderly, pregnant women and
  anyone with immune-deficiency disease should avoid
  these because of the slight risk of salmonella.
- Note that some recipes contain alcohol. Check the
  ingredient list before serving to children.

NOTES

- Both metric and imperial measures are given for the
  recipes. Follow either set of measures, not a mixture
  of both, as they are not interchangeable.

- All spoon measures are level.
  1 tsp = 5ml spoon; 1 tbsp = 15ml spoon.

- Ovens and grills must be preheated to the specified
  temperature.

- Use sea salt and freshly ground black pepper unless
  otherwise suggested.

- Fresh herbs should be used unless dried herbs are
  specified in a recipe.

- Medium eggs should be used except where otherwise
  specified. Free-range eggs are recommended.

- Note that some recipes contain raw or lightly cooked
  eggs. The young, elderly, pregnant women and anyone
  with an immune-deficiency disease should avoid these
  because of the slight risk of salmonella.

Photographers: Steve Baxter (page 280); Martin Brigdale (page
262); Nicki Dowey (pages 19B, 20, 42-43, 45, 48, 67, 70-71, 76-77,
94, 96-100, 103-105, 107-108, 128-130, 135-136, 138-139, 164, 169,
174-177, 179, 203-206, 209-211-213, 233, 235-237, 239-240, 243,
255-260, 263, 265, 274, 276-278, 282-285, 295, 297-298, 300, 302,
306, 320-326, 328,347B, 354, 357-358, 360, 374-380, 382, 384-386,
388-391, 399-402, 404-409 and 425-433); Will Heap (page 281);
Fiona Kennedy (pages 49, 66, 69, 95, 362 and 387);
William Lingwood (page 109); Diana Miller (page 424);
Craig Robertson (pages 10-15, 18, 21-33, 36-41, 54-63, 80-93,
114-117, 120-125, 133, 144-157, 160-161, 166, 182-194,196-201,
216-231, 246-253, 270-273, 288-293, 301, 305, 310-319, 332-339,
343-346, 347T, 348-351, 366-371, 394-398, 403, 412-423, 436-438,
440-441 and 444-449); Lucinda Symons (pages 19T, 44, 46-47,
50-51, 64-65, 72-75, 102, 106, 112-113, 126-127, 131-132, 134, 137,
142, 158-159, 162, 165, 167-168, 170-173, 178, 195, 202, 207-208,
210, 232, 234, 238, 241-242,254, 261, 264, 266-267, 275, 279, 294,
296, 299, 303-304, 307, 327, 340-341, 352, 355-356, 361, 363,
372-373, 381 and 383); Kate Whitaker (page 359).

Home Economists: Joanna Farrow, Emma Jane Frost,
Teresa Goldfinch, Alice Hart, Lucy McKelvie, Kim Morphew,
Aya Nishimura, Bridget Sargeson, Stella Sargeson, Kate Trend and
Mari Mererid Williams.
Stylists: Tamzin Ferdinando, Wei Tang, Helen Trent and Fanny Ward.

CONTENTS

FOREWORD

I believe that anyone who loves to cook can attribute their fascination with food to an instrumental figure – usually familial or celebrity. For me, as for many, it is my dear mother. She nurtured the culinary spark in me from a young age, which, with her encouragement, grew into a full-blown flame by my teens. She was the one who ate my rock-like cakes and under-cooked breads, never directly pointing out my mistakes but rather filling my measuring cup with confidence, so to speak. It was this confidence that has helped me immeasurably in the kitchen. Time and time again, people are afraid to enter the kitchen because they're worried they might make a mistake, but it's only by trying, practising and being brave that you learn to be a better cook.

What I didn't realise at that tender age was that my mother's inspiration was not a person, but rather an institute – the Good Housekeeping Institute. She received a Good Housekeeping cookery book when she married and it has been at her side ever since – along with many new editions. I'm sure this scenario rings true for many, as the GHI was founded in 1924 and has been inspiring people to cook ever since. And still to this day, every single recipe has been triple-tested to rigorous standards, which is our guarantee to you that they will work first time round.

I hope this book stays by your side for years to come and that it gives you many happy and confident hours in the kitchen.

Meike.

Meike Beck
Cookery Editor
Good Housekeeping

BASIC EQUIPMENT AND UTENSILS

Chopping boards

These kitchen essentials come in two materials: wood and some type of plastic (usually polypropylene).

Having a range of sizes will give you more chopping options, with small boards for chopping or slicing small quantities. For most people, three boards should suffice, in sizes of: 15–23cm (6–9in), 20.5–30.5cm (8–12in) and 25.5–35.5cm (10–14in).

Wood Wooden boards are best made from a single plank of wood rather than several pieces glued together, as the joins may harbour bacteria. Some modern wooden boards nowadays are dishwasher-safe, although many of them are not. You should try to check beforehand if this is important to you.

Polypropylene These boards can be bought in colour-coded sets so that you can have separate boards for meat, fish, and fruit and vegetables. They are suitable for washing in the dishwasher.

Knives

Good knives are essential and there are three cardinal rules to follow when buying knives.
- Buy knives singly, rather than in a set: the different sizes chosen to represent one manufacturer's knife set might not suit you.
- Try them out before buying – you need to hold the knife to see if it feels comfortable and balanced in your hand.
- Don't try to save money: knives are an investment, and good blades never come cheap.

At the very minimum, there are five basic types of knife, which will set you up you for most tasks:
- A small paring knife.
- A carving knife suitable for filleting, slicing and boning.
- A large 'cook's' knife for general chopping and slicing.
- A bread knife with serrated edge.
- A utility knife.

> ### SHARP BLADES
>
> Keep your knives sharp or they will be difficult – and probably dangerous – to use. There are several types of sharpener available: the traditional steel or whetstone is adequate for most home cooks, but the best ones have a diamond coating that is particularly hard-wearing. Remember that, as a general rule to go by, it is best to sharpen knives little but often.

Scales

Accurate measurement is essential when following most recipes, particularly baking. Usually used to measure dry ingredients, the most accurate scale is the electronic type, capable of weighing up to 2kg (4½lb) or 5kg (11lb) in increments of 1–5g. Buy one with a flat platform on which you can put your own bowl or measuring jug and always remember to set the scale to zero before adding the ingredients.

Measuring jugs

These can be plastic or glass, and are available in sizes ranging from 500ml (18fl oz) to 2 litres (3½ pints), or even 3 litres (5¼ pints). Have two – a large one and a small one – marked with both metric and imperial.

Measuring cups

Commonly used in the US, these are used for measuring both liquid and dry ingredients. Cups are bought in sets of ¼, ⅓, ½ and 1 cups. A standard 1 cup measure is equivalent to about 250ml (9fl oz).

Measuring spoons

Useful for the smallest units, accurate spoon measurements go up to 15ml (1 tbsp). These may be in plastic or metal, and often come in sets attached together on a ring.

Mixing bowls

For small quantities, the bowls you use for soup, cereals and so on will suffice. However, when mixing larger quantities, such as cake or bread mixtures, you will need at least two large bowls, including one very large one with a diameter of up to 38cm (15in).

Stainless steel bowls work best when you are using a hand whisk, or when you need to place the bowl into a larger bowl filled with iced water for chilling down or to place it over simmering water.

Plastic or glass bowls are best if you need to use them in the microwave.

EASY SLICING

→ A mandolin offers the easiest way of making uniform, thin slices or shreds (see page 194). French metal ones are the best but also pricey.
→ Smaller mandolins, which usually have a plastic frame holding the blades, are less versatile but also cheaper.
→ A mezzaluna – a curved board and knife – is good for chopping herbs.

Steel bowls with a rubber foot will keep their grip on the worksurface.

Bowls with gently tapered sides – much wider at the rim than at the base – will be useful for mixing dough and can also be used as salad bowls.

Spoons

For general mixing, the cheap and sturdy wooden spoon still can't be beaten, but equivalents made from thermoplastic materials are heatproof and may suit you better. The spoon should be stiff, so that it can cope with thick foods such as polenta and dough.

A large metal spoon for folding ingredients together and a slotted spoon for skimming and lifting ingredients out of liquids are also invaluable items to have.

Spatulas

You should have at least three: one metal for use in ordinary pans and one acrylic (to withstand high temperatures), and one suitable for non-stick pans.

Metal spatulas should be sturdy enough to lift heavy foods, such as a joint that you are browning before braising it.

Tongs

Most cooks will recommend that you buy at least one pair of tongs. You are bound to find them invaluable and, if this is your first ever pair, you will wonder how you managed without them in the kitchen up until now.

The all-metal ones with scalloped edges on the gripping heads are particularly good. They can be used for lifting food in and out of pans and for turning – which is especially useful for frying because spitting fat can be very dangerous.

OTHER EXTRAS

- Fine sieve
- Colander
- Steamer
- Bulb baster (metal is best)
- Apple corer
- Vegetable peeler
- Wire whisks
- Pastry brush
- Rolling pin
- Graters: fine and coarse
- Poultry shears (or sturdy kitchen scissors)
- Digital instant-read thermometer

POTS, PANS AND BAKEWARE

There is a huge variety of cooking vessels available, made from different materials. The main choices are:
- Stainless steel (with an inner core of another metal to improve heat conduction).
- Cast iron (plain or enamelled).
- Aluminium (usually anodised for stick-resistance and lower reactivity with food).

Frying pans

The most practical choices are aluminium or stainless steel with a non-stick coating. A range of sizes is useful: 20.5cm (8in), 24–25.5cm (9½–10in) and 30cm (11½in).

Look for pans with a thick base, for even and efficient heating. Non-stick coatings reduce oil and fat usage, but must be used with non-metal utensils to prevent scratches, and shouldn't be allowed to get very hot when empty.

Cast-iron pans

These may be enamelled or plain. Although heavy, they are favoured for their slow, steady conduction of heat – and some can be used in the oven.

Sauté pans

Consider buying one of these; its straight sides make it better than a frying pan for braising on the hob.

Pans

For most purposes, especially for general all-purpose pans and stockpots, stainless steel is best. You need at least three sizes of pan: small (about 16cm/6¼in in diameter), medium (about 24cm/9½in in diameter), and one large pan for making stock and pasta. Non-stick properties are generally less important in pans, but can be useful when making sauces or egg-based dishes. Anodised aluminium, which is stick-resistant, is another good choice for smaller pans.

Pressure cookers

A pressure cooker cooks more quickly than an ordinary saucepan and is useful for making stock, cooking root vegetables and pulses and tenderising tough cuts of meat. They have manual and automatic lid-lock systems to prevent steam escaping from the pan, so the water boils at a higher temperature, reducing cooking time.

Stainless-steel pressure cookers are the most expensive, but they are hard-wearing. Aluminium cookers are cheaper, but they can discolour and are not dishwasher safe. Both sorts can be used on all types of hob, but not on induction, unless they have a special magnetic base. Hi-dome pressure cookers tend to be aluminium and their extra height makes them especially suitable for making jams and pickles.

Casseroles

Cast iron is the material of choice for a flameproof casserole. It conducts heat slowly and steadily, and its thick walls and bases protect the food from high oven heat.

These casseroles are enamelled and must be treated with care. Although expensive, if treated well, they will last for decades. It's worth having at least two, one for small dishes and one larger one. The oval-shaped dishes are best for larger casseroles.

Bakeware

As well as being thin enough to conduct heat quickly and efficiently, bakeware should be sturdy enough not to warp. Most bakeware is made from aluminium, and it may have enamel or non-stick coatings.

Roasting tins Enamelled steel is excellent, and many have non-stick coatings, which make cleaning easier. It's worth having several sizes:

- A small one for just a few pieces of meat or vegetables.
- A medium-size tin for chickens and small joints.
- A very large one for turkeys or cooking for a crowd.

Baking trays Shallower than a roasting tin, these are good for cooking potatoes and vegetables that don't produce a lot of liquid during cooking.

Cake tins Available in many shapes and sizes, tins may be single-piece, loose-based or springform.

Loaf tins Available in various sizes, but one of the most useful is probably a 900g (2lb) tin.

Pie tins and muffin tins You should have both single-piece tins and loose-based tins for flans and pies.

Baking dishes Usually ceramic or Pyrex, you should have them in several sizes, ranging from 15–23cm (6–9in) to 25.5–35.5cm (10–14in).

SILICONE

A newer material for muffin pans and other bakeware is flexible, oven-safe silicone. It is safe to touch straight from the oven, is inherently non-stick and is also flexible – making it a lot easier to remove muffins and other bakes from their pans than it used to be.

ELECTRICAL EQUIPMENT

For quick preparation, a food processor is extremely useful. When it comes to all electrical kitchen appliances, however, the amount of space you have is a consideration.

Food processor For certain tasks, such as making breadcrumbs or pastry or for chopping large quantities of onions or nuts, food processors are unbeatable. Most come with a number of attachments – dough hooks, graters, slicers – which are well worth having even if only for occasional use.

Blenders These are less versatile than food processors, but unmatched for certain tasks, such as puréeing fruit, vegetables and soups, and for making smoothies.

The traditional jug blender is great but some cooks prefer a 'stick' blender, which can be used directly in a pan, bowl or jug.

Freestanding mixers Some cooks don't see the need for electric mixers whereas others swear by them. They may well be a good investment if you do a lot of baking, but decide first whether you have space in your kitchen. They take up a lot, and are big and heavy to store until needed

Electric hand mixers Useful for creaming together butter and sugar in baking and for making meringues. They don't take up a lot of space and can be packed away easily.

Bread machines Kneading bread by hand takes very little time and effort but bread machines are useful for making and baking bread if you have limited time. Doughs can also be prepared by the machine and then shaped and baked in the oven.

Ice cream makers Even if you make ice cream only a few times a year, a good machine will save lots of time and produce better results. The type with two freezing tubs enables you to make two flavours at once, or a larger quantity of a single flavour.

Microwave ovens One of the most useful innovations in cooking, but also one of the most under-utilised, a microwave oven can be used for thawing, reheating and cooking. There are various types of oven available, all with different power levels. Generally speaking, the higher the wattage the faster the oven will work, but the internal dimensions also affect the speed of energy transfer. Use manufacturers guidelines, but the best way to learn how to use your oven is through your experience.

Slow cookers Ideal for cook-ahead meals – put the recipe ingredients in it in the morning and a hot meal will be waiting in the evening. Cheaper cuts of meat will benefit from the long, slow cooking, while the lower temperatures minimise the risk of scorching foods in the bottom of the pan, which might otherwise happen in the oven. Available in various shapes and sizes.

SAUCES, DRESSINGS AND ACCOMPANIMENTS

The addition of rich gravies and sauces can transform both savoury and sweet dishes – from the simplest drizzle of balsamic dressing over a salad, a spoonful of refreshing salsa served with grilled fish or chicken, a dollop of creamy mayonnaise for dunking chips into or fresh pesto tossed with pasta, to lashings of custard poured over fruit pies or crumbles or a swirl of raspberry coulis or chocolate sauce with ice cream. This chapter is packed with recipes and easy-to-follow techniques for all the classic sauces and accompaniments you will ever want to make. There's essential advice plus variations and troubleshooting tips on saving a split or curdled sauce, and handy hints on freezing and ideas for creating stunning decorative effects for special meals.

SAVOURY SAUCES

Sauces and gravies add the finishing touch to many dishes, adding moisture to roast meats or a smooth texture and contrasting flavour that complements grilled meats, fish and vegetables.

White wine gravy

Perfect served with roast chicken.

To serve eight, you will need 4 tbsp plain flour, 500ml (18fl oz) chicken stock, 150ml (¼ pint) dry white wine, 2 tbsp redcurrant jelly, salt and ground black pepper.

1 When the chicken is cooked, skim the fat from the juices in the roasting tin. In a bowl, mix 3 tbsp of the juices with the flour to make a paste.

2 Pour the chicken stock, white wine and redcurrant jelly into the roasting tin and scrape the residue from the base of the tin using a wooden spoon.

3 Return the roasting tin to the heat and whisk in the flour mixture. Simmer gently for 5–10 minutes, then season to taste with salt and pepper and pour into a jug to serve.

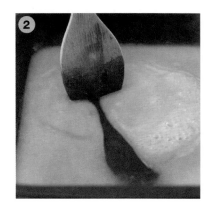

Rich red wine gravy

This rich gravy goes well with roasted chicken or meat such as beef.

To serve eight, you will need 4 tbsp plain flour, 300ml (½ pint) red wine, 1.1 litres (2 pints) chicken or beef stock, salt and ground black pepper.

1 When the roast is cooked, strain the juices from the roasting tin into a bowl and skim off any fat, reserving 3 tbsp of the fat.

2 Return the fat to the tin and whisk in the flour. Cook over a medium heat until the flour browns. Remove from the heat, stir in wine or port until smooth. Bubble for 2–3 minutes.

3 Stir in the chicken or meat juices and the stock, then bubble for 10–15 minutes until reduced by half and the gravy is smooth. Skim off any fat and season with salt and pepper.

Cheat's mint jelly

This is an ingenious short cut to the classic accompaniment for roast lamb.

To serve eight, you will need, 3 gelatine sheets, 200ml (7fl oz) clear apple juice, 1 tbsp white wine vinegar, 1 tsp dried mint.

1 Put the gelatine sheets in a bowl, cover with cold water and leave to soak for 5 minutes.

2 Meanwhile, line a small loaf tin or serving dish with clingfilm, then lightly grease the clingfilm with oil. Pour the apple juice into a small pan, then add the wine vinegar and dried mint.

3 Lift out the gelatine (discard the soaking water), add to the pan and heat gently until the gelatine dissolves. Pour the mixture into the prepared tin or dish and leave to cool completely, then chill until set.

4 To serve, invert on to a small board or plate and remove the tin or dish and clingfilm. Cut into squares and serve.

Special mint jelly

To serve eight, you will need zest and juice of 1 large orange, 20g (¾oz) freshly chopped mint, 450g (1lb) redcurrant jelly, 4 tbsp balsamic vinegar.

1 Put the orange zest and juice into a pan. Add half the mint and the redcurrant jelly and vinegar. Cook over a low heat for 5 minutes until smooth. Strain into a serving bowl and stir in the remaining mint.

VARIATIONS

Simple mint sauce
Finely chop 20g (¾oz) fresh mint and mix with 1 tbsp each olive oil and white wine vinegar.

Mint sauce

To serve eight, you will need 1 small bunch of mint, stalks removed, 1–2 tsp golden caster sugar, to taste, 1–2 tbsp wine vinegar, to taste.

1 Finely chop the mint leaves and put into a bowl with the sugar. Stir in 1 tbsp boiling water and put to one side for about 5 minutes to dissolve the sugar.

2 Add the wine vinegar to taste. Leave to stand for about 1 hour before serving.

Cumberland sauce

To serve eight, you will need the finely pared zest and juice of 1 orange, finely pared zest and juice of 1 lemon, 4 tbsp redcurrant jelly, 1 tsp Dijon mustard, 4 tbsp port, pinch of ground ginger (optional), salt and ground black pepper.

1 Cut the citrus zests into fine julienne strips and put into a small pan. Add cold water to cover and simmer for 5 minutes, then drain.

2 Put the orange and lemon juices, citrus zests, redcurrant jelly and mustard into a pan and heat gently, stirring, until the sugar has dissolved. Leave to simmer for 5 minutes, then add the port.

3 Leave to cool. Season with salt and pepper to taste and add a little ginger if you like.

Anchovy sauce

For 300ml (½ pint) sauce, you will need 15g (½ oz) butter, 15g (½ oz) flour, 150ml (¼ pint) milk, 150ml (¼ pint) fish stock, 1-2 tsp anchovy essence, a squeeze of lemon juice, red food colouring (optional), salt and ground black pepper.

1 Melt the butter in a pan, stir in the flour and cook gently for 1 minute, stirring.

2 Remove the pan from the heat and gradually stir in the milk and fish stock. Bring to the boil slowly and continue cooking, stirring all the time, until the sauce comes to the boil and thickens.

3 Simmer very gently for a further 2–3 minutes. Stir in anchovy essence to taste, the lemon juice and a few drops of red food colouring to tint it a pale pink, if you like. Season with salt and pepper.

COOK'S TIP

Serve hot with plaice, brill or turbot.

Bread sauce

To serve eight, you will need
1 quartered onion, 4 cloves, 2 bay
leaves, 450ml (¾ pint) milk, 175g (6oz)
fresh breadcrumbs, 50g (2oz) butter,
200ml (7fl oz) crème fraîche, salt and
ground black pepper.

1 Stud each onion quarter with a
clove, then put in a pan with 1 bay leaf
and the milk. Gently heat on the
lowest setting for 15 minutes.

2 Remove the pan from the heat and
discard the onion quarters, cloves and
bay leaf.

3 Stir the breadcrumbs, butter and
crème fraîche into the milk. Season
with salt and black pepper. Sprinkle
with grated nutmeg, drizzle with oil
and serve. Alternatively, store in the
fridge for up to two days.

Béchamel sauce

For 300ml (½ pint) sauce, you
will need 1 slice of onion, 6 black
peppercorns, 1 bay leaf, 1 blade of
mace, 300ml (½ pint) semi-skimmed
milk, 15g (½oz) butter, 15g (½oz) plain
flour, a pinch of freshly grated nutmeg,
salt and ground black pepper.

1 Put the onion, peppercorns, bay
leaf, mace and milk in a pan. Bring
almost to the boil, then remove from
the heat, cover and leave to infuse for
20 minutes. Strain.

2 Melt the butter in a pan over a low
heat. Add the flour and cook, stirring,
for 1 minute; do not colour.

3 Remove from the heat and slowly
pour in the milk, whisking. Season with
salt, pepper and nutmeg.

4 Return to the heat and cook,
stirring, until the sauce is thickened
and smooth. Simmer for 12 minutes.

VARIATIONS

- **Simple white sauce**
  Omit the seasonings except
  salt and pepper.
- **Thick binding sauce**
  Increase the butter and
  flour to 25g (1oz) each.
- **Cheese sauce** Stir in 50g
  (2oz) grated Cheddar or
  Gruyère cheese and a pinch
  of powdered mustard.
- **Parsley sauce** Stir in 2 tbsp
  finely chopped parsley.
- **Onion sauce** At step 4,
  stir in a large, finely diced,
  sautéed onion.

Hollandaise sauce

To serve six, you will need 4 tbsp white wine vinegar, a blade of mace, 1 slice of onion, 1 bay leaf, 6 black peppercorns, 3 medium egg yolks, 150g (5oz) unsalted butter, a little lemon juice, salt and white pepper.

1 Put the vinegar, mace, onion, bay leaf and peppercorns in a pan. Bring to the boil and reduce to 1 tbsp. Cut the butter into ten pieces.

2 Put the egg yolks in a heatproof bowl with one piece of butter and a pinch of salt. Beat, then strain in the vinegar mixture. Place over a pan of hot water, making sure it doesn't touch the water. Whisk for 3 minutes until pale and starting to thicken.

3 Add a piece of butter and beat until absorbed. Repeat with the remaining pieces of butter. Season and add lemon juice to taste. Serve.

PERFECT RESULTS

- → Make sure the sauce doesn't get too hot during cooking; if in doubt, dip the base of the bowl in very cold water for a couple of seconds.
- → Beat in each piece of butter completely before adding the next.
- → If the sauce begins to curdle, add an ice cube, then beat the sauce again.

Béarnaise sauce

To serve four to six, you will need 4 tbsp white wine vinegar, 2 finely chopped shallots, a few sprigs of fresh tarragon, 6 black peppercorns, 2 medium egg yolks, 75g (3oz) unsalted butter at room temperature, 2 tsp freshly chopped parsley or chervil (optional), salt and ground white pepper.

1 Put the vinegar, shallots, tarragon and peppercorns in a pan. Bring to the boil and reduce to 1 tbsp.

2 Cut the butter into ten pieces. Put the egg yolks in a heatproof bowl with one piece of butter and a pinch of salt. Beat, then strain in the vinegar. Place over a pan of hot water. Whisk for 3–4 minutes until pale and starting to thicken.

3 Add a piece of butter and beat in until completely absorbed. Repeat with the remaining butter. Season with salt and pepper to taste. Stir in the chopped herbs, if using. Serve.

Simple tomato sauce

To serve eight, you will need 2 chopped Spanish onions, 4 tbsp olive oil, 2 crushed garlic cloves, 2 × 400g cans chopped plum tomatoes, 2 tbsp torn basil leaves, salt and ground black pepper.

1 Gently fry the onions in the oil for 10 minutes. Add the garlic and cook for a further 10 minutes, stirring occasionally, until very soft.

2 Add the tomatoes and season. Bring to the boil, reduce the heat and simmer gently for 30 minutes or until the sauce is thick and pulpy. Add the basil and check the seasoning.

Pesto

Use on pasta or in salad dressings, mixed into crème fraîche for dips, or spread on toasted ciabatta and topped with cheese and tomato.

To serve four, you will need 50g (2oz) roughly torn fresh basil leaves, 1–2 garlic cloves, 25g (1oz) pinenuts, 6 tbsp extra-virgin olive oil, 2 tbsp freshly grated Parmesan, salt and ground black pepper, lemon juice to taste (optional).

1 Put the basil leaves in a food processor with the garlic, pinenuts and 2 tbsp olive oil. Process to a fairly smooth paste.

2 Gradually add the remaining oil and season with salt and pepper.

3 Transfer to a bowl and stir in the Parmesan. Check the seasoning and add a squeeze of lemon juice if you like. Store in the fridge for up to three days, cover with a thin layer of olive oil and seal tightly.

VARIATIONS

- **Coriander pesto** Use fresh coriander instead of basil and add 1 seeded, finely chopped chilli with the garlic. Omit the Parmesan cheese.
- **Rocket pesto** Replace the basil with rocket leaves and add 1 tbsp freshly chopped parsley.
- **Sun-dried tomato pesto** Replace half the basil with 50g (2oz) sun-dried tomatoes, drained of oil and roughly chopped. Blend.

FRUIT SAUCES

Tart fruit sauces complement meat well. They are traditionally served with poultry, game and fatty meats such as pork, duck and goose, which are suited to the astringency of fruit sauces.

Cranberry sauce

To serve eight, you will need 225g (8oz) fresh cranberries, grated zest and juice of 1 orange, 4 tbsp fine-shred marmalade, 125g (4oz) light muscovado sugar, 50ml (2fl oz) port.

1 Put all the ingredients in a pan.

2 Bring to the boil, reduce the heat and simmer for 5–10 minutes, stirring occasionally, until thick. Chill.

Apple sauce

This is the perfect accompaniment for roast pork or goose.

To serve eight, you will need about 450g (1lb) cooking apples (such as Bramleys), 2 tbsp sugar (or to taste), 25g (1oz) butter.

1 Peel, core and slice the apples and put them in a pan with 2–3 tbsp water.

2 Cover and cook gently for about 10 minutes, stirring occasionally, until soft and reduced to a pulp.

3 Beat the pulp with a wooden spoon until smooth, then pass it through a sieve if you want a very smooth sauce. Stir in sugar to taste and then the butter. Serve warm.

VARIATIONS

- Apple sauce can be seasoned with a little cinnamon, nutmeg or mace.
- You can use dessert apples instead of cooking apples. Granny Smiths and Cox's Orange Pippin would both be good choices.
- Sweeten the sauce with honey instead of sugar if you wish.

FREEZING TIP

Both these fruit sauces can be frozen for up to one month. Follow the instructions on page 444 for freezing sauces.

MAYONNAISE & FLAVOURED BUTTERS

The simplest of accompaniments, mayonnaise goes well with salads, poached fish and poultry, while a slice of flavoured butter makes a delicious topping for grilled meats, fish and vegetables.

Mayonnaise

For 250ml (9fl oz), you will need 2 large egg yolks, 1 tsp English mustard, 200ml (7fl oz) sunflower oil, 100ml (3½fl oz) virgin olive oil, 1 tsp white wine vinegar or lemon juice, salt and ground black pepper.

1 Put the egg yolks in a 900ml (1½ pint) bowl. Stir in the mustard, 1 tsp salt and plenty of black pepper.

2 Combine the oils and add 1 tsp to the egg yolks. Whisk thoroughly, then add another 1 tsp and whisk until thickened. Continue adding about half the oil, 1 tbsp at a time. Whisk in the vinegar or lemon juice, then add the oil in a thin, steady stream until the mayonnaise is thick.

3 Check the seasoning, adding more vinegar or lemon juice if necessary. Cover and keep in the fridge for up to four days.

VARIATIONS

➺ **Aïoli** Add 4 crushed garlic cloves, 1 tbsp lemon juice and ½ tsp salt to the egg yolks in step 1 and stir to combine. Add 300ml (½ pint) light olive oil, as in step 2.

➺ **Tartare sauce** Add 2 tsp chopped tarragon, 4 tsp each chopped capers, gherkins and parsley, and 2 tbsp lemon juice to the mayonnaise.

COOK'S TIPS

Sometimes mayonnaise splits or curdles but it's easy to fix:

➺ Add a splash of cold water (about 1 tbsp) and stir in with a spoon, then continue with the recipe.

➺ If this doesn't work, put another egg yolk into a clean bowl and gradually whisk in the curdled mixture 1 tbsp at a time.

Flavoured butter

Allow 25g (1oz) soft unsalted butter per serving.

1 Beat in the flavourings (see Variations, right). Turn out on to clingfilm, shape into a log and wrap tightly. Chill in the fridge for at least 1 hour. (Freeze for up to 1 month.)

2 Slice the log into pieces, about 5mm (¼in) thick and serve.

VARIATIONS

For 125g (4oz) unsalted butter:

➺ **Anchovy butter** 6 mashed anchovy fillets.

➺ **Herb butter** 2 tbsp finely chopped herbs, a squeeze of lemon juice.

➺ **Garlic butter** 1 crushed garlic clove, 2 tsp finely chopped fresh parsley.

SALSAS

Finely chopped fresh herbs and raw ingredients make salsas a tasty addition to meat and fish. They are quick to make and have a refreshing flavour, and you can create endless variations.

Guacamole

To serve eight, you will need 2 ripe avocados, 2 small tomatoes, seeded and chopped (see page 188), juice of 2 limes, 2 tbsp extra-virgin olive oil, 2 tbsp freshly chopped coriander, salt and ground black pepper, tortilla chips, or pitta bread and, vegetable sticks to serve.

1 Cut the avocados in half, remove the stones and peel away the skin. Tip the flesh into a bowl and mash with a fork.

2 Quickly add the tomatoes, lime juice, oil and chopped coriander. Mix well and season with salt and pepper to taste. Cover and chill in the fridge until ready to serve.

3 Serve the guacamole with tortilla chips or warm pitta bread and vegetable sticks.

ABOUT SALSAS

All salsas:
- are a type of relish, containing mostly raw ingredients, for serving alongside a meat or fish dish
- are highly flavoured, so you only need a little for each serving
- always contain at least one form of acid, to give them 'bite'.

VARIATIONS

Mango salsa

Combine 1 diced mango, 1 small head of diced fennel, 1 seeded and finely diced fresh chilli, 1 tbsp balsamic vinegar, juice of ½ lime, 2 tbsp each freshly chopped flat-leafed parsley and mint in a bowl and season generously with salt and ground black pepper.

Salsa verde

This piquant sauce is good for grilled fish and meat.

To serve four, you will need a small handful of parsley, about 40g (1½oz), 6 tbsp fresh white breadcrumbs, 5 tbsp extra-virgin olive oil, 1 tsp capers, 1 gherkin, 2 tbsp lemon juice, 1 tbsp chopped chives.

1 Put all the ingredients into a food processor. Process until combined.

2 Transfer to a bowl, check the seasoning and adjust as necessary.

SALAD DRESSINGS

Whether you prefer your dressing tart and piquant or rich and creamy, always dress and toss your salad just before serving, and avoid overdressing – instead, simply aim to coat the leaves well.

Balsamic dressing

To serve four, you will need 2 tbsp balsamic vinegar, 4 tbsp extra-virgin olive oil, salt and ground black pepper.

1 Whisk the vinegar and oil in a small bowl. Season with salt and pepper to taste.

2 If not using immediately, whisk briefly before drizzling over salad.

COOK'S TIPS

— Add 1 tsp cold water to the dressing to help it to emulsify easily.
— To get a really good emulsion, shake the dressing vigorously in a screw-topped jar.

French dressing

To make 100ml (3½fl oz), you will need 1 tsp Dijon mustard, a pinch of sugar, 1 tbsp red or white wine vinegar, 6 tbsp extra-virgin olive oil, salt and ground black pepper.

1 Put the mustard, sugar and vinegar in a small bowl and season with salt and pepper. Whisk until well combined, then gradually whisk in the oil until thoroughly combined.

VARIATIONS

— **Herb dressing** Use half the mustard, replace the vinegar with lemon juice, and add 2 tbsp chopped herbs, such as parsley, chervil and chives.
— **Garlic dressing** Add 1 crushed garlic clove to the dressing.

Blue cheese dressing

To serve four, you will need 50g (2oz) Roquefort cheese, 2 tbsp low-fat yogurt, 1 tbsp white wine vinegar, 5 tbsp extra-virgin olive oil.

1 Crumble the cheese into a food processor with the yogurt, vinegar and olive oil.

2 Whiz for 1 minute until thoroughly combined. Season to taste.

SWEET SAUCES

Sweet sauces can transform simple sweet dishes and desserts such as home-made ice cream, stewed or poached fruit and soufflés into decadent desserts and luscious puddings with very little effort.

Vanilla custard

Perfect as an accompaniment to hot desserts, such as crumbles, cobblers and pies, a simple vanilla custard can be served hot or cold.

To serve eight, you will need 600ml (1 pint) full-fat milk, 1 vanilla pod or 1 tbsp vanilla extract, 6 large egg yolks, 2 tbsp golden caster sugar, 2 tbsp cornflour.

1 Put the milk in a pan. Split the vanilla pod and scrape the seeds into the pan, then drop in the pod. If using vanilla extract, pour it in. Bring to the boil, then turn off the heat and leave to cool for 5 minutes.

2 Put the egg yolks, sugar and cornflour in a bowl and whisk to blend. Remove the vanilla pod from the milk and gradually whisk the warm milk into the egg mixture.

3 Rinse out the pan. Pour the custard back in and heat gently, whisking constantly, for 2–3 minutes. The mixture should thicken enough to coat the back of a wooden spoon in a thin layer. Remove the pan from the heat.

4 If you are not serving the custard immediately, pour it into a jug. Cover the surface with a round of wet greaseproof paper to keep a skin from forming, then cover with clingfilm and chill. To serve hot, reheat very gently.

PERFECT CUSTARD

- To avoid curdling, don't let the custard overheat during cooking.
- To control the heat better, use a double boiler instead of a pan.
- If you want a much thinner consistency, omit the cornflour.
- Custard may be made up to four hours in advance. Cover and chill until needed.

Chocolate sauce

Simple to make and delicious drizzled over ice cream or a bowl of fresh berries.

To serve four, you will need 75g (3oz) good-quality dark chocolate, 140ml (4½fl oz) double cream.

1 Put the chocolate in a small heatproof bowl over a pan of gently simmering water. Pour the cream over the top.

2 Leave the chocolate to stand over the heat for about 10 minutes until completely melted – don't stir while it is melting. Once melted, stir the chocolate and cream together until smooth, then serve immediately.

MELTING CHOCOLATE

- ➥ However tempting, be sure to leave the chocolate alone while it is melting: stirring will make it thicken into a sticky mess (see page 366).
- ➥ The heat should be at its lowest setting.
- ➥ Make sure the base of the bowl is not touching the water.

VARIATIONS

- ➥ Use a mint-flavoured chocolate instead of plain.
- ➥ Add a shot of espresso to the chocolate and cream while they are melting.
- ➥ Pour a slug of orange-flavoured liqueur into the chocolate and cream while they are melting.

Butterscotch sauce

To serve eight, you will need 50g (2oz) butter, 50g (2oz) golden caster sugar, 75g (3oz) light muscovado sugar, 150g (5oz) golden syrup, 125ml (4fl oz) double cream, a few drops vanilla extract, juice of ½ lemon.

1 Heat the butter, sugars and syrup gently, stirring, until melted. Cook for 5 minutes, then remove from the heat.

2 Stir in the cream, vanilla and lemon, stir over a low heat for 1–2 minutes.

Rum sabayon

This mousse-like sauce is good served with cakes and puddings. (You can also make it with sweet wine or liqueur.)

To serve eight, you will need 75g (3oz) golden caster sugar, 3 medium egg yolks, 140ml (4½fl oz) double cream, 2 tbsp dark rum, the zest of 1 lemon, 2 tbsp lemon juice.

1 Put the sugar in a pan with 100ml (3½fl oz) water. Heat over a low heat until the sugar dissolves, then boil for 7–8 minutes until syrupy.

2 Beat the egg yolks in a bowl until they are thick and pale. Whisking constantly, gradually drizzle in the syrup. Whisk until cool.

3 Whip the cream until stiff, then add the rum, lemon zest and juice. Fold into the egg mixture. Cover and chill until needed.

PERFECT SABAYON

- Don't let the syrup colour while you're boiling it.
- Add the syrup very gradually to the eggs: if they get too hot, they will curdle.

Rum mascarpone

This sauce is great with baked fruit.

To serve six, you will need 250g (9oz) well-chilled mascarpone, 2–3 tbsp light muscovado sugar, 2–3 tbsp dark rum.

1 Spoon the mascarpone into a bowl and stir in the sugar.

2 Add the rum. Cover and leave in a cool place.

Brandy butter

To serve eight to ten, you will need 125g (4oz) unsalted butter, 125g (4oz) light muscovado sugar, sieved, 6 tbsp brandy.

1 Put the butter in a bowl and beat until very soft. Gradually beat in the sugar until very light and fluffy.

2 Beat in the brandy, a spoonful at a time. Chill for at least 3 hours.

Raspberry coulis

This simple fruit purée is great with ice cream and meringues.

To serve four to six, you will need 225g (8oz) raspberries, 2 tbsp Kirsch or framboise eau de vie, icing sugar, to taste.

1 Put the raspberries in a blender or food processor with the Kirsch or eau de vie. Whiz until they are completely puréed.

2 Transfer the purée to a fine sieve and press and scrape it through the sieve until nothing is left but the dry pips.

3 Sweeten with icing sugar to taste and chill until needed.

VARIATIONS

⟿ Use different soft fruits and liqueurs. For example, try crème de cassis with blackcurrants or amaretto with apricots.

⟿ Make a cooked sauce by simmering fruit half-covered in water with half its weight of sugar. When soft, sieve and sharpen with lemon juice. If you wish, you can thicken it with cornflour, about 1 tsp per 300ml (½ pint) sauce.

DECORATIVE EFFECTS

Sauces don't just have to be served as a simple accompaniment to sweet and savoury dishes, they can be used to stunning effect too – drizzled, dripped, trailed and piped to give a truly professional finish.

Teardrops and hearts

1 Put a few spoonfuls of sauce on the serving plate and tip it so that the sauce spreads out in an even layer.

2 Drop small blobs of the second sauce 2.5–5cm (1–2in) from the rim of the plates, to form a circle.

3 Using a small knife, or a skewer, draw the knife tip through the 'blobs' of sauce to form a tail.

Feathering

1 Put a few spoonfuls of the base sauce on your serving plates and tip the plates so that the sauce spreads out in an even layer.

2 Working quickly but carefully, apply concentric circles of decorative sauce to the base.

3 Take a small knife, or a skewer, and run it through the sauces from the edge of the plate to the centre of the circles. Turn the plate and repeat until you have a symmetrical pattern of feather shapes.

PERFECT DECORATIONS

— For maximum effect, use two sauces of contrasting colour – one as a base and one as decoration. Good examples would be custard (as a base) with fruit coulis, chocolate sauce or butterscotch sauce (as decoration).

— To make your life easier before a dinner party, decorate the plates ahead of time and then refrigerate them until needed.

— Applying the decorative sauce is easiest with a fine-nozzled piping bag (for thicker sauces) or a plastic squeeze-bottle (like those used for sauces in fish and chip shops) for thinner sauces.

Drizzling

An easy and attractive decoration, this can be done with either one or two sauces.

1 Using a plastic bottle or a small spoon, scatter fine 'ribbons' of sauce, in a pattern of roughly parallel lines, all over the plate.

2 If using a second sauce of a contrasting colour, scatter the ribbons at an angle to the first.

3 Alternatively, use one sauce as a base sauce to cover the plate and drizzle the other sauce over the top.

4 Rather than drizzling the sauce on the plate, sauces can also look attractive drizzled over dishes such as ice cream and desserts.

COLOURED SAUCES

Choose two sauces that contrast well together. Spoon the first sauce over half the plate. Spoon the second sauce over the other half and tip the plate in one direction and then another so that the sauces gently flow against each other in a softened shape.

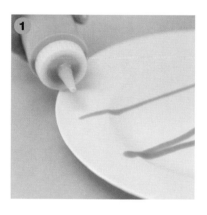

Piping

1 Pipe a wavy border on the plate with the darker sauce, then spoon a thinner pale sauce or cream into the centre and tip the plate to allow it to fill up the border.

2 Alternatively, pipe a decorative pattern such as a spiral around a dessert or main course to give a stunning effect.

RIPPLING

Spoon the base sauce on to the plate, then spoon a contrasting sauce in a circle over the top. Using a knife or skewer, gently stir the circle of sauce so that it ripples into the base sauce.

STOCKS AND SOUPS

A truly sensational soup is usually dependent on using a really good, well-flavoured stock. This chapter guides you through all the basics of making the four essential stocks – vegetable, meat, chicken and fish – and includes hints and tips on degreasing, storing, freezing and getting the best results every time. The illustrated step-by-step techniques then demonstrate the basics of soup-making, from blending, puréeing and thickening to making simple garnishes, before moving on to the delicious soups in the recipe section. With a great selection to choose from, try your hand at making chilled Gazpacho with tortilla chips, filling Fast fish soup, Asian-style Hot and sour soup or warming Scotch broth.

MAKING STOCK

Good stock can mark the difference between a good dish and a great one. It gives depth of flavour to many dishes. There are four main types of stock: vegetable, meat, chicken and fish.

Vegetable stock

For 1.2 litres (2 pints), you will need 225g (8oz) each onions, celery, leeks and carrots, all chopped, 1 bouquet garni (2 bay leaves, a few thyme sprigs, 1 small bunch parsley), 10 black peppercorns, ½ tsp salt.

1 Put all the ingredients in a pan and pour in 1.7 litres (3 pints) cold water. Bring slowly to the boil and skim the surface. Partially cover, reduce the heat and simmer for 30 minutes. Adjust the seasoning. Strain the stock through a fine sieve and leave to cool.

Meat stock

For 900ml (1½ pints), you will need 450g (1lb) each meat bones and stewing meat, 1 onion, 2 celery sticks and 1 large carrot, all sliced, 1 bouquet garni (2 bay leaves, a few thyme sprigs and a small bunch parsley), 1 tsp black peppercorns, ½ tsp salt.

1 Preheat the oven to 220°C (200°C fan oven) gas 7. Put the meat and bones in a roasting tin and roast for 30–40 minutes, turning now and again, until they are well browned.

2 Put the bones in a large pan with the remaining ingredients and add 2 litres (3½ pints) cold water. Bring slowly to the boil and skim the surface. Partially cover, reduce the heat and simmer for 4–5 hours. Adjust the seasoning. Strain through a muslin-lined sieve and cool quickly. Degrease (see opposite) before using.

Chicken stock

For 1.2 litres (2 pints), you will need 1.6kg (3½lb) chicken bones, 225g (8oz) each sliced onions and celery, 150g (5oz) chopped leeks, 1 bouquet garni (2 bay leaves, a few thyme sprigs, 1 small bunch parsley), 1 tsp black peppercorns, ½ tsp salt.

1 Put all the ingredients in a large pan with 3 litres (5¼ pints) cold water.

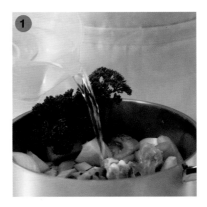

2 Bring slowly to the boil and skim the surface. Partially cover, reduce the heat and simmer gently for 2 hours. Adjust the seasoning if necessary.

3 Strain the stock through a muslin-lined sieve into a bowl and cool quickly. Degrease (see opposite) before using.

WHAT MAKES A GOOD STOCK?

Most stocks are made by cooking bones or fish trimmings with vegetables. Vegetables and herbs add flavour to any stock. Use onions, leeks, carrots and celery but avoid strongly flavoured vegetables such as cabbage and turnip, or those that disintegrate, such as potatoes. If you plan to make your own stock:

- Ask your butcher or fishmonger for bones and trimmings. They can be frozen for up to six months until you have enough to make stock.
- Stock can be stored in the fridge for three days or frozen for up to four months (see page 444), so it is worth making a large quantity.
- If you have made a lot of stock for freezing, reduce it after cooking so that it takes up less freezer space. First degrease it (see opposite), then put it in a clean pan and simmer over a medium heat until it's reduced by about three-quarters. Leave to cool completely before storing.

Fish stock

For 900ml (1½ pints), you will need 900g (2lb) fish bones and trimmings, washed, 2 carrots, 1 onion and 2 celery sticks, all sliced, 1 bouquet garni (2 bay leaves, a few thyme sprigs, 1 small bunch parsley), 6 white peppercorns, ½ tsp salt.

1 Put all the ingredients in a large pan with 900ml (1½ pints) cold water. Bring slowly to the boil and skim the surface.

2 Partially cover, reduce the heat and simmer gently for 30 minutes. Adjust the seasoning if necessary.

3 Strain through a muslin-lined sieve into a bowl and cool quickly. Fish stock tends not to have much fat in it and so does not usually need to be degreased. However, if it does seem to be fatty, you will need to remove this by degreasing it (see technique below).

VARIATION

Court bouillon is an enriched fish stock that is perfect for poaching fish (see page 82). Simply add 150ml (¼ pint) dry white wine and 3 tbsp white wine vinegar to the fish stock recipe at step 1.

Degreasing stock

Meat and poultry stock needs to be degreased. (Vegetable stock does not.) You can mop the fat from the surface using kitchen paper, but the following methods are easier and more effective. There are three main methods that you can use: ladling, pouring and chilling.

1 Ladling While the stock is warm, place a ladle on the surface. Press down to allow the fat floating on the surface to trickle over the edge until the ladle is full. Discard the fat, then repeat until all the fat has been removed.

2 Pouring For this you need a degreasing jug or a double-pouring gravy boat, which has the spout at the base of the vessel. When you fill the jug or gravy boat with a fatty liquid, the fat rises. When you pour, the stock comes out while the fat stays behind in the jug.

3 Chilling This technique works best with stock made from meat, whose fat solidifies when cold. Put the stock in the fridge until the fat becomes solid, then remove the pieces of fat using a slotted spoon.

COOK'S TIPS

- To get a clearer liquid when making fish, meat or poultry stock, strain the cooked stock through four layers of muslin in a sieve.
- If you want to keep stock for more than three days, transfer to a pan and reboil gently for five minutes to make it safe for further storage. Cool and put in a clean bowl then chill for a further three days.
- When making meat or chicken stock, make sure there is a good ratio of meat to bones. The more meat you use, the more flavour.

MAKING SOUPS

Soups are nutritious and full of flavour and can be light for a first course or substantial for a main course, containing pulses, vegetables, meat, chicken or fish. A basic soup is simple to make.

Puréeing soups

1 Using a jug blender Allow the soup to cool, then fill the jug about half full, making sure that there is more liquid than solids. Cover the lid with a teatowel and hold it on tightly. Blend until smooth, then add more solids and blend again until all the soup is smooth. (If you have a lot of soup, transfer each batch to a clean pan.)

2 Using a stick blender Leave the soup to cool. Stick the blender deep down into the soup, switch it on, and keep it moving so that all the soup is puréed.

3 Using a mouli The mouli-légumes is a traditional favourite of chefs, who require a perfectly uniform texture in their soups. It makes a fine purée although it takes longer than using a blender. Fit the fine plate to the mouli-légumes and set it over a bowl with a teatowel underneath to keep it from moving on the table. Fill the bowl of the mouli about halfway, putting in more solids than liquid. Work in batches if you have a particularly large quantity of soup. When the solids are puréed, repeat with the liquid.

4 Using a sieve If you don't have a blender or mouli-légumes, you can purée soup by pushing it through a sieve, although this will take a much longer time.

SIMPLE VEGETABLE SOUP

You can use almost any mixture of vegetables to make soup.
To make a basic soup for four, fry 1 or 2 finely chopped onions in 2 tbsp oil or 1 tbsp oil and 25g (1oz) butter, then add 1 or 2 crushed garlic cloves if you like. Add 450g (1lb) chopped mixed vegetables, such as leeks, potatoes, celery, fennel, canned tomatoes and parsnip (these can be chopped finely or cut into larger dice for a chunky soup). Add 1.1 litres (2 pints) home-made stock. Bring to the boil, reduce the heat and simmer for 20–30 minutes until the vegetables are tender. Leave chunky or blend until smooth if you prefer.

Chunky soups

1 Cut up the vegetables into bite-sized pieces. Heat oil or butter in the soup pan and cook the onions and garlic until soft and lightly coloured.

2 Add the remaining ingredients, putting in the vegetables that need the longest cooking first. Pour in some stock and bring to the boil.

3 Reduce the heat and simmer gently until all the ingredients are tender. If too much liquid cooks away, just add more (adding a lid will help minimise evaporation – but do not use a brightly-coloured soup, as colour may be lost).

4 If any ingredients need brief cooking, add them at the very end. Using something starchy in the soup will thicken the broth, or you can use any of the techniques on page 40.

Partially puréed soups

1 For a smooth yet chunky soup, purée one-third to half of it, then stir back into the soup.

2 Alternatively, chop the vegetables, putting a few choice pieces to one side. While the soup is cooking, cook these pieces until tender and refresh in cold water. Before serving, cut into smaller pieces and add to the soup.

Thickening soups

You can thicken soup before serving to give it a smoother texture and more richness.

1 Cornflour Because cornflour is maize flour stripped of everything except the purest starch, it requires little cooking. Measure the cornflour into a bowl – you will need 1–2 tbsp cornflour per 1 litre (1¾ pints) soup. Add about double the volume of cold water and whisk until the cornflour is completely dissolved. Stir into the soup and heat briefly. (Potato starch can be used in the same way as cornflour.)

2 Egg and cream Cream adds texture and richness, but to thicken a soup, egg yolks and cream work better. Remove the soup from the heat. Using one yolk per 4 tbsp double or whipping cream, whisk them together in a bowl. Add a little of the hot soup – not too much, or the egg will curdle. Whisk well, add more soup and whisk again. When you have a cupful of liquid, pour it back into the soup. You can turn on the heat again, but don't let the soup simmer or the egg yolk will curdle.

3 Breadcrumbs Add fresh or dry breadcrumbs to the soup during cooking, a handful at a time. Cook for 20 minutes or so, then add more if you need to. Purée the soup if you want a smooth texture. (A handful of cooked rice or mashed potato works in the same way, but make sure they cook for a long time until tender.)

4 Beurre manié This butter and flour paste is useful for thickening soups and sauces. Using equal parts of butter and flour – you will need 1–2 tbsp of each for a soup – cream the butter in a bowl with a wooden spoon then mix in the flour thoroughly to make a smooth paste. Add to the soup gradually in small pieces, stirring well with each addition. Add only as much as you need to get the desired consistency. (You can store any left over beurre manié in a sealed container for up to three days in the fridge or freeze for up to six months.)

SIMPLE GARNISHES

A garnish can make a huge difference to the presentation of a soup. It might be as simple as a sprinkling of herbs, a drizzle of cream, or some quickly cooked croûtons scattered over the top.

Toasted croûtons

1 Cut the crusts off sliced white bread, then cut into dice 1–2cm (½–¾in) square. Put the bread on a baking sheet and drizzle lightly with oil, then toss well with your hands.

2 Spread the bread dice in a single layer and bake at 200°C (180°C fan oven) mark 6 for 8–10 minutes until lightly browned.

Fried croûtons

Croûtons fried in a generous amount of oil will crispen all over.

1 Cut the crusts off sliced white bread, then cut into dice 1–2cm (½–¾in) square.

2 Heat the oil medium-hot in a frying pan. Fry in a single layer, stirring constantly, until brown all over. Drain on kitchen paper.

Fresh herbs

A simple sprinkling of fresh herbs makes a delicious garnish for soups. Fresh herb flowers can also make a pretty and unusual garnish.

1 Chop the herbs just before serving, and choose a herb that complements that flavour of soup, for example, basil with tomato, chives with creamy soups, or coriander with Asian-style soups.

CREAM

Cream and other dairy products such as yogurt and crème fraîche can also make a simple garnish, drizzled or spooned on to soup just before serving. They also add body and texture, so use sparingly if the soup already includes cream.

GAZPACHO WITH TORTILLA CHIPS

Serves 8
Preparation 25–30 minutes, plus chilling
Techniques see also making breadcrumbs (page 318)

900g (2lb) ripe tomatoes
4 garlic cloves
50g (2oz) fresh white breadcrumbs
6 tbsp extra-virgin olive oil
juice of 1½ small limes
1 red chilli, seeded and chopped
2 cucumbers, seeded and chopped
2 bunches spring onions, chopped
1 red pepper, deseeded and chopped
600ml (1 pint) tomato juice
6 tbsp freshly chopped coriander
salt and ground black pepper
175g bag tortilla chips to serve

To garnish
1 large avocado
juice of ½ small lime
140ml (4½fl oz) soured cream
a few fresh coriander sprigs

1 Score a cross in the skin at the base of each tomato, then put into a bowl. Pour over enough boiling water to cover them, leave for 30 seconds, then transfer to a bowl of cold water. Peel, discarding the skins, then cut into quarters. Discard the seeds.
2 Put all the gazpacho ingredients into a large bowl and mix well, then whiz together in batches in a food processor until smooth. Transfer to a bowl or jug. Season generously with salt and pepper and stir the soup well. Cover and chill for at least 2 hours or overnight.
3 Just before serving, peel and roughly dice the avocado, then toss in lime juice to coat. Serve the soup garnished with soured cream, the avocado, a sprinkling of black pepper and coriander. Serve the tortilla chips separately.

COOK'S TIP
Don't be tempted to make the garnish too far in advance. The delicate pale green flesh of avocado discolours when exposed to air so is best prepared shortly before serving.

NUTRITION PER SERVING
181 cals | 13g fat (2g sats) | 14g carbs | 0.6g salt

VICHYSSOISE WITH SPINACH CREAM

Serves 4–6
Preparation 20 minutes, plus chilling
Cooking time 40 minutes
Techniques see also peeling prawns (page 87), making stock (page 36), preparing leeks (page 183)

1kg (2¼lb) trimmed leeks, chopped
50g (2oz) butter
350g (12oz) onions, roughly chopped
1.1 litres (2 pints) vegetable stock
140ml (4½fl oz) double cream
225g (8oz) potatoes, sliced
salt and ground black pepper
cooked peeled prawns and fresh basil sprigs to garnish

For the spinach cream
15g (½oz) butter
125g (4oz) spinach leaves
zest of 1 lemon
140ml (4½fl oz) double cream

1 Rinse the leeks in cold water, drain and put to one side. Melt the butter in a large heavy-based pan and add the onions and leeks. Cook, stirring, for 10 minutes. Add the stock, cream and potatoes. Bring to the boil, then reduce the heat, cover and simmer for 30–40 minutes until the vegetables are tender.
2 Cool slightly, then process in batches until smooth (see page 38). Pass through a fine sieve if you like, then season generously with salt and pepper. Chill in the fridge for 6 hours or overnight.
3 Meanwhile, to make the spinach cream, heat the butter in a pan, then add the spinach and lemon zest. Cook, stirring, for 5 minutes. Add the cream and bubble for 1–2 minutes. Whiz in a blender or food processor until smooth. Season, then chill.
4 Ladle the soup into chilled bowls and spoon in the spinach cream. Garnish with prawns and basil, sprinkle with black pepper and serve.

GET AHEAD
Complete the recipe to the end of step 3, cool, cover and chill overnight.
To use Complete the recipe.

NUTRITION PER SERVING FOR 4
610 cals | 54g fat (33g sats) | 25g carbs | 1g salt

NUTRITION PER SERVING FOR 6
407 cals | 36g fat (22g sats) | 17g carbs | 0.6g salt

MULLIGATAWNY SOUP

Serves 8
Preparation 5 minute
Cooking time 40 minutes
Techniques see also making stock (page 36), cooking rice (page 246)

3 rashers streaky bacon, rinded and finely chopped
550g (1¼lb) chicken portions
600ml (1 pint) chicken stock
1 carrot, sliced
1 celery stick, chopped
1 apple, cored and chopped
2 tsp curry powder
4 peppercorns, crushed
1 clove
1 bay leaf
1 tbsp plain flour
150ml (¼ pint) milk
50g (2oz) long-grain rice, cooked, and
crusty bread to serve

1 Fry the bacon in a large pan until the fat begins to run. Do not allow the bacon to become brown.
2 Add the chicken and brown well. Drain the meat on kitchen paper and pour off the fat.
3 Return the bacon and chicken to the pan and add the stock and the next seven ingredients. Cover the pan and simmer for about 30 minutes or until the chicken is tender.
4 Remove the chicken and leave to cool a little. Cut off the meat and return it to the soup. Discard the clove and bay leaf and reheat the soup gently.
5 Mix the flour with a little cold water. Add to the soup with the milk and reheat without boiling.
6 Ladle the soup into warmed bowls, spoon a mound of rice into each one and serve immediately with crusty bread.

NUTRITION PER SERVING
252 cals | 13g fat (4g sats) | 4.3g carbs | 0.9g salt

HOT AND SOUR SOUP

Serves 4

Preparation 20 minutes

Cooking time 30–35 minutes

Techniques see also making stock (page 36), preparing fresh ginger (page 437)

1 tbsp vegetable oil
2 turkey breasts, about 300g (11oz),
or the same quantity of tofu, cut into strips
5cm (2in) piece fresh root ginger, peeled and grated
4 spring onions, finely sliced
1–2 tbsp Thai red curry paste
75g (3oz) long-grain wild rice
1.1 litres (2 pints) hot weak chicken or vegetable stock
    or boiling water
200g (7oz) mangetouts, sliced
juice of 1 lime
4 tbsp roughly chopped coriander to garnish

1 Heat the oil in a deep pan. Add the turkey or tofu and cook over a medium heat for 5 minutes or until browned. Add the grated ginger and spring onions and cook for a further 2–3 minutes. Stir in the curry paste and cook for 1–2 minutes to warm the spices.

2 Add the rice and stir to coat in the curry paste. Pour the hot stock or boiling water into the pan. Stir once, then bring to the boil. Reduce the heat and simmer, covered, for 20 minutes.

3 Add the mangetouts and cook for a further 5 minutes or until the rice is cooked. Just before serving, squeeze in the lime juice and stir to mix. Ladle into bowls and sprinkle with the coriander.

NUTRITION PER SERVING
255 cals | 10g fat (1g sats) | 19g carbs | 0.7g salt

FAST FISH SOUP

Serves 4
Preparation 10 minutes
Cooking time about 15 minutes
Techniques see also preparing leeks (page 183), preparing chillies (page 189), preparing prawns (page 87), preparing mussels and clams (page 90)

1 leek, trimmed and finely chopped
4 fat garlic cloves, crushed
3 celery sticks, finely chopped
1 small fennel bulb, finely chopped
1 red chilli, seeded and finely chopped
3 tbsp olive oil
50ml (2fl oz) dry white wine
about 750g (1lb 11oz) mixed fish and shellfish, such as haddock and monkfish fillets, peeled and deveined raw prawns, and fresh mussels (optional), scrubbed, cleaned and open or damaged ones discarded
4 tomatoes, chopped
20g (¾oz) freshly chopped thyme
salt and ground black pepper

1 Put the leek into a large pan and add the garlic, celery, fennel, chilli and oil. Cook over a medium heat for 5 minutes or until the vegetables are soft and beginning to colour.
2 Stir in 1.1 litres (2 pints) boiling water and the wine. Bring to the boil, then reduce the heat, cover the pan and simmer for 5 minutes.
3 Cut the white fish into large chunks. Add to the soup with the tomatoes and thyme. Continue to simmer gently until the fish has just turned opaque. Add the prawns, simmer for 1 minute, then add the mussels, if you're using them.
4 As soon as all the mussels have opened (discard any that do not), season the soup with salt and pepper. Ladle into warmed bowls and serve immediately.

VARIATIONS
Stir in 2 tbsp Pernod instead of wine.
Garlic croûtes Traditionally served with fish soup, they can be made while the soup is simmering. Toast small slices of baguette, spread with garlic mayonnaise and sprinkle with grated cheese. Float in the hot soup just before serving.

NUTRITION PER SERVING
269 cals | 10g fat (2g sats) | 6g carbs | 0.4g salt

QUICK WINTER MINESTRONE

Serves 4
Preparation 10 minutes
Cooking time 5 minutes
Techniques see also making stock (page 36), preparing vegetables (pages 182–194)

2 tbsp olive oil
1 small onion, finely chopped
1 carrot, chopped
1 celery stick, chopped
1 garlic clove, crushed
2 tbsp chopped fresh thyme
1 litre (1¾ pints) vegetable stock
400g can chopped tomatoes
400g can borlotti beans, drained
125g (4oz) minestrone pasta
175g (6oz) Savoy cabbage, shredded
salt and ground black pepper
fresh pesto, toasted ciabatta and extra-virgin
    olive oil to serve

1 Heat the oil in a large pan. Add the onion, carrot and celery. Cook for 8–10 minutes until softened, then add the garlic and thyme and fry for another 2–3 minutes.
2 Add the stock, tomatoes and half the borlotti beans. Mash the remaining beans, stir into the soup and simmer for 30 minutes, adding the minestrone pasta and cabbage for the last 10 minutes of cooking time.
3 Check the seasoning, then serve the soup in individual bowls with a dollop of fresh pesto on top and slices of toasted ciabatta drizzled with extra-virgin olive oil on the side.

NUTRITION PER SERVING
334 cals | 11g fat (2.5g sats) | 47g carbs | 1.5g salt

PARSNIP SOUP WITH CHEESE CRISPS

Serves 8
Preparation 30 minutes
Cooking time 1 hour
Techniques see also making stock (page 36), making vegetable crisps (page 198)

40g (1½oz) butter
150g (5oz) onion, roughly chopped
225g (8oz) floury potatoes, such as King Edward, peeled and chopped
400g (14oz) parsnips, peeled and chopped
4 tsp paprika, plus extra to dust
1.1 litres (2 pints) vegetable stock
450ml (¾ pint) milk
4 tbsp double cream
65g (2½oz) sliced chorizo sausage, cut into fine strips
salt and ground black pepper

For the Parmesan crisps
1 large parsnip, about 75g (3oz), peeled
vegetable oil, to fry
3 tbsp freshly grated Parmesan

1 Melt the butter in a large heavy-based pan. Add the onion and cook over a gentle heat for 5 minutes. Add the potatoes, parsnips and paprika. Mix well and cook gently, stirring occasionally, for 15 minutes or until the vegetables begin to soften. Add the stock, milk and cream and season. Bring to the boil, then reduce the heat and simmer for about 25 minutes or until the vegetables are very soft. Add 50g (2oz) chorizo.
2 Leave the soup to cool a little, then whiz in a blender or food processor until smooth. The soup can be thinned with additional stock or milk, if you like. Check the seasoning and put back in the pan.
3 Preheat the oven to 200°C (180°C fan oven) mark 6. Using a swivel vegetable peeler, peel off long, wide strips of parsnip until there is nothing left to peel. Pour the oil into a large pan or deep-sided frying pan to a depth of 2.5cm (1in) and heat to a medium temperature. Fry the parsnip strips in batches until light golden and crisp. Drain on kitchen paper and sprinkle lightly with salt. Arrange the strips in six piles on a baking sheet, then sprinkle with half the Parmesan and the remaining chorizo. Cook the Parmesan crisps in the oven for 3–5 minutes until the cheese just begins to melt.
4 Reheat the soup. Serve topped with the Parmesan Crisps, sprinkled with the remaining Parmesan and dusted with paprika.

FREEZING TIP
Prepare to the end of step 2, then cool, pack and freeze.
To use Thaw the soup overnight at cool room temperature. Then complete the recipe.

NUTRITION PER SERVING
111 cals | 81g fat (35g sats) | 72g carbs | 3g salt

CULLEN SKINK

Serves 4 (as a main meal soup)
Preparation 10 minutes
Cooking time 1½ hours
Techniques see also chopping onions (page 182, chopping herbs (page 436)

1 Finnan haddock, weighing about 350g (12oz), skinned
1 medium onion, chopped
600ml (1 pint) milk
700g (1½lb) potatoes
a knob of butter
salt and ground black pepper
freshly chopped flat-leafed parsley to garnish
crusty bread to serve

1 Put the haddock into a medium pan, just cover it with about 900ml (1½ pints) boiling water and bring back to the boil. Add the onion, then reduce the heat, cover and simmer for 10–15 minutes until the haddock is tender. Drain off the liquid and put to one side.
2 Remove the bones from the haddock and flake the flesh, then put to one side. Return the bones and strained stock to the pan with the milk. Cover and simmer gently for a further hour.
3 Meanwhile, peel and roughly chop the potatoes, then cook in lightly salted boiling water until tender. Drain well, then mash.
4 Strain the liquid from the bones and return it to the pan with the flaked fish. Add the mashed potato and the butter and stir well to give a thick creamy consistency. Adjust the seasoning and garnish with parsley. Serve with crusty bread.

COOK'S TIP
Ask the fishmonger to skin the haddock for you.

NUTRITION PER SERVING
309 cals | 6g fat (4g sats) | 40g carbs | 1g salt

COCK-A-LEEKIE SOUP

Serves 8
Preparation 30–40 minutes
Cooking time 1 hour 20 minutes
Techniques see also preparing vegetables (pages 182–194)

1 oven-ready chicken, about 1.4kg (3lb)
2 onions, roughly chopped
2 carrots, roughly chopped
2 celery sticks, roughly chopped
1 bay leaf
25g (1oz) butter
900g (2lb) leeks, trimmed and sliced
125g (4oz) ready-to-eat stoned prunes, sliced
salt and ground black pepper
freshly chopped parsley to serve

For the dumplings
125g (4oz) self-raising white flour
a pinch of salt
50g (2oz) shredded suet
2 tbsp freshly chopped parsley
2 tbsp freshly chopped thyme

1 Put the chicken into a pan in which it fits quite snugly. Add the chopped vegetables, bay leaf and chicken giblets (if available). Add 1.7 litres (3 pints) water and bring to the boil, then reduce the heat, cover the pan and simmer gently for 1 hour.
2 Meanwhile, melt the butter in a large pan, add the leeks and fry gently for 10 minutes or until softened.
3 Remove the chicken from the pan. Strain the stock and put to one side. Strip the chicken from the bones and shred roughly. Add to the stock with the prunes and softened leeks.
4 To make the dumplings, sift the flour and salt into a bowl. Stir in the suet, herbs and about 5 tbsp water to make a fairly firm dough. Lightly shape the dough into 2.5cm (1in) balls. Bring the soup just to the boil and season well. Reduce the heat, add the dumplings and cover the pan with a lid. Simmer for about 15–20 minutes until the dumplings are light and fluffy. Serve scattered with chopped parsley.

NUTRITION PER SERVING
280 cals | 4g fat (1g sats) | 40g carbs | 0.2g salt

SCOTCH BROTH

Serves 8
Preparation 15 minutes
Cooking time 2 hours
Techniques see also preparing vegetables (pages 182–194)

1 piece of marrow bone, about 350g (12oz)
1.4kg (3lb) piece of beef skirt (ask your butcher for this)
300ml (½ pint) broth mix (to include pearl barley, red lentils, split peas and green peas), soaked according to the pack instructions
2 carrots, finely chopped
1 parsnip, finely chopped
2 onions, finely chopped
¼ white cabbage, finely chopped
1 leek, trimmed and finely chopped
1–2 tbsp salt
ground black pepper
2 tbsp freshly chopped parsley to serve

1 Put the marrow bone and beef skirt into a 5.7 litre (10 pint) stock pot and add 2.6 litres (4½ pints) cold water – there should be enough to cover the meat.
2 Bring the water to the boil. Remove any scum from the surface with a spoon and discard. Reduce the heat to low, add the broth mix and simmer, partially covered, for 1½ hours, skimming the surface occasionally.
3 Add the carrots, parsnip, onions, cabbage, leek and another 600ml (1 pint) cold water. Cover to bring to the boil quickly, then reduce the heat and simmer for 30 minutes.
4 Remove the marrow bone and piece of beef from the broth. Add a few shreds of beef to the broth if you like. Season the broth well with the salt and some pepper and stir in the chopped parsley. Ladle into warmed bowls and serve hot.

COOK'S TIP
This is really two meals in one, a starter and a main course. The beef flavours the stock and is removed before serving. Later you divide up the meat and serve it with mashed potatoes, swedes or turnips.

NUTRITION PER SERVING
173 cals | 2g fat (trace sats) | 35g carbs | 2.3g salt

EGGS, CREAM AND CHEESE

Eggs are a wonderfully versatile ingredient that can be enjoyed on their own – cooked simply – or used in literally hundreds of different ways. In this chapter, you can learn all the basics from simple boiling, poaching and frying through to more complex techniques such as making omelettes, pancakes, soufflés and meringues. Once you've mastered the basics, try the delicious recipes such as Mixed mushroom frittata, Twice-baked soufflés, Queen of puddings, Crème caramel and sweet, nutty Toasted hazelnut meringue cake.

Cheese and cream both combine wonderfully with eggs, and have many other uses in everyday cooking, but knowing which types to use for what can be a puzzle. This chapter guides you through the basics, and introduces you to recipes such as Glamorgan sausages, Cheese ramekins and Classic tiramisù.

BASIC EGG PREPARATION

There are only three essentials to basic egg preparation: cracking, separating and whisking – and once you have mastered these simple techniques you will be able to cook eggs in lots of different ways.

Separating

You'll need to separate eggs for making a sauce such as mayonnaise, a soufflé, meringue, or some cakes. It's easy, but it requires some care.

1 Crack the egg more carefully than usual: right in the middle to make a break between the two halves that is just wide enough to get your thumbnail into.

2 Holding the egg over a bowl with the large end pointing down, carefully lift off the small half. Some of the white will drip and slide into the bowl while the yolk sits in the large end of the shell.

3 Carefully slide the yolk into the smaller end, then back into the large end to allow the remaining white to drop into the bowl. Take care not to break the yolk; even a speck can stop the whites from whisking up.

Whisking

1 Use an electric or hand whisk. Make sure that there is no trace of yolk in the whites and that the whisk and bowl are spotlessly clean and dry. At a low speed, use the whisk in a small area of the whites until it starts to become foamy.

2 Increase the speed and work the whisk through the whites until glossy and soft rounded peaks form. Do not over-whisk as the foam will become dry and grainy.

COOKING WITH EGGS

There are numerous ways to cook with eggs – from the simplest techniques such as boiling, poaching and scrambling, to more complex techniques such as making omelettes, soufflés and meringues.

Boiling: method 1

1 Bring a small pan of water to the boil. Once the water is boiling, add a medium egg. For a soft-boiled egg, cook for 6 minutes; for a salad egg, cook for 8 minutes; and for a hard-boiled egg, cook for 10 minutes.

2 Remove the egg from the water with a slotted spoon and serve.

Boiling: method 2

1 Put a medium egg in a small pan and cover with cold water. Put on a lid and bring to the boil. When the water begins to boil, remove the lid and cook for 2 minutes for a soft-boiled egg, 5 minutes for a salad egg, and 7 minutes for a hard-boiled egg.

2 Remove the egg from the water with a slotted spoon and serve.

PERFECT BOILED EGGS

There are two ways to boil an egg: starting in boiling water or starting in cold water. Both work well as long as you follow certain rules:
- The egg must be at room temperature.
- For both methods, cover the eggs with water, plus 2.5cm (1in) or so extra.
- If starting in boiling water, use an 'egg pick', if you like, to pierce the broad end of the shell. This allows air in the pocket at the base of the egg to escape and avoids cracking.
- Gently lower in the eggs using a long spoon to avoid cracking them.
- Cook at a simmer rather than a rolling boil.

Coddling

A variation of soft-boiled eggs, coddled eggs are very soft and have tender whites. They are particularly good for using when the eggs are going to be cooked again after peeling, such as in a pie or for recipes such as Scotch eggs.

1 Using a slotted spoon, gently lower the whole eggs into a pan of simmering water, then remove the pan from the heat.

2 Leave the eggs to stand in the water for 4–5 minutes, where they will cook gently with the residual heat of the water.

Poaching

1 Heat about 8cm (3¼ in) of lightly salted water in a shallow frying pan to a bare simmer. Crack a very fresh egg into a cup, then slip it into the water. (The whites in a fresh egg are firmer and will form a 'nest' for the yolk while older egg whites are watery and spread out in the pan.)

2 Cook for 3–4 minutes until the white is barely set. Remove the egg with a slotted spoon and drain on kitchen paper.

Scrambling

1 Allow 2 eggs per person. In a bowl, beat the eggs well but lightly with a fork and season with salt and ground black pepper.

2 Melt a knob of butter in a small heavy-based pan over a low heat – use a heat diffuser if necessary. (Using a non-stick pan minimises the amount of butter you need to use.)

3 Pour in the eggs and start stirring immediately, using a wooden spoon or a flat-headed spatula to break up the lumps as they form. Keep the eggs moving about as much as possible during cooking.

4 As the eggs start to set, scrape the bottom of the pan to keep the egg from overcooking and break up any larger lumps that may form. Your aim is to have a smooth mixture with no noticeable lumps.

5 Scrambled eggs may be well cooked and quite firm, or very 'loose' and runny; this is a matter of taste. They will continue to cook even when taken off the heat, so remove them from the pan when they are still a little softer than you want to serve them.

COOK'S TIP

Microwave scrambled eggs
Put the eggs, milk, if you like, and butter into a bowl and beat well. Cook at full power for 1 minute (the mixture should be just starting to set around the edges), then beat again. Cook again at full power for 2–3 more minutes, stirring every 30 seconds, until the eggs are cooked the way you like them.

Frying

1 Heat a good knob of butter or a little oil over a medium-high heat. Break the egg into a shallow bowl, then slide gently into the pan.

2 Cook for 2–3 minutes, gently shaking the pan to slosh the butter or oil over the egg white. Adjust the heat so that the egg doesn't become too brown underneath while the yolk remains cool. For a firm yolk, carefully turn the egg over and cook for a few seconds more.

Baking

You can crack eggs into individual dishes or into a large shallow pan and bake them. They may be cooked on their own, or baked with meat or vegetable accompaniments.

1 Generously smear individual baking dish(es) or one large baking dish with butter.

2 Put in any accompaniments, if using (see box on Variations and accompaniments, right). If using vegetable-based accompaniments, use the back of a spoon to make a hollow or hollows in which to break the egg or eggs. Carefully crack the egg or eggs into the hollows.

3 Bake for 8–10 minutes at 200°C (180°C fan oven) mark 6, or 15–18 minutes at 180°C (160°C fan oven) mark 4, until the whites are just set; the yolks should still be quite runny.

VARIATIONS AND ACCOMPANIMENTS

- Eggs are delicious baked on a simple bed of sautéed vegetables (such as ratatouille), lightly browned diced potatoes with onions, and also on well-cooked spinach.
- Accompaniments must be fully cooked before they are transferred to the dish and the raw eggs put on top.
- Other simple additions include chopped fresh herbs or a few shreds of crisp bacon.
- If liked, drizzle a small spoonful of cream and a good grinding of black pepper on top of the eggs before baking.

MAKING OMELETTES

There are numerous different types of omelette – from the classic folded omelette made from simple beaten eggs to thick omelettes such as Spanish tortilla and Italian frittata.

Classic omelette

1 To make an omelette for one person, heat a heavy-based 18cm (7in) frying pan or omelette pan. Using a fork, beat 2 eggs and season.

2 Add 15g (½oz) butter to the pan and let it sizzle for a few moments without browning, then pour in the eggs and stir a few times with a fork.

3 As the omelette begins to stick at the sides, lift it up and allow the uncooked egg to run into the gap.

4 When the omelette is nearly set and the underneath is brown, loosen the edges and give the pan a sharp shake to slide the omelette across.

5 Add a filling (such as grated cheese or fried mushrooms), if you like, and fold the far side of the omelette towards you. Tilt the pan to slide the omelette on to the plate and serve.

PERFECT OMELETTES

- ➔ Don't add butter until the pan is already hot, otherwise it will brown too much.
- ➔ Beat the eggs lightly.
- ➔ Use a high heat.

Potato and chorizo tortilla

To serve four, you will need 6 tbsp olive oil, 450g (1lb) very thinly sliced potatoes, 225g (8oz) thinly sliced onions, 2 chopped garlic cloves, 50g (2oz) chorizo, cut into strips, 6 large eggs, salt and ground black pepper.

1 Heat the oil in an 18cm (7in) non-stick frying pan. Add the potatoes, onion and garlic and stir to coat. Cover. Cook gently for 15 minutes, stirring occasionally, until the potato is soft. Season with salt.

2 Preheat the grill. Add the chorizo to the pan. Beat the eggs and season with salt and ground black pepper, then pour into the pan and cook for about 5 minutes until the edges are beginning to brown and the egg looks about three-quarters set.

3 Put the tortilla under the hot grill and quickly brown the top. Remove from the grill and leave to cool. Loosen the edges of the tortilla and serve cut into wedges.

MAKING SOUFFLÉS

Light fluffy soufflés made with whisked egg whites folded into a richly flavoured egg custard may be sweet or savoury. For a perfect rise, use a traditional straight-sided soufflé dish.

Cheese soufflé

To serve four, you will need 25g (1oz) butter, plus extra to grease, 1 tbsp freshly grated Parmesan, 200ml (7fl oz) milk, 6 black peppercorns, a few onion and carrot slices, 1 bay leaf, 2 tbsp plain flour, 2 tsp Dijon mustard, large pinch of cayenne pepper, 4 large eggs, separated, plus 1 egg white, 75g (3oz) finely grated mature Cheddar cheese, salt and ground black pepper.

1 Butter four ramekins. Coat the bottom and sides with Parmesan. Put the milk, peppercorns, onion, carrot and bay leaf in a pan. Bring to the boil, remove from the heat, cover and leave for 30 minutes. Strain. Preheat the oven to 180°C (160°C fan oven) mark 4.

2 Melt the butter in a pan. Stir in the flour and mustard. Add salt, pepper and cayenne and cook for 1 minute, stirring. Take off the heat and stir in the milk. Slowly bring to the boil and cook, stirring, until thick. Cool slightly, then beat in the egg yolks, one at a time. Stir in all but 1 tbsp of the cheese.

3 Whisk the egg whites until they stand in soft peaks.

4 Mix a large spoonful of egg white into the sauce, then gently fold in the remaining egg whites.

5 Spoon into the dish(es). Sprinkle with the reserved cheese. Stand the dishes on a baking sheet. Cook for 20 minutes or until golden brown, risen and just firm to the touch. Serve.

PERFECT SOUFFLÉS

- → Run a knife around the inside of the dish before baking to help achieve the classic 'hat' effect.
- → To prepare ahead, prepare the soufflé to the end of step 2 and leave to stand for several hours before baking.
- → Ensure you have a well-flavoured and well-seasoned sauce because the egg white will dilute the flavour.
- → When you fold the sauce and egg whites together, work very gently to avoid knocking the air out of the egg whites.

MAKING MERINGUES

Sweet and simple to make, meringues have just two ingredients, egg whites and sugar, and they have a lovely freshness that's often lacking in store-bought ones. Stored carefully, they will keep well.

Simple meringues

For 12 meringues, you will need 3 medium egg whites, 175g (6oz) caster sugar.

1 Preheat the oven to 170°C (150°C fan oven) mark 3. Cover a baking sheet with baking parchment. Put the egg whites into a large clean bowl.

2 Whisk them until soft peaks form. Add a spoonful of sugar and whisk until glossy.

3 Keep adding the sugar a spoonful at a time, whisking thoroughly after each addition until you have used half the sugar. The mixture should be thick and glossy.

4 Sprinkle the remaining sugar over the mixture and then gently fold in using a metal spoon.

5 Hold a dessertspoon in each hand and pick up a spoonful of mixture in one spoon, then scrape the other one against it to lift the mixture off. Repeat the process a few times, to form a rough oval shape. Using the empty spoon, push the oval on to the baking sheet; hold it just over the sheet so that it doesn't drop from a great height. Continue this process with the remaining mixture to make 12 meringues.

6 Put the meringues in the oven and bake for 15 minutes, then turn the oven off and leave them in the oven to dry out overnight.

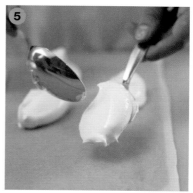

VARIATIONS

- For a richer flavour, add 1 tsp vanilla extract or 50g (2oz) ground almonds, pistachios or toasted hazelnuts.
- You can add a tiny amount of food colouring to make them a pale pink, lilac, and so on.
- Shape the meringues using a pastry bag instead of dessertspoons, if you like.
- Poaching the meringues keeps them soft throughout, perfect for serving on a pool of custard to make Floating Islands. To poach meringues, form them into ovals using two soup spoons and poach in a pan of simmering water for about 3 minutes.

PERFECT MERINGUES

- Baking meringues is best done in the evening, or whenever you know you won't be needing your oven for a good few hours, as they must be left to dry in the turned-off oven for several hours.
- Get a pan of water simmering gently before you start making your meringues, and line a large baking sheet with greaseproof paper or a silicone baking mat.
- Make sure your mixing bowl is spotlessly clean, as the tiniest trace of grease can keep the whites from whisking up properly. Also, check that your electric whisk is absolutely clean.
- If using a free-standing mixer with a whisk attachment, rather than a hand-held whisk, put the bowl of the mixer over the pan of simmering water. Dry it off and return it to the mixer stand.
- Don't rush the whisking process. If the egg whites are not beaten long enough, they won't hold their shape when baked.

Pavlova

This meringue variation has a chewy texture from the addition of vinegar and cornflour, which soften it, eliminating the crunchiness of ordinary meringue.

You will need 4 medium egg whites, 225g (8oz) golden caster sugar, 1 tbsp cornflour, 1 tbsp vanilla extract, 2 tsp white wine vinegar.

1 Preheat the oven to 130°C (110°C fan oven) mark ½. Take a large sheet of baking parchment and a large baking sheet. Draw a 20.5cm (8in) circle on the paper, then turn the paper over and place it on the baking sheet.

2 In a clean grease-free bowl, beat the egg whites until stiff peaks form.

3 Add the sugar, 1 tbsp at a time, until the mixture is stiff and glossy. Mix together the cornflour, vanilla and vinegar in a small bowl and sprinkle over the meringue mixture. Whisk for another minute.

4 Put a little dab of meringue under each corner of the parchment, to secure it to the baking sheet. Using a metal spoon, make a continuous ring of meringue inside the edge of the marked circle. Fill the empty circle with meringue, then flatten it out as evenly as possible with a palette knife or spatula.

5 Bake until it's firm about the edges and slightly soft in the centre (about 1¼ hours). Leave to cool.

Pavlova toppings

1 Whip 280ml (9½fl oz) double cream in a bowl until it gently holds its shape and spread it over the cooked, cooled pavlova.

2 Top with fresh seasonal fruits. In summer, berries such as strawberries, raspberries and blueberries make an excellent choice. You can also try chopped mango and whole redcurrants or sliced kiwi fruit and halved white seedless grapes.

MAKING BATTERS

Batters can serve a number of purposes, and are remarkably versatile for something so simple. All you need to remember when working with them is to mix quickly and lightly.

Pancakes

To make eight pancakes, you will need 125g (4oz) plain flour, a pinch of salt, 1 medium egg, 300ml (½ pint) milk, oil and butter to fry.

1 Sift the flour and salt, make a well in the middle and whisk in the egg. Work in the milk, then leave to stand for 20 minutes. Heat a pan and coat lightly with fat. Coat thinly with batter.

2 Cook for 1½–2 minutes until golden, carefully turning once.

Drop scones

For 15–18 pancakes, you will need 125g (4oz) self-raising flour, 2 tbsp caster sugar, 1 medium egg, beaten, 150ml (¼ pint) milk, a little vegetable oil to grease.

1 Mix the flour and sugar in a bowl. Make a well in the centre and mix in the egg and a little milk to achieve the consistency of thick cream.

2 Oil a griddle or heavy frying pan and heat it until medium-hot. Drop some of the batter in small rounds on to the griddle or pan and cook at a steady heat until bubbles rise to the surface (2–3 minutes).

3 Turn and cook for another 2–3 minutes, then remove to a clean teatowel. Cover with another teatowel to keep them moist, and continue cooking the scones until you have used all the batter.

USING CREAM

Cream, the fat globules in milk, is one of the richest and most luxurious of foodstuffs, capable of enhancing the texture and body of any dish to which it is added.

Cooking with cream

Cream may curdle when heated so if you are using it in cooking, do not let the mixture reach boiling point after cream has been added. Double cream is the best to use in cooking, as it is less likely to curdle. All creams have a short shelf life and should be kept in the fridge.

Use in its various types, to add to sauces, soups, savoury and sweet dishes; as a main ingredient in ice creams and other desserts; as a topping or decoration for fruit, cakes, puddings and breakfast cereals; and added to drinks.

Clotted cream

This very rich cream keeps for much longer than ordinary cream. It is too thick to pour but can be used as a main ingredient of a cream tea, served with scones and jam; in ice cream, or as a dessert topping.

Aerosol cream

Use aerosol cream just before serving, as it won't hold its shape for long periods and quickly melts; it is not suitable for decoration. Keep in the fridge once opened and use within a few days. It should not be regarded as a substitute for freshly whipped cream.

TYPES OF CREAM

- Single cream (around 18% fat) cannot be whipped, but it is excellent for pouring.
- Whipping cream and double cream can be whipped. Whipping cream has the lower fat content of the two (around 38% compared to 48% in double), and gives a lighter result.
- Extra-thick cream has been homogenised, so is not suitable for whipping – use as a rich spooning cream.

Whipping cream

Cream will whip more quickly if it and the bowl to be used are chilled first. Take care not to over-whip – stop every now and again to test the consistency; cream stiffens very quickly and it is too late when the cream turns to butter consistency. For most uses it is ready when the cream just holds its shape, but is still floppy. At this stage the maximum amount of air is incorporated. Over-beating of cream will result in a poor texture in dishes such as cold soufflés and mousses, and it will also make it more difficult to fold in cream evenly.

soft peak stage

1 Pour the cream into a large, deep bowl. Use an electric or hand whisk at a low speed and whip just until the cream clings to the whisk when lifted out of the bowl. Stop now and again to test the consistency.

stiff peak stage

1 Pour the cream into a large, deep bowl. Use an electric or hand whisk at a low speed and whisk until the cream clings firmly to the whisk when lifted out of the bowl. Stop now and again to test the consistency.

USING CHEESE

There is a huge variety of cheese available today, from the traditional hard varieties such as Cheddar, Leicester or Parmesan, to the soft, fresh, blue and continental varieties.

How to choose cheese

Avoid any cheese that has a strong ammonia odour. Hard or semi-hard cheese that has beads of moisture on the surface, or a dry, cracked rind, should be rejected. Semi-soft cheeses should yield to gentle pressure and any powdery bloom on the rind should be evenly coloured and slightly moist.

Buy only as much as you need (even if it's just a sliver) for consumption within a few days. Refrigeration at home will dry out the cheese.

If buying pre-packed cheese, check that it does not look sweaty or excessively runny and that it is within the life of its date stamp. If the date is many weeks ahead, it may mean that the cheese is immature; this may not matter if you intend to serve the cheese at this immature stage or to store it for using when mature.

Glamorgan sausages

To serve four, you will need 150g (5oz) grated Caerphilly cheese, 200g (7oz) fresh white breadcrumbs, 3 finely chopped spring onions, 1 tbsp freshly chopped flat-leafed parsley, leaves from 4 thyme sprigs, 3 large eggs, 1 separated, vegetable oil, salt and ground black pepper.

1 Preheat the oven to 140°C (120°C fan oven) mark 1. Mix the cheese with 150g (5oz) breadcrumbs, the spring onions and herbs in a large bowl. Season well. Add the 2 whole eggs plus the extra yolk and mix well. Cover and chill for 5 minutes. Lightly beat the egg white in a shallow bowl. Tip the rest of the breadcrumbs on to a large plate.

2 Take 2 tbsp of the cheese mixture and shape into a small sausage, about 4cm (1½in) long. Roll first in the egg white, then in the breadcrumbs to coat. Repeat to make 12 sausages in total.

3 Heat 2 tsp oil in a large heavy-based pan until hot and fry the sausages in two batches for 6–8 minutes, turning until golden all over. Keep warm in the oven while cooking the rest. Serve with salad and chutney.

COOKING WITH CHEESE

The less cooking cheese has, the better. Overheating tends to make it tough and indigestible, so when making a dish such as cheese sauce, always heat the cheese very gently and do not cook longer than is necessary to melt it. Most hard cheeses are excellent for grating and melting. Soft cheeses such as Camembert won't grate, but can be used baked or melted into sauces. Semi-soft cheeses, such as Edam are excellent for grilling.

THE CHEESEBOARD

Some people prefer a plate of cheese and biscuits rather than pudding. At an informal supper you could offer a cheeseboard instead of dessert along with some fresh fruit. For more formal occasions, offer the cheeseboard as a separate course, either before pudding or as an alternative alongside dessert. As a rule of thumb, include one hard, one blue and one or two soft cheeses.

VEGETARIAN CHEESES

Some vegetarians prefer to avoid cheeses that have been produced by the traditional method, because this uses animal-derived rennet. Most supermarkets and cheese shops now stock an excellent range of vegetarian cheeses, produced using vegetarian rennet.

EGGY BREAD

Serves 1–2
Preparation 5 minutes
Cooking time 10 minutes
Techniques see also using cheese (page 65)

75ml (2½fl oz) milk
1 small egg
2 slices wholemeal bread
25g (1oz) butter
125g (4oz) Caerphilly cheese, grated
2 tbsp pickle
3 pickled onions, chopped

1 Preheat the grill. Beat together the milk and egg. Dip both slices of bread into the egg mixture, coating well on both sides.
2 Melt the butter in a large frying pan and fry the bread until golden brown on both sides. Keep warm.
3 Mix together the cheese, pickle and pickled onions. Spread the cheese mixture over the bread, then grill until golden and bubbling. Serve immediately.

NUTRITION PER SERVING
434 cals | 130g fat (18g sats) | 23g carbs | 2.2g salt **V**

CREAMY BAKED EGGS

Serves 4
Preparation 5 minutes
Cooking time 15–18 minutes
Techniques see also baking eggs (page 57)

butter to grease
4 sun-dried tomatoes
4 medium eggs
4 tbsp double cream
salt and ground black pepper

1 Preheat the oven to 180°C (160°C fan oven) mark 4. Grease four individual ramekins.
2 Put 1 tomato in each ramekin and season with salt and pepper. Carefully break an egg on top of each, then drizzle 1 tbsp cream over each egg.
3 Bake for 15–18 minutes – the eggs will continue to cook once they have been taken out of the oven.
4 Leave to stand for 2 minutes before serving.

NUTRITION PER SERVING
161 cals | 14g fat (7g sats) | 3g carbs | 0.2g salt

MIXED MUSHROOM FRITTATA

Serves 4
Preparation 15 minutes
Cooking time 15–20 minutes
Techniques see also preparing mushrooms (page 187),
chopping herbs (page 436)

1 tbsp olive oil
300g (11oz) mixed mushrooms, sliced
2 tbsp freshly chopped thyme
zest and juice of ½ lemon
50g (2oz) watercress, chopped
6 medium eggs, beaten
salt and ground black pepper

1 Heat the oil in a large deep frying pan over a medium
heat. Add the mushrooms and thyme and stir-fry for 4–5
minutes until starting to soften and brown. Stir in the lemon
zest and juice, then bubble for 1 minute. Reduce the heat.
2 Preheat the grill. Add the watercress to the beaten eggs,
season with salt and pepper and pour into the pan. Cook
on the hob for 7–8 minutes until the sides and base are
firm but the centre is still a little soft.
3 Transfer to the grill and cook for 4–5 minutes until just
set. Cut into wedges to serve.

COOK'S TIP
This frittata tastes especially good served with
chunks of stoneground, wholegrain bread and a crisp
green salad.

NUTRITION PER SERVING
149 cals | 12g fat (3g sats) | 0g carbs | 0.3g salt

CHEESE RAMEKINS

Serves 4
Preparation 10 minutes
Cooking time 10–15 minutes
Techniques see also using cheese (page 65), making breadcrumbs (page 318), separating and whisking eggs (page 54)

50g (2oz) Double Gloucester cheese, grated
50g (2oz) Cheshire cheese, grated
4 tbsp single cream or milk
50g (2oz) cooked ham, finely chopped
50g (2oz) fresh wholemeal breadcrumbs
few drops of Worcestershire sauce
a pinch of ground mixed spice
butter to grease
2 medium eggs, separated
salt and ground black pepper
crusty bread and mixed salad to serve

1 Preheat the oven to 200°C (180°C fan oven) mark 6. Put the cheeses into a bowl, then beat in the cream or milk, the ham, breadcrumbs, Worcestershire sauce and mixed spice. Season to taste. Grease four ramekins and stand them on a baking sheet.
2 Beat the egg yolks into the mixture. Whisk the egg whites until stiff, then fold into the mixture.
3 Spoon into the ramekin dishes and cook in the oven for 10–15 minutes until golden and risen. Serve at once with crusty bread and a mixed salad.

NUTRITION PER SERVING
224 cals | 14g fat (8g sats) | 10g carbs | 1.4g salt

TWICE-BAKED SOUFFLÉS

Serves 8
Preparation 20 minutes
Cooking time 1¼ hours
Techniques see also preparing cauliflower (page 192),
separating eggs (page 54)

25g (1oz) ground almonds
50g (2oz) butter, plus extra to grease
250g (9oz) cauliflower florets
150ml (¼ pint) milk
40g (1½oz) plain flour
75g (3oz) Cheddar cheese, finely grated
75g (3oz) Emmenthal cheese, finely grated
3 large eggs, separated
285ml (9½fl oz) double cream
1 tbsp grainy mustard
salt and ground black pepper
rocket leaves and cherry tomatoes to serve
olive oil and balsamic vinegar to drizzle

1 Preheat the oven to 180°C (160°C fan oven) mark 4.
Cook the almonds under a grill, turning until lightly toasted.
Grease and baseline eight 150ml (¼ pint) ramekins with
greaseproof paper. Dust with the almonds.
2 Cook the cauliflower in salted boiling water for 5–10
minutes until tender. Drain, plunge into iced water and drain
again, then blend with the milk for 2–3 minutes until
smooth. Melt the butter in a pan, add the flour and mix to a
smooth paste. Stir in the cauliflower purée and bring to the
boil. Cool a little, then beat in the cheeses and egg yolks.
Season with salt and pepper.
3 Whisk the whites to a soft peak and fold in. Spoon the
mixture into the ramekins, put into a roasting tin and fill
halfway up the sides with hot water. Cook for 20–25
minutes until firm to the touch. Turn off the oven. Remove
from the roasting tin and cool completely. Run a knife
around the edge of the soufflés and turn out on to a
baking sheet.
4 Preheat the oven to 200°C (180°C fan oven) mark 6.
Pour the cream into a wide pan, bring to the boil and
bubble until syrupy and reduced by one-third. Add the
mustard and season. Spoon a little cream over the soufflés
and bake for 15–20 minutes until golden. Serve with rocket
leaves and cherry tomatoes drizzled with olive oil and
balsamic vinegar.

FREEZING'S TIP
Prepare the recipe to the end of step 3, then wrap
separately and freeze.
To use Complete the recipe. Cook the soufflés from
frozen at 200°C (180°C fan oven) mark 6 for 25–30
minutes until golden.

NUTRITION PER SERVING
385 cals | 35g fat (20g sats) | 7g carbs | 0.7g salt

LEEK AND PEA FLAN

Serves 4
Preparation 15 minutes
Cooking time about 1 hour
Techniques see also preparing leeks (page 183), using cheese (page 65), using pastry (page 290)

450g (1lb) leeks, trimmed and sliced
125g (4oz) fresh or frozen shelled peas
150ml (¼ pint) milk
150g (5oz) natural yogurt
3 medium eggs
175g (6oz) plain wholemeal flour, plus extra to dust
125g (4oz) Cheddar cheese, grated
75g (3oz) butter
salt and ground black pepper

1 Preheat the oven to 190°C (170°C fan oven) mark 5. Cook the leeks and peas in a little lightly salted water in a tightly covered medium pan until tender. Drain well.
2 Put the leeks, peas, milk and yogurt into a blender or food processor and whiz until smooth.
3 Beat 2 of the eggs into the purée and season to taste. Lightly beat the remaining egg in a small bowl.
4 Put the flour and half the cheese into a bowl. Rub in the butter until the mixture resembles fine breadcrumbs, then bind together with the remaining egg.
5 Roll out the pastry on a lightly floured worksurface and use to line a 23cm (9in) flan dish. Pour in the leek mixture, sprinkle the remaining cheese over the top and cook in the oven for 50–55 minutes until golden.

NUTRITION PER SERVING
519 cals | 31g fat (17g sats) | 38g carbs | 1.6g salt

CLASSIC TIRAMISÙ

Serves 8
Preparation 20 minutes, plus chilling
Techniques see also separating eggs (page 54),
whipping cream (page 64)

4 medium egg yolks
75g (3oz) golden caster sugar
200g tub mascarpone
1 tbsp vanilla extract
300ml (½ pint) double cream, whipped until softly peaking
100ml (3½fl oz) grappa
200g pack sponge fingers or Savoiardi biscuits
450ml (¾ pint) warm strong black coffee
1 tbsp cocoa powder

1 Using an electric hand-held beater, whisk the egg
yolks and sugar in a large bowl until pale and thick, about
5 minutes. Add the mascarpone and vanilla extract and beat
until smooth. Fold in the double cream and grappa.
2 Spread half the mascarpone mixture over the bottom of
eight small serving dishes. Dip the sponge fingers, in turn,
into the coffee and arrange on the mascarpone layer. Top
with the remaining mascarpone mixture.
3 Cover and chill in the fridge for at least 2 hours. Dust
with cocoa, just before serving.

NUTRITION PER SERVING
420 cals | 33g fat (18g sats) | 24g carbs | 0.3g salt Ⓥ

QUEEN OF PUDDINGS

Serves 4
Preparation 20 minutes, plus standing
Cooking time about 1¼ hours
Techniques see also separating eggs (page 54), making breadcrumbs, (page 318), making meringues (pages 60–1)

4 medium eggs
600ml (1 pint) milk
125g (4oz) fresh breadcrumbs
3–4 tbsp raspberry jam
75g (3oz) caster sugar

1 Separate 3 eggs and beat together the 3 egg yolks and 1 whole egg. Add to the milk and mix well. Stir in the fresh breadcrumbs.
2 Spread the jam on the bottom of a pie dish. Pour in the milk mixture and leave for 30 minutes. Preheat the oven to 150°C (130°C fan oven) mark 2.
3 Bake in the oven for 1 hour or until set. Put the egg whites into a clean, grease-free bowl and whisk until they form stiff peaks. Fold in the sugar, then pile on top of the custard and return to the oven for a further 15–20 minutes until the meringue is set.

NUTRITION PER SERVING
387 cals | 9g fat (3g sats) | 65g carbs | 1g salt **V**

CRÈME CARAMEL

Serves 6
Preparation 15 minutes
Cooking time 20–30 minutes, plus cooling
Techniques see also separating eggs (page 54), extracting seeds from vanilla pods (page 438)

175g (6oz) granulated sugar
600ml (1 pint) whole or semi-skimmed milk
1 vanilla pod, split lengthways, or a few drops of
   vanilla extract
4 large eggs, plus 4 egg yolks
50–65g (2–2½oz) golden caster sugar, to taste

1 Warm six ramekins. To make the caramel, put the granulated sugar into a heavy-based pan and heat gently until melted, brushing any sugar down from the side of the pan. Increase the heat and boil rapidly for a few minutes until the syrup turns to a rich golden brown caramel, gently swirling the pan to ensure even browning. Immediately, dip the base of the pan into cool water to prevent further cooking.
2 Pour a little caramel into each of the warmed ramekins and quickly rotate to coat the base and part way up the sides. Leave to cool.
3 To make the custard, put the milk and vanilla pod in a pan and heat until almost boiling; if using vanilla extract, add after heating the milk.
4 Meanwhile, beat the eggs, egg yolks and caster sugar in a bowl until well mixed. Stir in the hot milk. Strain, then pour into the ramekins.
5 Stand the ramekins in a roasting tin containing enough hot water to come halfway up the sides. Bake at 170°C (150°C fan oven) mark 3 for 20–30 minutes until just set and a knife inserted into the centre comes out clean. Remove from the tin and leave to cool.
6 To turn out, free the edges by pressing with the fingertips then run a knife around the edge of each custard. Put a serving dish over the top, invert and lift off the ramekin; the caramel will have formed a sauce around the custard.

TRY SOMETHING DIFFERENT
Make one large crème caramel in a 15cm (6in) soufflé dish; bake as above for 1 hour or until just set. After cooling, chill for several hours. Transfer to room temperature 30 minutes before serving.

NUTRITION PER SERVING
300 cals | 10g fat (3g sats) | 45g carbs | 0.3g salt Ⓥ

CRÈME BRÛLÉE

Serves 6
Preparation 15 minutes, plus infusing and chilling
Cooking time 30–35 minutes, plus cooling
Techniques see also separating eggs (page 54), extracting seeds from vanilla pods (page 438)

600ml (1 pint) double cream
1 vanilla pod, split lengthways
4 large egg yolks
125g (4oz) golden caster sugar

1 Pour the cream into a pan, add the vanilla pod and bring slowly to the boil. Remove from the heat, cover and leave to infuse for at least 30 minutes. Stand six ramekins in a roasting tin.
2 Beat the egg yolks with 1 tbsp caster sugar in a bowl. Pour in the vanilla-infused cream, stirring constantly. Strain into a jug, then pour into the ramekins. Surround with hand-hot water to come halfway up the sides of the ramekins. Bake at 150°C (130°C fan oven) mark 2 for 30–35 minutes. Cool, then chill in the fridge for at least 4 hours or, even better, overnight.
3 Preheat the grill to high Sprinkle the remaining sugar evenly on top of the custards to form a thin layer. Put under the very hot grill for 2–3 minutes until it caramelises. (Alternatively, you can wave a cook's blowtorch over the surface to caramelise the sugar.) Leave to cool for 1 hour, but do not chill – the caramel will form a crisp layer on the surface. Serve within 2–3 hours.

NUTRITION PER SERVING
580 cals | 52g fat (34g sats) | 25g carbs | 0.1g salt **V**

BAKED RASPBERRY MERINGUE PIE

Serves 8
Preparation 15 minutes
Cooking time 8 minutes
Techniques see also separating eggs (page 54),
preparing berries (page 219)

8 trifle sponges
450g (1lb) raspberries, lightly crushed
2–3 tbsp raspberry liqueur
3 medium egg whites
150g (5oz) golden caster sugar

1 Preheat the oven to 230°C (210°C fan oven) mark 8.
Put the trifle sponges in the bottom of a 2 litre (3½ pint)
ovenproof dish. Spread the raspberries on top and drizzle
with the raspberry liqueur.
2 Whisk the egg whites in a clean grease-free bowl until
stiff peaks form. Gradually whisk in the sugar until the
mixture is smooth and glossy. Spoon the meringue mixture
over the raspberries and bake for 6–8 minutes until golden.

COOK'S TIP
If you don't have any raspberry liqueur,
you can use another fruit-based liqueur such as
Grand Marnier instead.

NUTRITION PER SERVING
176 cals | 2g fat (1g sats) | 37g carbs | 0.1g salt **V**

TOASTED HAZELNUT MERINGUE CAKE

Serves 8
Preparation 10 minutes, plus cooling
Cooking time about 30 minutes
Techniques see also toasting nuts (page 228),
separating eggs (page 54)

oil to grease
175g (6oz) skinned hazelnuts, toasted
3 large egg whites
175g (6oz) golden caster sugar
250g carton mascarpone cheese
285ml (9½fl oz) double cream
3 tbsp Baileys Irish Cream liqueur, plus extra to serve
140g (4½oz) frozen raspberries
340g jar redcurrant jelly

1 Preheat the oven to 190°C (170°C fan oven) mark 5.
Lightly oil two 18cm (7in) sandwich tins and baseline with
baking parchment. Whiz the hazelnuts in a food processor
until finely chopped.
2 Put the egg whites into a clean grease-free bowl and
whisk until stiff peaks form. Whisk in the sugar, a spoonful
at a time. Using a metal spoon, fold in half the nuts. Divide
the mixture between the tins and spread evenly. Bake in the
middle of the oven for about 30 minutes, then leave to cool
in the tins for 30 minutes.
3 To make the filling, put the mascarpone cheese in a
bowl. Beat in the cream and liqueur until smooth. Put the
raspberries and redcurrant jelly into a pan and heat gently
until the jelly has melted. Sieve, then cool.
4 Use a palette knife to loosen the edges of the
meringues, then turn out on to a wire rack. Peel off the
baking parchment and discard. Put a large sheet of baking
parchment on a board and sit one meringue on top, flat
side down. Spread a third of the mascarpone mixture over
the meringue, then drizzle with raspberry purée. Top with
the other meringue, then cover the whole cake with the
rest of the mascarpone mixture. Sprinkle with the remaining
hazelnuts. Carefully put the cake on to a serving plate and
drizzle with more liqueur, if you like.

FREEZING TIP
Freezing the meringue makes it slightly softer but no less
tasty. Make the cake up to the end of step 4 but don't put on
serving plate or drizzle with more liqueur. Using the paper, lift
the cake into the freezer, then freeze until solid. Once solid,
freeze in a sturdy container for up to one month.
To use Thaw overnight in the refrigerator,
then complete the recipe.

NUTRITION PER SERVING
598 cals | 38g fat (16g sats) | 57g carbs | 0.1g salt **V**

FISH AND SHELLFISH

Healthy and delicious, but often intimidating for the home cook, this chapter takes the mystery out of preparing and cooking fish and shellfish. There are clearly illustrated, easy-to-follow step-by-step instructions for all the basic techniques – from preparing and cooking fish, peeling and butterflying prawns and cooking and removing the meat from crabs and lobsters to cleaning and cooking mussels and clams, opening scallops and oysters, and cleaning and preparing squid, cuttlefish and octopus. The comprehensive recipe collection builds on these skills with delicious recipes such as Red mullet baked in paper, Crab cakes with mayonnaise, Tuna with coriander rice, Potted prawns, Fish and chips, Old-fashioned fish pie and Thai green shellfish curry.

PREPARING ROUND FISH

Round fish include all those fish with a round body such as cod, herring, mackerel and trout. Most fishmongers will prepare them for you but it is very simple to clean, bone and fillet them yourself.

Cleaning and boning

1 Cut off the fins with scissors. Using the blunt edge of a knife, scrape the fish from tail to head and rinse off the loose scales. (The scaled fish should feel smooth.)

2 Insert a sharp knife at the hole towards the rear of the stomach and slit the skin up to the gills. Ease out the entrails. Use scissors to snip out anything that remains. With the knife, cut along the vein under the backbone. Wash the cavity under running water.

3 Working from the belly side of the fish, cut along one side of the backbone, then remove as many fine bones as possible and separate the backbone from the flesh.

4 Turn the fish over and repeat on the other side of the backbone. Carefully snip the backbone with scissors, then remove.

Filleting

1 Using a very sharp knife, cut through the flesh down to the backbone just behind the head.

2 Working from the head end, insert the knife between the flesh and the ribs on the back of the fish.

3 Holding the knife flat on the ribs, cut all the way down to the tail until the flesh is completely detached along the full length of the fish.

4 Lift the detached portion of flesh and, with the knife again placed flat on the ribs, cut until the flesh is detached from the bones and remove the fillet.

5 Turn the fish over and repeat on the other side, again working from head to tail, to remove the second fillet from the fish.

COOK'S TIP

Some cooks find it easier to remove the second fillet by keeping the fish with the unboned side down and working the knife under the ribs on both back and belly side of the fillet.

PREPARING FLAT FISH

These techniques are suitable for flat-shaped fish such as turbot, plaice and sole. Flat fish is often used filleted for recipes and sometimes rolled around a stuffing. For this, it also needs to be skinned.

Cleaning and skinning

1 To gut, slit open the skin just behind the head of the fish where the stomach sac begins. Work your fingers in and pull the entrails out, then snip out the remainder with scissors.

2 Thick-skinned fish, such as sole, can be skinned by hand. Make a nick right down to the backbone where the body meets the tail. Work your fingers under the skin until you have lifted enough to get a grip on.

3 Holding the tail in one hand, pull on the flap in the direction of the head. The skin should come away in a single sheet.

4 Thinner-skinned fish can be filleted first, then skinned using a knife. Put the fillet on a board with the skin down and the tail towards you. Make a nick in the tail flesh, just deep enough to cut through to the skin, and lift the little flap of flesh with the knife.

5 Hold the knife on the skin at a very shallow angle, almost parallel to the worksurface, and work it between flesh and skin to remove the skin in a single piece.

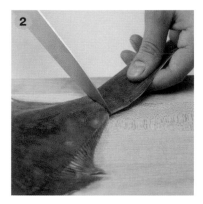

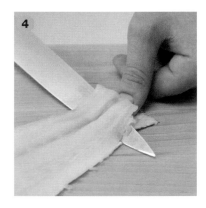

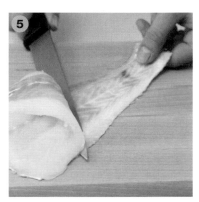

Filleting

1 Insert a sharp knife between the flesh and ribs on one side of the backbone. Holding the knife nearly parallel to the backbone, cut between the backbone and the flesh until detached. Turn the fish round and repeat on the other side.

2 Turn the fish over and repeat on the other side. Smaller fish may only provide two fillets.

COOKING FISH

Fish is wonderfully versatile and can be cooked in many ways – from the simplest steaming and poaching to quick stir-frying, crispy deep-frying and delicious roasting, baking and braising.

Steaming

A large traditional bamboo steamer is usually suitable for steaming small fish or pieces of fish, but a wok fitted with a bamboo, wood or metal trivet is often useful for steaming larger whole fish.

1 Put the fish on a lightly oiled heatproof plate that will hold it comfortably and will fit comfortably inside the steamer.

2 Season the fish with salt and ground black pepper or marinate (see box below).

3 Bring the water in the steamer to the boil over a medium heat. Put the fish in its plate in the steamer, put the lid on tightly and cook until the fish is just cooked through. Allow about 10 minutes of cooking per 2.5cm (1in) thickness.

Poaching

Fish can be poached whole or in pieces. If you're cooking a large fish such as salmon, you will need a salmon poacher. Smaller fish or pieces can be cooked in a large frying pan or in a roasting dish.

1 Put the fish in the pan and add enough poaching liquid (see page 37) to just cover it.

2 Bring it to the boil, then turn the heat right down so that the liquid is just simmering. The fish will need about 10 minutes of cooking per 2.5cm (1in) thickness.

3 Remove the fish carefully to a serving platter and allow it to drain well. Pour off the water before saucing and serving.

MARINADES

- Because fish is already tender, marinades are used for flavour and not to tenderise. Therefore, fish only requires to be marinated briefly – about 10 minutes is usually enough.
- If you are cooking whole fish, slash the skin diagonally on both sides so that the marinade can penetrate the flesh underneath it. While cooking, spoon the marinade over the fish to get the most flavour.
- The simplest marinades are best: try combining vegetable oil, soy sauce and garlic, or extra-virgin olive oil, lemon juice and chopped shallots.

Pan-frying whole fish

1 Put in enough oil to fill the pan to a depth of about 5mm (¼ in). Put the pan over a medium-high heat. Dust small whole fish with flour, then slip them carefully into the hot oil.

2 When they are lightly browned and looking crisp underneath, turn them using two spatulas. Cook until the second side is brown and the flesh just cooked through.

Pan-frying fillets or steaks

1 Put in enough oil to fill the pan to a depth of about 3mm (⅛ in) and heat over a medium-high heat. Add the fish to the pan. If you like, you can dust the fish with flour first.

2 Cook for a few minutes, then lift, using tongs, to check the colour underneath. If it is brown, turn the fish over completely and fry until cooked through.

Searing

1 Put in enough oil (or a mixture of oil and clarified butter) to fill the pan to a depth of about 3mm (⅛ in). Add the fish to the pan and fry.

2 Fry firm-fleshed fish such as tuna and salmon, or shellfish such as scallops, over a very high heat so that it cooks quickly – or stays undercooked in the middle while browning deeply on the outside.

Stir-frying

Choose a firm fish such as monkfish as more delicate fish will break up.

1 Cut into bite-sized pieces. Heat a wok or large pan until very hot.

2 Add oil to coat. Add the fish and toss over a high heat for 2 minutes until just cooked. Remove to a bowl. Cook vegetables and flavourings. Return the fish to heat through.

Deep-frying

1 Prepare the fish for frying (either small whole fish or fish pieces) and chill. Prepare the seasoned flour, batter or coating. Heat vegetable oil in a deep-fryer to 180°C (test by frying a small cube of bread; it should brown in 40 seconds). Start battering or coating your fish.

2 Carefully lower the fish into the oil, taking care not to splash. Don't put too many pieces of fish into the pan at once (if you do, the temperature drops and the fish takes longer to cook and becomes greasy).

3 As the fish becomes golden and crisp, remove it with a slotted spoon and drain on kitchen paper. Serve immediately or keep warm in the oven until everything is cooked.

COATINGS AND BATTERS

Flour, egg and breadcrumbs For a light coating, roll the food in flour seasoned with salt and pepper. For a crunchy coating, dip the floured food in beaten egg, then coat with dry breadcrumbs.

Coating batter You will need 125g (4oz) plain flour, sifted, pinch of salt, 1 medium egg, 150ml (¼ pint) milk. Mix the flour, salt, egg and enough milk for a stiff batter that will coat the back of a spoon; beat until smooth. Dip the food into the batter, drain slightly, then put into the hot fat.

Tempura batter For this delicate batter, you will need 125g (4oz) plain flour, 125g (4oz) cornflour, pinch of salt, 1 medium egg yolk, 300ml (½ pint) sparkling water. Lightly whisk the ingredients (the batter should be lumpy). Deep-fry at 170°C (a cube of bread should brown in 40 seconds).

Roasting

Good for firm fish, such as salmon and cod, at least 4cm (1½in) thick.

1 Preheat the oven to 190°C (170°C fan oven) mark 5. Arrange the fish on an oiled baking sheet. Whisk together 2 parts olive oil to 1 part lemon juice. Brush over the fish.

2 Roast for 10 minutes per 2.5cm (1in) thickness of fish until cooked.

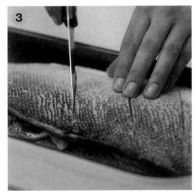

Baking

This method is suitable for cooking whole fish and larger pieces of fish. Cooking times will vary according to the weight and thickness of fish. To bake a whole salmon for six to eight, you will need 2.5kg (5½lb) salmon, filleted, 1 bulb fennel, cored and sliced, 2 tbsp extra-virgin olive oil, 1 lemon, thinly sliced, a few sprigs of dill, 4 tbsp dry white wine, black pepper.

1 Cook the fennel gently in half the olive oil for about 10 minutes until softened, then leave to cool. Meanwhile, preheat the oven to 190°C (170°C fan oven) mark 5.

2 Using tweezers, remove any remaining pin-bones from the salmon. Lay one fillet in a roasting dish, skin side down. Lay the lemon slices on top with the fennel, dill and a grinding of black pepper and spoon over the wine. Lay the other fillet on top, skin side up.

3 Score the skin every 5cm (2in) with a sharp knife. Brush with the remaining oil and scrunch pieces of foil against the fleshy parts of the fish, leaving the skin exposed.

4 Bake the fish for 30–40 minutes until the skin is opaque and the flesh firm to the touch. To test if it is cooked, slip a knife into the scored fish – it should be opaque.

5 Serve hot or cold with minted new potatoes and mayonnaise.

Braising

This is a good method when you want a fairly hearty dish that has its own sauce.

To serve four, you will need 1 tbsp oil, 15g (½oz) butter, 1 onion, chopped, 2 garlic cloves, crushed, 2 tbsp each freshly chopped parsley and thyme, 400g can chopped tomatoes, 1 large, flat fish, such as turbot or sole, about 900g (2lb).

1 Put the oil and butter in a large frying pan and cook the onion and garlic until soft.

2 Add the herbs and tomatoes to the pan, and cook until the tomatoes are fairly thick.

3 Lay the fish over the vegetables and spoon the tomatoes over it. Cook for another 5–10 minutes until the fish is just cooked through.

PERFECT BRAISED FISH

— Choose thick, fairly firm-fleshed fish if you are cooking it in pieces – cod, haddock, monkfish, hake and whiting are all good choices. Shellfish, squid and cuttlefish are also suitable.

— You can choose a variety of vegetables to cook in braised dishes. Make sure that all the other ingredients are cooked and their flavours well developed before you add the fish.

— Once you add the fish to the pan, don't move it about too much as the flesh can easily break up. Be careful when removing it from the pan.

Grilling

Suitable for thick cuts such as fillets and steaks; small to medium whole fish such as sardines and mackerel; and flat fish on the bone such as plaice. Leave the skin on fillets.

1 Brush the outside of the fish with oil or marinade (see page 82).

2 Set the grill to high and cook until the fish starts to turn golden, then turn carefully. Allow 4–5 minutes for fillets and 10–15 minutes for thick steaks, cutlets and whole fish.

PREPARING PRAWNS

Full of flavour and perhaps at their best served simply, raw prawns are delicious served boiled, steamed, stir-fried, grilled and used in soup. They can be cooked in or out of their shells.

Peeling and butterflying

1   To shell prawns, pull off the head and put to one side. Using pointed scissors, cut through the soft shell on the belly side.

2   Prise the shell off, leaving the tail attached. (Add to the head; it can be used later for making stock.)

3   Using a small sharp knife, make a shallow cut along the length of the back of the prawn. Using the point of the knife, carefully remove and discard the black vein (the intestinal tract) that runs along the back of the prawn.

4   To 'butterfly' the prawn, cut halfway through the flesh lengthways from the head end to the base of the tail, and open up the prawn.

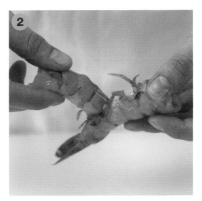
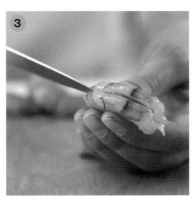

LANGOUSTINES AND CRAYFISH

- Related to the prawn, langoustines and crayfish can be shelled in the same way as prawns. To extract the meat from langoustine claws, pull off the small pincer from the claws, then work with small scissors to cut open the main section all the way along its length. Split open and carefully pull out the flesh in a single piece. To extract the meat from large crayfish claws, crack them open using a hammer or lobster cracker, then remove the meat.
- Also known as scampi, langoustines are at their best when just boiled or steamed, and then eaten from the shells. They can also be used in a shellfish soup.
- Crayfish are sold either live or cooked. To cook, boil in court bouillon for 5–10 minutes. Remove from the stock and cool. Eat crayfish from the shell or in a soup.

PREPARING CRABS

The amazing taste of fresh crab makes this one of the favourite shellfish and it is also reasonably priced. Avoid frozen crab, as the flesh is watery, and prepare your own for the best flavour.

Preparing and cooking

1 Live crabs must be humanely killed before cooking. Put the crab on a board, with the belly facing up. Take a large chef's knife and plunge it straight down into the crab's head, right between or just below the eyes.

2 Put the crab in a pan of boiling water and cook for 5 minutes per 450g (1lb). Alternatively, steam for 8 minutes per 450g (1lb).

3 To serve whole, simply set on the table with crackers and crab picks for diners to use themselves.

4 To remove the cooked meat for a recipe, put the crab on a board, with the belly facing up. Twist off the legs and claws. Lift off and discard the 'apron' (tail) – long and pointed in a male, short and broad in a female.

5 Pull the body out of the shell and remove and discard the feathery gills and grey stomach sac. Cut the body into pieces and pick out the meat using your fingers and a crab pick or small knife. Scrape the brown meat from the shell, keeping it separate from the white meat. If there is roe in a female, keep that separate, too.

6 Crack the claws with the back of a large knife, and pull out the meat in a single piece or in large chunks.

7 Cut through the shells of the legs with scissors, then cut through the opposite side. Pull off the shell halves to expose the meat and remove.

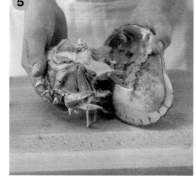

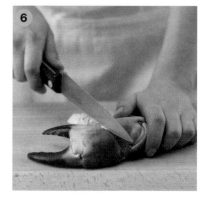

PREPARING LOBSTERS

The king of the crustaceans, lobster has a wonderfully sweet flavour and is excellent served simply: cold with a salad and mayonnaise or a sauce, or hot with butter.

Preparing and cooking

1 To kill a lobster humanely before grilling, boiling or baking, put it on a chopping board and hold the body firmly. Take a large chef's knife and plunge it straight down into the lobster's head, right between or just below the eyes. (It is inhumane to simply plunge it into boiling water or to put it into cold water and then bring it up to the boil.)

2 To cook the lobster whole, put it into a pot of boiling water and cook for 15–20 minutes.

3 If you are going to split the raw lobster for grilling or baking, cut the freshly killed lobster right through the head, then cut all the way down the length of the tail to split it in two.

4 Remove the head sac, which lies just behind the eyes, and discard. If you wish, you can remove the black coral (tomalley) and the green intestine, which lie inside the back of the shell just behind the head sac, or they may be left in place for cooking.

5 If you want the tail meat in one piece, split the head to where the tail begins, then use scissors to cut through the soft shell of the belly, down to the tail.

6 Pull the tail meat out with your fingers. Clean the head as in step 3. Cut off the claws and spiny legs. Crack the claws with a hammer or lobster cracker and remove the meat. Save the shells to make stock.

BUYING SHELLFISH

Shellfish should be as fresh as possible and should have a mild, fresh smell of the sea.

- Live lobsters are dark blue in colour and turn bright pink when cooked. When buying a live lobster, choose one with all its claws and legs intact.
- The common brown crab is most often found in fishmongers, but there are many varieties. When buying live crabs, look for a really lively one and make sure all its legs are intact.
- Prawns are sold ready-cooked and raw. Try to buy fresh ones when you can as they have the best taste and texture.
- When choosing molluscs, choose those with tightly closed, undamaged shells. Mussels, clams, scallops and oysters sold fresh are still alive and an open shell may indicate the shellfish is far from fresh. Tap the shell – it should close. If not, discard it.

PREPARING MUSSELS AND CLAMS

Two of the most popular shellfish, mussels and clams take moments to cook. Careful preparation is important, so give yourself enough time to get the shellfish ready.

Cooking mussels

1 Scrape off the fibres attached to the shells (beards). If the mussels are very clean, give them a quick rinse under the cold tap. If they are very sandy, scrub them with a stiff brush.

2 If the shells have sizeable barnacles on them, it is best (though not essential) to remove them. Rap them sharply with a metal spoon or the back of a washing-up brush, then scrape off.

3 Discard any open mussels that don't shut when sharply tapped; this means they are dead and could be dangerous to eat.

4 In a large heavy-based pan, fry 2 finely chopped shallots and a generous handful of parsley in 25g (1oz) butter for about 2 minutes or until soft. Pour in 1cm (½in) dry white wine.

5 Add the mussels to the pan and cover tightly with a lid. Steam for 5–10 minutes until the shells open. Immediately take the pan away from the heat.

6 Using a slotted spoon, remove the mussels from the pan and discard any that haven't opened, then boil the cooking liquid rapidly to reduce. Pour over the mussels and serve immediately.

Cooking clams

Small clams are usually used as an ingredient; larger clams can be eaten raw in the shell.

1 To cook, rinse or lightly scrub the clams. Place in a large bowl of cold salted water (2 tbsp salt per 1 litre/ 1¾ pints water). Leave to stand for a few hours to allow the clams to open and release any sand and grit.

2 Cook as for mussels, then use according to the recipe.

PREPARING SCALLOPS AND OYSTERS

Both of these delicately flavoured shellfish are contained within shells that can be a little tricky to open.
Ask your fishmonger to prepare them if you prefer. The fish themselves have a marvellous taste.

Opening scallops

Scallops can be eaten raw, either seasoned or marinated in citrus juice with seasonings (see page 82). They take very little cooking, usually between 5 and 10 minutes.

1 Hold the scallop with the flat half of the shell facing up. Firmly ease a very sharp small knife between the shells at a point close to the hinge.

2 Keeping the knife angled towards the flat shell, cut all along the shell surface until the two shells can be separated easily. Cut along the bottom of the rounded shell to release its contents. Cut loose the meat and the grey/orange coral and discard everything else.

3 Rinse off any grit, cut the coral from the round meat, and cut the little scrap of muscle from the edge of the meat.

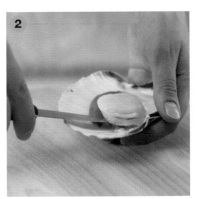

Opening oysters

Oysters can be fried, poached and grilled, or eaten straight from the shell with red wine vinegar flavoured with shallots, or just with lemon juice.

1 Hold the oyster in one hand with the flat half of the shell facing up, using a towel to protect your hand. Insert an oyster knife in the hinge and twist.

2 When the upper shell comes off, scrape off any shell and cut under the oyster to release it from the shell.

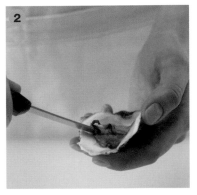

PREPARING SQUID AND CUTTLEFISH

Sliced into rings or left whole and stuffed, squid is a popular, flavourful and easily available fish. The less common cuttlefish also has a good flavour and is especially good in stews.

Cleaning and preparing

1 If you want to save the ink for using in a dish, position the head over a bowl and cut open the ink sac so that the ink can drain into it, then put the ink to one side

2 Cut off the tentacles just behind the 'beak'.

3 Pull out the beak and clean the tentacles well, getting off as many of the plastic-like rings from the suckers as you can.

4 Reach inside the body and pull out the internal organs, including the plastic-like 'pen' (in squid) or cuttle bone (in cuttlefish).

5 Scrape and pull off the loose, slippery skin covering the body. Rinse the body thoroughly to remove all internal organs, sand and other debris.

6 Detach the wings and put to one side, then cut up the tentacles and body as required in your recipe. Generally speaking, the longer the squid or cuttlefish is going to be cooked, the larger the pieces should be.

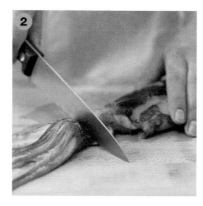

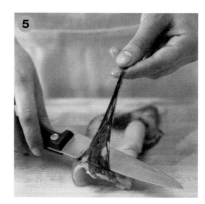

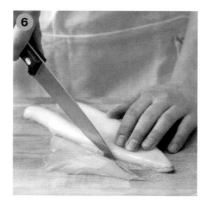

COOK'S TIP

Small squid are the sweetest and are generally best if cooked for a very short time: fried with a flour or batter coating, stir-fried, grilled or barbecued. Smaller cuttlefish can be treated in the same way. Larger cuttlefish and very large squid can be stewed.

PREPARING OCTOPUS

Small octopus can be cooked briefly like squid, but mostly they should be cooked slowly for a long time to make them tender. Cooking in red wine helps to tenderise large octopus.

Cleaning and preparing

1 Cut off the tentacles just behind the 'beak' (mouth).

2 Pull out the beak and clean the tentacles well, getting off as many of the plastic-like rings from the suckers as you can.

3 Turn the body inside out to expose the sac containing the internal organs. Pull out the sac and rub, scrape and pull off the loose, slippery skin covering the body. Rinse the body thoroughly to remove all internal organs, sand and other debris.

4 Cut up the tentacles and body as required in your recipe.

HOW TO BUY THE BEST FISH

For the best results, fish should be as fresh as possible. It's often hard to tell in the supermarket how fresh a piece of fish is but there are some key signs to look for. A really fresh fish will have:
- An even covering of scales with no patches and no damage to the fins.
- Bright and clear eyes and bright red gills.
- Flesh that feels firm rather than soft and spongy.
- Individual fillets should be moist, shiny and plump.

SMOKED SALMON PARCELS

Serves 6
Preparation 40 minutes
Cooking time 6 minutes
Techniques see also opening scallops (page 91), preparing vegetables (pages 182–194), zesting citrus fruits (page 217), making salad dressings (page 27)

6 large scallops or 12 small queen scallops with corals
    attached, about 225g (8oz) total weight
1 large ripe avocado
1 garlic clove, crushed
4 small spring onions, finely chopped
1 green chilli, seeded and chopped
1 tbsp grapeseed oil
zest and juice of 1 lime, plus extra to squeeze
6 large slices of smoked salmon, about 300g (11oz)
    total weight and 23cm (9in) in length
salt and ground black pepper
rocket leaves and lime wedges to garnish

For the coriander dressing
25g (1oz) fresh coriander sprigs
1 small garlic clove, crushed
50ml (2fl oz) grapeseed oil
1 tbsp lime juice
pinch of caster sugar

1 To make the coriander dressing, put all the ingredients in a blender and process until smooth. Put to one side.
2 To make the parcels, remove any tough membrane from the scallops and season with salt and pepper. Put in a steamer and cook for about 5 minutes or until the flesh is just white. Alternatively, put the scallops on a heatproof plate, cover with another plate and steam over a pan of simmering water for about 3 minutes on each side. Drain and set on kitchen paper to cool.
3 Put the avocado, garlic, spring onions, chilli, oil and lime zest and juice in a bowl. Mash the avocado with a fork, then mix together and season.
4 Lay the salmon slices on a worksurface, put a large scallop or two small ones on each slice and spoon the avocado mixture on top. Roll the salmon around the filling.
5 To serve, put the parcels on serving plates and squeeze a little lime juice over each. Drizzle with the coriander dressing, garnish with rocket and sprinkle with pepper.

NUTRITION PER SERVING
219 cals | 13g fat (2g sats) | 3g carbs | 2.5g salt

CUMBERLAND STUFFED HERRINGS WITH MUSTARD SAUCE

Serves 4
Preparation 10 minutes
Cooking time 30 minutes
Techniques see also preparing round fish (page 80), making breadcrumbs (page 318), preparing onions (page 182)

4 herrings with roe, or small mackerel, about 225g (8oz)
    each, head and fins removed, and cleaned
300ml (½ pint) milk
25g (1oz) fresh breadcrumbs
1 small onion, finely chopped
25g (1oz) butter
3 tbsp plain flour
1 tsp prepared English mustard
1 tsp white wine vinegar
salt and ground black pepper
green beans to serve

1 Preheat the oven to 180°C (160°C fan oven) mark 4. Put the roes into a small pan with the milk. Bring to the boil, then reduce the heat and simmer gently for 5 minutes. Strain, putting the milk to one side. Finely chop the roes.
2 Open out the fish on a board, inner side down, and press lightly down the middle to loosen the backbone. Gently ease the backbone away.
3 Mix together the breadcrumbs and onion and add the chopped roes. Season to taste and spread on the flesh side of the fish. Fold the fish over to enclose the stuffing. Cover and cook in the oven for 20 minutes or until tender.
4 Meanwhile, put the butter, flour and the reserved milk into a pan. Heat, whisking continuously, until the sauce thickens, boils and is smooth. Reduce the heat and simmer for 1–2 minutes. Stir in the mustard and vinegar, adjust the seasoning and serve with the fish and green beans.

NUTRITION PER SERVING
576 cals | 37g fat (12g sats) | 18g carbs | 1.7g salt

RED MULLET BAKED IN PAPER

Serves 2
Preparation 5 minutes
Cooking time 30 minutes
Techniques see also preparing onions (page 182), preparing mushrooms (page 187), zesting citrus fruits (page 217), chopping herbs (page 436)

2 red mullet, about 225g (8oz) each
1 tbsp freshly chopped flat-leafed parsley
1 small onion, sliced
50g (2oz) mushrooms, chopped
finely grated zest and juice of 1 lemon
salt and ground black pepper
boiled new potatoes and broccoli to serve

1 Preheat the oven to 180°C (160°C fan oven) mark 4. Cut two squares of greaseproof paper large enough to wrap the fish. Place the fish on top, then add the remaining ingredients. Fold the paper to make a secure parcel.
2 Place the parcels on a baking sheet and bake for 30 minutes or until the fish is tender. Serve the fish in their parcels with boiled potatoes and broccoli.

NUTRITION PER SERVING
259 cals | 9g fat (0g sats) | 2g carbs | 1.1g salt

CRAB CAKES WITH MAYONNAISE

Serves 4
Preparation 30 minutes, plus chilling
Cooking time 15 minutes
Techniques see also preparing vegetables (pages 182–194), preparing crab (page 88), making breadcrumbs (page 318), making mayonnaise (page 25)

1 tbsp sunflower oil
3 spring onions, finely sliced
2 garlic cloves, crushed
1 red chilli, seeded and chopped
350g (12oz) crabmeat
2 tsp tomato ketchup
4 tbsp mayonnaise
1 tsp Worcestershire sauce
50g (2oz) fresh white breadcrumbs
vegetable oil to fry
salt and ground black pepper
spring onion curls, crushed, sliced red chilli and
    lime wedges to garnish

For the chilli mayonnaise
2 tbsp sweet chilli sauce
1 tbsp freshly chopped coriander
zest and juice of 1 lime
5 tbsp mayonnaise

For the coating
50g (2oz) seasoned flour
1 large egg, beaten
125g (4oz) fresh white breadcrumbs

1 To make the chilli mayonnaise, combine the ingredients in a bowl. Season, cover and chill. Put to one side.
2 To make the crab cakes, heat the sunflower oil in a pan, add the spring onions and cook, stirring, for 3 minutes. Remove from the heat and stir in the garlic and chilli. Transfer to a large bowl and cool. Add the crabmeat, ketchup, mayonnaise, Worcestershire sauce and breadcrumbs and stir until well combined. Season.
3 Using your hands, shape the mixture into 12 cakes and put on a baking sheet. Cover and chill for at least 1 hour.
4 To make the coating, dip the cakes into the seasoned flour, then the beaten egg and breadcrumbs. Put back on the baking sheet and chill for 30 minutes.
5 Heat 2.5cm (1in) vegetable oil in a pan. Fry the cakes in batches for 2–3 minutes on each side until golden. Remove the cakes from the pan and drain on kitchen paper. Season, garnish with the spring onion curls, chilli and lime wedges, and serve with the chilli mayonnaise.

NUTRITION PER SERVING
620 cals | 37g fat (5g sats) | 50g carbs | 3.2g salt

TUNA WITH CORIANDER RICE

Serves 4
Preparation 10 minutes
Cooking time about 5 minutes
Techniques see also cooking rice (page 246), preparing fresh ginger (page 437), searing fish (page 831)

250g (9oz) basmati rice
8 × 125g (4oz) tuna steaks
5cm (2in) piece fresh root ginger, peeled and grated
1 tbsp olive oil
100ml (3½fl oz) orange juice
300g (11oz) pak choi, roughly chopped
a small handful of freshly chopped coriander
ground black pepper
lime wedges to garnish

1 Cook the rice according to the pack instructions.
2 Meanwhile, put the tuna steaks in a shallow dish. Add the ginger, oil and orange juice and season well with pepper. Turn the tuna over to coat.
3 Heat a non-stick frying pan until really hot. Add four tuna steaks and half the marinade. Cook for 1–2 minutes on each side until just cooked. Repeat with the remaining tuna and marinade. Remove the fish from the pan and keep warm.
4 Add the pak choi to the frying pan and cook for 1–2 minutes until wilted. When the rice is cooked, drain and stir the coriander through. Serve the tuna with the pak choi, rice and pan juices, and garnish with lime wedges.

COOK'S TIP
Basmati rice should be washed before cooking to remove excess starch and to give really light, fluffy results. Check out the technique for rinsing rice on page 246.

NUTRITION PER SERVING
609 cals | 15g fat (4g sats) | 51g carbs | 0.6g salt

DILL SALMON

Serves 4
Preparation 2 minutes
Cooking time 5–7 minutes
Techniques see also making mayonnaise (page 25), chopping herbs (page 436), skinning fish (page 81), grilling fish (page 86)

4 tbsp Dijon mustard-flavoured mayonnaise
4 tbsp finely chopped fresh dill
4 tbsp clear honey
1 tbsp lemon juice
4 thick skinless salmon fillets, about 150g (5oz) each
tomato salad to serve

1 Preheat the grill to high. Put the mayonnaise into a bowl with the dill, honey and lemon juice and mix together.
2 Put the salmon fillets on to a baking sheet and spread the mayonnaise mixture over the top. Grill for 5–7 minutes, depending on the thickness, until just cooked. Serve with tomato salad.

COOK'S TIP
There's no need to turn the salmon over halfway through – just remember to keep a close eye on it and reduce the heat if necessary, so that the honey in the sauce doesn't burn.

NUTRITION PER SERVING
422 cals | 28g fat (5g sats) | 12g carbs | 0.4g salt

SIMPLE SMOKED HADDOCK

Serves 4
Preparation 10 minutes
Cooking time about 10 minutes
Techniques see also preparing garlic (page 183), chopping herbs (page 436), pan-frying fish (page 83), zesting citrus fruits (page 217)

25g (1oz) unsalted butter
1 tbsp olive oil
1 garlic clove, thinly sliced
4 thick smoked haddock or cod fillets,
    about 175g (6oz) each
a small handful of freshly chopped parsley (optional)
finely grated zest of 1 small lemon, plus lemon wedges
    to serve

1 Heat the butter, oil and garlic in a large non-stick pan until the mixture starts to foam and sizzle. Put the fish into the pan, skin side down, and fry over a high heat for 10 minutes – this will give a golden crust underneath the fish.
2 Turn the fish over and scatter the parsley, if using, and lemon zest over it, then fry for a further 30 seconds. Put each cooked fillet on to a plate and spoon over some of the buttery juices. Serve with the lemon wedges and a green vegetable, such as romanesco broccoli.

COOK'S TIP
Smoked fish is quite salty so always taste the sauce before seasoning with any extra salt.

NUTRITION PER SERVING
217 cals | 9g fat (4g sats) | 1g carbs | 3.4g salt

POTTED PRAWNS

Serves 6
Preparation 15 minutes, plus chilling
Cooking time 10 minutes
Techniques see also chopping herbs (page 436)

600g (1lb 5oz) cooked small prawns
250g (9oz) butter
¼ tsp ground mace
½ tsp each cayenne pepper and freshly grated nutmeg
1 tbsp Worcestershire sauce
2 tbsp freshly chopped chives
salt and ground black pepper
6 slices white bread to serve

1 Dry the prawns on kitchen paper. Clarify the butter by gently melting it in a small pan. Spoon off the white scum, then pour the clear butter into another pan, discarding any milky residue.
2 Add the mace, cayenne pepper, nutmeg and Worcestershire sauce to the clarified butter, season with salt and pepper, then heat through for 3 minutes without letting the mixture boil. Remove from the heat and leave to cool slightly. Stir in most of the chives.
3 Divide the prawns among six 100ml (3½fl oz) ramekins and top with the flavoured butter. Sprinkle the remaining chives on top. Chill overnight.
4 Preheat the grill. Put the bread on a baking sheet and toast until golden. Cut off the crusts and slice each piece horizontally through the centre to make two slices. Toast the uncooked sides until golden. Carefully slice each piece in half diagonally and serve with the prawns.

NUTRITION PER SERVING
466 cals | 35g fat (22g sats) | 17g carbs | 2g salt

GRILLED LOBSTER

Serves 2
Preparation 20 minutes
Cooking time 15 minutes
Techniques see also preparing lobster (page 89)

1 killed fresh lobster, about 700g (1½lb)
25g (1oz) butter, softened, plus melted butter to brush
    and serve
salt and cayenne pepper

1 Preheat the grill. Split the lobster lengthways. Remove the
head sac, which lies just behind the eyes, and discard. Remove
the black coral (tomalley) and the green intestine, which lie
inside the back of the shell just behind the head sac.
2 Brush the shell and flesh with melted butter and grill the
flesh side for 8–10 minutes, then turn the lobster and grill
the shell side for 5 minutes.
3 Dot the flesh with small pieces of softened butter,
sprinkle with a little salt and cayenne pepper and serve
immediately, with melted butter.

COOK'S TIPS

➙ If you are able to buy a live lobster from
   your fishmonger, choose one that has all
   claws and legs intact.
➙ To kill a lobster humanely, put it into the freezer
   for 5 minutes, then put it on a chopping board
   and hold the body firmly. Take a large chef's
   knife and plunge it straight down into the
   lobster's head, right between or just below
   the eyes.

NUTRITION PER SERVING
186 cals | 120g fat (7g sats) | 0g carbs | 1.6g salt

OVEN-POACHED COD WITH HERBS

Serves 4
Preparation 10 minutes
Cooking time 10 minutes
Techniques see also preparing vegetables (pages 182–194), chopping herbs (page 436), making stock (page 36), mashing potatoes (page 196)

10 spring onions, sliced
2 garlic cloves, crushed
6 tbsp shredded fresh mint
6 tbsp freshly chopped flat-leafed parsley
juice of ½ lemon
150ml (¼ pint) fish, chicken or vegetable stock
4 cod fillets, about 200g (7oz) each
salt and ground black pepper
lemon wedges to garnish
mashed potato to serve

1 Preheat the oven to 230°C (210°C fan oven) mark 8. Combine the spring onions (putting some of the green part to one side), garlic, mint, parsley, lemon juice and stock in an ovenproof dish that can hold the cod in a single layer.
2 Put the cod on the herb and garlic mixture and turn to moisten. Season with salt and pepper, then roast for 8–10 minutes.
3 Sprinkle with the reserved spring onion, garnish with lemon wedges and serve with mashed potato.

COOK'S TIP
One of the best ways to lock in the flavours of fish and vegetables is to bake them in foil in the oven. Place the food on a sheet of oiled foil large enough to enclose it, then bring up the sides of the foil and seal securely.

NUTRITION PER SERVING
177 cals | 2g fat (trace sats) | 2g carbs | 0.6g salt

MUSSEL AND POTATO STEW

Serves 4
Preparation 15 minutes
Cooking time 15 minutes
Techniques see also preparing mussels (page 90), chopping herbs
(page 436)

25g (1oz) butter
200g pack rindless back bacon rashers, cut into strips
700g (1lb 9oz) white potatoes, cut into large chunks
198g can sweetcorn kernels, drained
1kg (2¼lb) mussels, tapped, and open or damaged ones
 discarded
140ml (4½fl oz) single cream
1 tbsp freshly chopped parsley
salt and ground black pepper

1 Melt the butter in a large pan. Add the bacon and
cook, stirring, until the strips separate. Add the potatoes
and 150ml (¼ pint) water and season lightly with salt and
pepper. Cover with a tight-fitting lid and cook for about
10 minutes or until the potatoes are almost tender.
2 Add the sweetcorn and mussels to the pan, cover, bring
to the boil, reduce the heat and simmer for 2–3 minutes
until the mussels open. Discard any mussels that don't open.
Add the cream and chopped parsley, and serve.

COOK'S TIP
To make sure mussels are safe to eat: check them
carefully before cooking for cracks and split shells.
Discard these, and any that do not close when sharply
tapped. Any mussels that remain closed after cooking
should also be discarded.

NUTRITION PER SERVING
472 cals | 23g fat (11g sats) | 42g carbs | 2.8g salt

FISH AND CHIPS

Serves 4
Preparation 30 minutes
Cooking time 40–50 minutes
Techniques see also coatings and batters (page 84), making mayonnaise (page 25), deep-frying fish (page 84), making potato chips (page 198)

900g (2lb) Desirée potatoes, peeled
2–3 tbsp olive oil
sea salt flakes
sunflower oil to deep-fry
2 × 128g packs batter mix
1 tsp baking powder
¼ tsp salt
330ml bottle of lager
4 plaice fillets, about 225g (8oz) each, skin on,
   trimmed and cut in half
plain flour to dust
2 garlic cloves, crushed
8 tbsp mayonnaise
1 tsp lemon juice
salt and ground black pepper
lemon wedges and chives to garnish

1 Preheat the oven to 240°C (220°C fan oven) mark 9. Cut the potatoes into chips. Put them in a pan of boiling salted water, cover and bring to the boil. Boil for 2 minutes, drain well, then turn on to kitchen paper to remove the excess moisture. Tip into a large non-stick roasting tin, toss with the olive oil and season with sea salt. Roast for 40–50 minutes until golden and cooked, turning from time to time.
2 Half-fill a deep-fat fryer with sunflower oil and heat to 190°C. Put the batter mix into a bowl with the baking powder and salt and gradually whisk in the lager. Season the plaice and lightly dust with plain flour. Dip two of the fillets into the batter and deep-fry in the hot oil until golden. Keep hot in the oven while you deep-fry the remaining plaice fillets.
3 Mix together the garlic, mayonnaise and lemon juice in a bowl and season well. Serve the garlic mayonnaise with the plaice and chips, garnished with lemon wedges and chives.

NUTRITION PER SERVING
1185 cals | 79g fat (18g sats) | 73g carbs | 3.2g salt

OLD-FASHIONED FISH PIE

Serves 4
Preparation 20 minutes
Cooking time 50 minutes
Techniques see also boiling eggs (page 55), chopping herbs (page 436), cooking and mashing potatoes (pages 195–6)

450g (1lb) haddock, cod or coley fillets
300ml (½ pint) milk, plus 6 tbsp
1 bay leaf
6 black peppercorns
2 onion slices
65g (2½oz) butter
3 tbsp flour
150ml (¼ pint) single cream
2 medium eggs, hard-boiled, shelled and chopped
2 tbsp freshly chopped flat-leafed parsley
900g (2lb) potatoes, cooked and mashed
1 medium egg
salt and ground black pepper

1 Put the fish into a frying pan, pour the 300ml (½ pint) milk over it and add the bay leaf, peppercorns, onion slices and a good pinch of salt. Bring slowly to the boil, then reduce the heat, cover and simmer for 8–10 minutes until the fish flakes when tested with a fork.
2 Using a fish slice, lift the fish out of the pan and put on a plate. Flake the fish, discarding the skin and bone. Strain and put the milk to one side. Preheat the oven to 200°C (180°C fan oven) mark 6.
3 Melt 40g (1½oz) of the butter in a pan, stir in the flour and cook gently for 1 minute, stirring. Remove the pan from the heat and gradually stir in the reserved milk. Bring to the boil slowly and continue to cook, stirring until the sauce thickens. Season with salt and pepper.
4 Stir in the cream and fish, together with any juices. Add the chopped eggs and parsley and adjust the seasoning. Spoon the mixture into a 1.1 litre (2 pint) pie dish or similar ovenproof dish.
5 Heat the 6 tbsp milk and remaining butter in a pan, then beat into the potatoes. Season and leave to cool slightly.
6 Spoon the cooled potato into a large piping bag fitted with a large star nozzle. Pipe shell-shaped lines of potato across the fish mixture. Alternatively, spoon the potato on top and roughen the surface with a fork.
7 Put the dish on a baking sheet and cook in the oven for 10–15 minutes until the potato is set.
8 Beat the egg with a good pinch of salt, then brush over the pie. Put back into the oven for 15 minutes or until golden brown.

TRY SOMETHING DIFFERENT

- Stir 125g (4oz) grated Cheddar cheese into the sauce.
- Beat 125g (4oz) grated Cheddar or Red Leicester cheese into the mashed potatoes.
- Stir 175g (6oz) canned sweetcorn, drained, and ¼ tsp cayenne pepper into the fish mixture.
- Fry 125g (4oz) sliced button mushrooms in 25g (1oz) butter for 3 minutes. Stir into the fish mixture.
- Sprinkle the potato topping with 50g (2oz) mixed grated Parmesan and fresh breadcrumbs after the first 10–15 minutes.
- Cover the pie with puff pastry instead of the potatoes.

NUTRITION PER SERVING
610 cals | 28g fat (15g sats) | 56g carbs | 1.4g salt

BAKED MACKEREL WITH GOOSEBERRY SAUCE

Serves 4
Preparation 10 minutes
Cooking time 25–30 minutes
Techniques see also preparing round fish (page 80)

15g (½oz) butter
225g (8oz) gooseberries, topped and tailed
4 mackerel, about 350g (12oz) each, cleaned and
    heads removed
lemon juice, to taste
1 medium egg, beaten
salt and ground black pepper

1 Preheat the grill. Melt the butter in a medium pan and add the gooseberries. Cover tightly and cook over a low heat, shaking the pan occasionally, until the gooseberries are tender.
2 Meanwhile, season the mackerel inside and out with salt, plenty of pepper and lemon juice. Make two or three slashes in the skin on each side of the fish, then grill for about 15–20 minutes, depending on size, turning once, until tender.
3 Purée the gooseberries in a blender or food processor, or press through a sieve. Pour the purée into a clean pan, beat in the egg, then reheat gently, stirring. Season to taste. Put the mackerel on warmed plates and spoon the sauce beside the fish.

NUTRITION PER SERVING
841 cals | 61g fat (1g sats) | 5g carbs | 1.3g salt

THAI GREEN SHELLFISH CURRY

Serves 6
Preparation 5 minutes
Cooking time 15 minutes
Techniques see also making coconut milk (page 231), making vegetable stock (page 36), opening scallops (page 91), preparing prawns (page 87)

1 tbsp vegetable oil
1 pack fresh Thai herbs (containing 1 lemongrass stalk,
    2 Thai chillies, coriander leaves, 2 lime leaves),
    all chopped
1–2 tbsp green Thai curry paste
400ml can coconut milk
450ml (¾ pint) vegetable stock
375g (13oz) queen scallops with corals
250g (9oz) raw tiger prawns, peeled with tails on
salt and ground black pepper
coriander leaves to garnish
jasmine rice to serve

1 Heat the oil in a wok and fry the Thai herbs for 30 seconds. Add the curry paste and fry for 1 minute.
2 Add the coconut milk and stock and bring to the boil. Reduce the heat and simmer for 5–10 minutes until reduced a little. Season well with salt and pepper.
3 Add the scallops and tiger prawns, bring to the boil, then reduce the heat and simmer gently for 2–3 minutes until cooked. Spoon into bowls of Thai jasmine rice and garnish with coriander.

COOK'S TIP
Jasmine rice is also known as Thai fragrant rice and has a distinctive taste and texture. It is traditionally served with Thai food and is available in supermarkets and Asian stores.

NUTRITION PER SERVING
156 cals | 5g fat (1g sats) | 6g carbs | 0.8g salt

FISH MASALA

Serves 4
Preparation 15 minutes
Cooking time about 20 minutes
Techniques see also preparing vegetables (page 182–194), preparing fresh ginger (page 437), chopping herbs (page 436), making garam masala (page 229)

1 onion, quartered
2 garlic cloves
1–2 hot green chillies, halved and seeded
    if you like
2.5cm (1in) piece fresh root ginger, peeled
    and halved
4 tbsp freshly chopped coriander
juice of 2 limes
1 tbsp coriander seeds
1 tsp fenugreek seeds
1 tsp ground turmeric
2 tbsp vegetable oil
5 large juicy tomatoes, peeled and chopped
1 tbsp garam masala
4 white fish steaks, such as cod, haddock, halibut
about 2 tbsp plain white flour, to coat
oil to shallow-fry
salt

1 Put the onion, garlic, chillies, ginger, chopped coriander and lime juice in a blender or food processor and whiz to make a fairly thick paste. Crush the coriander and fenugreek seeds using a pestle and mortar, then add to the spice paste with the turmeric and mix well.
2 Heat the oil in a large frying pan. Add the spice paste and cook, stirring constantly, for 5 minutes. Stir in the chopped tomatoes, garam masala and salt to taste. Cook for about 5 minutes or until the tomatoes have broken down and their liquid has evaporated.
3 Coat the fish steaks with the flour. Heat the oil in another frying pan. Add the fish steaks and quickly brown on both sides. Transfer the fish steaks to the frying pan containing the sauce, arranging them in a single layer. Spoon a little of the sauce over each fish steak and cover the pan with a lid or a baking sheet. Simmer gently for 8–10 minutes, depending on the thickness of the fish, until the fish is cooked right through. Serve.

NUTRITION PER SERVING
328 cals | 16g fat (2g sats) | 12g carbs | 0.6g salt

POULTRY AND GAME BIRDS

Chicken is a real staple of the family kitchen and the other poultry and game birds make a popular treat too – whether it's a festive roast turkey or goose, or a delicious recipe with duck or guinea fowl. This chapter guides you through the basic preparation techniques from cleaning, trussing and spatchcocking to boning, jointing and cutting escalopes. The cooking section demonstrates all the techniques from roasting, carving and stuffing to frying, grilling, pot-roasting, steaming and marinating, before building on the basics with the comprehensive recipe collection. Try delicious Stuffed chicken breasts, Poussins with pancetta, artichoke and potato salad, Lemon and herb roast turkey, Crispy duck salad or Goose with roasted apples.

BUYING POULTRY AND GAME BIRDS

Poultry and game birds are available all year round to feast on, but as a lot of game birds are unfarmed, there are seasonal fluctuations.

How to buy and store poultry

Most poultry and game birds from the butcher or supermarket are sold already plucked, drawn and ready for the oven. Look for birds with no signs of damage or blemishes. If the birds are not wrapped in plastic, check that they smell pleasant. Generally, the larger the bird, the greater proportion of meat to bone there will be – and therefore better value. Check that the birds have a neat shape, an even colour and no bruises or tears on the skin. The body should look meaty and plump.

Some whole birds are bought with a packet of giblets (neck, liver, heart and crop) tucked inside the carcass.

Remove and store them in a sealed container in the fridge, to use within a day. Put the bird in a shallow dish, cover with clingfilm and store in the fridge. Use within two days, or according to the 'use by' date on its label. Poultry from the supermarket can be left in its original packaging.

Where possible, when you are buying poultry and game birds, try to support your local butcher. You will be rewarded with great produce and choice.

Poultry comparison chart
1 Duck; 2 Guinea fowl; 3 Chicken
4 Poussin; 5 Pheasant

TYPES OF CHICKEN

Corn-fed These chickens are fed on corn rather than standard chicken feed and have golden yellow flesh and, often, an improved flavour. They weigh about 2kg (4½lb).

Roasting Usually young birds, chickens for roasting are tender and weigh about 2kg (4½lb).

Boiling These birds are usually about 18 months old and have tougher flesh that is better suited to long, slow cooking such as stewing, poaching, casseroling or pot-roasting. They usually weigh around 2.5–3kg (5½–6½lb).

Poussins Usually four to eight weeks old, they weigh only about 450g (1lb). Whole poussin can be roasted or spatchcocked and grilled; portions can be pan-fried, grilled, braised and pot-roasted.

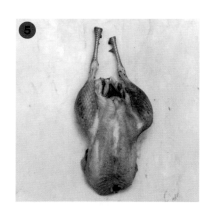

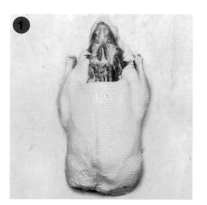

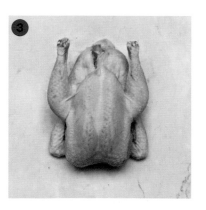

How to freeze and thaw poultry

Fresh chicken and poultry can be frozen successfully and safely. Be sure to follow the guidelines below:

- Always freeze poultry before its 'use by' date, preferably on the day of purchase.
- Follow any freezing or thawing instructions given.
- Wrap portions in individual freezer bags, seal tightly and label with the date of freezing. They can be stored in the freezer for up to three months.
- To thaw, put the poultry in a dish (to catch dripping juices) and leave overnight in the fridge until completely thawed, then cook within 24 hours.
- Do not re-freeze thawed poultry. You can, however, freeze it again after you have cooked it.

For larger whole birds such as turkey and geese, you will need to allow more thawing time:

- Remove the bird from its packaging and put it in a large dish to catch any juices. Cover and put in the fridge, checking and emptying the dish regularly.
- Follow the instructions on packaged birds for thawing times, or use the following as a guide:

2kg (4½lb) bird	20–24 hours
3kg (6½lb) bird	30–36 hours
4kg (8lb 13oz) bird	40–48 hours
5kg (11lb) bird	50–60 hours

Before you start cooking, check carefully that the bird is thoroughly thawed out:

- Put your hand inside the cavity to check that there are no ice crystals.
- Pierce the thickest part of the meat with a fork. If you feel ice crystals, thaw for a little longer.

How to buy and store game birds

Game birds are best eaten young. The feathers are a good guide, as young birds tend to have soft, even feathers. Also look for a plump breast, smooth legs and pliable spurs. Examine the birds for extensive damage by shot: signs are red/black entrance wounds on the breast and/or broken legs.

Game birds are traditionally hung for several days to deepen their gamey flavour and tenderise the flesh – an un-hung bird will be tough and tasteless. Most game from a butcher or supermarket will have been hung, but if you have a freshly shot bird, hang it yourself in a cool, airy place (see below).

A prepared bird can be stored in the fridge for one to two days. But birds that have been significantly damaged by shot will not keep as well, so cook as soon as possible.

COOK'S TIPS

- Look in the freezer aisle of the supermarket for packs of frozen chicken breasts and thighs. They're usually smaller fillets but cheaper as a result and make a good stand-by.
- Buy a whole chicken and joint it into pieces yourself (see page 116, or ask your butcher to do it). Use the carcass for stock.

HANGING TIMES FOR GAME BIRDS

Duck	2–3 days
Goose	2–9 days
Grouse	2–4 days
Partridge	3–5 days
Pheasant	3–10 days
Wood pigeon	Requires no hanging
Woodcock	3–5 days

PREPARING POULTRY

Chicken and other poultry and game birds may be bought whole for roasting or in pieces ready for cooking. It is often cheaper to buy a whole bird, then joint it yourself for cooking as required.

Cleaning and trussing

1 Before stuffing a bird for roasting, clean it thoroughly. Put the bird in the sink and pull out any loose fat with your fingers. Then run cold water through the cavity and dry the bird well using kitchen paper.

2 It is not necessary to truss poultry before roasting it but it gives the bird a neater shape for serving at the table. Cut the wishbone out by pulling back the flap of skin at the neck end and locating the tip of the bone with a small sharp knife. Run the knife along the inside of the bone on both sides, then on the outside. Take care not to cut deep into the breast meat. Use poultry shears or sharp-pointed scissors to snip the tip of the bone from the breastbone and then pull the bone away from the breast. Snip the two ends or pull them out by hand.

3 Pull off any loose fat from the neck or cavity. Put the wing tips under the breast and fold the neck flap on to the back of the bird. Thread a trussing needle and use it to secure the neck flap.

4 Push a metal skewer through the legs, at the joint between thigh and drumstick. Twist some string around both ends of the skewer and pull firmly to tighten.

5 Turn the bird over. Bring the string over the ends of the drumsticks, pull tight and tie to secure the legs in place.

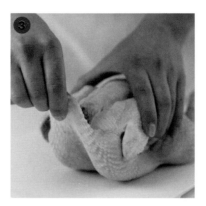

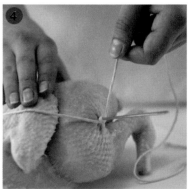

HYGIENE

Raw poultry and meat contain harmful bacteria that can spread easily to anything they touch.

- Always wash your hands, kitchen surfaces, chopping boards, knives and equipment before and after handling poultry or meat.
- Don't let raw poultry or meat touch other foods.
- Always cover raw poultry and meat and store in the bottom of the fridge, where they can't touch or drip on to other foods.

Spatchcocking

A technique to flatten smaller poultry and guinea fowl for grilling.

1 Hold the bird on a board, breast down. Cut through one side of the backbone with poultry shears. Repeat on other side and remove.

2 Turn bird over, press down until you hear breastbone crack. Thread skewers through legs and breasts.

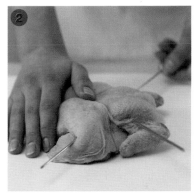

Boning

Boned poultry, stuffed and roasted, makes an attractive dish.

1 Using a meat knife with a curved blade, remove the wishbone (see step 2, page 114) and the first two sections of the wings.

2 Lay the chicken breast side down, with the back facing up, and cut down to the backbone along the whole length of the bird. Pulling skin and flesh away as you go, work a sharp knife between the flesh and bone down one side of the bird. Always cut in, towards the bone.

3 You will soon reach the joints connecting the thigh and wing to the body. Cut through both joints, taking care not to cut through the skin. Do not pierce the skin; it will be the casing for your cooked dish. Continue cutting down between the breast meat and ribcage, again taking care to cut towards the bone.

4 When you reach the tip of the breastbone, turn the bird around and repeat on the other side. Cut through the soft cartilage along the length of the breastbone to remove the boned flesh in a single piece.

5 To remove the wings and legs, cut the tendons at the end of the bones and then use a small chopping knife to scrape off the flesh along the full length of the bone. Pull out the bone. Do this twice with the legs to remove the thigh and drumstick.

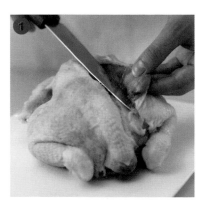

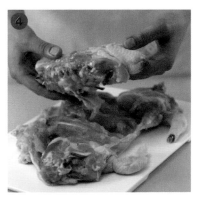

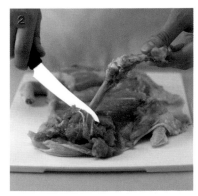

Jointing

You can buy pieces of chicken in the supermarket or butcher, but it is more economical to joint the bird yourself. Use the wing tips and bones to make stock (see page 36).

1 Using a sharp meat knife with a curved blade, cut out the wishbone and remove the wings in a single piece. Remove the wing tips.

2 With the tail pointing towards you and breast side up, pull one leg away and cut through the skin between leg and breast. Pull the leg down until you crack the joint between the thigh bone and ribcage.

3 Cut through that joint, then cut through the remaining leg meat. Repeat on the other side.

4 To remove the breast without any bone, make a cut along the length of the breastbone. Gently teasing the flesh away from the ribs with the knife, work the blade down between the flesh and ribs of one breast and cut it off neatly. (Always cut in, towards the bone.) Repeat on the other side.

5 To remove the breast with the bone in, make a cut along the full length of the breastbone.

6 Using poultry shears, cut through the breastbone, then cut through the ribcage following the outline of the breast meat. Repeat on the other side. Trim off any flaps of skin or fat.

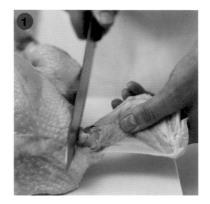
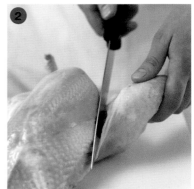

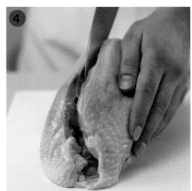

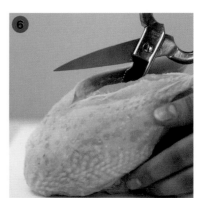

Slicing breast fillets

1 Cut or pull out the long strip of flesh lying on the inside of the breast. Slice it across the grain to the thickness required for your recipe. (Raw chicken should not be cut less than about 3mm/⅛in thick.)

2 Starting at the small tip of the breast, cut slices of the required thickness. Alternatively, cut into chunks or dice.

PERFECT SLICING

To make slicing easier, put breast fillets in the freezer for 30 minutes or so before slicing. The flesh will be much firmer and it will therefore be easier to slice it thinly.

Cutting escalopes

Escalopes are good for quick frying.

1 Cut or pull out the long strip of flesh lying on the inside of the breast fillet. (It can be used for stir-fries, stuffings, etc.)

2 Pressing the breast firmly on to the chopping board with the flat of one hand, carve a thin slice from underneath the breast using a sharp knife. (The knife blade should be parallel with the chopping board.) Remove that slice, then repeat until the breast meat is too small to slice.

3 To make escalopes, put the slices of chicken between two sheets of clingfilm or greaseproof paper and pound them with a meat mallet until they are about 3mm (⅛in) thick.

Skinning breast fillets

1 Firmly grab the flap of skin at the small end of the breast and pull towards the other end of the breast. Remove the skin and discard, then prepare or cook the fillet as required.

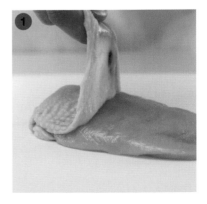

POULTRY AND GAME ROASTING TIMES

Chicken

To calculate the roasting time for a chicken, weigh the oven-ready bird (including stuffing, if using) and allow 20 minutes per 450g (1lb) plus 20 minutes extra, in an oven preheated to 200°C (180°C fan oven) mark 6.

Oven-ready weight	Serves	Cooking time (approx.)
1.4–1.6 kg (3–3½lb)	4–6	1½ hours
1.8–2.3kg (4–5lb)	6–8	1 hour 50 minutes
2.5–2.7kg (5½–6lb)	8–10	2¼ hours

Other poultry and feathered game

Preheat the oven to 200°C (180°C fan oven) mark 6.

Game	Serves	Cooking time (approx.)
Poussin	1–2	20 minutes per 450g (1lb)
Guinea fowl 1.4kg (3lb)	2–4	35 minutes per 1kg (2¼lb), plus 15 minutes
Duck 1.8–2.5kg (4–5½lb)	2–4	20 minutes per 450g (1lb)
Goose, small 3.6–5.4kg (8–12lb)	4–7	20 minutes per 450g (1lb)
Goose, medium 5.4–6.3kg (12–14lb)	8–11	25 minutes per 450g (1lb)
Grouse	1	25–35 minutes
Partridge	1	20–25 minutes
Pheasant	2–3	45–60 minutes

How to tell if poultry is cooked

Test by piercing the thickest part of the meat – usually the thigh – with a skewer. The juices that run out should be clear with no trace of pink; if they're not, return the bird to the oven and check at regular intervals. Duck and game birds are traditionally served with the meat slightly pink: if overcooked, the meat may be dry. When tested, the juices should have just a blush of pink.

Resting times

Once the bird is cooked, allow it to rest before carving. Lift it out of the roasting tin, put it on a plate and cover loosely with foil and a clean teatowel. Resting allows the juices to settle back into the meat, leaving it moist and easier to carve.

Chicken and duck	15 minutes
Turkey and goose	20–30 minutes
Grouse and small game birds	10 minutes

COOK'S TIP

When roasting duck or goose (above), spoon off the excess fat every 20–30 minutes. Keep the cooled fat in a covered bowl in the fridge: it lasts for months and is excellent for cooking roast potatoes.

GIBLET STOCK

To make 1.3 litres (2¼ pints), put the turkey giblets into a large pan. Add 1 halved carrot, 1 quartered onion, 1 halved celery stick, 1 bay leaf and 6 black peppercorns. Pour in 1.4 litres (2¼ pints) cold water, cover and bring to the boil. Reduce the heat and simmer for 30 minutes–1 hour, skimming occasionally. Strain through a sieve. Cool quickly, put into a sealable container and chill for up to three days.

COOKING A TURKEY

Cooking a turkey can be a daunting prospect, especially since quite often it is a once-a-year meal.

Turkey preparation

Take the turkey out of the fridge 45 minutes before stuffing it. Coat the turkey with butter and season. Wrap loosely in a 'tent' of foil, then cook in an oven preheated to 190°C (170°C fan oven) mark 5. Allow 45 minutes per 1kg (2¼lb), plus 20 minutes (see chart below for timings). Remove the foil about 1 hour before the end of cooking time to brown the bird. Baste regularly.

How to tell if the turkey is cooked

Pierce the thickest part of the leg with a skewer. The juices that run out should be clear with no traces of pink; if they're not, return the bird to the oven and check at regular intervals.

Resting

After cooking, allow to rest for 20–30 minutes before carving. Transfer from the roasting tin to a plate. Cover with foil and a clean teatowel. This allows the juices to settle back into the meat, leaving it moist and easier to carve.

Oven-ready weight of turkey

(at room temperature)	Approximate no. of servings	Approximate thawing time	Cooking time (foil-wrapped)
2.3–3.6kg (5–8lb)	6–10	15–18 hours	2–3 hours
3.6–5kg (8–11lb)	10–15	18–20 hours	3–3¼ hours
5–6.8kg (11–15lb)	15–20	20–24 hours	3¼–4 hours
6.8–9kg (15–20lb)	20–30	24–30 hours	4–5½ hours

Quantities for roasting	Serves
Chicken 2kg (4½lb)	about 5
Duck	allow 450g (1lb) per person
Goose 4.5kg (10lb)	6–8
Grouse	allow 1 bird per person
Guinea fowl	1 bird will serve 2–4
Partridge	allow 1 bird per person
Pheasant	1 bird will serve 2–3
Pigeon	allow 1 bird per person
Poussin	allow 1 bird per person
Quail	allow 2 birds per person
Turkey 3.5kg (7¾lb)	10
Woodcock	allow 1 bird per person

COOKING POULTRY

From the simplest, healthiest stir-frying, steaming and poaching to the most indulgent and luxurious deep-frying and roasting, there are numerous ways to make the most of the delicate taste of poultry.

Simple roast chicken

To serve four to six, you will need 1.4–1.6kg (3–3½lb) chicken, 5 garlic cloves, 4 lemon slices, juice of 2 lemons (squeezed halves put to one side), 2 tsp Dijon mustard, 4 sprigs each fresh rosemary and thyme, 1 sliced onion, 300ml (½ pint) chicken stock, 300ml (½ pint) dry white wine.

1 Make incisions all over the chicken except the breast. Loosen the breast skin. Crush 3 garlic cloves and slip under the skin with lemon slices, mustard and herbs.

2 Put the lemon halves in the cavity. Put the chicken in a roasting tin. Spoon 2 tbsp lemon juice into the cavity and pour the remaining juice over. Chill for a few hours. Take out of the fridge 30 minutes before cooking.

3 Preheat the oven to 200°C (180°C fan oven) mark 6. Put the chicken, breast down, on a rack in the tin. Add the onion, remaining garlic and 4 tbsp each stock and wine.

4 Roast for 20 minutes, turn and roast for 35 minutes or until juices run clear when the leg is pierced. Baste now and then, adding wine if needed.

5 Put the chicken on a platter and cover loosely with foil. Spoon off as much fat as possible, leaving behind the juices in the tin. Put the tin over a medium-high heat, add remaining stock and wine and scrape up the sediment from the tin. Simmer for 5 minutes to make gravy. Strain.

Roasting and testing

To calculate the roasting time for the chicken, see charts on page 118. Test if it is cooked by piercing the flesh with a skewer: the juices should run clear.

Carving

1 Hold the back of a carving fork against one side of the breast. Starting at the neck end, cut slices about 5mm (¼in) thick, then use the knife and fork to lift them on to a warmed serving plate.

2 To cut off the legs, cut the skin between the thigh and breast.

3 Pull the leg down to expose the joint between the thigh bone and ribcage, and cut through that joint. For small birds, cut through the joint between the thigh and drumstick.

4 To carve meat from the leg (for turkeys and very large chickens), remove it from the carcass as in step 2. Joint the two parts of the leg. Holding the drumstick by the thin end, stand it up on the carving board and carve slices roughly parallel with the bone. The thigh can be carved either flat on the board or upright.

CRANBERRY AND LEMON STUFFING

If you would like to cook the stuffing separately, try this recipe. You will need 25g (1oz) butter, 1 large onion, finely chopped, 1 garlic clove, crushed, 450g (1lb) best-quality sausages, 4 tbsp chopped parsley, 2 tbsp chopped sage, the zest of 2 lemons, 1 tbsp brandy or Calvados (optional), 75g (3oz) dried cranberries, salt and ground black pepper.

1 Melt the butter in a frying pan and sauté the onion for about 10 minutes or until softened but not coloured. Add the garlic and cook for 1 minute more, then transfer to a bowl and leave to cool.
2 Squeeze the sausage meat out of the skins into the bowl with the onions and garlic. Add all the remaining ingredients and season, then mix well, using your hands. Shape into 18 balls and place in muffin tins or pack into an oiled baking dish. Preheat the oven to 190°C (170°C fan oven) mark 5 and bake for 30 minutes or until cooked through and golden on top.

Pan-frying

This is a quick method for cooking chicken pieces and you can make a sauce with the pan juices at the end if you like.

1 Put in enough oil (or a mixture of oil and clarified butter) to fill the pan to a depth of about 5mm (¼in) and put the pan over a medium heat.

2 Season the chicken with salt and ground black pepper, then carefully add to the pan, flesh side down, and fry for 10–15 minutes until it's nicely browned. (Don't put too many pieces of chicken in the pan at once or the chicken will cook partly in its own steam.)

3 Turn the pieces over and cook on the skin side for another 10–15 minutes until the skin is brown and the flesh is cooked but still juicy all the way through.

4 Remove the chicken from the pan using a pair of tongs and keep warm. Pour off the excess oil and deglaze the pan.

5 Make a simple gravy using wine, stock, herbs and some chopped garlic or onion (see page 18).

Stir-frying

1 Cut the poultry into small, even-sized strips or dice no more than 5mm (¼in) thick. Heat a wok or large pan until very hot and add oil to coat the inside.

2 Add the chicken and cook, stirring constantly, until just done. Remove to a bowl. Cook the other ingredients you are using for the stir-fry, then return the poultry to the pan and cook for 1–2 minutes to heat through.

Deep-frying

1 Prepare the poultry for frying and chill. Prepare the seasoned flour, batter or coating (see page 82). Heat vegetable oil in a deep-fryer to 180°C (test by frying a small cube of bread; it should brown in 40 seconds). Start battering or coating each piece of poultry.

2 Using tongs, carefully lower the poultry into the oil. Don't add more than three or four pieces at a time (otherwise the temperature will drop and the poultry will take longer to cook and become greasy). Cook small chunks or strips for about 10 minutes, jointed pieces for about 15 minutes.

3 As the pieces become golden and crisp, remove them with a slotted spoon and drain on kitchen paper. Sprinkle with a little salt and serve immediately, or keep warm in the oven until everything is cooked.

PERFECT FRYING

➣ Coat each piece of food well and make sure that they are completely covered in the coating.

➣ To speed up the cooking time, cut the chicken into strips or chunks.

Grilling

This method is perfect for cooking pieces of poultry such as breast fillets or for poultry strips or chunks threaded on to skewers.

1 Marinate (see page 125) the poultry pieces for 30 minutes, drain and pat dry. Alternatively, brush the poultry with a flavoured oil. Put the pieces on a wire rack over a grill pan or roasting tin and set the pan under a preheated grill so that it is about 8cm (3¼in) from the heat source.

2 Every few minutes brush a little of the marinade or a teaspoon of oil over the poultry.

3 When cooked on one side, turn with tongs and cook the other side until cooked through. Avoid piercing the flesh when turning. Allow 12–20 minutes for a breast fillet or joint and 20–30 minutes for a spatchcocked bird. (There should be no pink juices when the flesh is pierced with a sharp knife.)

Casseroling

To serve four to six, you will need 1 jointed chicken, 3 tbsp oil, 1 chopped onion, 2 crushed garlic cloves, 2 each chopped celery sticks and carrots, 1 tbsp plain flour, 2 tbsp chopped tarragon or thyme, chicken stock and/or wine, salt and pepper.

1 Preheat the oven to 180°C (160°C fan oven) mark 4. Cut the chicken legs and breasts in half.

2 Heat the oil in a flameproof casserole and brown the chicken all over. Remove and pour off the excess oil. Add the onion and garlic and brown for a few minutes. Add the vegetables, then stir in the flour and cook for 1 minute. Add the herbs and season. Add the chicken and pour in stock and/or wine to come three-quarters of the way up the poultry. Cook for 1–1½ hours.

Pot-roasting

To serve four to six, you will need 2 tbsp vegetable oil, 1 onion, cut into wedges, 2 rashers rindless streaky bacon, chopped, 1.4–1.6kg (3–3½lb) chicken, 2 small turnips, cut into wedges, 6 carrots, halved, 1 crushed garlic clove, bouquet garni, 600ml (1 pint) chicken stock, 100ml (3½fl oz) dry white wine, small handful parsley, chopped, salt and pepper.

1 Preheat the oven to 200°C (180°C fan oven) mark 6. Heat the oil in a casserole dish. Fry the onion and bacon for 5 minutes. Set aside. Add the chicken and brown for 10 minutes, then put to one side. Fry turnips, carrots and garlic for 2 minutes, then add the bacon, onion and chicken.

2 Add the bouquet garni, stock, wine and season. Bring to the boil and transfer to the oven. Cook, basting now and then, for 1 hour 20 minutes or until the juices run clear. Lift out the chicken, stir in the parsley and carve.

PERFECT POT-ROASTS

- Pot-roasting is the perfect way to cook almost any poultry or game bird apart from duck or goose, which are too fatty and do not give good results, and turkey, which are too large to fit in the average casserole dish.
- Make sure that you use a large enough casserole and that the bird doesn't fit too closely to the sides of the dish.
- Watch out for overcooking – the closed pot cooks birds almost as fast as an ordinary roast chicken in the oven would cook.
- Check the liquid level in the casserole from time to time. If it's too dry, add a little more. Water is fine, stock or wine are even better.
- Timings for pot-roasted poultry: about 45 minutes (for small birds such as poussin) or 1–1½ hours (for chicken or guinea fowl).

Steaming

1 Cut the poultry into thick shreds or chunks, or use thighs, drumsticks or halved breasts. Marinate (see below), if you like, for at least 1 hour.

2 Arrange the poultry in a single layer on a heatproof dish that is small enough to fit inside the steamer. Place the dish in the steamer, cover and steam for 20–40 minutes until just cooked through.

Poaching

The quick and gentle method of poaching will produce a light broth.

1 Brown the bird in oil if you wish (this is not necessary but will give a deeper flavour), then transfer to a pan that will hold it easily: a large frying pan or sauté pan is good for pieces, a large pan or casserole for a whole bird.

2 Add 1 roughly chopped onion, 3 garlic cloves, 2 chopped carrots, 2 chopped celery sticks, 6 whole black peppercorns and a few sprigs of thyme, scattering them about the whole bird or between the pieces. Pour in just enough stock to cover, then simmer, uncovered, for about 1 hour (for a whole bird) or 30–40 minutes (for pieces).

3 Gently lift the bird out of the liquid. If you are planning to use the liquid as the basis for a sauce, reduce it by at least half.

MARINADES

- Used to flavour the flesh, marinades will not penetrate poultry skin so remove the skin or cut slashes in it.
- Use just enough marinade to coat the poultry generously – drowning it is wasteful, as it runs off and most will be left in the bottom of the container.
- To make a simple marinade, combine olive oil, lemon juice and chopped garlic, pour over chicken and marinate in the refrigerator for at least 1 hour.
- To make a spicy marinade, combine 1 crushed garlic clove, 2 tbsp ground coriander, 2 tbsp ground cumin, 1 tbsp paprika, 1 seeded and chopped hot red chilli, the juice of ½ lemon, 2 tbsp soy sauce and 8 thyme sprigs. Pour over 2kg (4½lb) chicken pieces, mix well and marinate in the fridge overnight.

COQ AU VIN

Serves 4
Preparation 45 minutes
Cooking time about 1 hour
Techniques see also jointing chicken (page 116)

750ml bottle full-bodied white wine, such as Burgundy
    or Chardonnay
4 tbsp brandy
2 bouquet garni (fresh parsley and thyme sprigs,
    1 bay leaf and a piece of parsley)
1 garlic clove, bruised
1 chicken, about 1.4kg (3lb), jointed, or 2 boneless
    breasts, halved, plus 2 drumsticks and 2 thighs
seasoned flour to coat
125g (4oz) butter
125g (4oz) rindless unsmoked bacon rashers, cut into strips
225g (8oz) baby onions, peeled with root ends intact
225g (8oz) brown-cap mushrooms, halved, or quartered
    if large
salt and ground black pepper
buttered noodles or rice to serve

For the beurre manié (see page 40)
25g (1oz) butter mixed with 25g (1oz) plain flour

1 Preheat the oven to 180°C (160°C fan oven) mark 4.
Pour the wine and brandy into a pan and add 1 bouquet
garni and the garlic. Bring to the boil, reduce the heat and
simmer until reduced by half. Leave to cool.
2 Coat the chicken joints lightly with the seasoned flour.
Melt half the butter in a large frying pan. When foaming,
add the chicken and brown all over (in batches if
necessary). Transfer to a flameproof casserole. Add the
bacon to the frying pan and fry until golden. Remove with
a slotted spoon and add to the chicken. Strain the cooled,
reduced wine mixture over the chicken and add the other
bouquet garni. Bring to the boil, cover and cook in the oven
for 30 minutes.
3 Meanwhile, melt the remaining butter in a frying pan
and fry the onions until tender and lightly browned. Add
the mushrooms and fry until softened. Add the onions and
mushrooms to the casserole, cover and cook for 10 minutes
or until the chicken is tender. Lift out the chicken and
vegetables with a slotted spoon and put into a warmed
serving dish. Cover and keep warm.
4 Bring the cooking liquid in the casserole to the boil.
Whisk in the beurre manié, a piece at a time, until the sauce
is shiny and syrupy. Check the seasoning. Pour the sauce
over the chicken and serve with buttered noodles or rice.

NUTRITION PER SERVING
787 cals | 51g fat (22g sats) | 24g carbs | 1.5g salt

MEDITERRANEAN ROAST CHICKEN

Serves 4
Preparation 40 minutes
Cooking time about 1 hour 25 minutes
Techniques see also preparing vegetables (pages 182–194)

900g (2lb) floury potatoes, such as Maris Piper,
    peeled and cut into chunks
125g (4oz) butter, softened
4 tbsp roughly chopped sage leaves, stalks reserved,
    plus extra leaves
4 tbsp roughly chopped thyme, stalks reserved,
    plus extra sprigs
1.4kg (3lb) chicken
juice of 1 lemon, halves reserved
2 fennel bulbs, cut into wedges
1 red onion, cut into wedges
salt and ground black pepper

1 Preheat the oven to 190°C (170°C fan oven) mark 5.
Put the potatoes in a large pan of salted cold water and
bring to the boil. Cook for 5 minutes.
2 Meanwhile, put the butter in a bowl and mix in the
chopped sage and thyme. Season well.
3 Lay the chicken on a board and put the lemon halves
and herb stalks into the cavity. Ease your fingers under
the skin of the neck end to separate the breast skin from
the flesh, then push the herby butter up under the skin,
reserving a little. Season well.
4 Put the chicken in a roasting tin, pour the lemon juice
over it, then top with the extra sage and thyme and
reserved butter. Drain the potatoes and shake in a colander
to roughen their edges. Put around the chicken with the
fennel and red onion. Roast for 1 hour 20 minutes or until
the juices run clear when the thickest part of the thigh is
pierced with a skewer. Carve and serve with the vegetables.

NUTRITION PER SERVING
843 cals | 58g fat (26g sats) | 42g carbs | 0.9g salt

STUFFED CHICKEN BREASTS

Serves 4
Preparation 5 minutes
Cooking time 20 minutes
Techniques see also steaming vegetables (page 195)

oil to grease
150g (5oz) ball mozzarella
4 chicken breasts, about 150g (5oz) each
4 sage leaves
8 slices Parma ham
new potatoes and steamed spinach to serve

1 Preheat the oven to 200°C (180°C fan oven) mark 6. Lightly grease a baking sheet. Slice the mozzarella into eight, then put two slices on each chicken piece. Top each with a sage leaf.
2 Wrap each piece of chicken in two slices of Parma ham, covering the mozzarella.
3 Put on to the prepared baking sheet and cook in the oven for 20 minutes. Serve with the potatoes and spinach.

COOK'S TIP
Sage has a naturally strong, pungent taste, so you need only a little to flavour the chicken. Don't be tempted to add more than just one leaf to each one as too much will overpower the finished dish.

NUTRITION PER SERVING
270 cals | 10g fat (6g sats) | trace carbs | 1g salt

TARRAGON CHICKEN WITH FENNEL

Serves 4
Preparation 10 minutes
Cooking time 45–55 minutes
Techniques see also preparing vegetables (pages 182–194), making stock (page 36), chopping herbs (page 436), casseroling poultry (page 124)

1 tbsp olive oil
4 chicken thighs
1 onion, finely chopped
1 fennel bulb, finely chopped
juice of ½ lemon
200ml (7fl oz) hot chicken stock
200g carton crème fraîche
a small bunch tarragon, roughly chopped
salt and ground black pepper

1 Preheat the oven to 200°C (180°C fan oven) mark 6. Heat the oil in a large flameproof casserole. Add the chicken thighs and fry for 5 minutes or until brown, then remove and put them to one side to keep warm.
2 Add the onion to the pan and fry for 5 minutes, then add the fennel and cook for 5–10 minutes until softened.
3 Add the lemon juice to the pan, followed by the stock. Bring to a simmer and cook until the sauce is reduced by half.
4 Stir in the crème fraîche and return the chicken to the pan. Stir once to mix, then cover and cook in the oven for 25–30 minutes. Stir the tarragon into the sauce, season to taste and serve.

NUTRITION PER SERVING
333 cals | 26g fat (15g sats) | 3g carbs | 0.5g salt

TANDOORI CHICKEN

Serves 4
Preparation 45 minutes, plus marinating
Cooking time 20 minutes
Techniques see also slicing chicken breast fillets (page 117),
preparing chillies (page 189), preparing fresh ginger (page 437)

4 tbsp groundnut oil, plus extra to oil
3 × 150g cartons natural yogurt
juice of ½ lemon
4 skinless chicken breasts, about 600g (1 ¼lb),
    cut into finger-width pieces
½ cucumber
salt and ground black pepper
mint leaves to garnish

For the tandoori paste
24 garlic cloves, about 125g (4oz), crushed
5cm (2in) piece fresh root ginger, peeled and chopped
3 tbsp each coriander seeds, cumin seeds, ground fenugreek
    and paprika
3 red chillies, seeded and chopped
3 tsp English mustard
2 tbsp tomato purée
1 tsp salt

1 Put all the ingredients for the tandoori paste into a food processor with 8 tbsp water and blend to a paste. Divide the paste into three equal portions, freeze two (put into separate freezer bags; they will keep for up to three months – see Freezing Tip) and put the other in a large bowl.
2 To make the tandoori chicken, add 1 tbsp oil, 2 cartons of yogurt and the lemon juice to the paste. Add the chicken and stir well to coat. Cover the bowl, chill and marinate the chicken for at least 4 hours.
3 Preheat the oven to 220°C (200°C fan oven) mark 7. Oil a roasting tin. Put the chicken in it, drizzle the remaining oil over the chicken and roast for 20 minutes or until cooked through.
4 Meanwhile, prepare the raita. Whisk the remaining carton of yogurt. Using a vegetable peeler, scrape the cucumber into very thin strips. Put the strips in a bowl and pour the whisked yogurt over them. Season, then chill until ready to serve. Garnish the chicken with mint sprigs and serve with the raita.

FREEZING TIP
To use the frozen paste, put the paste in a microwave and cook on Defrost for 80 seconds (based on 900W oven), or thaw at a cool room temperature for 1 hour.

NUTRITION PER SERVING
399 cals | 20g fat (4g sats) | 15g carbs | 1.8g salt

CORONATION CHICKEN

Serves 6
Preparation 20 minutes
Cooking time about 50 minutes
Techniques see also making stock (page 36), chopping herbs (page 436)

1 tbsp vegetable oil
1 onion, chopped
1 tbsp ground coriander
1 tbsp ground cumin
1½ tsp ground turmeric
1½ tsp paprika
150ml (¼ pint) dry white wine
500ml (18fl oz) chicken stock
6 boneless, skinless chicken breasts or thighs
2 bay leaves
2 fresh thyme sprigs
2 fresh parsley sprigs
salt and ground black pepper
3–4 tbsp freshly chopped flat-leafed parsley to garnish
mixed leaf salad and French bread to serve

For the dressing
150ml (¼ pint) mayonnaise
5 tbsp natural yogurt
2 tbsp mango chutney
125g (4oz) ready-to-eat dried apricots, chopped
juice of ½ lemon

1 Heat the oil in a large, heavy-based pan, add the onion and fry for 5–10 minutes until softened and golden. Add the spices and cook, stirring, for 1–2 minutes.
2 Pour in the wine, bring to the boil and let it bubble for 5 minutes to reduce right down. Add the stock and bring back to the boil.
3 Season the chicken with salt and pepper, then add to the pan with the bay leaves and herb sprigs. Cover and bring to the boil. Reduce the heat to low and poach the chicken for 25 minutes or until cooked through. Cool quickly by plunging the base of the pan into a sink of cold water, replacing the water as it warms up.
4 Meanwhile, to make the dressing, mix the mayonnaise, yogurt and mango chutney together in a bowl. Drain the cooled stock from the chicken and whisk 200ml (7fl oz) into the mayonnaise mixture. Add the apricots and lemon juice and season well.
5 Chop the chicken into bite-size pieces, then stir into the mayonnaise. Cover and chill until required. Garnish with chopped parsley and serve with salad and French bread.

NUTRITION PER SERVING
425 cals | 26g fat (4g sats) | 14g carbs | 0.6g salt

CHICKEN AND VEGETABLE TERRINE

Serves 8
Preparation 40 minutes, plus chilling
Cooking time 1 hour 2 minutes, plus chilling
Techniques see also preparing vegetables (pages 182–194)

900g (2lb) chicken joints
1 small slice white bread, crusts removed
450ml (¾ pint) double cream, chilled
1 small bunch of watercress
125g (4oz) small young carrots
125g (4oz) French beans, trimmed and stringed
275g (10oz) peas in the pod, shelled
75g (3oz) small, even-sized button mushrooms
200g (7oz) can artichoke hearts, drained
butter to grease
salt and ground black pepper
rocket leaves to garnish (optional)

For the sauce
225g (8oz) ripe tomatoes, peeled and quartered
125ml (4fl oz) vegetable oil
50ml (2fl oz) white wine vinegar
75ml (2½fl oz) tomato purée

1 Cut all the chicken flesh away from the bones; discard the skin and any fat. Finely mince the chicken with the bread. Chill for 30 minutes. Stir the cream, a little at a time, into the chicken mixture with salt and pepper to taste.
2 Trim the watercress and discard the coarse stalks. Stir one-third of the chicken mixture into the watercress. Cover both bowls and chill for 2 hours.
3 Preheat the oven to 170°C (150°C fan oven) mark 3. The careful preparation of vegetables is essential to the final presentation. Cut the carrots into neat matchstick pieces, 2.5cm (1in) by 3mm (⅛in). Cut the beans into similar-length pieces. Blanch the carrots, beans and peas for 2 minutes in separate pans of boiling water. Drain. Trim the mushroom stalks level with the caps. Cut the mushrooms across into slices 5mm (¼in) thick. Dice the artichoke hearts into 5mm (¼in) pieces.
4 Grease a 1.1 litre (2 pint) lidded terrine and base-line with a rectangular piece of greaseproof paper, and grease the top of the paper. Take half the watercress and chicken mixture and spread it evenly over the bottom of the terrine. Arrange the carrots in neat crossways lines over the top, then spread one-quarter of the chicken mixture carefully over the carrots.
5 Lightly seasoning the vegetables with salt and pepper as they are layered, sprinkle the peas over the chicken mixture in the dish and put another thin layer of chicken mixture on top. Next, put the mushrooms in crossways lines and top with the remaining watercress and chicken mixture. Arrange the artichokes on top, cover with half the remaining chicken mixture, arrange the beans in crossways lines and cover with the remaining chicken mixture.
6 Put a double sheet of greased greaseproof paper on top and cover tightly with the lid. Put the terrine in a roasting tin and add enough hot water to come halfway up the sides of the terrine. Cook in the oven for 1 hour or until firm.
7 Cool a little, drain off any juices, then invert the terrine on to a serving plate. Cool, then chill for 1 hour before serving.
8 Meanwhile, make the sauce. Purée the tomatoes in a blender or food processor with the oil, vinegar, tomato purée and seasoning. Rub through a sieve. Chill lightly before serving, then garnish with some rocket leaves, if you like.

NUTRITION PER SERVING
616 cals | 54g fat (23g sats) | 8g carbs | 0.6g salt

POUSSINS WITH PANCETTA, ARTICHOKE AND POTATO SALAD

Serves 6

Preparation 20 minutes, plus overnight marinating

Cooking time 1 hour 40 minutes, plus resting

Techniques see also zesting citrus fruits (page 217), crushing garlic (pages 183), chopping herbs (page 436)

grated zest of 1 lemon
5 large fresh rosemary sprigs, leaves stripped
4 tbsp white wine vinegar
150ml (¼ pint) fruity white wine
4 garlic cloves, crushed
3 tbsp freshly chopped oregano or a pinch of dried oregano
290g jar marinated artichokes, drained, oil reserved
3 poussins, about 450g (1lb) each
½ tsp cayenne pepper
450g (1lb) new potatoes, quartered
225g (8oz) pancetta, prosciutto or streaky bacon, roughly chopped
350g (12oz) peppery salad leaves, such as watercress, mustard leaf and rocket
salt and ground black pepper

1 Put the lemon zest and rosemary leaves into a large bowl with the vinegar, wine, garlic, oregano and 4 tbsp oil from the artichokes. Stir well. Using a fork, pierce the skin of the poussins in five or six places, then season well with black pepper and the cayenne pepper. Put the birds, breast side down, in the bowl and spoon the marinade over them. Cover and chill overnight.

2 Cook the potatoes in lightly salted boiling water for 2 minutes. Drain. Preheat the oven to 200°C (180°C fan oven) mark 6.

3 Lift the poussins from the marinade and put, breast side up, into a large roasting tin. Scatter the potatoes, pancetta or bacon and artichokes around them and pour the marinade over. Cook for 1½ hours, basting occasionally, or until golden and cooked through.

4 Cut each poussin in half lengthways and keep warm. Toss the salad leaves with about 5 tbsp warm cooking juices. Arrange the leaves on warmed plates, then top with the potatoes, pancetta, artichokes and poussins.

COOK'S TIP
Use the oil drained from the artichokes to make a salad dressing for another meal.

NUTRITION PER SERVING
442 cals | 27g fat (8g sats) | 13g carbs | 1.5g salt

LEMON AND HERB ROAST TURKEY

Serves 8
Preparation time 25 minutes
Cooking time 4½–5 hours, plus resting
Techniques see also cooking a turkey (page 119)

5.4–6.3kg (12–14lb) turkey, giblets removed for stock
(see page 118)
½ quantity Chestnut and Butternut Squash Stuffing,
thawed (see page 319)
125g (4oz) butter, softened
1 lemon, halved
3 fresh bay leaves
3 fresh sage leaves
2 fresh rosemary sprigs
8 rashers rindless streaky bacon, rolled into neat rolls
350g (12oz) chipolata sausages, twisted in two to make
cocktail sausages and snipped with scissors
salt and ground black pepper
a bunch of mixed herbs to garnish (optional)
Rich Red Wine Gravy to serve (see page 18)

1 Take the turkey out of the fridge 45 minutes before
stuffing it. Preheat the oven to 220°C (200°C fan oven)
mark 7. Put the turkey on a board, lift the neck flap, spoon
in the stuffing and secure (see page 119).
2 Put a large sheet of foil in a flameproof roasting tin. Put
the turkey on top and smear it all over with butter. Squeeze
the lemon juice over. Put the squeezed lemon halves and
bay leaves inside the turkey, with a sage leaf and a sprig of
rosemary, then snip over the remaining sage and rosemary.
Season with salt and pepper. Tie the turkey legs together
with string. Bring the foil over the turkey and crimp the
edges together, leaving plenty of space between the bird
and foil. Roast for 30 minutes. Reduce the oven temperature
to 170°C (150°C fan oven) mark 3 and roast for a further
3½ hours. Take the turkey out of the oven and increase the
temperature to 200°C (180°C fan oven) mark 6. Pull off the
foil and baste the turkey with the juices. Put the bacon rolls
and chipolatas around the turkey and roast for 40 minutes
more, basting halfway through. Check whether the turkey is
cooked (see page 119).
3 Tip the juices out of the turkey into the roasting tin.
Lift the turkey, bacon and sausages on to a warm platter,
cover with foil and a teatowel and leave in a warm place
for 30 minutes. Make the gravy. To garnish, stuff the turkey
cavity with a bunch of mixed herbs, if you like.

NUTRITION PER SERVING
457 cals | 25g fat (10g sats) | 2g carbs | 1.2g salt

ORANGE AND BAY TURKEY CROWN

Serves 8
Preparation 20 minutes, plus resting
Cooking time 2½ hours
Techniques see also making gravy (page 18)

2 onions, sliced
2 bay leaves, plus extra to garnish
2.7kg (6lb) oven-ready turkey crown
40g (1½oz) butter, softened
1 lemon, halved
2 tbsp all-purpose chicken seasoning
2 oranges, halved
150ml (¼ pint) dry white wine or chicken stock

1 Preheat the oven to 190°C (170°C fan oven) mark 5.
Arrange the onions in a large flameproof roasting tin, add
the bay leaves and sit the turkey on top. Spread the butter
over the turkey breast, then squeeze the lemon over. Throw
the halves into the tin. Sprinkle with the seasoning, then put
the orange halves in the tin around the turkey.
2 Pour the wine or stock into the roasting tin, followed by
250ml (9fl oz) hot water. Cover the turkey loosely with a
large sheet of foil. Make sure it's completely covered, but
with enough space between the foil and the turkey for air
to circulate.
3 Roast the turkey for 2 hours or until juices run clear
when the meat is pierced with a skewer (see Cook's Tip).
Remove the foil and put the turkey back in the oven for
30 minutes or until golden.
4 Lift the turkey on to a warmed carving dish, cover
loosely with foil to keep warm and leave it to rest for
15 minutes before carving. Keep the orange and lemon
halves to garnish. Don't wash up the tin – you'll need it
for making the gravy.

COOK'S TIP
To check that the turkey crown is cooked, pierce the
thickest part of the crown with a skewer. Press the
skin to release the juices – they should run clear and
golden with no traces of pink. If there are any pink
juices, put the turkey back in the oven for another
10–15 minutes until cooked.

NUTRITION PER SERVING
181 cals | 6g fat (3g sats) | 3g carbs | 0.2g salt

CRISPY DUCK SALAD

Serves 8
Preparation 30 minutes, plus cooling and overnight chilling
Cooking time 1 hour 25 minutes
Techniques see also zesting citrus fruits (page 217), making salad dressings (page 27)

6 duck legs, about 200g (7oz) each
2 fresh thyme sprigs
1 tsp peppercorns
2 bay leaves
2 tsp salt
125g (4oz) kumquats
125g (4oz) pecan nuts
finely grated zest and juice of 2 oranges
225g (8oz) cranberries
125g (4oz) caster sugar
4 tbsp white wine vinegar
9 tbsp sunflower oil
3 tbsp walnut oil
salt and ground black pepper
frisée leaves to serve

1 Preheat the oven to 180°C (160°C fan oven) mark 4. Put the duck legs into a large flameproof casserole, cover with cold water and bring to the boil. Reduce the heat and simmer for 10 minutes, skim the surface and add the thyme, peppercorns, bay leaves and salt. Cook in the oven for 45 minutes–1 hour until tender. Cool quickly in the liquor and chill overnight.

2 Preheat the grill. Quarter the kumquats. Put the nuts on a baking sheet and toast lightly under the grill. Put the orange zest in a frying pan with 200ml (7fl oz) orange juice, the cranberries and sugar. Bring to the boil, reduce the heat and simmer for 5 minutes or until the cranberries are tender. Drain the juice into a pan, reserving the berries. Bring the juice to the boil and bubble until syrupy, then return the cranberries to the pan.

3 In a small bowl, whisk the vinegar and oils and season with salt and pepper. Add the kumquats to the cranberry mixture with the oil and vinegar dressing and the pecan nuts. Put to one side. Skim the fat from the jellied duck liquor and put to one side. Cut the duck into thick shreds, leaving the skin on. Just before serving, heat 1 tbsp reserved duck fat in a large non-stick frying pan and fry half the duck for 5 minutes or until crisp and brown. Keep warm and repeat with the remaining duck. To serve, toss the duck with the cranberry mixture and serve with salad leaves.

NUTRITION PER SERVING
614 cals | 54g fat (10g sats) | 24g carbs | 0.1g salt

DUCK WITH RED ONION MARMALADE

Serves 4
Preparation 25 minutes, plus overnight marinating
Cooking time about 1 hour
Techniques see also preparing onions (page 182)

900ml (1½ pints) olive oil
4 duck legs with skin, marinated overnight (see Cook's Tips)
steamed cabbage and roast potato wedges to serve

For the red onion marmalade
125g (4oz) butter
550g (1¼lb) red onions, sliced
125g (4oz) kumquats, halved
125ml (4fl oz) sherry or wine vinegar
150g (5oz) golden caster sugar
grated zest and juice of 1 orange
300ml (½ pint) red wine
salt and ground black pepper

1 Preheat the oven to 170°C (150°C fan oven) mark 3. Heat the olive oil gently in a pan. Meanwhile, arrange the prepared duck legs in a single layer in a roasting dish – they should be touching. Pour the warmed oil over the duck legs, to cover completely. Roast in the oven for 45 minutes until the duck is cooked through.
2 Meanwhile, to make the onion marmalade, melt the butter in a pan, add the onions, kumquats and vinegar and simmer, covered, for 15–20 minutes until the onions are soft, stirring every now and then. Add the sugar, turn up the heat and cook for 10 minutes, stirring, to caramelise the onions. Add the orange zest, juice and wine, then cook gently, uncovered, for 20 minutes until all the liquid has evaporated. Season with salt and pepper.
3 Lift the duck out of the oil and pat dry. Heat a large frying pan and cook the duck over a medium heat for 10–15 minutes until golden and crisp. Serve with the onion marmalade, cabbage and roast potato wedges.

COOK'S TIPS
- The night before, put the duck legs in a single layer in a plastic container. Rub in 3 crushed garlic cloves, 2 tsp freshly chopped thyme and 1 tsp salt. Add 3 bay leaves. Cover and chill overnight. The next day, remove the duck, rub off excess salt and rinse under cold running water. Pat dry.
- Make the red onion marmalade, cover and chill for up to three days. Reheat to serve.

NUTRITION PER SERVING
979 cals | 79g fat (31g sats) | 53g carbs | 0.7g salt

GUINEA FOWL WITH PRUNES

Serves 6
Preparation 40 minutes, plus marinating
Cooking time 1½ hours
Techniques see also preparing vegetables (pages 182–194), making stock (page 36), preparing apples (page 216)

225g (8oz) onion, roughly chopped
125g (4oz) carrot, roughly chopped
125g (4oz) celery, roughly chopped
6–8 guinea fowl joints or cornfed chicken joints,
   2kg (4½lb) total weight
750ml (1¼ pints) red wine
1 tsp black peppercorns, crushed
1 tbsp freshly chopped thyme
2 bay leaves
175g (6oz) ready-to-eat dried prunes
3 tbsp vegetable oil
3 garlic cloves, crushed
1 tsp harissa paste
1 tbsp tomato purée
2 tbsp plain flour
300ml (½ pint) chicken stock
225g (8oz) streaky bacon, cut in strips
2 apples, cored and sliced
salt and ground black pepper
mashed potato to serve

1 Put the onion, carrot, celery, guinea fowl or chicken, 600ml (1 pint) wine, peppercorns, thyme and bay leaves in a large bowl. Cover and marinate for at least 3–4 hours. Put the remaining wine in another bowl with the prunes. Cover and soak for 3–4 hours.

2 Preheat the oven to 170°C (150°C fan oven) mark 3. Drain and dry the joints (put the vegetables and wine to one side). Heat 2 tbsp oil in a large flameproof casserole. Cook the joints in batches, skin side down, over a medium heat until brown, then turn and brown the underside. Remove from pan and put to one side. Add the marinated vegetables (keep the marinade to one side) and stir-fry for 5 minutes. Add the garlic, harissa and tomato purée and cook for 1 minute. Mix in the flour and cook for 1 minute. Pour in the reserved marinade and stock. Bring to the boil, stirring. Return the joints to the casserole, with the legs at the bottom. Bring to the boil, season well, cover and cook in the oven for 40 minutes.

3 Heat the remaining oil in a pan. Cook the bacon, stirring, for 5 minutes or until golden brown. Remove from the pan and put to one side. Cook the apple for 2–3 minutes on each side until golden. Put to one side. Remove the joints from the casserole. Strain the sauce and return to the pan with the joints. Add the prunes and any juices, the bacon and apple. Heat through in the oven for 10 minutes. Serve with mashed potatoes.

NUTRITION PER SERVING
811 cals | 49g fat (14g sats) | 24g carbs | 1.7g salt

GOOSE WITH ROASTED APPLES

Serves 8
Preparation 30 minutes
Cooking time 4¼ hours
Techniques see also preparing vegetables (pages 182–194)

6 small red onions
7 small red eating apples
5kg (11lb) oven-ready goose, washed, dried and
    seasoned inside and out
1 small bunch each sage and rosemary
1 bay leaf
sea salt and ground black pepper

For the stock
giblets removed from the goose
1 carrot and 1 celery stick, chopped
1 onion, quartered
1 bouquet garni
6 black peppercorns

For the gravy
30g pack Madeira Wine Gravy Mix
300ml (½ pint) red wine
200ml (7fl oz) giblet stock

1 For the stock, put the giblets in a pan, add the remaining ingredients and pour in 1.1 litres (2 pints) cold water. Cover and bring slowly to the boil, then reduce the heat and simmer for 1 hour. Strain and keep the liquid to one side.
2 Preheat the oven to 230°C (210°C fan oven) mark 8. Quarter one of the onions and two of the apples and put inside the goose with half the sage and rosemary and the bay leaf. Tie the legs together and push a long skewer through the wings to tuck them in.
3 Put the goose, breast side up, on a rack in a large roasting tin. Prick the breast all over and season. Put the remaining onions around the goose. Cover with foil. Cook for 15 minutes per 450g (1lb) plus 15 minutes (3 hours for a 5kg/11lb goose). Roast for 30 minutes. Reduce the heat to 190°C (170°C fan oven) mark 5.
4 Remove the fat from the tin, drizzle some over the goose, then chill the remainder in a jar (reserve for roasting potatoes). Roast the goose for 1 hour, remove fat again and chill. Cook the bird for 30 minutes, then remove the foil. Remove and chill fat again. Add the remaining apples. Sprinkle the goose with the remaining herbs and roast for 1 hour. Put on to a warm serving plate, cover with foil and leave to rest for 30 minutes. Remove the apples and onions and keep warm.

5 Make the gravy (see Finishing Touches). Cut the remaining apples and onions into wedges and serve with the goose and gravy.

FINISHING TOUCHES

To make the gravy, pour out all but 1 tbsp of the fat from the tin. Sprinkle in the gravy mix and whisk in the wine. Cook for 5 minutes, stirring. Whisk in the stock. Bring to the boil, add 1 roasted apple and onion and press down with a spoon. Reduce the heat and simmer for 10 minutes, then strain into a pan.

NUTRITION PER SERVING
646 cals | 41g fat (12g sats) | 11g carbs | 1g salt

MEAT AND GAME

Beef, lamb, pork, ham and game such as rabbit and venison make wonderfully hearty, delicious meals and are easy to prepare and cook when you know how. The detailed step-by-step techniques in this chapter guide you through all the basic preparation and cooking, with easy-to-follow photographs for perfect results every time. Packed with tips, hints and advice, ideas for stuffings and marinades, and handy tables of cooking times, here you will find everything you need to know about preparing and cooking meat. The recipe collection is packed with fabulous ideas too, including Classic roast beef, chunky Italian meatballs, Ginger and honey-glazed ham, Braised lamb shanks, Honey roast pork and Pheasant with cider and apples.

BUYING MEAT AND GAME

Whether you enjoy the delicate flavour of lamb, the robust taste of beef, or the richness of game, there's plenty to choose from with all the different cuts and joints available.

How to buy and store meat and game

Each animal can be divided into different cuts, all of which have their own characteristic flavour and texture. Cuts from parts of the animal that have worked hardest, for example the shin or neck, contain the toughest muscle tissue and usually require long, slow cooking. Cuts from parts that have worked the least, like the fore-rib or sirloin, are more tender and suit quicker cooking. It's important to choose the right cut when buying meat for a recipe – if you want beef for a speedy stir-fry, for example, you will need a tender, quick-cooking cut such as sirloin.

When buying meat and game, always check it first: it should look and smell fresh. The flesh should look moist but not watery, and pink, red or dark red according to variety (mature beef will be dark red, as will venison). Fat should be pale, creamy and firm – avoid meat where the fat is crumbly, waxy or yellowing. Look for meat that has been well cut and trimmed and remember that some fat will add flavour.

Meat should be wrapped and stored in the fridge, placed in a dish so that if any juices escape they cannot drip and contaminate other foods. Do not allow the meat to touch any other foods. Raw meat can generally be stored for three to five days, although offal and minced or processed meat such as sausages can deteriorate more quickly and should be used within two days. Meat that is bought sealed in a pack can be stored in the fridge unopened, making sure that it is eaten before the use-by-date.

COOK'S TIP

You need smaller quantities when buying cuts of meat off the bone: allow 100–150g (3½–5oz) per person. For meat on the bone, allow slightly more, anything from 175–350g (6–12oz) per person depending on the cut.

SAUSAGES FOR COOKING

Sausages can be made from a variety of meats, either finely or coarsely ground, but the most often used, alone or in combination, are pork, beef, veal and venison. As well as ground meat, sausages also contain some type of fat, herbs, spices, seasoning and cereal. The meat-to-fat ratio varies hugely between varieties of sausage, and from region to region, but a pork sausage should contain a minimum of 42% pork meat. Sausage skins can be either natural (intestine casing) or synthetic. Sausages are usually sold twisted into links. There are endless varieties of sausage, but the most famous of the pork-based are:

Cumberland sausages, traditionally sold in a coil, rather than twisted into links. With a chunky texture and peppery flavour, they are a great all-round sausage.

Lincolnshire sausages, with a chunky and open texture. Flavoured with thyme and sage.

Chipolatas, famous for being wrapped in bacon and served with the Christmas turkey. Slender sausages which are usually grilled rather than pan-fried or oven-roasted.

Chorizo, a distinctive red Spanish sausage, strongly flavoured with paprika. It has a coarse texture and hot, spicy flavour. Available both raw and cooked, smoked and unsmoked.

Frankfurters, lightly smoked German sausages with a fine texture, which includes salted bacon. They are the classic hot dog sausage. Toulouse, a pungent coarse sausage flavoured with wine, garlic and seasoning. Great in hot-pots or cassoulets, served with mash, and fried onions, too.

Toulouse sausage A coarse pork sausage from south-west France, it also contains smoked bacon and white wine. Highly seasoned and flavoured with garlic and herbs, it is a key ingredient in the bean stew cassoulet. It can also be eaten on its own, with potato salad and mustard.

Other meats and game

More unusual meats are to be found in butchers' shops and supermarkets nowadays, while some others are making a comeback. These include:

Rabbit

Rabbit is now widely farmed, but wild and farmed rabbit are strikingly different: farmed rabbit has pale and tender meat while the wild animals usually have flesh that is darker and much tougher. Farmed rabbit is often likened to chicken in flavour and texture. The meat is low in fat and cholesterol, making it a healthy option. Rabbit can be bought whole, or cut into pieces. To cook wild rabbit: braise, casserole, stew or add to pie fillings. To cook farmed rabbit: grill, sauté or roast. Young, tender rabbit can be treated in all the ways you would treat chicken, including roasting, grilling and sautéing. Because the meat is lean, however, it should be basted with oil and not overcooked.

Hare

Similar in appearance to rabbit, but much larger and with longer ears, hare has darker, more strongly flavoured flesh. As hare is unsuited to farming, only wild are available. Young hare (leveret) is best, and can be roasted, as saddle of hare. Older hare can be potted or casseroled and requires long, slow cooking to achieve tender results. A traditional English recipe is for jugged hare, which is marinated in wine and juniper berries, then cooked for a long time in a tightly covered earthenware jug or casserole.

Goat

Goat is not commonly found, but it is worth buying if you come across it. Like goat's cheese, the meat has a distinctive and pungent aroma. The meat of young goats (kids) is tender, juicy and lean, and can be cooked more quickly, but generally goat's meat is best suited to long, slow cooking such as stewing. Classic goat recipes include Jamaican goat curry, jerked leg of goat, Greek kid with avgolemono (egg and lemon sauce), and Filipino kalderetta (spicy goat stew). Braise, stew or casserole mature goat. Roast or barbecue young goat.

Venison

Venison is the meat from fallow, red and roe deer. The meat is dark red and lean, with a fine texture and a fairly strong flavour. Meat from older deer has a better flavour but requires long, slow cooking to achieve tender results. The meat from younger animals can be cooked more quickly. Venison is sold as joints and smaller cuts, cubed, minced, and processed into products such as sausages. Venison suits fruity sauces as well as earthier flavours such as red wine, mushrooms and marjoram. To keep venison meat moist and tender, marinate and then baste regularly during cooking. Pan-fry smaller cuts, roast larger joints. Otherwise braise, casserole, stew or add to pie fillings.

Boar

A type of wild pig, from which modern domesticated pigs are descended, boar is found throughout Europe and Asia, and is now also farmed. The meat is much darker and more strongly flavoured than pork (because the meat is not bled before cooking as it is for pork). The flesh is also leaner and must be cooked carefully to keep it from drying out. Boar is sold in various cuts and processed into products such as sausages and burgers. It goes well with robust flavourings such as thyme, rosemary, sage, juniper, garlic and red wine. Roast tender cuts; braise, stew or casserole tougher cuts or use in pie fillings. Use in sauces, or make into patties, meatballs and meatloaves.

FREEZING AND THAWING MEAT

Meat can be successfully and safely frozen, but be sure to follow the guidelines below:

- Always freeze meat before its 'use-by' date, preferably on the day of purchase.
- Follow any freezing or thawing instructions given.
- Wrap portions in individual freezer bags, seal tightly and label with the date of freezing. They can be stored in the freezer for up to three months.
- To thaw, put the meat in a dish to catch any juices and put in the fridge until completely thawed. Use within two days.
- Do not refreeze raw meat that has thawed. You can, however, freeze dishes made from thawed meat that you have then cooked.

PREPARING BEEF

From trimming and tying joints to tenderising steaks and barding and larding to ensure the moistest, tenderest results, there are lots of simple techniques to make sure you make the most of your beef.

Boning

The joints you are mostly likely to want to bone are rib and sirloin, so that they are easier to slice when cooked; they can also be rolled. The principle for preparing both joints is the same.

1 Put the joint on your chopping board with the bone facing down and the shorter vertebral bones facing upwards.

2 Use a long knife to make a thin cut all the way along the length of the spine. Cut towards the bone, working the knife between the bone and meat until you reach the ribs.

3 Lift the meat in one hand and cut between the ribs and meat, cutting towards the bone, to remove the meat in a single piece. Trim off the cartilage and fat.

Barding

Lean joints of meat can be barded – wrapped in a thin layer of fat to moisten the meat during cooking. If the butcher hasn't done this for you, it's easy to do at home.

You will need string and 3–4 sheets of pork fat, preferably back fat, large enough to cover the whole joint, dried herbs, ground black pepper.

1 Season the meat with freshly ground black pepper and dried herbs if you like. Wrap the sheets of fat around the joint so that both the sides and ends are covered.

2 Tie a piece of string around the length of the joint. Turn it 90 degrees and tie another piece in the same way, so that the fat is held in place.

3 Starting at one end, loop string around the meat, tie it securely and cut off. Make another loop about 5cm (2in) from the first. Continue along the length of the joint.

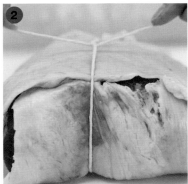
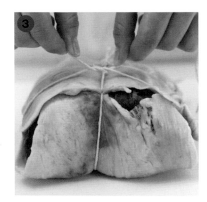

Larding

Threading narrow strips of fat through beef fillet is another way of guaranteeing juiciness. The fat is threaded through the joint using a larding needle.

1 Cut long strips of pork fat, preferably back fat, which will fit easily into the larding needle. Chill well or freeze.

2 Push the needle right through the joint, so that the tip sticks out at least 5cm (2in) through the other side.

3 Take a strip of fat, place it in the hollow of the larding needle, and feed it into the tip. When the fat can't go in any further, press down on the joint and pull the needle out. The fat should stay inside.

4 Repeat at 2.5cm (1in) intervals on all sides of the joint.

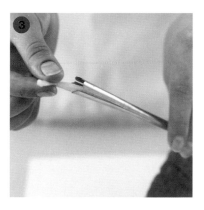

Trimming tips

There are certain rules that apply to trimming most cuts of meat.

1 Trim away excess fat, leaving no more than 5mm (¼in) on steaks, chops and roasting cuts – a little fat will contribute juiciness and flavour. When preparing meat for cutting into chunks, try to separate the individual muscles, which can be identified by the sinews running between each muscle.

Trimming a joint

1 Cut off the excess fat to leave a thickness of about 5mm (¼in). This isn't necessary for very lean cuts.

2 Trim away any stray pieces of meat or sinew left by the butcher.

3 If the joint has a covering of fat, you can lightly score it – taking care not to cut into the meat – to help the fat drain away during cooking.

Tying

Tie the joint if you are using a boned and rolled joint, or if you have boned the joint but want to roast it using the bones as a 'roasting rack'.

1 Tie a piece of string around the length of the joint, securing it to the bones if you are using them. If you are cooking a boned and rolled joint, turn it 90 degrees then tie another piece in the same way.

2 Starting at one end of the joint, loop string around the meat and tie it securely and firmly. Cut it off and make another loop about 5cm (2in) from the first.

3 Continue tying the joint in this way along the whole length of the joint until neatly and firmly secured.

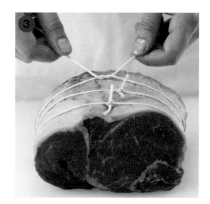

Seasoning

All joints can be seasoned for extra flavour. For pork, the meat should be seasoned and the rind rubbed with salt. Use a dry marinade (see page 155) or salt and black pepper.

1 Rub the joint with vegetable oil to help the seasonings stick.

2 Press on the seasonings in a thin, uniform layer.

Tenderising steak

Some cuts of steak benefit from tenderising. There are two ways to do it: by pounding or scoring.

1 To pound, lay the steaks in a single layer on a large piece of clingfilm or waxed paper. Lay another sheet on top of the slices and pound gently with a rolling pin, small frying pan or the flat side of a meat mallet.

2 Scoring is especially useful for cuts that have long, tough fibres, such as flank. It allows a marinade to penetrate more deeply into the meat. Lay the steak on the chopping board and, using a long, very sharp knife, make shallow cuts in one direction along the whole surface.

3 Make another set of cuts at a 45 degree angle to the first. Now turn the meat over and repeat on the other side.

USING A MALLET

You can tenderise very tough cuts of meat by beating them with the side of the meat mallet that has raised dimples on its surface. The dimples break down muscle fibre, effectively 'pre-chewing' it. Don't use clingfilm if you are tenderising with this method.

Mincing

If you don't have a mincer you can mince meat using a food processor or a knife.

1 Using a food processor Cut the meat into chunks about 2.5cm (1in) square. Put a handful of meat into the food processor and pulse for a few seconds at a time. Stop when the meat is just starting to form a ball on the sides of the bowl. Remove and put to one side, then repeat with the remaining meat.

2 Using a knife This is an old-fashioned method but actually a really excellent one. Trim off all fat and sinews and cut the meat into thin pieces. Chop with two large heavy knives or cleavers, using a decisive hammer action, until the meat resembles coarse mince.

PREPARING LAMB

From tender juicy noisettes of lamb for pan-frying to boned or butterflied leg of lamb for roasting, or rack of lamb tied in the French style or as an elegant guard or honour, lamb is wonderfully varied.

Butterflying a leg of lamb

1 Place the leg of lamb on a chopping board with the meaty side facing down and the bone facing up. With the thick end facing towards you, see if the chunky end of the pelvic bone is in place. If it is, cut it out by working all around it with a boning or paring knife – always cutting towards the bone – then pull or twist it out.

2 Using a boning knife, cut a long slit right down to the bone, starting from the thin end, until you reach the joint.

Then scrape and cut the meat from the bone, pulling it back with your fingers, until the bone is fully exposed.

3 Work the knife carefully around the bone, cutting away from the meat, to loosen it. Twist out the bone, then follow the same procedure with the other bone.

4 Flatten the meat with your hands. Holding one hand flat on the top of the thickest part, make a cut parallel

with the chopping board about midway through. Cut to within 2.5cm (1in) of the edge, then fold it out as if opening a book.

5 Repeat with the other thick part of the leg and fold out. If you like, secure the flaps of meat with skewers to make cooking easier.

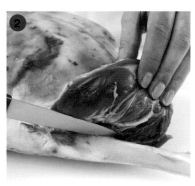

Tunnel-boning a leg of lamb

Here, the leg is boned but left whole so that the cavity can be stuffed. If necessary, cut out the pelvic bone as described above.

1 Starting from the thin end of the leg, insert a boning knife between the meat and bone and run it around the bone to cut through the connective tissue and free the bone from the surrounding meat.

2 When you reach the joint, twist the bone and pull it out.

3 Turn the leg around and use the same technique to cut out the thick bone. When you reach the end of the bone, it should pull out easily.

Preparing a rack of lamb

A rack of lamb comprises the seven or eight cutlets, chops from the neck end, served as a joint. It is one of the tastiest and most impressive lamb joints and easy to prepare. You can cook it just as it comes from the butcher, or as a French-style rack.

1 If necessary, pull off the papery outer membrane from the fat side of the rack. Trim away the excess fat. Look for a long strip of cartilage on one end of the rack and cut it out if it is there. Do the same with a long strip of sinew running the length of the rack under the ribs.

2 Make a cut right down to the bone across the fat side of the rack about 2.5–5cm (1–2in) from the tips of the bones. Place the knife in that cut and, holding the knife almost parallel to the ribs, slice off the meat as a single piece to expose the ends of the bones.

3 Insert the knife between one pair of bared ribs at the point of the initial cut. Push through it to cut the meat between the ribs. Continue in the same way with the other ribs.

4 Slice down on both sides of each rib to remove the strips of meat. When you've finished, turn the rack bone side up and scrape off the papery membranes from the backs of the ribs. This will leave the top parts of the bones clean.

ROASTING TIMES

A rack of lamb should always be cooked at a fairly high temperature so that it browns well without overcooking the thin 'eye' meat. Preheat the oven to 220°C (200°C fan oven) mark 7 and cook for 25–30 minutes. If you are cooking a single rack, an alternative is to brown the fat side first; this means that you can cook it at a lower temperature, 180°C (160°C fan oven) mark 4.

Guard of honour

1 Prepare the racks as described for rack of lamb (see page 149). Place with the bases pressed together and the exposed end-bones interlocking.

2 Tie the joint using a piece of string vertically between every two ribs. Roast as it is, or stuff the space between the two racks and cook at 220°C (200°C fan oven) mark 7 for 30–35 minutes.

Noisettes of lamb

Loin of lamb can be boned, rolled and sliced to make noisettes (usually with a layer of fat on the meat), both delicious and elegant. Buy them ready prepared or ask the butcher to do it – or try this simple version.

1 Use a thin-bladed knife to scrape and cut along the backbone until the tenderloin falls away. Remove and save for a stir-fry.

2 Turn the loin around and cut between the backbone and eye meat, always cutting towards the bone. Remove the meat in a single piece and trim the excess fat.

3 Roll the flat apron of fat around the eye and tie it securely with string at 2.5cm (1in) intervals.

4 Slice the loin about 2.5cm (1in) thick. Grill (for 8–12 minutes) or pan-fry (for 6–10 minutes).

COOK'S TIPS

— The small fillet on the underside of the loin is usually rolled up with the loin to make true noisettes. Otherwise, you can cut it off as a strip and use it (thinly sliced) in a stir-fry, while making this simplified version of noisettes of lamb, which will still be a delicious cut.

— Roast the boned loin as one whole piece rather than cutting it into individual noisettes.

— For a simpler version of medallions requiring no string, you can follow steps 1 and 2, then cut off all the fat and slice the meat. This may look a lot less elegant but is actually a much leaner cut and is therefore probably all the more desirable.

PREPARING PORK

From simple chops for stuffing to glorious tenderloin and crispy roast pork, the choice of techniques you can use with pork is endlessly varied and the results always delicious.

Removing the tenderloin

Like beef and lamb, pork has a piece of flesh running along the backbone on the other side of the ribs from the loin called the tenderloin. It is the most tender cut of all.

1 Place the loin skin side down on your chopping board and locate the long rounded strip of tenderloin meat. You can get your butcher to remove this for you, but it is also easy to do yourself.

2 Make a cut along the edge of the tenderloin closest to the backbone, taking care not to cut into the meat, then work the knife between meat and bone until you can pull away the tenderloin.

3 Cut off the thin strip of meat connected to the main section and save it for stock, if you like.

4 Using a sharp small knife, make a cut at the thick end of the tenderloin just underneath the thick, silvery membrane covering it on one side.

5 Taking care not to cut the meat, cut and pull off the membrane in long strips. Make sure every bit of membrane comes away. Trim away any loose scraps of meat and tidy the ends if they look at all ragged.

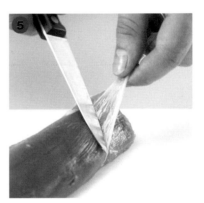

COOKING TENDERLOIN

The tenderloin is most often cut into medallions (see page 152), but it can also be cooked in a single piece with or without stuffing. To cook it unstuffed, brown it well on all sides and then finish cooking in an oven preheated to 200°C (180°C fan oven) mark 6 for about 10 minutes. To stuff it, make a deep cut through the centre of the tenderloin, open it like a book, then pound it gently with a small frying pan or meat mallet to flatten it out. Put the stuffing in the centre of the meat, then roll it up and tie with string. (A quick stuffing can be made with chopped onion cooked gently in oil until soft with a little freshly chopped sage or rosemary.) Cook the stuffed tenderloin as you would unstuffed, but for a little longer.

Cutting medallions

1 Cut the pork fillet into pieces about 1–2.5cm (½–1 in) thick and lay them in a single layer on a sheet of clingfilm or waxed paper.

2 Lay another sheet of clingfilm or waxed paper on top of the slices and pound gently with a rolling pin, small frying pan or the flat side of a meat mallet until they are about half their original thickness.

Stuffing chops

Chops at least 2.5cm (1 in) thick can be stuffed for extra flavour. Loin chops are best for this; chump chops are also good.

1 Remove the rind (skin) and trim off all but about 5mm (¼ in) of fat.

2 Press down with the flat of your hand and, using a small sharp knife, cut into the eye of the meat in the middle of the fat side of the chop.

3 Keep working the knife in until you reach the bone.

4 Cut through all of the eye meat to make a deep pocket. You can enlarge the pocket by cutting through some of the tail of the chop, but don't cut all the way through.

5 Shape the stuffing into thin flat patties if necessary. Open the pocket of the chop and slide the stuffing in, then secure with cocktail sticks.

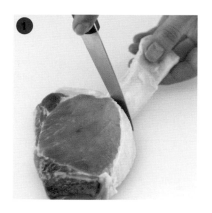

EASY STUFFINGS

Don't overfill the chops or the stuffing will spill out. Try some of the following ideas:

- Slivered garlic cooked in butter
- Sage leaves
- Soft goat's cheese mashed with chopped herbs
- Apple sauce
- Slices of peeled lemon or orange

Pork loin

1 Using a long thin-bladed knife, cut a long slit into fat from rib end just below the rind (skin), taking off as little fat as you can. Work the knife into the fat to remove the rind in a single sheet. Trim off all but 5mm (¼in) of fat.

2 Using a long thin-bladed knife, cut into the meat as far as you can go.

3 Turn the loin around and place the knife flat on the ribs. Following the line of the ribs, and always cutting towards the bone, cut through the meat until you reach the vertebrae.

4 Use a small sharp knife to scrape the pieces of meat connecting the loin to the underlying bones, and remove the meat. Trim off any ragged scraps.

5 If you want a fully trimmed loin that doesn't need rolling, cut off the flap meat from the eye. Trim away any visible fat and sinews.

6 The loin may be rolled with or without stuffing. To stuff, shape the stuffing into a thin sheet or cylinder. Lay the loin with the fat side down on the chopping board and put the stuffing on the line where the eye meets the flap meat.

7 Fold the flap of meat over the eye of loin and secure with skewers.

8 Tie the loin with string every 5cm (2in) and remove the skewers.

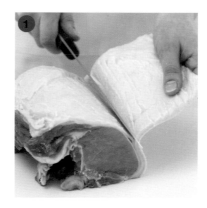

COOK'S TIPS

➺ Roast a boned loin with the bones as a roasting rack – they add flavour to gravy.

➺ Save the rind to make pork scratchings. Roast at 200°C (180°C fan oven) mark 6 for 15–25 minutes.

➺ Butchers use a Stanley knife – available from DIY stores – to score pork rind, because it is so sharp.

PREPARING AND COOKING HAM

Hams come in different sizes and cures. Some are sold cooked, while others are uncooked and some need to be soaked, so buy your ham from a butcher and ask his advice on preparation and cooking.

Baking

1 If the ham needs to be soaked, place it in a large container that will hold it comfortably with plenty of space for water. Pour cold water over to cover and weigh down the ham if necessary. Leave to soak overnight, then drain well.

2 Put the ham in a large flameproof casserole or stockpot, cover with cold water and bring to the boil. Skim off any surface scum. Reduce the heat and simmer gently for 25 minutes per 450g (1lb), checking occasionally to make sure it is completely covered with water.

3 Leave to cool in the water. Transfer the ham to a roasting tin. (Put the stock to one side for soup.)

4 Preheat the oven to 200°C (180°C fan oven) mark 6. Using a thin-bladed knife, remove the rind and neatly trim the fat so that there is a 5mm–1cm (¼–½in) layer of fat left on the meat.

5 Score the fat with parallel lines about 5cm (2in) apart, then score on the diagonal to make diamond shapes. Press a clove into the centre of each diamond.

6 Spread prepared English mustard as thinly and evenly as possible over the top of the ham. Sprinkle with soft brown sugar to make a light but even coating.

7 Bake the ham for about 30 minutes, until golden-brown.

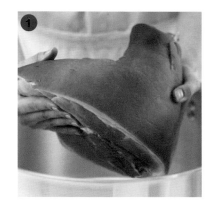
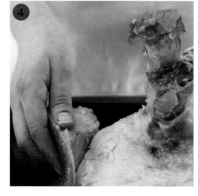

COOK'S TIPS

- Do not let the water continue to boil otherwise the meat will be tough.
- Add a few sprigs of parsley, a few peppercorns, a bay leaf and a chopped onion to the liquid.
- Or, braise in a covered casserole or bake in a tent of aluminium foil, if the ham is not too salty – 170°C (fan oven 150°C) mark 3.

PREPARING HARE AND RABBIT

Hare and rabbit are long thin animals with three sections of meat that need different types of cooking. This is reflected in the way that they are cut up for cooking.

Jointing

1 Chop off any pieces of bare bone from the legs and trim away the thin pieces of flesh from the ribcage.

2 Using a large heavy knife, cut off the hind legs, then cut into two. Cut through the joint to separate the thigh from the ankle and do the same with the forelegs.

3 If you are not cooking the saddle in a single piece, chop into three pieces of roughly equal size. For smaller pieces, cut each piece in half.

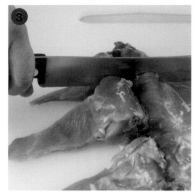

MARINADES FOR MEAT

Meat is good for marinating, either wet or dry, because its large surface area allows maximum exposure to the marinade. Begin marinating at least 8 hours in advance for small pieces of meat and 24 hours for thick joints.

Wet marinades
These almost always contain some form of acid, which has a modest tenderising effect (especially in thin cuts such as steak). Dry marinated meat thoroughly to remove liquid from the surface, and cook the marinade (skimming off the oil if necessary) as a sauce or deglazing liquid. The following recipe is simple and quick to make:

Herb and garlic marinade
This will marinate about 450g (1lb) meat. Use white wine for pork and rabbit, red for all other meats. You will need 2–3 crushed garlic cloves, 1 thinly sliced celery stick, 150ml (¼ pint) red or white wine, 50ml (2fl oz) extra-virgin olive oil, 50ml (2fl oz) red or white wine vinegar, ¼ tsp dried herbs, 1 bay leaf.

1 Whisk all the ingredients together. Pour over the meat, coating it thoroughly, and chill for at least 8 hours. Turn the meat regularly to ensure it marinates evenly.
2 Before cooking, drain the meat and dry on kitchen paper.

Good additions to wet marinades:
- Onions and shallots, chopped or sliced
- Asian spices, such as Chinese five-spice and star anise
- Chilli
- Sherry or sherry vinegar
- Brandy

Dry marinades
These are useful for roasts and pot roasts. They don't penetrate far into the meat, but give an excellent flavour on and just under the crust. Make them with crushed garlic, dried herbs or spices, and plenty of ground black pepper. Rub into the meat and marinate for at least 30 minutes or up to 8 hours.

COOKING MEAT AND GAME

For perfectly cooked meat choose the appropriate method for the cut. Tender cuts need quick cooking, such as grilling, whereas tougher cuts benefit from slower cooking, such as pot-roasting.

Grilling

1 Preheat the grill to high while you dry the meat (if marinated) and put it on a wire rack in the grill pan. If it has not been marinated, salt lightly.

2 Put the grill pan under the heat. Thin cuts should be about 2.5cm (1in) from the heat source, thicker cuts about 7.5cm (3in). Cook according to the table.

GRILLING TIMES

Note Cooking times are approximate, for a piece of meat 2.5cm (1in) thick.

Cut	Rare	Medium	Well done
Beef fillet	3–5 minutes	6–7 minutes	8–10 minutes
Other beefsteaks	5–6 minutes	8–12 minutes	15–18 minutes
Pork chops/steaks	8–10 minutes	10–14 minutes	
Lamb chops/steaks	8–10 minutes	10–14 minutes	
Lamb cutlets	6–10 minutes	8–12 minutes	

Griddling

1 Preheat the griddle for 3 minutes. Lightly brush the meat with vegetable oil on one side, then place on the griddle, oiled side down.

2 Cook for a few minutes. Lift the meat to see if it has formed blackened lines, then turn at a 45-degree angle to create a crisscross pattern. Repeat on the second side.

PERFECT GRILLS

- Get the griddle smoking hot before putting on the meat.
- You may find that you can cook without oil as long as you let the meat sear thoroughly before turning.

Stir-frying

1 Perfect for tender cuts. Trim the fat, then cut the meat into strips or dice no thicker than 5mm (¼in).

2 Heat a wok or large pan until hot and add oil to coat the inside. Add the meat and cook, stirring. Set aside. Cook the other ingredients you are using (such as vegetables and flavourings). Return the meat to the wok for 1–2 minutes, to heat through.

Pan-frying

1 Ideal for steaks or chops. Preheat a frying pan and season meat with salt.

2 Pour in enough vegetable oil to coat the base of the pan. Put in the meat without crowding. Do not move it for at least the first minute of cooking – it may stick.

3 When the meat is well browned, turn and cook on the other side.

Braising and pot-roasting

Tougher cuts require slow cooking. Braises and pot roasts are similar but braises need more liquid.

To serve six, you will need 3 tbsp olive oil, 6 lamb shanks, 1 large onion, 3 carrots, 3 celery sticks, all thickly sliced, 2 crushed garlic cloves, 2 × 400g cans chopped tomatoes, 150ml (¼ pint) white wine, salt and ground black pepper, 2 bay leaves.

1 Preheat the oven to 170°C (150°C fan oven) mark 3. Heat the oil in a large flameproof casserole and lightly brown the lamb shanks all over, two or three at a time. Remove from the pan and set aside. Add the onion, carrots, celery and garlic and cook until beginning to colour, then add the lamb, tomatoes and wine.

2 Stir well, season and add the bay leaves. Bring to the boil, cover, and transfer to the oven for 2 hours or until tender. Skim off fat if necessary.

PERFECT BRAISING AND POT-ROASTING

- Good cuts of beef include shin, chuck, blade, brisket and flank; good cuts of lamb include leg, shoulder, neck, breast and shank; good cuts of pork include shoulder, hand, spring, belly and loin.
- Casserole cooking can also be used with cuts you would normally roast. These simply need less time in the oven.
- Always use a low heat and check regularly to make sure that there is enough liquid to keep the meat from catching on the casserole.
- Braises often improve by being cooked in advance and then gently reheated before serving. If you've braised a whole piece of meat, you can slice it before reheating.

ROASTING AND CARVING MEAT

Ensure the joint is cooked correctly and has time to rest before carving to allow the juices to redistribute and give moist, tender results. When carving joints, slice evenly through the meat.

Rib of beef

Best cooked on the bone, a rib of beef makes a grand centrepiece to any special meal. A rib of beef joint can be any size from two to seven ribs and there are two ways to carve it. The first slices between the rib bones; the second separates the whole joint of meat from the bones, making it easier to carve. As with any meat, a well-rested rib of beef is easier to slice, as the meat has had time to relax.

Rib of beef:
method 1

1 Stand the joint with ribs uppermost and hold it steady with a carving fork.

2 Using long, smooth strokes, cut the meat in slices until you reach the first rib. Make a cut on the other side of the rib, for a slice of meat on the bone, then continue in the same way until the end of the joint is reached.

Rib of beef:
method 2

1 Stand the joint with the ribs flat on the board and hold it steady with a carving fork.

2 Place the knife blade parallel to the rib bones between the ribs and meat. Keeping the knife close to the bones, cut along the rib bones to separate them entirely from the meat. Discard the bones, place the meat carved side down on a board and carve in the usual manner.

Roasting a 2-bone rib of beef

To serve eight, you will need 2-bone rib of beef, 2.5–2.7kg (5½–6lb), 1 tbsp plain flour, 1 tbsp mustard powder, 150ml (¼ pint) red wine, 600ml (1 pint) beef stock, 600ml (1 pint) water from parboiled potatoes, salt and ground black pepper.

1 Preheat the oven to 230°C (210°C fan oven) mark 8. Put the beef, fat side up, into a roasting tin just large enough to hold the joint. Mix the flour with the mustard in a small bowl and season with salt and pepper, then rub the mixture over the beef. Roast in the centre of the oven for 30 minutes.

2 Move the beef to a lower shelf, near the bottom of the oven. Turn the oven down to 220°C (200°C fan oven) mark 7 and continue to roast for a further 2 hours, basting occasionally.

3 Put the beef on a carving dish, cover loosely with foil and leave to rest while you make the gravy. Skim off most of the fat from the roasting tin. Put the roasting tin on the hob, pour in the wine and boil vigorously until very syrupy. Pour in the stock and boil until syrupy. Add the vegetable water and boil until syrupy. There should be about 450ml (¾ pint) gravy. Taste and adjust the seasoning.

4 Remove the rib bone and carve the beef. Serve with gravy, Yorkshire puddings and vegetables.

ROASTING TIMES FOR BEEF

Preheat the oven to 220°C (200°C fan oven) mark 7. Weigh the joint to calculate the roasting time. Brown the beef in the hot oven for 20 minutes, then turn the oven down to 190°C (170°C fan oven) mark 5 and roast for the calculated time.

Cooking time per 450g (1lb)

Rare	15 minutes
Medium	20 minutes
Well done	25 minutes

Use these times as a guideline, but remember that cooking times will vary depending on how the meat has been aged and stored, the shape and thickness of the joint, and personal taste. Ovens vary as well. If a recipe gives a different oven temperature, follow the recipe for timing. Allow the meat to rest for at least 15 minutes before carving. A large joint can rest for 45 minutes without getting cold.

Leg of lamb

There are two ways to carve leg of lamb. The first gives slices with a section of the browned crust; the second starts with slices that are well done but gets progressively rarer.

COOK'S TIP

Don't forget to remove all string before carving any joint of meat. This also applies to any skewers or cocktail sticks that may have been used to secure the joint.

Leg of lamb:
method 1

1 Hold the shank and cut from that end, holding the knife flat on the bone, a 5cm (2in) into the meat. Cut down on to the bone to remove that chunk and slice thinly.

2 Start cutting thin slices from the meat on the bone, starting at the cut left by the chunk you removed. Hold the knife at right angles to the bone, then cut at a slight angle as you reach the thicker sections of meat.

3 When all the meat on that side has been removed, turn the leg and do the same on the other side.

Leg of lamb:
method 2

1 Hold the shank with the meatiest part of the leg facing up. Slice with the knife blade parallel to the bone. When you reach the bone, turn the leg over and continue slicing (knife blade parallel to the bone) until you reach the bone.

2 Remove the remainder of the meat from both sides in single pieces and slice thinly.

Pork with crackling

1 It is much easier to slice pork if you first remove the crackling. Remove the strings and position the carving knife just under the skin on the topmost side of the joint. Work the knife under the skin, taking care not to cut into the meat, until you can pull it off with your fingers.

2 Slice the meat, then break the crackling into servings.

PERFECT ROASTING

- Bring the meat to room temperature before cooking – remove from the fridge 2–3 hours ahead.
- Cook on a wire rack, or on a bed of sliced vegetables, so that the fat drops away.
- Roast fat side up.
- Check pan juices to make sure they don't dry up and scorch – this will ruin the gravy. Pour water into the roasting tin and reduce extra liquid later.
- When cooked, loosely cover the meat with foil and leave to rest for 20 minutes before carving. This makes the meat juicier and easier to carve.

ROASTING TIMES FOR LAMB AND PORK

All these timings are designed as a rough guide. They are based on a large joint, such as a leg of pork or leg of lamb, brought to room temperature before cooking. Smaller joints may take between 3 and 5 minutes less per 450g (1lb). Check the meat as it nears the end of its cooking time and don't be surprised if it needs a few minutes more or less. Allow the meat to rest for at least 15 minutes before carving. A large joint can rest for 45 minutes without getting cold.

Lamb	Oven temperature	Timing per 450g (1lb)
Medium-rare	180°C (160°C fan) mark 4	15–20 minutes
Well done	180°C (160°C fan) mark 4	20–25 minutes

Pork
Note Many cooks give pork an initial blast of heat – 220°C (fan oven 200°C) mark 7 – for 15–20 minutes. If you do this, watch it carefully near the end of its cooking time.

Medium-rare	190°C (170°C fan oven) mark 5	20–25 minutes
Well done	190°C (170°C fan oven) mark 5	25–30 minutes

CLASSIC ROAST BEEF

Serves 8
Preparation 20 minutes
Cooking time about 1½ hours, plus resting
Techniques see also making stock (page 36)

1 boned and rolled rib, sirloin, rump or topside of beef, about 1.8kg (4lb)
1 tbsp plain flour
1 tbsp mustard powder
salt and ground black pepper
fresh thyme sprigs to garnish
vegetables to serve

For the gravy
150ml (¼ pint) red wine
600ml (1 pint) beef stock

1 Preheat the oven to 230°C (210°C fan oven) mark 8. Put the beef in a roasting tin, with the thickest part of the fat uppermost. Mix the flour with the mustard powder, salt and pepper. Rub the mixture over the beef.
2 Roast the beef in the middle of the oven for 30 minutes.
3 Baste the beef and turn the oven down to 190°C (170°C fan oven) mark 5. Cook for a further 1 hour, approximately, basting occasionally. Meanwhile, prepare the Yorkshire pudding batter (see Cook's Tip).
4 Put the beef on a warmed carving dish, cover loosely with foil and leave to rest in a warm place. Increase the oven temperature to 220°C (200°C fan oven) mark 7 and cook the Yorkshire puddings.
5 Meanwhile, make the gravy. Skim off any remaining fat from the roasting tin. Put the tin on the hob, add the wine and boil until syrupy. Pour in the stock and, again, boil until syrupy; there should be about 450ml (¾ pint) gravy. Taste and adjust the seasoning.
6 Carve the beef into slices. Garnish with thyme and serve with the gravy, Yorkshire puddings and vegetables of your choice.

COOK'S TIP
Yorkshire puddings Sift 125g (4oz) plain flour and ½ tsp salt into a bowl. Mix in 150ml (¼ pint) milk. Add 2 medium eggs, beaten. Season with pepper. Beat until smooth. Whisk in another 150ml (¼ pint) milk. Pour 3 tbsp fat from the beef roasting tin and use to grease 8–12 individual Yorkshire pudding tins. Put the tins in a preheated oven at 220°C (200°C fan oven) mark 7 for 5 minutes or until the fat is almost smoking. Pour the batter into the tins. Bake for 15–20 minutes until well risen, golden and crisp.
Serve immediately.

NUTRITION PER SERVING
510 cals | 24g fat (9g sats) | 16g carbs | 0.5g salt

BEEF FILLET WITH ROQUEFORT SAUCE

Serves 6
Preparation 30 minutes
Cooking time about 1 hour 10 minutes, plus standing
Techniques see also preparing vegetables (pages 182–194)

125g (4oz) Roquefort cheese, crumbled
125g (4oz) unsalted butter, softened
900g (2lb) fillet of beef
7 tbsp vegetable oil
2 garlic cloves, crushed
2 large aubergines, 400g (14oz) each, cut lengthways
    into 1cm (½in) slices
150g (5oz) onion, finely chopped
150ml (¼ pint) medium-dry sherry
750ml (1¼ pints) beef stock
lemon juice to taste
salt and ground black pepper
Cheesy Polenta (see Cook's Tip) to serve

1 Gently stir the cheese into the butter. Cover and chill. Season the beef with salt and pepper. Heat 1 tbsp oil in a frying pan, add the beef and brown for 1–2 minutes on each side. Leave to cool.
2 Rub the beef with garlic. Brush each side of the aubergines with oil and fry in a non-stick frying pan for 4–5 minutes on each side until golden, then leave to cool. Wrap the aubergines around the beef and tie at intervals with string. Season and put to one side.
3 Preheat the oven to 220°C (200°C fan oven) mark 7. Heat 2 tbsp oil in the frying pan and cook the onion for 10 minutes or until golden. Add the sherry, bring to the boil and bubble to reduce by half. Add the stock, bring back to the boil and bubble for 10–15 minutes until reduced by half. Put to one side. Roast the beef for 30–40 minutes. Put the beef on a board, cover and leave to rest in a warm place for 10 minutes.
4 To make the sauce, reheat the sherry stock mixture, whisking in the Roquefort butter a little at a time. Add the lemon juice. Remove the string from the beef and slice. Stir any beef juices into the sauce. Serve the beef with the cheesy polenta and Roquefort sauce.

COOK'S TIP

Cheesy polenta Pour 900ml (1½ pints) milk into a large pan, add a pinch of salt and bring to the boil. Remove from the heat. Add 150g (5oz) polenta in a slow stream, stirring constantly. Simmer, stirring, for 5 minutes. Remove from the heat and stir in 4 tbsp olive oil and 75g (3oz) finely grated Parmesan. Season with salt and pepper.

NUTRITION PER SERVING
610 cals | 46g fat (2g sats) | 7g carbs | 1.1g salt

BRAISED BEEF

Serves 4
Preparation 20 minutes
Cooking time about 3½ hours
Techniques see also preparing vegetables (pages 182–194), chopping herbs (page 436)

175g (6oz) smoked pancetta or smoked streaky
    bacon, cubed
2 medium leeks, thickly sliced
1 tbsp olive oil
450g (1lb) braising steak, cut into 5cm (2in) pieces
1 large onion, finely chopped
2 carrots and 2 parsnips, thickly sliced
1 tbsp plain flour
300ml (½ pint) red wine
1–2 tbsp redcurrant jelly
125g (4oz) chestnut mushrooms, halved
ground black pepper
freshly chopped flat-leafed parsley
    to garnish

1 Preheat the oven to 170°C (150°C fan oven) mark 3. Fry the pancetta or bacon in a shallow flameproof casserole for 2–3 minutes until golden. Add the leeks and cook for a further 2 minutes or until the leeks are just beginning to colour. Remove with a slotted spoon and set aside.
2 Heat the oil in the casserole. Fry the beef in batches for 2–3 minutes until a rich golden colour on all sides. Remove from the casserole and put to one side. Add the onion and fry over a gentle heat for 5 minutes or until golden. Stir in the carrots and parsnips and fry for 1–2 minutes.
3 Return the beef to the casserole and stir in the flour to soak up the juices. Gradually add the wine and 300ml (½ pint) water, then stir in the redcurrant jelly. Season with pepper and bring to the boil. Cover with a tight-fitting lid and cook in the oven for 2 hours.
4 Stir in the fried leeks, pancetta and mushrooms, re-cover and cook for a further 1 hour or until everything is tender. Serve scattered with chopped parsley.

FREEZING TIP
Complete to the end of step 4, without the garnish. Put in a freezerproof container, cool and freeze for up to three months.
To use Thaw overnight at cool room temperature. Preheat the oven to 180°C (160°C fan oven) mark 4. Bring to the boil on the hob, cover tightly and reheat in the oven for about 30 minutes or until piping hot.

NUTRITION PER SERVING
524 cals | 25g fat (9g sats) | 27g carbs | 1.6g salt

CALF'S LIVER WITH FRIED SAGE

Serves 4
Preparation 5 minutes
Cooking time 5 minutes
Techniques see also cooking rice (page 246)

15g (¼oz) butter, plus a little olive oil for frying
12 sage leaves
4 thin slices calf's liver
1–2 tbsp balsamic vinegar
rice, with freshly chopped parsley stirred through,
    or grilled polenta to serve

1 Preheat the oven to 130°C (110°C fan oven) mark ½.
Melt the butter with a little oil in a heavy-based frying
pan and when hot add the sage leaves. Cook briefly for
1 minute or so until crisp. Remove, put in a single layer
in a shallow dish and keep warm in the oven.
2 Add a little extra oil to the pan, put in two slices of calf's
liver and cook quickly for 30 seconds on each side over a
high heat. Remove and put on a plate while you quickly
cook the remaining two slices.
3 Put all four slices back into the pan, splash the balsamic
vinegar over the top and cook for another minute or so.
Top with the crispy sage leaves. Serve immediately with rice
or polenta.

NUTRITION PER SERVING
88 cals | 6g fat (3g sats) | trace carbs | 0.1g salt

RACK OF LAMB WITH BALSAMIC GRAVY

Serves 8
Preparation 5 minutes
Cooking time 30–45 minutes, plus resting
Techniques see also crushing garlic (page 183), preparing rack of lamb (page 149)

4 fat garlic cloves, crushed
2 tbsp herbes de Provence
6 tbsp balsamic vinegar
12 tbsp olive oil
4 trimmed racks of lamb
salt and ground black pepper

1 Preheat the oven to 220°C (200°C fan oven) mark 7. Put the garlic in a bowl with the herbs, 2 tbsp vinegar and 4 tbsp oil. Season with salt and pepper.
2 Put the lamb in a roasting tin and rub the garlic mixture into both the fat and meat. Roast for 25–30 minutes if you like the meat pink, or cook for a further 5–10 minutes if you like it well done. Lift the lamb on to a warmed serving dish, cover with foil and leave to rest for 10 minutes.
3 Put the roasting tin on the hob over a medium heat and whisk in the remaining vinegar and oil, scraping up any sediment as the liquid bubbles. Pour the gravy into a small jug.
4 Slice the lamb into cutlets and serve with the gravy.

NUTRITION PER SERVING
410 cals | 37g fat (14g sats) | 1g carbs | 0.2g salt

STUFFED LEG OF LAMB

Serves 8
Preparation 40 minutes
Cooking time 3 hours–3 hours 40 minutes, plus resting
Techniques see also chopping herbs (page 436), chopping onions
(page 182), chopping musrooms (page 187), chopping
herbs (page 436)

1 leg of lamb, about 2.7kg (6lb), knucklebone removed
    but end bone left in
2 garlic bulbs
roast potatoes and vegetables to serve

For the stuffing
25g (1oz) butter
75ml (3fl oz) olive oil
1 small red onion, finely chopped
450g (1lb) chestnut mushrooms, finely chopped
4 tbsp freshly chopped flat-leafed parsley, 1 tbsp freshly
    chopped oregano and 6–8 thyme sprigs, leaves stripped
salt and ground black pepper

1 First make the stuffing. Melt the butter in a frying pan
with 2 tbsp oil. Fry the onion gently for 10–15 minutes until
soft. Add the mushrooms and cook for 15–20 minutes –
the mixture will become dryish – stirring all the time, until
the mushrooms begin to turn golden brown. Add the herbs
and cook for 1 minute. Season and leave to cool.
2 Preheat the oven to 190°C (170°C fan oven) mark 5.
Open out the lamb and spread the stuffing over the meat.
Reshape the lamb and secure with string. Put the lamb in
a roasting tin and season. Roast, basting occasionally, for
2½–3 hours.
3 About 1 hour before the end of the cooking time,
rub the whole garlic bulbs with the remaining oil. Put
them alongside the lamb and cook until very soft.
4 When the lamb is cooked to your liking, transfer to a
carving board, cover with a tent of foil and leave to rest
for 20 minutes. Keep the garlic warm until ready to serve.
5 Carve the lamb and garnish with the roasted garlic,
broken into cloves. Serve with roast potatoes and
vegetables of your choice.

GET AHEAD
Make the stuffing, cover and chill for up to one day.

NUTRITION PER SERVING
632 cals | 47g fat (15g sats) | 1g carbs | 0.4g salt

BRAISED LAMB SHANKS

Serves 6
Preparation 15 minutes
Cooking time 3 hours
Techniques see also preparing vegetables (pages 182–194)

3 tbsp olive oil
6 lamb shanks
1 large onion, chopped
3 carrots, sliced
3 celery sticks, sliced
2 garlic cloves, crushed
2 × 400g cans chopped tomatoes
125ml (4fl oz) balsamic vinegar
2 bay leaves
2 × 400g cans cannellini beans, drained and rinsed
salt and ground black pepper
steamed spinach to serve

1 Preheat the oven to 170°C (150°C fan oven) mark 3.
Heat the oil in a large flameproof casserole dish and brown
the lamb shanks, in two batches, all over. Remove and put
to one side.
2 Add the onion, carrots, celery and garlic to the casserole
dish and cook gently until softened and just beginning
to colour.
3 Return the lamb to the casserole and add the chopped
tomatoes and balsamic vinegar, giving the mixture a good
stir. Season with salt and pepper and add the bay leaves.
Bring to a simmer, cover and cook on the hob for 5 minutes.
4 Transfer to the oven and cook for 1½–2 hours or until
the lamb shanks are nearly tender.
5 Remove the casserole from the oven and add the
cannellini beans. Cover and return to the oven for a further
30 minutes. Serve with spinach.

NUTRITION PER SERVING
382 cals | 18g fat (6g sats) | 29g carbs | 1.2g salt

LAMB, PRUNE AND ALMOND TAGINE

Serves 6
Preparation 20 minutes, plus marinating
Cooking time 2½ hours
Techniques see also making stock (page 35), preparing vegetables (pages 182–194)

2 tsp each coriander and cumin seeds
2 tsp chilli powder
1 tbsp each paprika and ground turmeric
5 garlic cloves, chopped
6 tbsp olive oil
1.4kg (3lb) lamb leg steaks
75g (3oz) ghee or clarified butter
2 large onions, finely chopped
1 carrot, roughly chopped
900ml (1½ pints) lamb stock
300g (11oz) ready-to-eat prunes
4 each cinnamon sticks and bay leaves
50g (2oz) ground almonds
12 shallots
1 tbsp honey
salt and ground black pepper
toasted almonds and chopped flat-leafed parsley to garnish

1 Blend together the coriander, cumin, chilli powder, paprika, turmeric, garlic and 4 tbsp oil using a pestle and mortar or a blender. Coat the steaks with the paste and cover and chill for at least 5 hours.
2 Preheat the oven to 170°C (150°C fan oven) mark 3. Melt 25g (1oz) ghee or clarified butter in a large flameproof casserole, add the onions and carrot and cook until soft. Remove and put to one side. Fry the lamb on each side in the rest of the ghee or butter. Add a little of the stock to the casserole and bring to the boil, scraping up the sediment from the bottom. Return the onion and carrot to the casserole and add 100g (3½oz) prunes. Add the remaining stock to the pan with the cinnamon sticks, bay leaves and ground almonds. Season, cover and cook in the oven for 2 hours or until the meat is really tender.
3 Meanwhile, fry the shallots in the remaining oil and the honey until they turn a deep golden brown. Add to the casserole 30–40 minutes before the end of the cooking time.
4 Take the lamb out of the sauce and put to one side. Bring the sauce to the boil, bubble and reduce to a thick consistency. Return the lamb to the casserole. Add the remaining prunes, then bubble for 3–4 minutes. Garnish with almonds and parsley and serve.

COOK'S TIP
Clarified butter Heat butter in a small pan without colouring. Skim off the foam; the solids will sink. Strain the clear butter through a muslin-lined sieve. Leave for 10 minutes. Pour into a bowl, leaving any sediment behind. Cool, then store in a jar in the refrigerator for up to six months.

NUTRITION PER SERVING
652 cals | 44g fat (16g sats) | 31g carbs | 0.6g salt

IRISH STEW

Serves 4
Preparation 15 minutes
Cooking time 2 hours
Techniques see also making stock (page 36), chopping herbs (page 436)

700g (1½lb) middle neck lamb cutlets, fat trimmed
2 onions, thinly sliced
450g (1lb) potatoes, thinly sliced
1 tbsp freshly chopped parsley, plus extra to garnish
1 tbsp dried thyme
300ml (½ pint) lamb stock

1 Preheat the oven to 170°C (150°C fan) mark 3. Layer the meat, onions and potatoes in a deep casserole dish, sprinkling some herbs and seasoning between each layer. Finish with a layer of potato, overlapping the slices neatly.
2 Pour the stock over the potatoes, then cover with greaseproof paper and a lid. Cook for about 2 hours or until the meat is tender.
3 Preheat the grill. Take off the lid and remove the paper. Put under the grill and brown the top. Sprinkle with parsley and serve immediately.

NUTRITION PER SERVING
419 cals | 20g fat (9g sats) | 24g carbs | 0.6g salt

SHEPHERD'S PIE

Serves 4
Preparation 20 minutes
Cooking time about 55 minutes
Techniques see also preparing vegetables (pages 182–194), making stock (page 36)

2 tbsp sunflower oil
450g (1lb) lamb mince
1 large onion, chopped
50g (2oz) mushrooms, sliced
2 carrots, chopped
2 tbsp plain flour
1 tbsp tomato purée
1 bay leaf
300ml (½ pint) lamb stock
700g (1½lb) potatoes, cut into large chunks
25g (1oz) butter
60ml (2½fl oz) milk
50g (2oz) Lancashire or cheddar cheese, crumbled
  (optional)

1 Heat half the oil in a large pan and brown the mince over a medium-high heat – do this in batches otherwise the meat will steam rather than fry. Remove with a slotted spoon and put to one side.

2 Turn the heat to low and add the remaining oil. Gently fry the onion, mushrooms and carrots for 10 minutes, until softened. Stir in the flour and tomato purée and cook for 1 minute. Return the meat to the pan and add the bay leaf. Pour in the stock and bring to the boil, then reduce the heat, cover and simmer over a low heat for 25 minutes.

3 Preheat the oven to 200°C (180°C fan) mark 6. Cook the potatoes in lightly salted boiling water for 20 minutes, until tender. Drain and leave to stand in the colander for 2 minutes to steam dry. Melt the butter and milk in the potato pan and add cooked the potatoes. Mash until smooth.

4 Spoon the lamb mixture into a 1.7 litre (3 pint) ovenproof casserole dish. Remove the bay leaf and check the seasoning. Cover with the mashed potato and sprinkle the cheese over, if using. Bake for 15–20 minutes, until bubbling and golden. Serve immediately with green vegetables.

NUTRITION PER SERVING
513 cals | 27g fat (11g sats) | 44g carbs | 0.6g salt

HONEY ROAST PORK

Serves 4
Preparation 20 minutes
Cooking time 1 hour 40 minutes, plus resting
Techniques see also perfect roasting (page 158), preparing apples (page 216)

1kg (2¼lb) loin of pork, with crackling and four bones
4 tbsp olive oil
25g (1oz) butter
700g (1½lb) Charlotte potatoes, scrubbed and halved
1 large onion, cut into eight wedges
1 tbsp clear honey mixed with 1 tbsp wholegrain mustard
2 Cox apples, cored and each cut into six wedges
12 fresh sage leaves
175ml (6fl oz) dry cider
salt and ground black pepper

1 Preheat the oven to 240°C (220°C fan oven) mark 9. Using a paring knife, score the skin of the pork into thin strips, cutting about halfway into the fat underneath. Rub 1 tsp salt and 2 tbsp oil over the skin. Season well with pepper. Put the meat on a rack skin side up in a large roasting tin (or just in the tin). Roast for 25 minutes. Turn the oven down to 190°C (170°C fan oven) mark 5 and continue to roast for 15 minutes. Add the remaining oil and the butter to the roasting tin. Scatter the potatoes and onion around the meat, season and continue to roast for 45 minutes.
2 Brush the meat with the honey and mustard mixture. Add the apples and sage leaves to the tin and roast for 15 minutes or until the pork is cooked. Remove the pork from the tin and wrap completely with foil. Leave to rest for 10 minutes. Put the potatoes, onions and apples in a warmed serving dish and put back in the oven to keep warm.
3 Put the roasting tin on the hob, add the cider and stir well to make a thin gravy. Season.
4 Cut the meat away from the bone. Cut between each bone. Pull the crackling away from the meat and cut into strips. Carve the joint, giving each person some crackling, and a bone to chew. Serve with the gravy and potatoes, onion and apples.

> **NUTRITION PER SERVING**
> 830 cals | 55g fat (19g sats) | 40g carbs | 0.4g salt

BELLY OF PORK WITH CIDER

Serves 8
Preparation 30 minutes,
Cooking time about 4½ hours plus cooling and chilling
Techniques see also making stock (page 36), zesting citrus fruits (page 217)

2kg (4½lb) piece pork belly roast, on the bone
500ml bottle medium cider
600ml (1 pint) hot chicken stock
6–8 fresh rosemary sprigs
3 fat garlic cloves, halved
2 tbsp olive oil
grated zest and juice of 1 large orange and 1 lemon
3 tbsp light muscovado sugar
beurre manié (25g/1oz softened butter mixed with 1 tbsp
    plain flour, see page 40)
salt and ground black pepper
mixed vegetables to serve

1 Preheat the oven to 150°C (130°C fan oven) mark 2. Put the pork, skin-side up, in a roasting tin just large enough to hold it. Add the cider, stock and half the rosemary. Bring to the boil on the hob, then cover with foil and cook in the oven for 4 hours. Leave to cool in the liquid.
2 Strip the leaves from the remaining rosemary and chop. Put into a pestle and mortar with the garlic, oil, orange and lemon zest, 1 tsp salt and 1 tbsp sugar. Pound for 3–4 minutes to make a rough paste.
3 Remove the pork from the tin (keep the cooking liquid). Slice off the rind from the top layer of fat. Put to one side. Score the fat in a diamond pattern. Rub in the rosemary paste. Cover loosely with clingfilm. Chill until required. Meanwhile, make the crackling (see Cook's Tip) and the gravy. Strain the cooking liquid into a pan. Add the orange and lemon juice and the remaining 2 tbsp sugar, bring to the boil and bubble until reduced by half. Whisk the butter mixture into the liquid and boil for 4–5 minutes until thickened. Set aside. Reheat on the hob when required.
4 When almost ready to serve, preheat the oven to 220°C (200°C fan oven) mark 7. Cook the pork, uncovered, in a roasting tin for 20 minutes until piping hot. Carve the pork into slices and serve with the crackling, gravy and vegetables.

COOK'S TIP
Crackling Preheat the grill. Pat the rind dry with kitchen paper and put it (fat-side up) on a foil-lined baking sheet. Cook under the grill, about 10cm (4in) away from the heat, for 5 minutes. Turn over, sprinkle lightly with salt, then grill for 7–10 minutes until crisp. Cool, then cut the crackling into rough pieces. When ready to serve, wrap in foil and warm in the oven for the last 5 minutes of the pork cooking time.

NUTRITION PER SERVING
694 cals | 52g fat (19g sats) | 9g carbs | 0.5g salt

GINGER AND HONEY-GLAZED HAM

Serves 8–10
Preparation 1 hour
Cooking time 5¾ hours
Techniques see also preparing ham (page 154), preparing vegetables (pages 182–194), preparing fresh ginger (page 437), preparing mangoes (page 220)

4.5–6.8kg (10–15lb) unsmoked gammon on the bone
2 shallots, peeled and halved
6 cloves
3 bay leaves
2 celery sticks, cut into 5cm (2in) pieces
2 tbsp English mustard
5cm (2in) piece fresh root ginger, peeled and thinly sliced

For the glaze
225g (8oz) dark brown sugar
2 tbsp clear honey
8 tbsp brandy or Madeira

For the chutney
4 mangoes, peeled, sliced and chopped into 5cm (2in) chunks
1 tsp mixed spice
4 cardamom pods, seeds removed and crushed
½ tsp ground cinnamon
4 tbsp raisins

1 Put the gammon in a large pan. Add the shallots, cloves, bay leaves, celery and cold water to cover. Bring to the boil, then reduce the heat, cover and simmer gently for about 5 hours. Remove any scum with a slotted spoon. Lift the ham out of the pan, discard the vegetables and herbs, and cool.
2 Preheat the oven to 200°C (180°C fan oven) mark 6. Using a sharp knife, carefully cut away the ham's thick skin to leave an even layer of fat. Score a diamond pattern in the fat and put the ham into a roasting tin. Smother evenly with the mustard and tuck the ginger into the scored fat.
3 To make the glaze, put the sugar, honey and brandy or Madeira into a pan and heat until the sugar has dissolved. Brush over the ham.
4 In a bowl, mix together the chutney ingredients, add any remaining glaze, then spoon around the ham.
5 Cook the ham for 30–40 minutes, basting every 10 minutes. Remove the ham from the roasting tin and put to one side. Preheat the grill. Stir the chutney and put it under the grill for 5 minutes to allow the mango to caramelise. Transfer the chutney to a side dish for serving.

NUTRITION PER SERVING FOR 8
550 cals | 19g fat (6g sats) | 48g carbs | 5.5g salt

NUTRITION PER SERVING FOR 10
440 cals | 15g fat (5g sats) | 38g carbs | 4.4g salt

CUMIN-SPICED GAMMON

Serves 4
Preparation 5 minutes
Cooking time about 10 minutes
Techniques see also preparing papaya (page 221), zesting citrus fruits (page 217), preparing chillies (page 189), chopping herbs (page 436), preparing green beans (page 186)

large pinch each of ground cumin and paprika
2 tbsp olive oil
2 tsp light muscovado sugar
8 thin smoked gammon steaks, about 125g (4oz) each
2 large ripe papayas
zest and juice of 2 limes
½ red chilli, seeded and finely chopped
20g (¾oz) fresh mint, finely chopped
steamed green beans to serve

1 Preheat the grill. In a small bowl, mix together the cumin, paprika, oil and half the sugar. Put the gammon on to a non-stick baking sheet, then brush the spiced oil over each side.
2 Grill the gammon for about 5 minutes on each side, basting once or twice with the juices.
3 Meanwhile, cut each papaya in half, then seed and peel. Roughly chop half the flesh and put into a bowl. Purée the remaining fruit with the lime juice. Add to the bowl with the lime zest, chilli, mint and remaining sugar. Spoon the mixture on top of the gammon and serve with green beans.

VARIATIONS
- Use mango instead of the papaya. Make sure it's ripe before you buy it – give it a gentle squeeze to check.
- Try the spice rub and fruity relish with pork chops, or with meaty fish such as swordfish.

NUTRITION PER SERVING
566 cals | 31g fat (9g sats) | 4g carbs | 12.1g salt

ITALIAN MEATBALLS

Serves 4
Preparation 15 minutes
Cooking time 50 minutes
Techniques see also making breadcrumbs (page 318), mincing meat (page 147), chopping herbs (page 436), cooking noodles (page 273)

50g (2oz) ready-made breadcrumbs
450g (1lb) minced lean pork
1 tsp fennel seeds, crushed
¼ tsp chilli flakes, or to taste
3 garlic cloves, crushed
4 tbsp chopped flat-leafed parsley
3 tbsp red wine
oil-water spray
salt and ground black pepper
oregano leaves to garnish
noodles to serve

For the tomato sauce
oil-water spray
2 large shallots, finely chopped
3 pitted black olives, shredded
2 crushed garlic cloves
2 pinches of chilli flakes
250ml (9fl oz) stock
500g carton passata
2 tbsp each freshly chopped flat-leafed parsley, basil
    and oregano

1 To make the tomato sauce, spray a pan with the oil-water spray and add the shallots. Cook gently for 5 minutes. Add the olives, garlic, chilli flakes and stock. Bring to the boil, then reduce the heat, cover and simmer for 3–4 minutes.
2 Uncover and simmer for 10 minutes or until the shallots and garlic are soft and the liquid syrupy. Stir in the passata and seasoning. Bring to the boil, reduce the heat and simmer for 10–15 minutes, then stir in the herbs.
3 Meanwhile, put the breadcrumbs and remaining ingredients into a large bowl, season and mix together, using your hands, until thoroughly combined. (If you wish to check the seasoning, fry a little mixture, taste and adjust if necessary.)
4 Preheat the grill. With wet hands, roll the mixture into balls. Line a grill pan with foil, shiny side up, and spray with the oil-water spray. Cook the meatballs under the grill for 3–4 minutes on each side. Serve with the tomato sauce and noodles, garnished with oregano.

NUTRITION PER SERVING
248 cals | 6g fat (2g sats) | 20g carbs | 1.6g salt

PHEASANT WITH CIDER AND APPLES

Serves 8

Preparation 1 hour

Cooking time 1–1½ hours

Techniques see also chopping onions (page 182), preparing celery (page 185), preparing apples (page 216) making stock (page 36) preparing fresh ginger (page 437)

2 oven-ready pheasants, about 700g (1½lb) each, each cut into four portions
2 tbsp plain flour, plus extra to dust
50g (2oz) butter
4 streaky bacon rashers, rind removed
225g (8oz) onions, roughly chopped
275g (10oz) celery sticks, roughly chopped
4 eating apples, such as Granny Smith, cored, cut into large pieces and tossed in 1 tbsp lemon juice
1 tbsp dried juniper berries, lightly crushed
2.5cm (1in) piece fresh root ginger, peeled and finely chopped
300ml (½ pint) chicken stock
2 × 440ml cans dry cider
140ml (4½fl oz) double cream
salt and ground black pepper
fried apple wedges, thyme sprigs and juniper berries to garnish

1 Preheat the oven to 170°C (150°C fan oven) mark 3. Season each pheasant portion and dust lightly with flour. Melt the butter in a large flameproof casserole and brown the pheasant pieces in batches until deep golden brown. Remove and keep warm.

2 Put the bacon into the casserole and cook for 2–3 minutes until golden. Add the onions, celery, apples and lemon juice, juniper and ginger and cook for 8–10 minutes. Stir the flour into the vegetables and cook for 2 minutes, then add the stock and cider and bring to the boil. Return the pheasant to the casserole, cover and cook in the oven for 45 minutes–1 hour until tender.

3 Lift the pheasant out of the sauce and keep it warm. Strain the sauce through a sieve and return it to the casserole with the cream. Bring to the boil and bubble for 10–15 minutes until syrupy. Return the pheasant to the sauce and season with salt and pepper.

4 To serve, garnish the pheasant with the fried apple wedges, thyme sprigs and juniper berries.

GET AHEAD

➥ Complete the recipe to the end of step 3, cool quickly, then cover and chill for up to two days.

➥ To use, bring the pheasant to the boil and reheat in the oven at 180°C (160°C fan oven) mark 4 for 20–25 minutes.

NUTRITION PER SERVING
463cals | 27g fat (13g sats) | 13g carbs | 0.7g salt

PEPPERED WINTER STEW

Serves 6
Preparation 20 minutes
Cooking time 2¾ hours
Techniques see also preparing vegetables (pages 182–194), making stock (page 36)

25g (1oz) plain flour
900g (2lb) stewing beef, venison or lamb, cut into 4cm
    (1½in) cubes
5 tbsp oil
225g (8oz) button onions or shallots, peeled with root
    end intact
225g (8oz) onion, finely chopped
4 garlic cloves, crushed
2 tbsp tomato purée
125ml (4fl oz) red wine vinegar
75cl bottle red wine
2 tbsp redcurrant jelly
1 small bunch of fresh thyme, plus extra sprigs
    to garnish (optional)
4 bay leaves
1 tbsp coarsely ground black pepper
6 cloves
600–900ml (1–1½ pints) beef stock
900g (2lb) mixed root vegetables, such as carrots, parsnips,
    turnips and celeriac, cut into 4cm (1½in) chunks; carrots
    cut a little smaller
salt and ground black pepper

1 Preheat the oven to 180°C (160°C fan oven) mark 4.
Put the flour into a plastic bag, season with salt and pepper,
then toss the meat in it.
2 Heat 3 tbsp of the oil in a large flameproof casserole
over a medium heat and brown the meat well in small
batches. Remove and put to one side.
3 Heat the remaining oil and fry the button onions or
shallots for 5 minutes or until golden. Add the chopped
onion and the garlic and cook, stirring, until soft and golden.
Add the tomato purée and cook for a further 2 minutes,
then add the vinegar and wine and bring to the boil. Bubble
for 10 minutes.
4 Add the redcurrant jelly, thyme, bay leaves, 1 tbsp
pepper, cloves and meat to the pan, together with the
vegetables and enough stock to barely cover the meat
and vegetables. Bring to the boil, cover and cook in the
oven for 1¾–2¼ hours until the meat is very tender.
Serve hot, garnished with thyme sprigs, if you like.

NUTRITION PER SERVING
540 cals | 24g fat (7g sats) | 24g carbs | 1.5g salt

RABBIT CASSEROLE WITH PRUNES

Serves 6
Preparation 20 minutes, plus soaking
Cooking time 1¼ hours
Techniques see also jointing rabbit (page 155), preparing vegetables (pages 182–194), making stock (page 36)

175g (6oz) ready-to-eat pitted prunes
300ml (½ pint) red wine
3–4 tbsp olive oil
about 2.3kg (5lb) rabbit joints
1 large onion, chopped
2 large garlic cloves, crushed
5 tbsp Armagnac
450ml (¾ pint) light stock
few sprigs fresh thyme or 1 tsp dried thyme
2 bay leaves
140ml (4½fl oz) double cream
125g (4oz) brown-cap mushrooms, sliced
salt and ground black pepper
fresh thyme sprigs to garnish

1 Put the prunes and wine into a bowl. Cover and leave for about 4 hours, then strain, keeping the wine and prunes to one side.
2 Preheat the oven to 170°C (150°C fan oven) mark 3. Heat 3 tbsp oil in a flameproof casserole. Brown the rabbit joints a few at a time, then remove from the casserole. Add the onion and garlic with a little more oil, if necessary, and lightly brown. Return the rabbit to the casserole, add the Armagnac and warm through. Carefully light the Armagnac with a taper or long match, then shake the pan gently until the flames subside.
3 Pour in the stock and the wine from the prunes and bring to the boil. Add the sprigs of thyme (tied together), or the dried thyme, to the casserole with the bay leaves and plenty of seasoning. Cover the casserole tightly. Bake for about 1 hour or until tender.
4 Lift the rabbit out of the juices and keep warm. Boil the cooking juices until reduced by about a half. Add the cream and mushrooms and continue boiling for 2–3 minutes. Stir in the prunes and warm through. Adjust the seasoning and spoon the sauce over the rabbit to serve. Garnish with sprigs of fresh thyme.

NUTRITION PER SERVING
538 cals | 26g fat (13g sats) | 5g carbs | 0.3g salt

VEGETABLES

Nutritious, mouthwatering and essential to a healthy diet – vegetables are a must in every kitchen. From basic peeling, slicing, shredding, chopping and dicing to podding, coring, seeding and stuffing, the easy-to-follow techniques section explains every type of preparation for the various families of vegetables. The cooking section guides you through the essentials, including boiling, steaming, sautéing, stir-frying, deep-frying, braising, stewing, griddling, roasting and mashing, with essential tips and useful tables of cooking times. The recipes offer a choice of dishes for every occasion – from salads such as Warm new potato salad to Mediterranean kebabs, Brussels sprouts with chestnuts and shallots, Mixed vegetable tempura, Thai vegetable curry, Creamed spinach and Roasted stuffed peppers.

PREPARING ONIONS AND SHALLOTS

Similar in shape, aroma and flavour, onions and shallots are prepared in very similar ways. Their pungent taste makes them excellent flavouring ingredients.

Onions

1 Cut off the tip and base of the onion. Peel away all the layers of papery skin and any discoloured layers underneath.

2 Put the onion cut side down on the chopping board, then, using a sharp knife, cut the onion in half from tip to base.

3 **Slicing** Put one half on the board with the cut surface facing down and slice across the onion.

4 **Chopping** Slice the halved onions from the root end to the top at regular intervals. Next, make 2–3 horizontal slices through the onion, then slice vertically across the width.

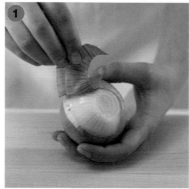

Shallots

As shallots are much smaller than onions, they are easier to slice and dice in the following way.

1 Cut off the tip and trim off the ends of the root. Peel off the skin and any discoloured layers beneath.

2 Holding the shallot with the root end down, use a small, sharp knife to make deep parallel slices almost down to the base while keeping the slices attached to it.

3 **Slicing** Turn the shallot on its side and cut off slices from the base.

4 **Dicing** Make deep parallel slices at right angles to the first slices. Turn it on its side and cut off the slices from the base. You should now have fine dice, but chop any larger pieces individually.

COOK'S TIPS

- When buying onions, press the neck end with a fingertip. If it is not rock-hard, the onion may be soft in the centre and therefore not at its best.
- To keep your hands from getting an onion smell, use your fingertips to hold the onion and touch the cut surfaces as little as possible.

PREPARING GARLIC AND LEEKS

Although garlic and leeks are also members of the onion family and share the same familiar pungent flavour and aroma, they are prepared in quite different ways to onions and shallots.

Garlic

1 Put the clove on the chopping board and put the flat side of a large knife on top of it. Press down firmly on the flat of the blade to crush the clove and break the papery skin.

2 Cut off the base of the clove and slip the garlic out of its skin. It should come away easily.

3 Slicing Using a rocking motion with the knife tip on the board, slice the garlic as thinly as you need.

4 Shredding and chopping Holding the slices together, shred them across the slices. Chop the shreds if you need chopped garlic.

5 Crushing After step 2, the whole clove can be put into a garlic press. To crush with a knife, roughly chop the peeled cloves and put them on the board with a pinch of salt.

6 Press down hard with the edge of a large knife tip (with the blade facing away from you), then drag the blade along the garlic while still pressing hard. Continue to do this, dragging the knife tip over the garlic to make a purée.

Leeks

As some leeks harbour a lot of grit and earth between their leaves, they need careful cleaning.

1 Cut off the root and any tough parts of the leek. Make a cut into the leaf end of the leek, about 7.5cm (3in) deep.

2 Hold under the cold tap while separating the cut halves to expose any grit. Wash well, then shake dry. Use the green tops for stock.

PREPARING SHOOTS, STEMS AND CORN

The delicate flavours of artichokes, asparagus and fennel are excellent in salads, main dishes or first courses. Celery is a useful vegetable for flavouring stocks and soups too.

Whole artichokes

1 Snap off the stalk so that it's level with the base of the leaves. Tear off any dry or discoloured leaves, and rinse in cold water.

2 Put the artichokes in a pan of salted water with 1 tsp lemon juice and weigh them down with a bowl so that they are completely covered. Boil for 40–45 minutes until an outer leaf pulls off easily.

Artichoke hearts

1 Heat a pan of salted water with 1 tbsp lemon juice per 1 litre (1¾ pints) of water.

2 Remove the stalk and outer leaves, then cut off the remaining leaves and trim away the green parts from the base. Rub with lemon juice and cook for 15–20 minutes until tender.

3 Drain, then scoop out the choke.

Asparagus

1 Cut the asparagus spears about 5cm (2in) from the stalk end, or where the white and green sections meet. Or cut off the stalk end and peel with a vegetable peeler or small sharp knife.

2 Heat a large pan of salted water that will hold the asparagus in a single layer. Put in the spears and cook for 5–8 minutes until tender.

COOK'S TIPS

- To prepare, snap off the woody tip of the stem; it will snap just where the stem becomes tender.
- To roast, drizzle with olive oil, a few spoonfuls water and a little salt and roast for 12 minutes at 200°C (180°C fan oven) mark 6.

Celery

1 To remove the strings in the outer green stalks, trim the ends and cut through the base to separate the stalks. Set aside the inner ones.

2 Cut into the base of the green outer stalks with a small knife and catch strings between the blade and your thumb. Pull up towards the top of the stalk to remove the string. Continue along the outside of stalk.

Fennel

1 Trim off the top stems and the base of the bulbs. Remove the core with a small, sharp knife if necessary.

2 The outer leaves may be discoloured and can be scrubbed gently in cold water, or you can peel away the discoloured parts with a knife or a vegetable peeler. Slice the fennel or cut it into quarters, according to your recipe.

Corn on the cob

Like peas, the sugar in corn starts to turn to starch soon after picking, so it is best eaten as soon as possible after picking or buying. To bake, microwave or barbecue corn, leave it in its husk. To boil, you will need to remove it from its husk.

1 To husk, pull away the green papery husks from the ear, a few at a time, until the whole ear is exposed.

2 Grasp the stalk and snap it off, taking all the husks with it. Rub the cob firmly with your hand to remove all the silky threads.

3 **Removing the kernels** Hold the ear upright in a large bowl, with the stalk sitting on the base of the bowl. Using a thin-bladed knife, cut off the kernels from top to bottom, turning the cob until they are all removed.

PREPARING PEAS, BEANS AND PODS

Quick and simple preparation means that you can enjoy summertime favourites, such as sweet young peas, mangetouts, beans and okra at their best.

Peas

1 Hold the pea pod in one hand with the stem pointing towards you. Press the curved 'seam' at the top of the pod to pop it open, and insert the tip of a thumbnail between the two halves to open up the pod.

2 Using your thumb, gently push the peas into a bowl. Rinse the peas in cold water before using.

COOK'S TIPS

- Cook peas as soon as possible after shelling.
- Allow 1kg (2¼lb) unshelled peas or broad beans for four servings.
- Mangetouts and sugarsnaps can be eaten whole. Top and tail; older specimens may benefit from stringing.

Broad beans

1 Hold the pod in one hand with the stem pointing towards you. Insert the tip of a thumbnail between the two halves and open up the pod. Using your thumb, gently push the beans into a bowl.

2 For older beans, it is best to remove the skin. Make a shallow nick in the skin of each bean, then pull off the skin and discard.

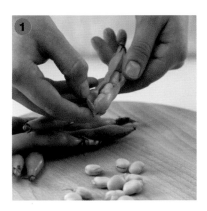

Runner beans

1 Small tender runner beans can be topped and tailed. Larger ones need to be stringed. Cut through the stem end so you can catch the string between the knife blade and your finger.

2 Pull off the string and discard. Cut on the diagonal into 5cm (2in) pieces or into fine strips lengthways using a bean slicer or a sharp knife.

OTHER BEANS

- Fine (French) beans simply need to be topped and tailed: snip off both ends to remove the stem and tail.
- Bobby beans – a thicker form of bean – can be topped and tailed if tender. Larger ones may need to be stringed.

Okra

1 For cooking okra whole Wash and remove any wispy black 'hair' on the pods. Trim the end of the caps, taking care not to pierce the pods.

2 For cooking okra split If you want the gelatinous texture inside the pod for thickening a stew, okra should be split. Wash well and remove any wispy black 'hair'. Trim the end of the caps and cut in half lengthways, from tip to cap.

MUSHROOMS

There are many different types of these edible fungi. The most common are cultivated white mushrooms, but there are also numerous wild varieties.

Cultivated mushrooms

Button, white, chestnut and flat mushrooms are all prepared in a similar way.

1 Wipe with a damp cloth or pastry brush to remove any dirt.

2 With button mushrooms, cut off the stalk flush with the base of the cap. For other mushrooms, cut a thin disc off the end of the stalk and discard. Chop or slice mushrooms.

3 If stuffing the mushrooms, snap off the stalk instead, then chop finely and use in the stuffing.

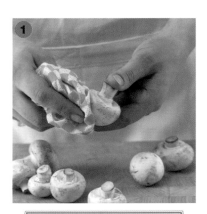

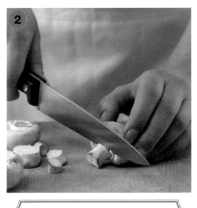

WILD AND SHIITAKE

Wild mushrooms are typically dirtier than cultivated mushrooms and need careful cleaning and trimming. Fill a bowl with cold water. Immerse the mushroom and shake vigorously to loosen dirt. Dry the mushroom carefully on kitchen paper and check for any remaining specks of dirt. Shiitake have a hard stalk that needs to be removed. Cut this from the softened mushroom, using a sharp knife.

DRIED

Soaking in hot water softens the mushrooms to make them usable. Put the mushrooms in a bowl and cover with hot but not boiling water. Leave to soak for 15–40 minutes (or according to the instructions on the pack) until the mushroom caps are soft and flexible. Rinse under cold water, checking for any dirt that might be trapped.

PREPARING VEGETABLE FRUITS

Tomatoes and full-flavoured Mediterranean vegetable fruits such as aubergines and peppers add a rich flavour to many dishes. Each have their individual preparation techniques.

Peeling tomatoes

1 Fill a bowl or pan with boiling water. Using a slotted spoon, add the tomato for 15–30 seconds, then remove to a chopping board.

2 Use a small sharp knife to cut out the core in a single cone-shaped piece. Discard the core.

3 Peel off the skin; it should come away easily depending on ripeness.

Cutting tomatoes

1 Use a small sharp knife to cut the core out in a single cone-shaped piece. Discard the core.

2 **Wedges** Halve the tomato and then cut into quarters or into three.

3 **Slices** Hold the tomato with the cored side on the chopping board for greater stability and use a serrated knife to cut into slices.

Seeding tomatoes

1 Halve the tomato through the core. Use a small, sharp knife or a spoon to remove the seeds and juice. Shake off the excess water.

2 Chop the tomato as required for your recipe and place in a colander for a minute or two, to drain off any excess liquid.

COOK'S TIP

If you are using tomatoes in a sauce that will be cooked for a long time, you can just roughly chop them without peeling and then, if you prefer it smooth, sieve the sauce after cooking.

Seeding peppers

The seeds and white pith of peppers taste bitter so should be removed.

1 Cut the pepper in half vertically and snap out the white pithy core and seeds. Trim away the rest of the white membrane with a knife.

2 Alternatively, cut off the top of the pepper, then cut away and discard the seeds and white pith.

SKINNING

Some people find pepper skins hard to digest. To peel raw peppers, use a swivel-handled peeler to cut off strips down the length of the pepper. Use a small knife to cut out any parts of skin that the peeler could not reach.

Chargrilling peppers

Charring imparts a smoky flavour and makes peppers easier to peel.

1 Hold the pepper, using tongs, over the gas flame on your hob (or under a preheated grill) until the skin blackens, turning until black all over.

2 Put in a bowl, cover and leave to cool (the steam will help to loosen the skin). Peel.

Chillies

Always wash your hands thoroughly with soap and water immediately after handling chillies.

1 Cut off the cap and slit open lengthways. Using a spoon, scrape out the seeds and the pith. (These are the hottest parts of the chilli.)

2 For diced chilli, cut into thin shreds lengthways, then cut crossways.

Avocados

Prepare avocados just before serving because their flesh discolours quickly once exposed to air.

1 Halve the avocado lengthways and twist the two halves apart. Tap the stone with a sharp knife, then twist to remove the stone.

2 Run a knife between the flesh and skin and pull away. Slice the flesh.

Cutting aubergines

1 Trim the aubergine to remove the stalk and end.

2 **Slicing** Cut the aubergine into slices as thick as the pieces you will need for your recipe.

3 **Cutting and dicing** Stack the slices and cut across them to the appropriate size for fingers. Cut in the opposite direction for dice.

Stuffing aubergines

1 To hollow out an aubergine for stuffing, cut off the stem and halve the aubergine lengthways.

2 Make deep incisions in the flesh, using a crisscross pattern, being careful not to pierce the skin.

3 Using a spoon, scoop out the flesh, leaving the skin intact, and use according to your recipe.

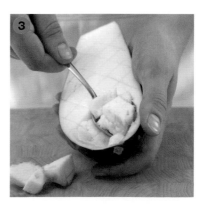

Courgettes

Cutting diagonally is an ideal, all-purpose shape if using courgettes in a stir-fry.

1 After washing under the cold tap, dry the courgette well and trim the base and the stem.

2 Trim off a piece at the base at a 45-degree angle, then repeat with the remaining courgette.

STUFFING

- To stuff courgettes whole, trim the base, then halve lengthways.
- To stuff courgettes in sections, trim the base and stem, then cut into 7.5cm (3in) sections. Stand on one end and use a melon baller to scoop out the flesh.

Peeling and cutting squash

1 For steaming, baking or roasting, keep the chunks fairly large – at least 2.5cm (1in) thick. Peel with a swivel-handled peeler or a chef's knife.

2 Halve the squash, then use a knife to cut through some of the fibrous mass connecting the seeds with the wall of the central cavity. Scoop out the seeds and fibres with a spoon, then cut the flesh into pieces.

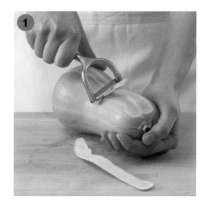

Cooking squash in the skin

1 Wash the squash, then cut in half or quarters.

2 Use a knife to cut through some of the fibrous mass connecting the seeds with the wall of the central cavity, then use a spoon to scoop out the seeds and fibres.

PREPARING CABBAGE AND BROCCOLI

Cauliflower, cabbage and broccoli – the cruciferous vegetables – make crisp, healthy and tasty accompaniments to main courses as well as working well in stir-fries and other vegetable dishes.

Cabbage

The crinkly leaved Savoy cabbage may need more washing than other varieties, because its open leaves catch dirt more easily than the tightly packed white and red cabbage. The following method is suitable for all cabbages.

1 Pick off any of the outer leaves that are dry, tough or discoloured. Cut off the base and, using a small sharp knife, cut out as much as possible of the tough inner core in a single cone-shaped piece.

2 If you need whole cabbage leaves, peel them off one by one. As you work your way down, you will need to cut out more of the core.

3 If you are cooking the cabbage in wedges, cut it in half lengthways then cut the pieces into wedges of the required size.

Broccoli

1 Slice off the end of the stalk and cut 1cm (½in) below the florets.

2 Peel the thick, woody skin from the stalks and slice in half or quarters lengthways. Cut off equal-sized florets with a small knife. If the florets are very large, or if you want them for a stir-fry, you can halve them by cutting lengthways through the stalk and pulling the two halves apart.

PREPARING ROOTS AND TUBERS

All roots and tubers are prepared in roughly the same way. Some should always be peeled, whereas for others peeling is optional – it will depend mostly on how you plan to cook them.

What to peel

Not all vegetables need to be peeled. Some vegetables become discoloured after peeling, and need to be placed in acidulated water (water and lemon juice) to slow the discolouration down:

- **Beetroot** are unpeeled when left whole, but peeled if sliced or shredded. They can be scrubbed if organic, otherwise peel.

- **Celeriac** needs to be peeled and then put into acidulated water.

- **Potatoes** can be peeled or scrubbed. If peeled, put them immediately into cold water.

- **Salsify** needs to be peeled and then put into acidulated water.

- **Sweet potatoes** can be peeled or scrubbed. If peeled, put them immediately into cold water.

- **Turnips** need to be peeled and then put into acidulated water.

Peeling roots and tubers

1 Using a swivel-headed peeler is the best method to peel most roots and tubers. However, celeriac has thick, irregular skin and is easier to peel using a knife.

2 Using a sharp knife, trim the ends off the vegetable.

3 Peel off the skin in long strips using a vegetable peeler.

Coring parsnips

Large parsnips have a tough woody core that takes longer to cook so it can be removed.

1 Trim both ends and use a sharp knife to halve the parsnip lengthways.

2 Run the knife along both sides of the core. Cut into the thick end of the parsnip, between core and walls, and gently work it up the core.

Slicing and dicing

Root vegetables often need to be cut into small pieces and a slice-and-stack approach works well.

1 First, peel and cut off the ends.

2 Cut slices off each of the rounded sides to make four flat surfaces that are stable on the chopping board.

3 Hold steady with one hand and cut lengthways into even slices so they are lying in a flat stack.

4 To dice the shreds, turn the stack at right angles and cut through in the opposite direction.

Slicing with a mandolin

1 Put the mandolin on a chopping board and set the blade to the required thickness. Push the pieces of vegetable across the blade with a swift, decisive motion, taking care to protect your fingers.

2 To make julienne (matchsticks), use either the fine or coarse julienne blade and swiftly push the pieces of vegetable across the blade.

COOKING VEGETABLES

Vegetables can be boiled, fried, sautéed, roasted, braised, stir-fried or steamed, providing endless variety. Some methods are more suited to certain vegetables than others, as explained below.

Boiling

This technique is suitable for most vegetables, but time them carefully as they can disintegrate or turn mushy if overcooked.

1 Prepare the vegetables and put them in plenty of salted cold water.

2 Cover, bring to the boil, then reduce the heat and simmer until cooked. Drain in a colander.

COOK'S TIP

- Don't boil very thin pieces of root vegetable – they are more likely to absorb a lot of water and disintegrate.
- Small new potatoes are the only type that takes well to boiling whole. Larger ones can start to disintegrate before they are fully cooked.

BOILING TIMES

Note All timings are for peeled vegetables sliced about 2.5cm (1in) thick, except where noted.

Vegetable	Timing
Beetroot (whole)	1–2 hours
Carrots	10–20 minutes
Celeriac	20–25 minutes
Corn on the cob	10–15 minutes
Green beans	4–6 minutes
Potatoes	15–20 minutes
Potatoes, new	10 minutes
Salsify	10–20 minutes
Sweet potatoes	10–15 minutes
Turnips	15–20 minutes

Microwaving

1 Cut vegetables into bite-sized pieces and put, no more than 12.5cm (5in) deep, into a microwave-proof bowl. Add a splash of water, season and cover with clingfilm. Cook at full power for 2 minutes. Toss, re-cover and cook for 2 minutes more.

2 Continue in 2-minute bursts until cooked al dente. Towards the end of cooking, switch to 1-minute bursts.

Steaming

This is a healthy cooking method, cooking the vegetables until just tender while retaining their nutrients.

1 Put the vegetables in a steamer basket set over a pan of simmering water, being careful that the water does not touch the basket.

2 Cover and cook until the vegetables are just tender.

STEAMING TIPS

- Use an uncrowded steamer so that air can circulate.
- Cut root vegetables into chunks or dice.
- Toss the vegetables now and then during steaming.
- If steaming frozen vegetables, move them around occasionally.

STEAMING TIMES

Note For soft results, add 2–3 minutes.

Vegetable	Timing
Leaf spinach	1–2 minutes
Peas, beans, carrots, cabbage, cauliflower and broccoli florets	about 5 minutes
Root vegetables	5–10 minutes

Mashing potatoes

To serve four, you will need 900g (2lb) floury potatoes such as Maris Piper, 125ml (4fl oz) full-fat milk, 25g (1oz) butter.

1 Peel the potatoes and cut into even-sized chunks. Put in a pan of cold salted water to cover, then bring to the boil, reduce the heat and simmer for 15–20 minutes until just tender. Test with a skewer or small knife. Drain.

2 Return the potatoes to the pan and cover with a clean teatowel for 5 minutes. Alternatively, warm the potatoes over a very low heat until all the moisture has evaporated.

3 Pour the milk into a small pan and bring to the boil. Pour on to the potatoes with the butter and season.

4 Mash the potatoes until smooth, light and fluffy.

Crushing potatoes

To serve six, you will need 18 new potatoes, halved, 3 large garlic cloves, chopped, 225ml (8fl oz) olive oil, 8 tbsp freshly chopped flat-leafed parsley, salt and black pepper.

1 Boil the potatoes until just soft. Drain. Heat the garlic in the oil until it starts to sizzle. Roughly mash the potatoes with a fork. Spoon the oil over. Season and add the herbs.

PERFECT MASH

- To mash vegetables you can use a mouli-légumes, a potato masher, or a ricer. The mouli and ricer give the smoothest results.
- Mashing and crushing are also suitable for parsnips, sweet potatoes and celeriac.

Sautéing

Sautéing browns vegetables lightly.

1 Cut into uniform pieces. Coat the base of a heavy-based pan with oil until medium-hot. Add the vegetables, toss quickly to coat with oil. Season.

2 Cover the pan and cook for 2–3 minutes until they start to soften. Remove the lid and stir every minute or so while the vegetables cook.

Stir-frying

Stir-frying is perfect for non-starchy vegetables, as the quick cooking preserves their colour, freshness and texture. You will need 450g (1lb) vegetables, 1–2 tbsp vegetable oil, 2 crushed garlic cloves, 2 tbsp soy sauce, 2 tsp sesame oil.

1 Cut the vegetables into even-sized pieces. Heat the oil in a large wok or frying pan until smoking-hot. Add the garlic and cook for a few seconds, then remove and put to one side.

2 Add the vegetables to the wok, then toss and stir them. Keep them moving constantly as they cook, which will take 4–5 minutes.

3 When the vegetables are just tender, but still with a slight bite, turn off the heat. Put the garlic back into the wok and stir well. Add the soy sauce and sesame oil, toss and serve.

Deep-frying

Carrots, broccoli, onions, courgettes, aubergines, mushrooms and cauliflower are all good deep-fried.

1 Prepare the vegetables and cut into small pieces, no more than 2cm (¾in) thick. If washed, dry well.

2 Heat vegetable oil in a deep-fryer to 190°C (a small cube of bread should brown in 20 seconds).

3 Coat the vegetables with flour, then dip into batter (see page 84).

4 Fry in batches, a few pieces at a time, until the batter is crisp and golden brown. Don't put too many vegetables in the pan at once (if you do, the temperature drops and the vegetables take longer to cook and become greasy). Drain on kitchen paper before serving.

Making potato chips

1 Heat vegetable oil in a deep-fryer to 160°C (a cube of bread should brown in 60 seconds). Cut potatoes into chips and dry on kitchen paper. Fry in batches for 6–7 minutes until soft. Drain on kitchen paper.

2 Turn up heat to 190°C (bread will brown in 20 seconds). Fry until golden brown. Drain well, sprinkle with salt and serve immediately.

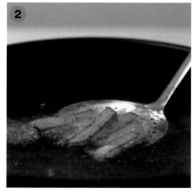

Making vegetable crisps

1 Using a mandolin, slice the potatoes or root vegetables very thinly. Heat vegetable oil in a deep-fryer to 190°C (a small cube of bread should brown in 20 seconds).

2 Gently lower the sliced vegetables into the oil and stir or shake the frying basket to separate them. Fry until golden, then lift out and drain on kitchen paper.

FRYING POTATOES

- Potatoes never need to be coated in batter.
- Use floury potatoes – Maris Piper is the best variety.
- Dry the sliced potatoes thoroughly before frying. Water on the surface can cause the fat to splatter.

Braising

1 Prepare the vegetables (see box right). Pack tightly in an ovenproof dish. Preheat the oven to 180°C (160°C fan oven) mark 4. Dot generously with butter and season with salt.

2 Pour in stock to come halfway up the vegetables. Cover and bake for 30–40 minutes until the vegetables are soft. Baste them with the buttery stock a few times during cooking.

Stewing

1 Cut the vegetables into large bite-sized pieces, no more than about 5cm (2in) square. Put them into a heatproof casserole (for oven cooking) or a heavy-based pan (for hob cooking). Add salt and pepper and flavourings, if you like (see box right), and mix well.

2 Preheat the oven to 180°C (160°C fan oven) mark 4 if you are cooking in the oven.

3 Pour in stock to come about three-quarters of the way up the vegetables. Cover the dish with a lid or foil and cook for 30–40 minutes until the vegetables are tender but not disintegrating.

4 Turn the vegetables once during cooking, and baste with the juices a few times.

Griddling and grilling

A few vegetables are perfect for cooking on a griddle or under the grill. Those that work well in both methods are courgettes and aubergines. Peppers (whole or halved) can be grilled and so can fennel, onions and sweet potatoes with careful slicing. Brush all vegetables with oil and use a medium-high heat.

To serve four, you will need 450g (1lb) courgettes, cut lengthways into 5mm (¼in) slices, or quartered if small, about 6 tbsp extra-virgin olive oil, ½ lemon, a small handful of fresh dill, finely chopped.

1 Preheat the griddle over a medium to high heat. Brush the courgettes with oil.

2 Cook the courgettes without disturbing them until they have deep brown seared lines underneath, about 2–3 minutes.

3 Turn them and griddle until seared underneath and tender, but still with a hint of bite.

4 Remove to a serving plate and squeeze lemon juice over to taste. Scatter with dill and serve.

PERFECT GRIDDLING

- Vegetables have a lovely flavour when cooked on the griddle, as well as attractive browned lines if you use a ridged griddle.
- The choice of vegetable is crucial in griddling: you have to use something that has a fairly even surface so that it will lie flat on the griddle and won't break up when it's turned. Top choices include sliced courgettes, aubergines, fennel and onion, whole small onions, large field mushrooms and asparagus.
- Don't slice the vegetables too thickly or they will burn before they get fully cooked – 1cm (½in) should be the maximum thickness.
- Lay the vegetables on a work board and brush them with oil so that it coats them thoroughly. Turn once when they have browned underneath.

Roasting potatoes

To serve eight to ten, you will need 1.8kg (4lb) potatoes, peeled and cut into large chunks, 3 tbsp vegetable oil, 75g (3oz) unsalted butter, 6 rosemary sprigs, 6 garlic cloves, salt and ground black pepper.

1 Preheat the oven to 200°C (180°C fan oven) mark 6. Put the potatoes in a pan of salted water, cover, bring to the boil, reduce the heat and simmer for 5–6 minutes until they start to soften. Drain and return to the pan over a low heat. Shake until the potatoes are dry and a little fluffy.

2 Heat the oil and butter in a roasting tin. Put the potatoes in the tin with the rosemary and garlic. Toss to cover evenly in oil and butter, and season. Cook for 1 hour, turning from time to time until the potatoes are brown and crisp. Adjust the seasoning and serve.

ROASTING OTHER VEGETABLES

Many vegetables are excellent when roasted, as long as they contain enough starch to brown well. Brush them with extra-virgin olive oil and season. Timings are for a 200°C (180°C fan oven) mark 6 oven.

Aubergines (halved)	30–40 minutes
Beef tomatoes (halved)	10–20 minutes
Courgettes (halved)	20–30 minutes
Green or yellow peppers (halved)	30–40 minutes
Mushrooms (large)	20–30 minutes
Onions (quartered, halved or small)	20 minutes

Roasting butternut squash

To serve four, you will need 2 squash, quartered and seeded, 2 tbsp olive oil, 2 tbsp thyme, 1 seeded and chopped red chilli, 25g (1oz) butter.

1 Preheat the oven to 220°C (200°C fan oven) mark 7. Drizzle the squash with oil. Roast for 40 minutes.

2 Combine the thyme, chilli and butter and dot over the squash.

WARM NEW POTATO SALAD

Serves 6
Preparation 15 minutes
Cooking time 15–20 minutes
Techniques see also chopping herbs (page 436)

650g (1lb 6oz) new potatoes, halved
1 heaped tbsp freshly chopped tarragon
caperberries to serve

For the caper dressing
1 heaped tbsp capers in sherry vinegar, rinsed
1 heaped tbsp Dijon mustard
4 tbsp extra-virgin olive oil
salt and ground black pepper

1 Put the potatoes in a large pan of lightly salted boiling water and cook for 15–20 minutes or until tender. Drain, cool slightly, then cut each into quarters lengthways and keep them warm.
2 Meanwhile, make the dressing. Put the capers, mustard and oil in a mini processor and blend until thick. Season well with salt and pepper.
3 Put the warm potatoes in a large salad bowl, add the dressing and tarragon and toss everything together.
4 Put the caperberries in the bowl with the potatoes and toss together.

VARIATIONS
Warm Pesto and Rocket Salad Omit the capers and mustard and make a dressing by mixing 4 tbsp pesto with 1 tbsp olive oil. Toss with the warm potatoes, along with a good handful of wild rocket instead of the tarragon and caperberries.

NUTRITION PER SERVING
148 cals | 8g fat (1g sats) | 18g carbs | 0.2g salt

ROASTED ROOT VEGETABLE SALAD

Serves 4
Preparation 20 minutes
Cooking time 40 minutes
Techniques see also preparing vegetables (pages 182–194), toasting nuts (page 228)

1 butternut squash, halved, seeded and cubed
1½ large carrots, cut into chunks
3 fresh thyme sprigs
1½ tbsp olive oil
2 red onions, cut into wedges
1 tbsp balsamic vinegar
410g can chickpeas, drained and rinsed
25g (1oz) pinenuts, toasted
100g (3½oz) wild rocket
salt and ground black pepper

1 Preheat the oven to 190°C (170°C fan oven) mark 5. Put the squash and carrots into a large deep roasting tin. Scatter the thyme over and drizzle with 1 tbsp oil. Season with salt and pepper and roast for 20 minutes.
2 Take the tin out of the oven, give it a good shake to make sure the vegetables aren't sticking, then add the onions. Drizzle the remaining oil over and toss to coat. Continue to roast for 20 minutes or until all the vegetables are tender.
3 Remove the roasted veg from the oven and discard any twiggy bits of thyme. Drizzle the vinegar over, stir in and leave to cool.
4 To serve, put the chickpeas into a large serving bowl. Add the cooled vegetables, the pinenuts and rocket (putting some to one side for a garnish). Toss everything together and garnish with a little rocket.

GET AHEAD
Make to the end of step 3 up to two days ahead.
Put in a container. Cool, cover and chill.
To use Complete the recipe.

NUTRITION PER SERVING
290 cals | 14g fat (2g sats) | 33g carbs | 0.7g salt Ⓥ

SUMMER VEGETABLE SALAD

Serves 10
Preparation 10 minutes
Cooking time about 10 minutes
Techniques see also preparing vegetables (pages 182–194), chopping herbs (page 436), making salad dressings (page 27)

900g (2lb) mixed green vegetables, such as French beans, peas, sugarsnap peas, asparagus and broccoli
¼ cucumber, halved, seeded and sliced
1 tbsp freshly chopped flat-leafed parsley
salt

For the dressing
1 tbsp white wine or sherry vinegar
1 tsp English mustard powder
3 tbsp extra-virgin olive oil

1 Cook the beans in a large pan of boiling salted water for 5 minutes, then add all the other vegetables. Bring the water back to the boil and cook for a further 3–4 minutes. Drain well and put immediately into a bowl of ice-cold water.
2 Whisk the dressing ingredients together.
3 To serve, drain the vegetables, then toss in the dressing with the cucumber and parsley.

GET AHEAD
Make the recipe to the end of step 2 up to one day ahead. Chill the dressing and keep the cooked vegetables, covered in cold water, until needed.
To use Complete the recipe.

NUTRITION PER SERVING
54 cals | 4g fat (1g sats) | 3g carbs | 0g salt **V**

ASPARAGUS WITH LEMON DRESSING

Serves 5
Preparation 15 minutes
Cooking time 5 minutes
Techniques see also zesting citrus fruits (page 217), making salad dressings (page 27), preparing asparagus (page 184)

finely grated zest of ½ lemon
2 tbsp lemon juice
3 tbsp extra-virgin olive oil
pinch of golden caster sugar
250g (9oz) fine-stemmed asparagus, ends trimmed
salt and ground black pepper

1 Put the lemon zest into a screw-topped jar, add the lemon juice, oil and sugar, then shake to mix.
2 Half-fill a frying pan with boiling salted water. Add the asparagus, then cover and simmer for 5 minutes or until just tender.
3 Remove the asparagus with a large slotted spoon. If serving the asparagus cold, plunge it into a large bowl of iced water (this will help to keep its bright green colour), then drain.
4 To serve, arrange the asparagus in a concentric pattern in a large shallow bowl, with tips outwards and ends overlapping in the centre. Season with salt and pepper and drizzle with the dressing.

NUTRITION PER SERVING
73 cals | 7g fat (1g sats) | 1g carbs | 0g salt

MEDITERRANEAN KEBABS

Serves 4
Preparation 15 minutes
Cooking time 10 minutes
Techniques see also preparing courgettes (page 191), preparing peppers (page 189), preparing couscous (page 250) chopping herbs (page 436)

1 large courgette, cut into chunks
1 red pepper, seeded and cut into chunks
12 cherry tomatoes
125g (4oz) halloumi cheese, cubed
100g (3½oz) natural yogurt
1 tsp ground cumin
2 tbsp olive oil
squeeze of lemon
1 lemon, cut into eight wedges
couscous tossed with freshly chopped flat-leafed parsley
    to serve

1   Preheat the grill. Put the courgette into a large bowl with the red pepper, cherry tomatoes and halloumi cheese. Add the yogurt, cumin, oil and a squeeze of lemon. Mix together.
2   Take eight presoaked skewers (see Cook's Tip) and push a lemon wedge on to each one, then divide the vegetables and cheese among the skewers. Grill the kebabs, turning regularly, for 8–10 minutes until the vegetables are tender and the halloumi is nicely charred. Serve with couscous.

COOK'S TIP
If using wooden skewers, soak them in water for at least 30 minutes before using to prevent them burning during grilling.

NUTRITION PER SERVING
177 cals | 13g fat (5g sats) | 8g carbs | 1.2g salt

ROASTED POTATOES AND PARSNIPS

Serves 8
Preparation 25 minutes
Cooking time about 1 hour
Techniques see also roasting vegetables (page 201)

1.4kg (3lb) small, even-sized potatoes, scrubbed
800g (1lb 12oz) small parsnips, peeled
50g (2oz) goose fat
1–2 tbsp black mustard seeds
1 tbsp sea salt

1 Cut out small wedges from one side of each of the potatoes and parsnips (this will help make them extra crispy). Put them into a pan of salted cold water, bring to the boil and cook for 6 minutes. Drain well.
2 Preheat the oven to 200°C (180°C fan oven) mark 6. Heat the goose fat in a roasting tin for 4–5 minutes until sizzling hot. Add the potatoes, toss in the fat and roast for 30 minutes. Add the parsnips and sprinkle with the mustard seeds and sea salt. Roast for a further 30–35 minutes, turning after 20 minutes, until the vegetables are golden.

FREEZING TIP
Complete step 1. Spread out the vegetables on a baking tray and leave to cool, then freeze on the tray. Once frozen, put them into a plastic bag and freeze for up to three months.
To use Cook from frozen, allowing an additional 15–20 minutes total cooking time.

NUTRITION PER SERVING
251 cals | 8g fat (3g sats) | 43g carbs | 1.9g salt

BRUSSELS SPROUTS WITH CHESTNUTS AND SHALLOTS

Serves 8
Preparation 15 minutes
Cooking time 12 minutes
Techniques see also preparing shallots (page 182)

900g (2lb) small Brussels sprouts, trimmed
1 tbsp olive oil
8 shallots, finely chopped
200g pack peeled cooked chestnuts
15g (½oz) butter
a pinch of freshly grated nutmeg
salt and ground black pepper

1 Add the sprouts to a large pan of lightly salted boiling water, bring back to the boil and blanch for 2 minutes. Drain the sprouts and refresh with cold water.
2 Heat the oil in a wok or sauté pan. Add the shallots and stir-fry for 5 minutes or until almost tender.
3 Add the sprouts to the pan with the chestnuts and stir-fry for about 4 minutes to heat through.
4 Add the butter and nutmeg, and season generously with salt and pepper. Serve immediately.

COOK'S TIP
If you have to store Brussels sprouts, prepare them for cooking and keep in the fridge in a polythene bag. For convenience, blanch the Brussels sprouts ahead, then pan-fry just before serving. This helps to retain their colour and texture.

NUTRITION PER SERVING
140 cals | 5g fat (1g sats) | 8g carbs | 0.3g salt

LEMON AND ORANGE CARROTS

Serves 8
Preparation 5 minutes
Cooking time 10–15 minutes
Techniques see also preparing root vegetables (page 193), chopping herbs (page 436)

900g (2lb) carrots, cut into long batons
150ml (¼ pint) orange juice
juice of 2 lemons
150ml (¼ pint) dry white wine
50g (2oz) butter
3 tbsp light muscovado sugar
4 tbsp freshly chopped coriander to garnish

1 Put the carrots, orange and lemon juices, wine, butter and sugar in a pan. Cover and bring to the boil.
2 Remove the lid and cook until almost all the liquid has evaporated – this should take about 10 minutes. Serve sprinkled with the coriander.

FREEZING TIP
Cook the carrots for only 5 minutes and cool. Freeze with the remaining liquid.
To use Thaw for 5 hours and reheat in a pan for 5–6 minutes or microwave on full power at 900W for 7–8 minutes.

NUTRITION PER SERVING
127 cals | 6g fat (3g sats) | 17g carbs | 0.2g salt

CREAMED SPINACH

Serves 6
Preparation 15 minutes
Cooking time 5 minutes

900g (2lb) spinach leaves, stalks removed
4 tbsp crème fraîche
salt and ground black pepper

1 Cook the spinach with just the water clinging to the leaves in a covered pan for 3–4 minutes until just wilted.
2 Stir in the crème fraîche and season with salt and pepper to taste. Serve at once.

NUTRITION PER SERVING
80 cals | 5g fat (3g sats) | 3g carbs | 0.2g salt

MIXED VEGETABLE TEMPURA

Serves 6
Preparation 20 minutes
Cooking time 20 minutes
Techniques see also making tempura batter (page 84), preparing vegetables (pages 182–194), deep-frying vegetables (page 198)

1.8 litres (3¼ pints) vegetable oil
150g pack Tempura Mix
330ml bottle of Japanese lager (or a substitute lager)
40g (1½oz) sesame seeds
1 tsp salt
150g (5oz) sweet potato, cut into fine matchsticks
1 onion, cut into wedges
150g (5oz) baby leeks, washed and cut into
  5cm (2in) pieces
1 red pepper, seeded and cut into 12 wedges
200g (7oz) fine green beans, trimmed
Thai sweet chilli dipping sauce

1 Heat the oil in a deep-fat fryer on the chip setting, or until 190°C. Preheat the oven to 110°C (90°C fan oven) mark ¼. Put the pack of tempura mix into a bowl and gradually whisk in the lager to make a smooth batter. Add the sesame seeds and salt.
2 Drop six pieces of vegetable into the tempura batter to coat, then, using a slotted spoon, put into the hot oil. Cook for 3 minutes or until golden and puffy. Drain on kitchen paper, then keep warm in the oven. Repeat with the remaining vegetables. Serve with a bowl of chilli dipping sauce.

VARIATIONS
Other good vegetables for using for tempura include broccoli and cauliflower florets, yellow peppers, cut into wedges, and carrots and butternut squash, cut into fine matchsticks.

NUTRITION PER SERVING
282 cals | 16g fat (2g sats) | 27g carbs | 0.9g salt

ROASTED STUFFED PEPPERS

Serves 4
Preparation 20 minutes
Cooking time 50 minutes
Techniques see also preparing vegetables (pages 182–194), chopping herbs (page 436), making breadcrumbs (page 318)

4 Romano peppers
40g (1½oz) butter
350g (12oz) chestnut mushrooms, roughly chopped
3 tbsp olive oil
4 tbsp finely chopped chives
100g (3½oz) feta cheese
50g (2oz) fresh white breadcrumbs
25g (1oz) freshly grated Parmesan
salt and ground black pepper

1 Preheat the oven to 180°C (160°C fan oven) mark 4. Halve the peppers, keeping the stalks on, and carefully cut out the seeds. Use a little of the butter to grease a shallow ovenproof dish and put in the peppers side by side, ready to be filled.
2 Fry the mushrooms in the remaining butter and 1 tbsp oil until they are golden and there's no excess liquid left in the pan. Stir in the chives, then spoon the mixture into the pepper halves.
3 Crumble the feta cheese over the mushrooms. Mix the breadcrumbs and Parmesan in a bowl, then sprinkle over the top.
4 Season with salt and pepper and drizzle with the remaining oil, then roast for 45 minutes or until golden and tender. Serve warm.

FREEZING TIP
Prepare up to the end of step 3 and freeze in a freezerproof container for up to one week.
To use Thaw the peppers overnight in the fridge and complete the recipe.

NUTRITION PER SERVING
375 cals | 25g fat (11g sats) | 27g carbs | 1.5g salt

THAI VEGETABLE CURRY

Serves 4
Preparation time 15 minutes
Cooking time 15 minutes
Techniques see also preparing fresh ginger (page 437), making coconut milk (page 231), preparing vegetables (pages 182–194), chopping herbs (page 436), cooking rice (page 246)

2–3 tbsp Thai red curry paste
2.5cm (1in) piece fresh root ginger, peeled
    and finely chopped
50g (2oz) cashew nuts
400ml can coconut milk
3 carrots, cut into thin batons
1 broccoli head, cut into florets
20g (¾oz) fresh coriander, roughly chopped
zest and juice of 1 lime
2 large handfuls of washed spinach leaves
basmati rice to serve

1 Put the curry paste into a large pan. Add the ginger to the pan with the cashew nuts. Stir over a medium heat for 2–3 minutes.
2 Add the coconut milk, cover and bring to the boil. Stir the carrots into the pan, reduce the heat and simmer for minutes, then add the broccoli florets and simmer for a further 5 minutes or until the vegetables are tender.
3 Stir the coriander and lime zest into the pan with the spinach. Squeeze the lime juice over and serve with basmati rice.

NUTRITION PER SERVING
203 cals | 12g fat (2g sats) | 16g carbs | 0.6g salt

FRUIT AND NUTS

Fresh, sweet, juicy fruit can be prepared and cooked in many different ways. The step-by-step techniques guide opens by showing you how to peel, core, slice, pit, seed and hull all the different fruits and then demonstrates the basic cooking techniques, from poaching, stewing and pan-frying to deep-frying, baking and grilling – along with advice on making smoothies and purées. This is followed by an essential guide to preparing nuts, including special advice on preparing chestnuts and coconut. The recipe section puts these techniques to work in dishes such as White nut roast, Baked apples, Summer pudding and American-style plum cobbler.

PREPARING ORCHARD FRUITS

When they are used for cooking, all these fruits are usually peeled and cored. Quince is very hard and is always cooked, never eaten raw – unlike its relatives, the apple and pear.

Apples and quinces

1 To core an apple, push an apple corer straight through the apple from the stem to base. Remove the core and use a small sharp knife to pick out any stray seeds or seed casings. To core a quince, halve the quince and then cut out the core.

2 To peel, hold the fruit in one hand and run a swivel peeler under the skin, starting from the stem end and moving around the fruit, taking off the skin until you reach the base. (Quinces for making jelly do not need to be peeled.)

3 To slice, halve the cored apple. For flat slices, hold the apple cut side down and slice with the knife blade at right angles to the hollow left by the core. For crescent-shaped slices, stand the fruit on its end and cut slices into the hollow as if you were slicing a pie.

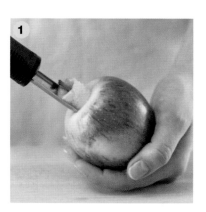

Pears

1 To core, use a teaspoon to scoop out the seeds and core through the base of the pear. Trim away any remaining fragments with a small knife. If you halve or quarter the pear, remove any remaining seeds.

2 To peel, cut off the stem. Peel off the skin in even strips from tip to base. If not using immediately, toss the pears in lemon juice.

3 To slice, halve the cored, peeled pear lengthways. Check for any remaining fragments of core, then slice with the pear halves lying cut side down on the board.

4 To make pear fans, slice at closely spaced intervals from the base to about 2.5cm (1in) from the tip, making sure you don't cut all the way through.

PRESERVING COLOUR

Apples and quinces are easy to work with because they are very firm-fleshed, but their flesh starts to discolour quickly and turn brown when exposed to air. Toss with lemon juice if you are not going to use the prepared fruit immediately.

PREPARING CITRUS FRUITS

Citrus zest is an important flavouring and is simple to prepare. The segments or slices of citrus are also used in recipes and need to be prepared so that no skin, pith or membrane remains.

Zesting

1 Wash and thoroughly dry the fruit. Using a vegetable peeler, cut away the zest (the coloured outer layer of skin) taking care to leave behind the bitter white pith. Continue until you have removed as much as you need.

2 Stack the slices of zest on a board and shred or dice as required using a sharp knife.

EASY ZESTING

— To use a zester, press the blade into the citrus skin and run it along the surface to take off long shreds.

— To use a grater, rub the fruit over the grater, using a medium pressure to remove the zest without removing any of the white pith.

Segmenting

1 Cut off a slice at both ends of the fruit, then cut off the peel, just inside the white pith.

2 Hold fruit over a bowl to catch the juice and cut between the segments just inside the membrane to release the flesh. Continue until all the segments are removed. Squeeze the juice from the membrane into the bowl and use as required.

Slicing

1 Cut off a slice at both ends of the fruit, then cut off the peel, just inside the white pith as described above.

2 Gently hold the fruit on its side on the chopping board and use a serrated knife to cut slices no less than 5mm (¼ in) thick.

SPRAYED FRUIT

Most citrus fruit is sprayed with wax and fungicides or pesticides. When using the zest, wash the lemon with a tiny drop of washing-up liquid and warm water, then rinse with clean water.

PREPARING STONE FRUITS

The most difficult aspect of dealing with stone fruits is that really ripe fruits can be very soft. Handle them with care whenever you are lucky enough to find fully ripe fruits.

Pitting cherries

1 To eat raw, cherries need only to be stemmed and washed. If your recipe requires you to remove the stones, a cherry stoner will do this neatly, but it is important to take care to position the fruit correctly on the cherry stoner.

2 First, remove the stems from the cherries, and then wash the fruits and pat dry on kitchen paper.

3 Put each cherry on the stoner with the stem end facing up. Close the stoner and gently press the handles together so that the metal rod pushes through the fruit, pressing out the stone.

4 Alternatively, if you do not have a cherry stoner, cut the cherries in half and remove the stones with the tip of a small, pointed knife.

Stoning larger fruits

Peaches, nectarines, plums, greengages and apricots can all be handled in the same way.

1 Following the cleft along one side of the fruit, cut through to the stone all around the fruit.

2 Twist gently to separate the halves. Ease out the stone with a small knife. Rub the flesh with lemon juice.

Peeling peaches

1 Peaches may be peeled for use in desserts. Put in a bowl of boiling water for 15 seconds–1 minute (depending on ripeness). Don't leave in the water for too long, as heat will soften the flesh. Put in cold water.

2 Work a knife between the skin and flesh to loosen the skin, then gently pull to remove. Rub the flesh with lemon juice.

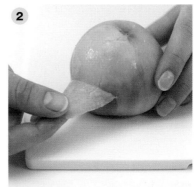

PREPARING BERRIES AND CURRANTS

Soft fruits – strawberries, blackberries, raspberries and currants – are generally quick to prepare.
Always handle ripe fruits gently, as they can be delicate.

Washing berries

Most soft fruits can be washed very gently in cold water. Shop-bought blackberries will usually have the hull removed. If you have picked blackberries yourself the hulls and stalks may still be attached, so pick over the berries carefully and remove any that remain. Raspberries are very delicate, so handle very carefully; remove any stalks and hulls. Leave strawberries whole.

1 Place the berries in a bowl of cold water and allow any small pieces of grit, dust or insects to float out.

2 Transfer the fruit to a colander and rinse gently under fresh running water. Drain well, then leave to drain on kitchen paper.

Hulling strawberries

1 Wash the strawberries gently and dry on kitchen paper. Remove the hull (the centre part that was attached to the plant) from the strawberry using a strawberry huller or a small sharp knife.

2 Put the knife into the small, hard area beneath the green stalk and gently rotate to remove a small, cone-shaped piece.

Stripping currants

Blackcurrants, redcurrants and whitecurrants can all be stripped quickly and simply from the stem in the same way.

1 Using a fork, strip all the currants off the stalks by running the fork down the length of the stalk.

2 Put the currants into a colander and wash them gently.

PREPARING EXOTIC FRUITS

Sweet, fragrant exotic fruits are wonderful eaten raw but are also delicious in numerous desserts. Each fruit is unique and requires its own individual preparation technique.

Pineapples

1 Cut off the base and crown of the pineapple, and stand the fruit on a chopping board.

2 Using a medium-sized knife, peel away a section of skin going just deep enough to remove all or most of the hard, inedible 'eyes' on the skin. Repeat all the way around.

3 Use a small knife to cut out any remaining traces of the eyes.

4 You can buy special tools for coring pineapples but a 7.5cm (3in) biscuit cutter or an apple corer works just as well. Cut the peeled pineapple into slices.

5 Place the biscuit cutter directly over the core and press down firmly to remove the core. If using an apple corer, cut out in pieces, as it will be too wide to remove in one piece.

Mangoes

1 Cut a slice to one side of the stone in centre. Repeat on the other side.

2 Cut parallel lines into the flesh of one slice, almost to the skin. Cut another set of lines to cut the flesh into squares.

3 Press on the skin side to turn the fruit inside out, so that the flesh is thrust outwards. Cut off the chunks as close as possible to the skin. Repeat with the other half.

Papaya

1 Using a sharp knife, halve the fruit lengthways and use a teaspoon to scoop out the shiny black seeds and fibres inside the cavity.

2 If using in a salad, peel the fruit using a swivel-headed vegetable peeler, then gently cut in half using a sharp knife. Remove the seeds using a teaspoon and slice the flesh, or cut into cubes.

Passion fruit

1 The seeds are edible but if you want the fruit for a purée, you will need to sieve them. Halve the passion fruit and scoop the seeds and pulp into a food processor or blender. Process for 30 seconds, until the mixture looks soupy.

2 Pour into a sieve over a bowl, and press down hard on pulp with the back of a spoon to release the juice.

Pomegranate

1 Cut off base of fruit, trying not to cut into cells containing seeds, and make four shallow cuts into the skin with a small sharp knife. Break the pomegranate in half, then quarters.

2 Bend the skin of each quarter backwards to push the seeds out into a bowl. Remove any left behind with a teaspoon. Remove any of the bitter pith that remains on the seeds.

COOK'S TIP

To extract the juice, roll the pomegranate on a board, then halve over a bowl and let the juice drip out. Put the pulp in a sieve and press the seeds lightly to extract the juice. Do not press hard or the juice will have a bitter taste. Take care: the juice stains.

PREPARING OTHER FRUITS

There are several other fruits, including melons, gooseberries, grapes and figs, that do not fit into any particular category or family of fruit. They are simple to prepare and delicious to eat.

Melons

1 Halve the melon by cutting horizontally through the middle.

2 Use a spoon to scoop out the seeds and fibres, and pull or cut out any that remain.

3 **Balling** Cut into the flesh close to the hollow left by the seeds with a melon baller to scoop out a ball. Continue along the perimeter of the hollow until you have come full circle. Keep scooping until you have scooped out all of the soft flesh. (Avoid the harder flesh just under the skin.)

4 **Slicing** Cut each seeded half into slices of the required thickness. Trim off the skin in a single piece, taking care to remove the harder flesh just inside it (the knife will meet more resistance here than when it meets the softer flesh).

Gooseberries

Gooseberries should always be cooked and sweetened.

1 Remove the stems and flower ends and put in a pan. Add sugar to taste – about 50g (2oz) per 125g (4oz) fruit for a dessert, 25g (1oz) per 125g (4oz) for a sauce. Pour in water to a quarter the depth of the fruit.

2 Cook over a medium heat, stirring occasionally, until about half the berries have collapsed.

Grapes

1 Seeding grapes Cut grapes in half from stalk-end to base. Remove seeds.

2 Peeling grapes Keep grapes in bunches and dip into boiling water for 10 seconds, then iced water for another 10 seconds.

3 Remove from the stalk and catch a piece of skin between your thumb and the knife and pull to remove.

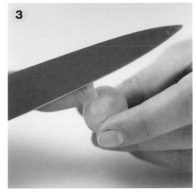

Figs

1 Washing One of the most fragile of fruits, figs call for very careful handling. To wash, put the fig in a bowl of cold water and, holding it loosely, shake briefly underwater. Gently rub the skin to remove any traces of grit then dry gently but thoroughly with kitchen paper.

2 Peeling Cut off the stem end, taking care not to cut into any of the flesh. Starting from the stalk end, catch a piece of skin between your thumb and the blade of a small sharp knife. Pull down to remove a strip of skin, then catch another piece of skin and remove it. Continue until peeled.

3 Halving and quartering Figs can be cooked under the grill or in a tart. Either way, it is best to leave the skin on but to cut the figs into pieces. Trim off the stem, then halve the fig lengthways. For quarters, cut both halves lengthways again.

4 Removing the pulp If you are making a sauce, purée or coulis, you need to remove the pulp from the fig. Halve the fruit lengthways. Starting from the base, use a teaspoon to dig into the flesh just underneath the skin. Follow the contours of the skin to scoop out the flesh in a single piece, taking care not to mash the pulp or cut the skin.

COOK'S TIP

Figs have a very soft, edible skin, which helps keep the fruit together if you are cooking it. If you are in doubt about whether figs should be peeled, cut off a small section of skin and eat it. If it's chewy and leathery, peel it. If it is soft and tender, it doesn't need to be peeled.

COOKING FRUIT

Most fruits taste marvellous raw, although a few always need to be cooked. Nearly all fruits make superb desserts when they are baked, poached, stewed, deep-fried or pan-fried.

Poaching

To serve four, you will need 300g (11oz) sugar, 4 ripe pears, 1 lemon, halved.

1 Put the sugar in a large measuring jug and fill with cold water to make 1 litre (13/4 pints). Transfer to a pan and heat gently, stirring now and then, until the sugar has dissolved.

2 Peel and halve the pears, then gently toss with lemon juice.

3 Pour the sugar syrup into a wide-based pan and bring up to a simmer. Put in the pears, cut sides down. They should be completely covered with syrup; add a little more syrup if necessary.

4 Simmer the fruit very gently for 30–40 minutes until the pears are soft when pierced with a knife. Serve hot, warm or cold.

OVEN POACHING

- You can poach fruit in the oven as well. Put the pears in a shallow ovenproof dish and add the syrup as described. Cook at 150°C (130°C fan oven) mark 2 for 30–40 minutes.
- Under-ripe fruit takes much longer to cook than ripe fruit. Test for doneness regularly, especially in the final stages of cooking.

COOK'S TIPS

Pears, apples and stone fruits are all well suited to gentle poaching in a sugar syrup. The secrets to successful poaching are to:
- Never let the liquid boil rapidly.
- Never overcook the fruit.

Stewing

To serve four, you will need 450g (1lb) prepared fruit (chunks of apples and rhubarb, whole gooseberries, halved plums), 1 tbsp lemon juice, sugar (see box on Sweetening, right).

1 Put the fruit in a non-stick stainless steel pan with the sugar. Add flavourings and 2 tbsp water. Bring to the boil over a medium heat, then reduce the heat and simmer gently, partly covered, until the fruit is soft, stirring often.

SWEETENING

The type of fruit, its ripeness and personal taste will dictate how much sugar is required. However, as a general rule:
- Fruit that you can eat raw will need less sugar.
- Fruits that you wouldn't eat raw such as rhubarb will need more sugar.

Pan-frying

Suitable for apples, pineapple, bananas and stone fruits, this can make a quick dessert or a tasty side dish for pork and game.

To serve four, you will need 450g (1lb) fruit, 25g (1oz) unsalted butter, 4 tbsp golden caster sugar, 1 tbsp lemon juice.

1 Prepare fruit and cut into pieces no more than 2cm (¾in) thick.

2 Melt the butter in a heavy frying pan and add the fruit. Stir to coat with butter, then cover and cook just long enough to heat through.

3 Uncover the pan and sprinkle on the sugar. Stir to coat well, and continue cooking, stirring regularly, until the fruit is soft but not mushy. Sprinkle with the lemon juice and toss just before serving.

Deep-frying

Bananas and apples are best-known for deep-frying, but other fruits are equally good if coated in batter, too. Other good choices for cooking this way include pears, pineapple and skinned peaches or nectarines.

1 Heat vegetable oil in a deep-fryer to 190°C (test by frying a small cube of bread; it should brown in about 20 seconds).

2 Cut the fruit into small pieces, about 1cm (½in) thick. Dry them completely on kitchen paper if they have been washed.

3 Coat the fruit with icing sugar, then dip into the batter (page 84).

4 Fry, a few pieces at a time, until the batter is crisp and golden brown.

5 Lift out the fruit using a slotted spoon and drain well on kitchen paper before serving.

PERFECT FRYING

- Make sure the oil is at the correct temperature.
- Don't crowd the pieces in the pan (if you do, the temperature drops and the fruit takes longer to cook and becomes greasy).
- If you have washed the fruit, dry it thoroughly before coating.
- Don't coat the fruit with batter more than a couple of minutes before cooking.

Baking

The key to success to baking fruit is in keeping the cooking time short, so that the delicate flesh of the fruit doesn't break down completely. Preheat the oven to 200°C (180°C fan oven) mark 6.

1 Prepare the fruit and put in a single layer in a buttered baking dish or individual dishes. Put a splash of water in the bottom of the dish(es). (For extra flavour, you can use fruit juice or wine instead of water, if you prefer.) Sprinkle the tops with sugar (and other flavourings such as spices, citrus zest or vanilla, if you like). Dot with butter.

2 Bake the fruit until just tender when pierced with a knife or skewer; this should take 15–25 minutes depending on the fruit and the size of the pieces. Leave to rest for a few minutes before serving.

GOOD FRUITS FOR BAKING

Fruit	Preparation
Apples (dessert or cooking)	cored and halved or quartered
Apricots	whole or halved and stoned
Bananas	peeled and halved, or in their skins
Berries	whole
Nectarines and peaches	halved and stoned
Pears	cored and halved or quartered
Pineapple	cored and cut into large chunks
Plums	whole or halved and stoned

Grilling

Cooking fruit under the grill is a quick and delicious method.

1 Preheat the grill to high. Prepare the fruit and put in the grill pan (or a roasting tin) in a single layer. Sprinkle generously with sugar.

2 Set the grill pan under the grill about 10cm (4in) from the heat. Grill until the top is lightly caramelised and the fruit has softened, 5–8 minutes. Serve hot or warm.

MAKING SMOOTHIES AND PURÉES

Fruit, whether cooked or raw, can be transformed into a smooth sauce by puréeing. It also makes a healthy breakfast or snack that is bursting with flavour when used in a smoothie.

Making smoothies

To serve four, you will need 4 passion fruit, 150ml (¼ pint) low-fat yogurt, 4 bananas, 225g (8oz) grapes.

1 Halve the passion fruit and scoop the pulp into a blender. Add the remaining ingredients. Crush 8 ice cubes and add to the blender.

2 Process until smooth and pour into glasses. Serve immediately.

Puréeing in a blender

Some fruit can be puréed raw, while others are better cooked. Wait until cooked fruit cools.

1 Blend a spoonful of fruit until smooth, then add another spoonful and blend. Add rest of fruit in batches.

2 For a very smooth purée, pass through a fine sieve.

Puréeing using a mouli

The fine plate of a mouli-légumes does a good job of puréeing, although it is slightly more laborious than a blender.

1 Set the mouli over a bowl and, working in batches, ladle in the fruit.

2 Turn the handle until the fruit has gone through, then repeat until all the fruit has been puréed.

PREPARING NUTS

Most nuts are sold ready-prepared, but if you plan to store them for any length of time, choose nuts in their shells, which keep for longer.

Blanching and skinning

After nuts have been shelled, they are still coated with a skin, which, although edible, tastes bitter. This is easier to remove if the nuts are blanched or toasted.

1 Blanching Put the shelled nuts in a bowl and cover with boiling water. Leave for 2 minutes.

2 Drain and remove the skins either by rubbing between your hands in a teatowel or squeezing between your thumb and index finger.

3 Toasting Preheat the oven to 200°C (180°C fan oven) mark 6. Put the shelled nuts on a baking sheet in a single layer, and bake for 8–15 minutes until the skins are lightly coloured. Remove skins by rubbing in a teatowel or squeezing between your thumb and index finger.

Chopping

Unless you want very large pieces, the easiest way to chop nuts is in the food processor. Only chop about 75g (3oz) of nuts at a time.

1 Put the nuts in a food processor and pulse at 10-second intervals.

2 Chop to the size of coarse breadcrumbs. Store in an airtight container for up to two weeks.

Slicing and slivering

Although you can buy sliced and slivered nuts, it's easy enough to make your own.

1 Put the nuts on a board. Using a chef's knife, carefully slice the nuts as thinly as required.

2 To make slivers, carefully cut the slices in the same way to make narrow matchsticks.

Making spiced nuts

These simply toasted nuts with a spicy, oily coating are great served with drinks at a party.

To make a 500ml jar, you will need 4 tbsp vegetable oil, 2 tsp caster sugar, 2 tsp English mustard powder, 2 tsp garam masala, ½ tsp hot chilli powder, 350g (12oz) mixed nuts (almonds, pecan nuts, cashews, hazelnuts, Brazil nuts), 50g (2oz) pumpkin seeds, 50g (2oz) sunflower seeds, 1 tsp sea salt.

1 Preheat the oven to 200°C (180°C fan oven) mark 6. Pour the vegetable oil into a roasting tin and heat for 3 minutes.

2 Meanwhile, mix together the sugar, mustard, garam masala and chilli powder, then add to the oil in the tin and roast for 1 minute.

3 Add the nuts and seeds to the tin, and stir to coat thoroughly in the spices, then roast for 10–15 minutes until golden.

4 Transfer the nuts to a bowl lined with kitchen paper, sprinkle with salt, and leave to cool. Serve immediately, or store in an airtight container for up to two weeks.

COOK'S TIP

Garam masala
Grind together 10 green cardamom pods, 1 tbsp black peppercorns and 2 tsp cumin seeds. Store in an airtight container and use within one month.

PREPARING CHESTNUTS

A richly flavoured nut, the chestnut is used for stuffings and other sweet and savoury dishes. Chestnuts need to be cooked and peeled before eating or using as an ingredient.

Slitting the shells

Whatever you are planning to do with chestnuts, they need to be cut open first.

1 Using a very sharp small knife, make a slit in the flat side of the nut, through the skin but not too deeply into the flesh.

2 Make a second cut across the first to make a cross-shaped cut.

Boiling

This is the simplest way to prepare chestnuts for stuffings or for cooking.

1 Put scored chestnuts in a pan and cover with water. Bring to the boil, then reduce the heat and simmer for 15–20 minutes until half-cooked. (They will feel soft but with some resistance at the centre.)

2 Drain. When cool enough to handle, skin using a small knife

Roasting

These are best eaten immediately but can also be used for stuffings.

1 Preheat the oven to 200°C (180°C fan oven) mark 6. Slit the shells.

2 Put the nuts in a roasting pan in a single layer and bake for 20–25 minutes until the flesh is cooked and the edges of the cuts are slightly blackened. Cool a little, then peel.

COOK'S TIP

After skinning boiled chestnuts, you can cook them further.
- Fry gently in butter in a covered pan.
- Simmer in salted water or stock until just tender.
- For stuffings, chop using a knife or food processor.

PREPARING COCONUT

The moist flesh of fresh coconut can be eaten as it is or grated to use in recipes. Check the coconut for freshness when you buy it by shaking it to make sure it has liquid inside.

Cracking

1 Find the three 'eyes' on one end and make holes with a skewer or screwdriver. Drain the juice into a bowl or jug.

2 Crack the shell by hitting between the eyes with a hammer or cleaver, then tap around the circumference. Break open, then split into smaller pieces. Using a small sharp knife, dig out flesh by cutting just under shell.

Grating

In countries where fresh coconut is extensively used, cooks use a special grater that produces perfectly fluffy shreds. You can grate coconut by hand or in the food processor.

1 By hand A rotary grater is easier to use than a flat grater because of the tough fibres of the coconut. Cut the coconut into pieces and feed through the grater.

2 Using a food processor Cut the coconut into fairly small pieces and process no more than a handful at a time. Pulse the processor until the coconut forms dry, fluffy shreds.

Coconut milk

1 Weigh the grated coconut flesh and put it into a bowl. Pour 100ml (3½fl oz) boiling water over for each 100g (3½oz) coconut. Leave to stand for 30 minutes.

2 Line a large sieve with a double layer of muslin and pour the liquid through it. Gather up the four corners of the muslin and twist hard to squeeze out every bit of juice.

WHITE NUT ROAST

Serves 8
Preparation 20 minutes
Cooking time about 1 hour
Techniques see also making breadcrumbs (page 318)

40g (1½oz) butter
1 onion, finely chopped
1 garlic clove, crushed
225g (8oz) mixed white nuts, such as brazils, macadamias, pinenuts and whole almonds, ground in a food processor
125g (4oz) fresh white breadcrumbs
grated zest and juice of ½ lemon
75g (3oz) sage Derby cheese or Parmesan, grated
125g (4oz) cooked, peeled (or vacuum-packed) chestnuts, roughly chopped
½ × 400g can artichoke hearts, roughly chopped
1 medium egg, lightly beaten
2 tsp each freshly chopped parsley, sage and thyme, plus extra sprigs
salt and ground black pepper

1 Preheat the oven to 200°C (180°C fan oven) mark 6. Melt the butter in a pan and cook the onion and garlic for 5 minutes or until soft. Put into a large bowl and put to one side to cool.
2 Add the nuts, breadcrumbs, zest and juice of the lemon, cheese, chestnuts and artichokes. Season well and bind together with the egg. Stir in the herbs.
3 Put the mixture on to a large piece of buttered foil and shape into a fat sausage, packing tightly. Scatter with the extra herb sprigs and wrap in the foil.
4 Cook on a baking sheet for 35 minutes, then unwrap the foil slightly and cook for a further 15 minutes until turning golden.

FREEZING TIP

Complete the recipe to step 3, cool, cover and freeze for up to one month.
To use Cook from frozen for 45 minutes, then unwrap the foil slightly and cook for a further 15 minutes until turning golden.

NUTRITION PER SERVING
371 cals | 28g fat (9g sats) | 20g carbs | 0.8g salt

NUT AND CRANBERRY TERRINE

Serves 8
Preparation 45 minutes, plus cooling
Cooking time 1 hour 10 minutes
Techniques see also toasting nuts (page 228), preparing vegetables (pages 182–194), making breadcrumbs (page 318), cooking rice (page 246)

125g (4oz) long-grain rice
4 tbsp olive oil
1 onion, finely chopped
1 leek, trimmed and thinly sliced
4 celery sticks, thinly sliced
4 tbsp chopped mixed fresh herbs, such as sage, parsley and thyme
40g (1½oz) walnuts, toasted and roughly ground
125g (4oz) dolcelatte cheese, crumbled
1 large egg, beaten
40g (1½oz) fresh white breadcrumbs
125g (4oz) fromage frais or crème fraîche
Hot Water Crust Pastry (see Cook's Tip)
salt and ground black pepper
bay leaves to garnish

For the topping
125g (4oz) redcurrant jelly
1 tsp lemon juice
125g (4oz) cranberries or redcurrants, thawed if frozen

1 Cook the rice for 10 minutes or until just tender. Refresh under cold water, drain and put to one side. Heat the oil in a frying pan. Add the onion, leek, celery and herbs and fry gently for 10 minutes until softened. Transfer to a bowl. Add the rice, walnuts, cheese, egg, breadcrumbs and fromage frais or crème fraîche. Season and stir well.
2 Preheat the oven to 220°C (200°C fan oven) mark 7. Roll out the pastry to a 25.5 × 20.5cm (10 × 8in) rectangle and use to line a 900g (2lb) loaf tin, pressing the dough into the corners. Trim the overhanging pastry and set aside.
3 Spoon the rice mixture into the pastry case and smooth the surface. Divide the pastry trimmings in half, roll each piece into a long thin rope and twist the two ropes together. Dampen the pastry edges and top with the pastry twist, pressing down gently. Cook in the oven for 45–50 minutes until golden and a skewer inserted into the centre comes out hot. Leave to cool.
4 To make the topping, heat the redcurrant jelly with the lemon juice and 1 tbsp water until melted, then simmer for 3 minutes. Remove from the heat and stir in the fruit.
5 Turn the loaf tin upside down and tap gently. Spoon the topping over and leave to set. When cold, garnish with bay.

COOK'S TIP
Hot Water Crust Pastry Sift 225g (8oz) plain flour and a pinch of salt into a bowl and make a well in the middle. Heat 50g (2oz) white vegetable fat and 100ml (3½fl oz) water in a pan until it comes to the boil. Pour into the flour and work together, using a wooden spoon. When cool enough to handle, knead until smooth; use while still warm and pliable.

NUTRITION PER SERVING
495 cals | 28g fat (12g sats) | 52g carbs | 0.7g salt

NUTTY BEAN BURGERS

Serves 6
Preparation 20 minutes, plus standing
Cooking time 25 minutes
Techniques see also chopping onions (page 182), crushing garlic (page 183), chopping herbs (page 436), making breadcrumbs (page 318)

2 tbsp olive oil
I small onion, chopped
I garlic clove, crushed
2 tsp freshly chopped thyme
400g can red kidney beans, rinsed and drained
400g can butter beans, rinsed and drained
50g (2oz) chopped mixed nuts
40g (1½oz) fresh white breadcrumbs
I tbsp dark soy sauce
I tbsp lemon juice
oil to shallow-fry
6 soft burger buns, split
salt and ground black pepper
selection of relishes and mixed salad to serve

1 Heat the olive oil in a frying pan. Add the onion, garlic and chopped thyme and fry for 10 minutes or until softened and golden.
2 Add the canned beans to the pan. Fry gently for a further 5 minutes, then transfer to a food processor and process briefly to form a rough paste; turn into a bowl.
3 Add the nuts, breadcrumbs, soy sauce and lemon juice, stir until evenly combined and season generously with salt and pepper. Cover and leave to stand for several hours to allow the flavours to develop.
4 Divide the bean mixture into six equal portions and shape into burgers.
5 Heat a little oil in a heavy-based frying pan and fry the burgers in batches for 2–3 minutes on each side until golden and cooked through. Drain on kitchen paper and keep warm while frying the rest.
6 Serve in burger buns, with your favourite relishes and a mixed salad.

NUTRITION PER SERVING
450 cals | 13g fat (2g sats) | 70g carbs | 3.5g salt **V**

RHUBARB AND PEAR CRUMBLE

Serves 8
Preparation 25 minutes
Cooking time 40–45 minutes
Techniques see also preparing pears (page 216)

450g (1lb) rhubarb, cut into 2.5cm (1in) pieces
2 ripe pears, peeled, cored and roughly chopped
75g (3oz) Demerara sugar
1 tsp ground cinnamon
50g (2oz) chilled butter
75g (3oz) self-raising flour
2 shortbread fingers
50g (2oz) whole hazelnuts
500g (1lb 2oz) Greek yogurt to serve

1 Preheat the oven to 180°C (160°C fan oven) mark 4.
Put the fruit into a small shallow baking dish and sprinkle
with 25g (1oz) sugar and the cinnamon. Mix together well.
2 Next, make the crumble mixture. Put the butter in a
food processor, add the flour and remaining sugar and whiz
until it looks like rough breadcrumbs. (Alternatively, rub the
fat into the flour by hand or using a pastry cutter, then stir
in the sugar.)
3 Break the shortbread fingers into pieces and add to
the processor with the hazelnuts (or crush the shortbread
with a rolling pin and chop the hazelnuts). Whiz again for
4–5 seconds until the crumble is blended but still looks
rough. Sprinkle the crumble over the fruit, spreading it
up to the edges and pressing down with the back of a
wooden spoon.
4 Bake in the oven for 40–45 minutes until the topping is
golden brown and crisp. Serve with yogurt.

VARIATION
Creamy vanilla custard is another traditional accompaniment
to fruit crumbles. Make your own using the recipe and
technique on page 28.

NUTRITION PER SERVING
262 cals | 17g fat (7g sats) | 25g carbs | 0.3g salt **V**

BAKED APPLES

Serves 6
Preparation 5 minutes, plus soaking
Cooking time 15–20 minutes
Techniques see also preparing apples (page 216)

125g (4oz) hazelnuts
125g (4oz) sultanas
2 tbsp brandy
6 large Bramley apples, cored
4 tbsp soft brown sugar
100ml (3½fl oz) apple juice
thick cream to serve

1 Preheat the grill. Preheat the oven to 190°C (170°C fan oven) mark 5. Spread the hazelnuts over a baking sheet and toast under the hot grill until golden brown, turning them frequently. Put the hazelnuts in a clean teatowel and rub off the skins, then chop the nuts. Put to one side.
2 Soak the sultanas in the brandy and put to one side for 10 minutes. Using a small sharp knife, score around the middle of each apple to stop them from bursting, then stuff each apple with equal amounts of brandy-soaked sultanas. Put the apples in a roasting tin and sprinkle with the brown sugar and apple juice. Bake in the oven for 15–20 minutes until soft.
3 Serve the apples with the toasted hazelnuts and a dollop of cream.

NUTRITION PER SERVING
280 cals | 13 fat (1g sats) | 36g carbs | 0g salt **V**

DRUNKEN PEARS

Serves 4
Preparation 20 minutes
Cooking time 50 minutes
Techniques see also preparing pears (page 216), zesting citrus fruits (page 217)

4 Williams or Comice pears
140g (4½oz) granulated sugar
300ml (½ pint) dry red wine
150ml (¼ pint) sloe gin
1 cinnamon stick
zest of 1 orange
6 star anise
Greek yogurt or whipped cream to serve (optional)

1 Peel the pears, cut out the calyx at the base of each and leave the stalks intact. Put the sugar, wine, sloe gin and 300ml (½ pint) water into a small pan and heat gently until the sugar dissolves.
2 Bring to the boil, then add the cinnamon stick, orange zest and star anise. Add the pears, then reduce the heat to low, cover and poach for 30 minutes or until tender.
3 Lift the pears into a bowl and reduce the liquid to about 200ml (7fl oz) or until syrupy. Pour over the pears and serve warm or chilled with Greek yogurt or whipped cream, if you like.

NUTRITION PER SERVING
305 cals | trace fat (0g sats) | 52g carbs | 0g salt **Ⓥ**

CRANBERRY CHRISTMAS PUDDING

Serves 12
Preparation 20 minutes, plus overnight soaking
Cooking time 6 hours
Techniques see also zesting citrus fruits (page 217), making breadcrumbs (page 318)

200g (7oz) currants
200g (7oz) sultanas
200g (7oz) raisins
75g (3oz) dried cranberries or cherries
grated zest and juice of 1 orange
50ml (2fl oz) rum
50ml (2fl oz) brandy
1–2 tsp Angostura bitters
1 small apple, grated
1 carrot, grated
175g (6oz) fresh breadcrumbs
100g (3½oz) plain flour, sifted
1 tsp mixed spice
175g (6oz) light vegetarian suet
100g (3½oz) dark muscovado sugar
50g (2oz) blanched almonds, roughly chopped
2 medium eggs
butter to grease
fresh or frozen cranberries (thawed if frozen),
    fresh bay leaves and icing sugar to decorate
Brandy Butter (see page 31) to serve

1 Put the dried fruit, orange zest and juice in a large bowl. Pour the rum, brandy and Angostura bitters over. Cover and leave to soak in a cool place for at least 1 hour or overnight.

2 Add the apple, carrot, breadcrumbs, flour, mixed spice, suet, sugar, almonds and eggs to the bowl of soaked fruit. Use a wooden spoon to mix everything together well. Grease a 1.8 litre (3¼ pint) pudding basin and line with a 60cm (24in) square piece of muslin. Spoon the mixture into the basin and flatten the surface. Gather the muslin up and over the top, twist and secure with string. Put the basin on an upturned heatproof saucer or trivet in the base of a large pan. Pour in enough boiling water to come halfway up the side of the basin. Cover with a tight-fitting lid and simmer for 6 hours. Keep the water topped up. Remove the basin from the pan and leave to cool. When the pudding is cold, remove from the basin, then wrap it in clingfilm and a double layer of foil. Store in a cool, dry place for up to six months.

3 To reheat, steam for 2½ hours; check the water level every 40 minutes and top up if necessary. Leave the pudding in the pan, covered, to keep warm until needed. Decorate with cranberries and bay leaves, dust with icing sugar. Serve with Brandy Butter.

NUTRITION PER SERVING
448 cals | 17g fat (7g sats) | 68g carbs | 0.3g salt

AMERICAN-STYLE PLUM COBBLER

Serves 6
Preparation 25 minutes
Cooking time 40 minutes
Techniques see also stoning fruit (page 218)

900g (2lb) plums, halved and stoned
150g (5oz), golden caster sugar, plus 3 tbsp
1 tbsp cornflour
250g (9oz) self-raising flour
100g (3½oz) chilled unsalted butter, diced
175ml (6fl oz) buttermilk or whole natural yogurt

1 Preheat the oven to 200°C (180°C fan oven) mark 6.
Cut the plums into chunky wedges. Tip into an ovenproof
dish measuring 25.5 × 18 × 7.5cm (10 × 7 × 3in) and toss
together with 3 tbsp sugar and the cornflour.
2 Whiz the flour, butter and 100g (3½oz) sugar in a
food processor until the mixture forms fine crumbs.
(Alternatively, rub the fat into the flour by hand or using a
pastry cutter, then stir in the sugar.) Add the buttermilk or
yogurt and blend for a few seconds until just combined.
3 Scatter clumps of the squidgy dough over the plums,
leaving some of the fruit exposed. Sprinkle the cobbler with
the remaining sugar and bake in the oven for 40 minutes or
until the fruit is tender and the topping is pale golden.

FINISHING TOUCHES
A scoop of vanilla ice cream makes an indulgent addition to
a bowl of plum cobbler. Try making your own home-made
ice cream using the recipe and technique on page 394.

NUTRITION PER SERVING
451 cals | 15g fat (9g sats) | 76g carbs | 0.3g salt **V**

SUMMER GRATIN

Serves 4
Preparation 15 minutes
Cooking time 15 minutes
Techniques see also stoning fruit (page 218), preparing berries (page 219), separating eggs (page 54)

3 ripe peaches, halved, stoned and sliced
225g (8oz) wild strawberries or raspberries
3 tbsp Kirsch or Eau de Vie de Mirabelle
4 large egg yolks
50g (2oz) sugar

1 Put the peach slices in a bowl with the strawberries or raspberries and 2 tbsp Kirsch or Eau de Vie.
2 Put the egg yolks, sugar, remaining Kirsch and 2 tbsp water in a heatproof bowl set over a pan of barely simmering water. Whisk for 5–10 minutes or until the mixture leaves a trail and is warm in the centre. Remove from the heat. Preheat the grill.
3 Arrange the fruit in four shallow heatproof dishes and spoon the sauce over. Cook under the grill for 1–2 minutes or until light golden. Serve immediately.

NUTRITION PER SERVING
168 cals | 4g fat (1g sats) | 27g carbs | 0g salt

SUMMER PUDDING

Serves 8
Preparation 10 minutes, plus overnight chilling
Cooking time 10 minutes
Techniques see also preparing berries and currants (page 219)

800g (1lb 12oz) mixed summer berries,
   such as 250g (9oz) each redcurrants
   and blackcurrants and 300g (11oz) raspberries
125g (4oz) golden caster sugar
3 tbsp crème de cassis
9 thick slices of slightly stale white bread, crusts removed

1 Put the redcurrants and blackcurrants into a medium pan. Add the sugar and cassis. Bring to a simmer and cook for 3–5 minutes until the sugar has dissolved. Add the raspberries and cook for 2 minutes. Once the fruit is cooked, taste it – there should be a good balance between tart and sweet.
2 Meanwhile, line a 1 litre (1¾ pint) bowl with clingfilm. Put the base of the bowl on one piece of bread and cut around it. Put the circle of bread in the base of the bowl.
3 Line the inside of the bowl with more slices of bread, slightly overlapping to avoid any gaps. Spoon in the fruit, making sure the juice soaks into the bread. Keep back a few spoonfuls of juice in case the bread is unevenly soaked when you turn out the pudding.
4 Cut the remaining bread to fit the top of the pudding neatly, using a sharp knife to trim excess bread from around the edges. Wrap in clingfilm, weigh down with a saucer and a tin can and chill overnight.
5 To serve, unwrap the outer clingfilm, upturn the pudding on to a serving plate and remove the inner clingfilm. Drizzle with the reserved juice and serve with crème fraîche or clotted cream.

NUTRITION PER SERVING
173 cals | 1g fat (trace sats) | 38g carbs | 0.4g salt

LEMON AND PASSION FRUIT FOOL

Serves 6
Preparation 20 minutes
Techniques see also preparing passion fruit (page 221), slivering nuts (page 229)

6 tbsp good-quality lemon curd
4 ripe passion fruits
140ml (4½fl oz) double cream
1 tbsp icing sugar
200g (7oz) Greek yogurt
toasted flaked almonds to decorate

1 Put the lemon curd into a small bowl. Halve the passion fruit and spoon the pulp into a sieve resting over a bowl. Stir to separate the seeds from the juice. Add 1 tbsp of the passion fruit juice to the lemon curd and mix well.
2 In a large bowl, whip the cream with the icing sugar until soft peaks form. Stir in the yogurt.
3 Put a dollop of yogurt cream into each of four small glasses. Layer with a spoonful of lemon curd mixture and 1 tsp passion fruit juice. Repeat to use up all the ingredients. Decorate with toasted flaked almonds and serve.

NUTRITION PER SERVING
244 cals | 18g fat (10g sats) | 21g carbs | 0.1g salt

EXOTIC FRUIT SALAD

Serves 4
Preparation 10 minutes
Techniques see also preparing exotic fruits (page 220), preparing melons (page 222), zesting citrus fruits (page 217)

2 oranges
1 mango, peeled, stoned and chopped
450g (1lb) peeled and diced fresh pineapple
200g (7oz) blueberries
½ Charentais melon, cubed
grated zest and juice of 1 lime

1 Using a sharp knife, peel the oranges, remove the pith and cut into segments. Put into a bowl.
2 Add the mango to the bowl with the pineapple, blueberries and melon.
3 Add the lime zest and juice, and gently mix together. Serve immediately.

TRY SOMETHING DIFFERENT
Use 2 papayas, peeled, seeded and chopped, instead of the pineapple. Mix the seeds of 2 passion fruit with the lime juice before adding to the salad.

NUTRITION PER SERVING
122 cals | 1g fat (0g sats) | 29g carbs | 0.1g salt

RICE, GRAINS AND PULSES

Wholseome and healthy, grains, beans, lentils and pulses can be a nutritious staple in your everyday diet and they are so easy to prepare. The step-by-step technique section in this chapter explains how to prepare and cook perfect rice every time including making risotto, paella and sushi, as well as other grains such as couscous, bulgur wheat, barley, quinoa, wheat grain and polenta. It also shows you how easy it is to soak, cook and sprout your own beans. The recipes put these skills to good use in wonderful dishes such as Smoked haddock kedgeree, Spiced chicken pilau, Prawn and lemon risotto, Cheesy polenta with tomato sauce, Summer couscous, Spicy pork and bean stew and Spicy bean and tomato fajitas.

COOKING RICE

There are two main types of rice: long-grain and short-grain. Short-grain rice is used for dishes such as risotto, sushi and paella. Long-grain rice is used as an accompaniment.

Preparing long-grain rice

Long-grain rice needs no special preparation, though basmati should be washed to remove excess starch.

1 Put in a bowl and cover with cold water. Stir until this becomes cloudy, then drain and repeat the washing process until the water is clear.

2 Soak the rice for 30 minutes, then drain before cooking.

Cooking long-grain rice

1 Measure the rice by volume and put it in a pan with a pinch of salt with twice the volume of boiling water (or boiling stock).

2 Bring to the boil. Reduce the heat to low, and set the timer for the time stated on the pack. It needs to cook *al dente*: tender but with a hint of bite at the centre.

3 When the rice is cooked, fluff up the grains by gently tossing with a fork; this keeps the grains from sticking together. The rice can be left, covered, for a few minutes.

PERFECT RICE

- Use 50–75g (2–3oz) raw rice per person – or measure by volume 50–75ml (2–2½fl oz).
- If you cook a lot of rice, you may want to invest in a special rice steamer. They are available in Asian supermarkets and some kitchen shops and give good, consistent results.

VARIATION

Cooking the rice in stock, with additional aromatics such as herbs, garlic or spices, will add flavour.

MAKING RISOTTO

Italian risotto is made with medium-grain arborio, vialone nano or carnaroli rice, which release starch to give a rich, creamy texture. It is traditionally cooked on the hob, but can also be cooked in the oven.

Basic risotto

To serve four, you will need
1 chopped onion, 50g (2oz) butter,
900ml (1½ pints) hot chicken stock,
225g (8oz) risotto rice, 50g (2oz)
grated Parmesan, plus extra to serve.

1 Gently fry the onion in the butter for 10–15 minutes until it is very lightly coloured. Heat the stock in a pan and keep at a simmer. Add the rice to the butter and stir for 1–2 minutes until well coated.

2 Add a ladleful of stock and stir constantly until absorbed. Add the remaining stock a ladleful at a time, stirring, until the rice is al dente (tender but still with bite in the centre), about 20–30 minutes. You may not need all the stock.

3 Stir in the grated Parmesan and serve immediately, with extra cheese passed separately.

PERFECT RISOTTO

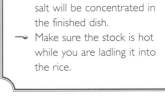

- Use home-made stock, preferably with minimal salt – the stock cooks away, so the salt will be concentrated in the finished dish.
- Make sure the stock is hot while you are ladling it into the rice.

Easy oven risotto

This method has the advantage over classic risotto because it requires no attention or stirring during cooking.

To serve four, you will need 40g (1½oz) unsalted butter, 1 finely chopped garlic clove, 1 finely chopped onion, 1 rosemary sprig, leaves finely chopped, 225g (8oz) risotto rice, 900ml (1½ pints) hot chicken stock, 50g (2oz) freshly grated Parmesan.

1 Preheat the oven to 150°C (130°C fan) mark 2. Melt half the butter in a flameproof casserole and fry the garlic, onion and rosemary for 8 minutes until soft and golden.

2 Add the rice and stir for 2 minutes. Pour in the stock, bring to the boil, cover and bake for 20 minutes. To serve, stir in the remaining butter and the cheese.

MAKING PAELLA

No two Spanish cooks make this classic dish in exactly the same way and the choice and quantities of ingredients vary from home to home. It is usually made in a large flat pan with a dimpled bottom.

Simple paella

Traditionally, paella is made using a medium-grain rice but this version uses long-grain rice.

To serve six, you will need about 1 litre (1¾ pints) chicken stock, ½ tsp saffron, 6 boneless skinless chicken thighs, 5 tbsp extra-virgin olive oil, 1 large onion, chopped, 4 large garlic cloves, crushed, 1 tsp paprika, 2 sliced red peppers, 400g can chopped tomatoes, 350g (12oz) long-grain rice, 200ml (7fl oz) dry sherry, 500g (1lb 2oz) cooked mussels, 200g (7oz) cooked tiger prawns, the juice of ½ lemon, salt and ground black pepper, lemon wedges and parsley sprigs to serve.

1 Heat the stock, then add the saffron and leave to infuse for 30 minutes. Meanwhile, cut the chicken thighs into three pieces.

2 Heat half the oil in a large frying pan and, working in batches, fry the chicken for 3–5 minutes until pale golden brown. Set the chicken aside.

3 Reduce the heat slightly and add the remaining oil. Fry the onion for 5 minutes until soft. Add the garlic and paprika and stir for 1 minute. Add chicken, peppers and tomatoes.

4 Stir in the rice, then add one-third of the stock and bring to the boil. Season with salt and pepper.

5 Reduce the heat to a simmer. Cook, uncovered, stirring continuously, until most of the liquid is absorbed.

6 Add the remaining stock a little at a time, letting it become absorbed into the rice before adding more. (This should take about 25 minutes.) Add the sherry and continue cooking for another 2 minutes – the rice should be quite wet, as it will continue to absorb liquid.

7 Add the mussels and prawns to the pan, including all their juices, with the lemon juice. Stir them in and cook for 5 minutes to heat through. Adjust the seasoning and garnish with lemon wedges and sprigs of fresh parsley.

MAKING SUSHI

Japanese sushi is made with special short- or medium-grain rice, which has a higher moisture content and stickier consistency, making it perfect for rolling up inside seaweed to make elegant sushi rolls.

Classic sushi rolls

To make four rolls (24 pieces), you will need 150g (5oz) Japanese sushi rice, 2 tbsp rice vinegar, 4 tbsp mirin (rice wine), 1 tbsp caster sugar, 4 sheets nori (seaweed), 1 tbsp wasabi paste, soy sauce, wasabi and pickled ginger to serve.

For the filling you will need 150g (5oz) smoked salmon, ½ cucumber, 2 large spring onions.

1 Put the rice in a pan with 350ml (12fl oz) cold water. Bring to the boil, cover, reduce the heat and simmer for 10 minutes or until the water has evaporated. Remove from the heat and stir in the vinegar, mirin and sugar. Leave to cool, then fluff up with chopsticks.

2 Cut the salmon into long thin strips. Peel and seed the cucumber and cut into strips. Thinly shred the spring onions.

3 Lay a sheet of nori, shiny side down, in the centre of a sushi mat. Spread a quarter of the rice across two-thirds of the nori.

4 Make an indentation along the top of the rice and spread with a little wasabi paste, then lay a quarter of the salmon, cucumber and spring onion across the width.

5 Using your thumbs to pick up the mat, roll it away from you, pressing gently but firmly on the filling as you roll to make a neat cylinder. Unroll the mat and repeat with the remaining nori and fillings.

6 Wet the blade of a very sharp knife. Trim the ends of each roll, cut each one into three equal-sized pieces, then cut each third in half at an angle. Serve with soy sauce, wasabi and pickled ginger.

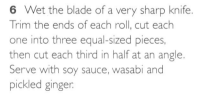

COOKING OTHER GRAINS

With any grain, the cooking time depends heavily on how the grain has been processed. Both wheat and barley come in several forms, so you need to check which type you have bought.

Couscous

Often mistaken for a grain, couscous is actually a type of pasta that originated in North Africa. It is perfect for serving with stews and casseroles, or making into salads. The tiny pellets do not require any cooking and can simply be soaked.

1 Measure the couscous in a jug and add 1½ times the volume of hot water or stock.

2 Cover the bowl and leave to soak for 5 minutes. Fluff up with a fork before serving.

3 If using for a salad, leave the couscous to cool completely before adding the other salad ingredients.

Bulgur wheat

A form of cracked wheat, bulgur has had some or all of the bran removed. It is pre-boiled during manufacturing and may be boiled, steamed or soaked. It is good served as a grain or used in salads.

1 **Simmering bulgur** Cover in water by about 2.5cm (1in). Bring to the boil, then reduce the heat and simmer for 10–15 minutes until just tender. Drain.

2 **Steaming bulgur** Place the bulgur in a steamer lined with a clean teatowel and steam over boiling water for 20 minutes or until the grains are soft.

3 **Soaking bulgur** Put the bulgur in a deep bowl. Cover with hot water and mix with a fork. Leave for 20 minutes, checking to make sure there is enough water. Drain and fluff up with a fork.

Barley

There are three types of barley, all of which may be cooked on their own, or in a soup or stew.

1 **Whole barley** Soak the barley overnight in twice the volume of water, then drain well. Put the barley in a heavy-based pan, pour boiling water over and simmer for about 1½ hours or until tender. Check the liquid, adding more if necessary.

2 **Scotch (pot) barley** Rinse well, then simmer gently in boiling water for 45–50 minutes until tender.

3 **Pearl barley** This barley has had all of its outer husk removed and needs no soaking. Rinse the barley and put it into a pan with twice the volume of water. Bring to the boil. Reduce the heat and simmer until tender, about 25–30 minutes.

Quinoa

This nutritious South American grain makes a great alternative to rice.

1 Put the quinoa in a bowl of cold water. Mix well, soak for 2 minutes and drain. Put in a pan with twice its volume of water. Bring to the boil.

2 Reduce the heat and simmer for 20 minutes. Remove from the heat, cover and leave to stand for 10 minutes.

Wheat grain

Also known as whole wheat and wheat berries, wheat grain needs to be soaked overnight, followed by long, slow simmering. You can sometimes find pre-cooked varieties that will cut down on soaking and cooking time.

1 Soak the wheat grain overnight in twice the volume of water, then drain well.

2 Measure the grain in a measuring cup, then put in a heavy-based pan with twice the volume of water (or use unsalted stock instead of water to add flavour to the grain).

3 Bring to the boil, reduce the heat and simmer until tender, about 45 minutes. Check the liquid regularly to make sure it is not boiling away, and add more if necessary. Drain well.

QUANTITIES

Allow 50–75g (2–3oz) raw grain per person. Or, if measuring by volume, allow 50–75ml (2–2½fl oz).

COOKING POLENTA

This classic Italian staple made of coarse ground cornmeal may be cooked to make a grainy purée to be served immediately, or cooled and then fried or grilled. Here are some quick ways to cook it.

Traditional polenta

1 Fill a pan with 1.1 litres (2 pints) water and add ¼ tsp salt. Pour in 225g (8oz) polenta and set it over the heat.

2 As the water starts to heat up, stir the polenta. Bring to the boil, reduce the heat to a simmer and continue cooking, stirring every few minutes, for 15–20 minutes until it comes away from the sides of the pan.

Grilling polenta

1 Make traditional polenta (see above), then pour into an oiled baking dish. Smooth the surface with a spatula and leave to cool.

2 Cut polenta into squares and brush the pieces with olive oil.

3 Preheat the grill or frying pan and cook for 5–10 minutes until hot and browned on both sides.

Baking polenta

1 Preheat the oven to 200°C (180°C fan oven) mark 6. Fill a pan with 1.1 litres (2 pints) water and add ¼ tsp salt. Pour in 225g (8oz) polenta and set it over the heat. Bring to the boil, stirring, then reduce the heat and simmer for 5 minutes.

2 Pour the polenta into an oiled baking dish, cover with foil and bake for 45–50 minutes. Brown under grill.

> ### PERFECT POLENTA
> → Use coarse cornmeal if you want a slightly gritty texture, or use fine cornmeal for a smooth texture.
> → If you are serving the traditional polenta straight from the pan, have all the other dishes ready – the polenta needs to be eaten straightaway otherwise it becomes thick and difficult to serve.

USING BEANS AND LENTILS

Many dried beans and peas need to be soaked overnight before cooking, and doing so will shorten their cooking time. However, quicker-cooking lentils do not need soaking.

Cooking beans

1 Pick through the beans to remove any grit or small stones.

2 Put the beans in a bowl or pan and pour cold water over to cover generously. Leave to soak for at least 8 hours, then drain. (If you are in a hurry, pour boiling water over and leave the beans to cool in the water for 1–2 hours.)

3 Put the soaked beans in a large pan and add water to cover by at least 5cm (2in). Bring to the boil and boil rapidly for 10 minutes.

4 Skim off the scum that rises to the top, then reduce the heat and leave to simmer until the beans are soft inside. They should be tender but not falling apart. Check the water periodically to make sure there's enough to keep the beans well covered. Drain well. If using in a salad, leave to cool completely.

COOKING TIMES

These vary for dried beans. Older beans will take longer to cook, so use them within their best-before date.

Chickpeas	1–2 hours
Beans:	
red kidney,	
cannellini,	
borlotti,	
butter,	
flageolet beans	1–3 hours
Red lentils	20 minutes
Green lentils	30–40 minutes

TIMESAVER

If you don't have time to soak lentils, buy microwave sachets or canned lentils, which have already been soaked and cooked. Look for those with no added salt and sugar.

Sprouting beans

Mung beans, green or Puy lentils and alfalfa are all popular for home sprouting and are good in salads and stir-fries. You will only need about 3 tbsp beans to sprout at one time.

1 Pick through the beans to remove any grit or stones, then soak in cold water for at least 8 hours. Drain and place in a clean (preferably sterilised) jar. Cover the top with a dampened piece of cloth, secure and leave in a warm, dark place.

2 Rinse the sprouting beans twice a day. The sprouts can be eaten when there is about 1cm (½in) of growth, or they can be left to grow for a day or two longer. When they are sprouted, leave the jar on a sunny windowsill for about 3 hours – this will improve both their flavour and their nutrients. Then rinse and dry them well. They can be kept for about three days in the fridge. Always rinse the beans well before using them.

SMOKED HADDOCK KEDGEREE

Serves 4
Preparation 10 minutes
Cooking time 20 minutes
Techniques see also cooking rice (page 246), boiling eggs (page 55), chopping herbs (page 436)

175g (6oz) long-grain rice
450g (1lb) smoked haddock fillets
2 medium eggs, hard-boiled and shelled
75g (3oz) butter
salt and cayenne pepper
freshly chopped parsley to garnish
mixed leaf salad to serve

1 Cook the rice in a pan of fast-boiling salted water until tender. Drain well and rinse under cold water.
2 Meanwhile, put the haddock in a large frying pan with just enough water to cover. Bring to simmering point, then simmer for 10–15 minutes until tender. Drain, skin and flake the fish, discarding the bones.
3 Chop one egg and slice the other into rings. Melt the butter in a pan. Add the cooked rice, fish, chopped egg, salt and cayenne pepper, and stir over a medium heat for 5 minutes or until hot. Pile on to a warmed serving dish and garnish with parsley and the sliced egg. Serve with a mixed leaf salad.

NUTRITION PER SERVING
429 cals | 20g fat (11g sats) | 38g carbs | 3.1g salt

SPICED CHICKEN PILAU

Serves 4
Preparation 15 minutes
Cooking time 35 40 minutes
Techniques see also preparing vegetables (pages 182–194), preparing poultry (pages 114–117), toasting nuts (page 228)

2 tbsp olive oil
2 garlic cloves, crushed
2 onions, sliced
2 tbsp medium curry powder
6 skinless boneless raw chicken thighs, or 450g (1lb) skinless cooked chicken, cut into strips
350g (12oz) – or a measuring jug filled to 450ml (¾ pint) – American easy-cook rice
2 tsp salt
pinch of saffron
50g (2oz) sultanas
225g (8oz) ripe tomatoes, roughly chopped
50g (2oz) pinenuts, toasted

1 Heat the oil in a large heavy-based pan (a paella pan is ideal). Add the garlic and onions, then cook for 5 minutes to soften. Remove half the onions and put to one side.
2 Add the curry powder and cook for 1 minute, then add the chicken and stir. Cook for 10 minutes if the meat is raw, or for 4 minutes if you're using cooked chicken, stirring from time to time until browned.
3 Add the rice to the pan, stir to coat in the oil, then add 900ml (1½ pints) boiling water, the salt and saffron. Cover and bring to the boil, then reduce the heat to low and cook for 20 minutes or until the rice is tender and most of the liquid is absorbed.
4 Stir in the reserved onions and the sultanas, tomatoes and pinenuts. Cook for a further 5 minutes to warm through, then serve.

COOK'S TIP
The word pilau comes from the Persian pilaw. The dish originated in the east and consists of rice flavoured with spices and cooked in stock, to which vegetables, poultry and fish have been added.

NUTRITION PER SERVING
649 cals | 18g fat (2g sats) | 87g carbs | 2.8g salt

PRAWN AND LEMON RISOTTO

Serves 4
Preparation 15 minutes
Cooking time 40 minutes
Techniques see also preparing vegetables (pages 182–194), making stock (page 36), zesting citrus fruits (page 217)

225g (8oz) sugarsnap peas, sliced diagonally
175g (6oz) baby courgettes, sliced diagonally
2 tbsp olive oil
1 onion, finely chopped
¼ tsp saffron (optional)
225g (8oz) arborio (risotto) rice
1 garlic clove, crushed
225g (8oz) brown-cap mushrooms, quartered
zest and juice of 1 lemon
750ml (1¼ pints) hot fish, chicken or vegetable stock
300g (11oz) cooked peeled prawns
3 tbsp finely chopped chives
salt and ground black pepper
spring onion curls (see Cook's Tips) and grated lemon
    zest to garnish

1 Put the sugarsnap peas and courgettes in a large pan of boiling salted water, then bring to the boil. Cook for 1–2 minutes, then drain and plunge into ice-cold water.
2 Heat the oil in a medium non-stick pan, then add the onion and saffron, if using. Cook over a medium heat for 10 minutes or until soft. Add the rice, garlic and mushrooms, and cook, stirring, for 1–2 minutes. Season with salt and pepper.
3 Add the grated lemon zest and about one-third of the stock (see Cook's Tips). Simmer gently, stirring frequently, until most of the liquid has been absorbed. Add another one-third of the stock, then repeat the process.
4 Add the remaining stock. Cook, stirring, for 10 minutes or until the rice is tender and most of the stock has been absorbed. Add the prawns, drained vegetables, 1–2 tbsp lemon juice and the chives, then heat for 3–4 minutes. Garnish with spring onion curls and grated lemon zest.

COOK'S TIPS
- Adding the stock gradually gives the risotto its deliciously creamy texture.
- To make spring onion curls, thinly slice the onions lengthways, soak in ice-cold water for 30 minutes, then drain well.

NUTRITION PER SERVING
396 cals | 8g fat (1g sats) | 57g carbs | 0.6g salt

FRUITY RICE PUDDING

Serves 6
Preparation 10 minutes
Cooking time 1 hour, plus cooling and chilling
Techniques see also vanilla (page 428)

125g (4oz) pudding rice
1.1 litres (2 pints) full-fat milk
1 tsp vanilla extract
3–4 tbsp caster sugar
200ml (7fl oz) whipping cream
12 tbsp wild lingonberry sauce

1 Put the rice in a pan with 600ml (1 pint) cold water.
Bring to the boil, then reduce the heat and simmer until the
liquid has evaporated. Add the milk, bring back to the boil,
then reduce the heat and simmer for 45 minutes or until
the rice is very soft and creamy. Leave to cool.
2 Add the vanilla extract and sugar to the rice. Lightly
whip the cream and fold through the pudding. Chill in the
fridge for 1 hour.
3 Divide a third of the rice mixture among six glass
tumblers, top with a spoonful of lingonberry sauce and
repeat the process, finishing with a spoonful of lingonberry
sauce. Chill until ready to serve.

VARIATION
Although wild lingonberry sauce is recommended here, a
spoonful of any fruit sauce or compote such as strawberry
or blueberry will taste delicious.

NUTRITION PER SERVING
352 cals | 21g fat (13g sats) | 34g carbs | 0.2g salt

CHEESY POLENTA WITH TOMATO SAUCE

Serves 6
Preparation 15 minutes
Cooking time 45 minutes, plus cooling
Techniques see also making polenta (page 252), chopping herbs (page 436)

oil to grease
225g (8oz) polenta
4 tbsp freshly chopped herbs, such as oregano,
    chives and flat-leafed parsley
100g (3½oz) freshly grated Parmesan
salt and ground black pepper
fresh Parmesan shavings to serve

For the tomato and basil sauce
1 tbsp vegetable oil
3 garlic cloves, crushed
500g carton creamed tomatoes or passata
1 bay leaf
sprig of fresh thyme
caster sugar
3 tbsp freshly chopped basil, plus extra to garnish

1 Lightly oil a 25.5 × 17cm (10 × 6½in) dish. In a large
pan, bring 1.1 litres (2 pints) water and ¼ tsp salt to the
boil. Sprinkle in the polenta, whisking constantly. Reduce the
heat and simmer, stirring frequently, for 10–15 minutes until
the mixture leaves the sides of the pan.
2 Stir in the herbs and Parmesan, and season to taste
with salt and pepper. Turn into the prepared dish and leave
to cool.
3 Next, make the tomato and basil sauce. Heat the oil in a
pan and fry the garlic for 30 seconds (do not brown). Add
the creamed tomatoes or passata, the bay leaf, thyme and a
large pinch of sugar. Season with salt and pepper, bring to
the boil, reduce the heat and simmer, uncovered, for 5–10
minutes. Remove the bay leaf and thyme sprig, and add the
chopped basil.
4 To serve, cut the polenta into pieces and lightly brush
with oil. Preheat a griddle or grill and fry for 3–4 minutes
on each side, or grill under the grill for 7–8 minutes on
each side. Serve with the tomato and basil sauce, fresh
Parmesan shavings and chopped basil.

GET AHEAD
Complete to the end of step 3. Cover and chill separately
for up to two days.
To use Complete the recipe.

NUTRITION PER SERVING
246 cals | 9g fat (4g sats) | 30g carbs | 0.5g salt **V**

SUMMER COUSCOUS

Serves 4
Preparation 10 minutes
Cooking time about 20 minutes
Techniques see also preparing vegetables (pages 182–194), toasting nuts (page 228), chopping herbs (page 436)

175g (6oz) baby plum tomatoes, halved
2 small aubergines, thickly sliced
2 large yellow peppers, seeded and roughly chopped
2 red onions, cut into thin wedges
2 fat garlic cloves, crushed
5 tbsp olive oil
250g (9oz) couscous
400g can chopped tomatoes
2 tbsp harissa paste
25g (1oz) toasted pumpkin seeds (optional)
1 large bunch of coriander, roughly chopped
salt and ground black pepper
warm flatbreads and Greek yogurt
   to serve

1 Preheat the oven to 230°C (210°C fan oven) mark 8. Put the vegetables and garlic into a large roasting tin, drizzle over 3 tbsp oil and season with salt and pepper. Toss to coat. Roast for 20 minutes or until tender.
2 Meanwhile, put the couscous into a separate roasting tin and add 300ml (½ pint) cold water. Leave to soak for 5 minutes. Stir in the tomatoes and harissa, and drizzle with the remaining oil. Pop in the oven next to the vegetables for 4–5 minutes to warm through.
3 Stir the pumpkins seeds, if you like, and the coriander into the couscous and season. Add the vegetables, stir through and serve with warm flatbreads and a dollop of Greek yogurt.

NUTRITION PER SERVING
450 cals | 21g fat (3g sats) | 49g carbs | 0g salt

ROASTED TOMATO BULGUR SALAD

Serves 6
Preparation 15 minutes, plus soaking
Cooking time 15 minutes
Techniques see also chopping herbs (page 436)

175g (6oz) bulgur wheat
700g (1lb 9oz) cherry tomatoes or baby plum tomatoes
8 tbsp extra-virgin olive oil
a handful each of mint and basil, roughly chopped,
    plus basil sprigs to garnish
3–4 tbsp balsamic vinegar
1 bunch spring onions, sliced
salt and ground black pepper

1 Put the bulgur wheat in a bowl and add boiling water to cover by 1cm (½in). Leave to soak for 30 minutes.
2 Preheat the oven to 220°C (200°C fan oven) mark 7. Put the tomatoes in a small roasting tin, drizzle with half the oil and add half the mint. Season with salt and pepper, and roast for 10–15 minutes until beginning to soften.
3 Put the remaining oil and the vinegar into a large bowl. Add the warm pan juices from the roasted tomatoes and the soaked bulgur wheat.
4 Stir in the remaining chopped herbs and the sliced spring onions, and check the seasoning. (You may need a little more vinegar depending on the sweetness of the tomatoes.)
5 Carefully toss in the tomatoes and serve garnished with basil sprigs.

COOK'S TIP
Bulgur wheat is widely used in Middle Eastern cooking and has a light, nutty flavour and texture. It is available in several different sizes – from coarse to fine.

NUTRITION PER SERVING
265 cals | 16g fat (2g sats) | 29g carbs | 0g salt

SPICY BEAN AND TOMATO FAJITAS

Serves 6
Preparation 15 minutes
Cooking time 25 minutes
Techniques see also making stock (page 36), preparing avocados (page 190)

2 tbsp sunflower oil
1 onion, sliced
2 garlic cloves, crushed
½ tsp hot chilli powder
1 tsp ground coriander
1 tsp ground cumin
1 tbsp tomato purée
400g can chopped tomatoes
225g can red kidney beans, drained and rinsed
300g can borlotti beans, drained and rinsed
300g can flageolet beans, drained and rinsed
150ml (¼ pint) hot vegetable stock
2 ripe avocados, quartered and chopped
juice of ½ lime
1 tbsp freshly chopped coriander, plus extra sprigs
    to garnish
6 ready-made flour tortillas
150ml (¼ pint) soured cream
salt and ground black pepper
lime wedges to serve

1 Heat the oil in a large pan. Add the onion and cook gently for 5 minutes. Add the garlic and spices and cook for a further 2 minutes.
2 Add the tomato purée and cook for 1 minute, then add the tomatoes, beans and hot stock. Season well with salt and pepper, bring to the boil, reduce the heat and simmer for 15 minutes, stirring occasionally.
3 Put the avocado into a bowl, add the lime juice and the chopped coriander and mash together. Season to taste.
4 To warm the tortillas, either wrap them in foil and heat in the oven at 180°C (160°C fan oven) mark 4 for 10 minutes, or put on a plate and microwave on full power for 45 seconds.
5 Spoon the beans down the centre of each tortilla. Add a little avocado and soured cream, then fold the two sides in so that they overlap. Garnish with coriander sprigs and serve with lime wedges.

NUTRITION PER SERVING
508 cals | 20g fat (6g sats) | 71g carbs | 1.6g salt 🆅

SPECIAL FRIED RICE

Serves 4
Preparation 5 minutes
Cooking time 10–15 minutes
Techniques see also cooking rice (page 246), preparing cabbage (page 192)

2 x 250g packs of microwavable rice or 200g (7oz) long-grain rice, cooked, rinsed and drained
1 tbsp sesame oil
6 tbsp nasi goreng paste (see Cook's Tip)
200g (7oz) green cabbage, shredded
250g (9oz) cooked and peeled large prawns
2 tbsp light soy sauce
1 tbsp sunflower oil
2 medium eggs, beaten
2 spring onions, thinly sliced
1 lime, cut into wedges, to serve

1 Cook the rice according to the pack instructions.
2 Heat the sesame oil in a wok or large pan and fry the nasi goreng paste for 1–2 minutes. Add the cabbage and stir-fry for 2–3 minutes. Add the prawns and stir briefly, then add the rice and soy sauce and cook for a further 5 minutes, stirring occasionally.
3 Heat the sunflower oil in a non-stick frying pan, about 25.5cm (10in) in diameter, and add the eggs. Swirl around to cover the base of the pan in a thin layer and cook for 2–3 minutes until set.
4 Roll up the omelette and cut it into strips. Serve the rice scattered with strips of omelette and spring onions, and pass round the lime wedges to squeeze over it.

COOK'S TIP
Nasi goreng paste can be bought at large supermarkets and Asian food shops.

NUTRITION PER SERVING
412 cals | 18g fat (3g sats) | 46g carbs | 1.9g salt

SPICY PORK AND BEAN STEW

Serves 4
Preparation 15 minutes
Cooking time 50–55 minutes
Techniques see also preparing vegetables (pages 182–194), making stock (page 36)

3 tbsp olive oil
400g (14oz) pork escalopes, cubed
1 red onion, sliced
2 leeks, cut into chunks
2 celery sticks, cut into chunks
1 tbsp harissa paste
1 tbsp tomato purée
400g can cherry tomatoes
300ml (½ pint) hot vegetable or chicken stock
400g can cannellini beans, drained and rinsed
1 marinated red pepper, sliced
salt and ground black pepper
chopped flat-leafed parsley to garnish
Greek yogurt and lemon wedges to serve

1 Preheat the oven to 180°C (160°C fan oven) mark 4. Heat 2 tbsp oil in a flameproof casserole and fry the pork in batches until golden. Remove from the pan and put to one side.
2 Heat the remaining oil in the pan and fry the onion for 5–10 minutes until softened. Add the leeks and celery, and cook for about 5 minutes. Return the pork to the pan, and add the harissa and tomato purée. Cook for 1–2 minutes, stirring all the time. Add the tomatoes and stock. Season well with salt and pepper. Bring to the boil, then transfer to the oven. Cook for 25 minutes.
3 Add the drained beans and red pepper to the mixture and put back in the oven for 5 minutes to warm through. Garnish with parsley and serve with a dollop of Greek yogurt and lemon wedges for squeezing over.

COOK'S TIP
For a simple accompaniment, serve with chunks of crusty baguette or wholegrain bread.

NUTRITION PER SERVING
373 cals | 14g fat (3g sats) | 32g carbs | 1.2g salt

SMOKED SESAME TOFU

Serves 4
Preparation 20 minutes, plus marinating
Cooking time 12 minutes
Techniques see also preparing vegetables (page 182–194)

2 tbsp toasted sesame seeds
2 tbsp tamari (see Cook's Tips)
1 tsp light muscovado sugar
1 tsp rice wine vinegar
1 tbsp sesame oil
225g (8oz) smoked tofu, cubed (see Cook's Tips)
½ small white or green cabbage, shredded
2 carrots, peeled and cut into strips
200g (7oz) bean sprouts
4 roasted red peppers, roughly chopped
2 spring onions, shredded
brown rice to serve

1 Put the sesame seeds into a bowl, add the tamari, sugar, vinegar and ½ tbsp sesame oil. Mix together, then add the smoked tofu and stir to coat. Set aside to marinate for 10 minutes.
2 Heat a large wok or non-stick frying pan, add the marinated tofu, reserving the marinade and fry for 5 minutes until golden all over. Remove from the wok with a slotted spoon and put to one side.
3 Heat the remaining oil in the wok, add the cabbage and carrots and stir-fry for 5 minutes. Stir in the bean sprouts, peppers, spring onions, cooked tofu and reserved marinade and cook for a further 2 minutes. Serve with brown rice.

COOK'S TIPS
- Tamari is a wheat-free Japanese soy sauce. It is available in large supermarkets and Asian food shops.
- Tofu, also known as beancurd, is made from the 'milk' obtained from boiled, mashed soya beans. There are two main types: firm, which can be sliced or cut into cubes, and silken, which is softer and good for mashing or puréeing. Fresh tofu should be stored in the fridge and used within a few days.

NUTRITION PER SERVING
208 cals | 11g fat (2g sats) | 19g carbs | 1.4g salt

AUBERGINE AND LENTIL CURRY

Serves 4
Preparation 10 minutes
Cooking time 40–45 minutes
Techniques see also preparing vegetables (pages 182–194), making stock (page 36), chopping herbs (page 436)

3 tbsp olive oil
2 aubergines, cut into 2.5cm (1in) chunks
1 onion, chopped
2 tbsp mild curry paste
3 × 400g cans chopped tomatoes
200ml (7fl oz) hot vegetable stock
150g (5oz) red lentils
100g (3½oz) spinach leaves
25g (1oz) fresh coriander, roughly chopped
2 tbsp Greek 0 per cent fat yogurt

1 Heat 2 tbsp oil in a large pan and fry the aubergine chunks until golden. Remove from the pan and put to one side.
2 Heat the remaining oil and fry the onion for 8–10 minutes until soft. Add the curry paste and stir-fry for a further 2 minutes.
3 Add the tomatoes, stock, lentils and aubergine to the pan. Bring to the boil, then reduce the heat to a low simmer, half-cover with a lid and simmer for 25 minutes or according to the lentil pack instructions.
4 At the end of cooking, stir through the spinach, coriander and yogurt. Serve.

COOK'S TIP
When buying aubergines, choose those that are firm, shiny and blemish-free, with a bright green stem.

NUTRITION PER SERVING
335 cals | 15g fat (3g sats) | 39g carbs | 0.2g salt

MOROCCAN CHICKPEA STEW

Serves 4
Preparation 10 minutes
Cooking time 40 minutes
Techniques see also preparing vegetables (pages 182–194), making stock (page 36), chopping herbs (page 436)

1 red pepper, halved and seeded
1 green pepper, halved and seeded
1 yellow pepper, halved and seeded
2 tbsp olive oil
1 onion, finely sliced
2 garlic cloves, crushed
1 tbsp harissa paste
2 tbsp tomato purée
½ tsp ground cumin
1 aubergine, diced
400g can chickpeas, drained and rinsed
450ml (¾ pint) vegetable stock
4 tbsp roughly chopped fresh flat-leafed parsley,
    plus a few sprigs to garnish
salt and ground black pepper

1 Preheat the grill and lay the peppers, skin side up, on a baking sheet. Grill for around 5 minutes until the skin begins to blister and char. Put the peppers in a plastic bag, seal and put to one side for a few minutes. When cooled a little, peel off the skins and discard, then slice the peppers and put to one side.
2 Heat the oil in a large heavy-based frying pan over a low heat. Add the onion and cook for 5–10 minutes until soft. Add the garlic, harissa, tomato purée and cumin and cook for 2 minutes.
3 Add the peppers to the pan with the aubergine. Stir everything to coat evenly with the spices and cook for 2 minutes. Add the chickpeas and stock, season well with salt and pepper and bring to the boil. Reduce the heat and simmer for 20 minutes.
4 Just before serving, stir the parsley through the chickpea stew. Serve in warmed bowls, garnished with parsley sprigs.

NUTRITION PER SERVING
232 cals | 9g fat (1g sats) | 29g carbs | 3g salt

LEMON HUMMUS WITH BLACK OLIVES

Serves 4
Preparation 15 minutes
Techniques see also zesting citrus fruits (page 217)

2 × 400g cans chickpeas, drained and rinsed
1 garlic clove (use fresh garlic when possible,
    see Cook's Tip), crushed
grated zest and juice of 1 lemon
4 tbsp olive oil
25g (1oz) pitted black olives, roughly chopped
1 tsp paprika, plus a little extra to serve
sticks of raw vegetables and breadsticks to serve

1 Put the chickpeas and garlic into a food processor. Add the lemon zest and juice and process to combine. With the motor running, drizzle in the oil to make a thick paste. If the hummus is too thick, add 1–2 tbsp cold water and blend again.

2 Spoon into a bowl and stir in the olives and paprika. Serve with a sprinkling of extra paprika with raw vegetables and breadsticks for dipping.

COOK'S TIP
Fresh garlic has juicy, mild cloves and is available from May and throughout the summer. It is the best garlic to use for making pesto, salsa verde, garlic mayonnaise and chilled soups

NUTRITION PER SERVING
284 cals | 16g fat (2g sats) | 25g carbs | 1.2g salt

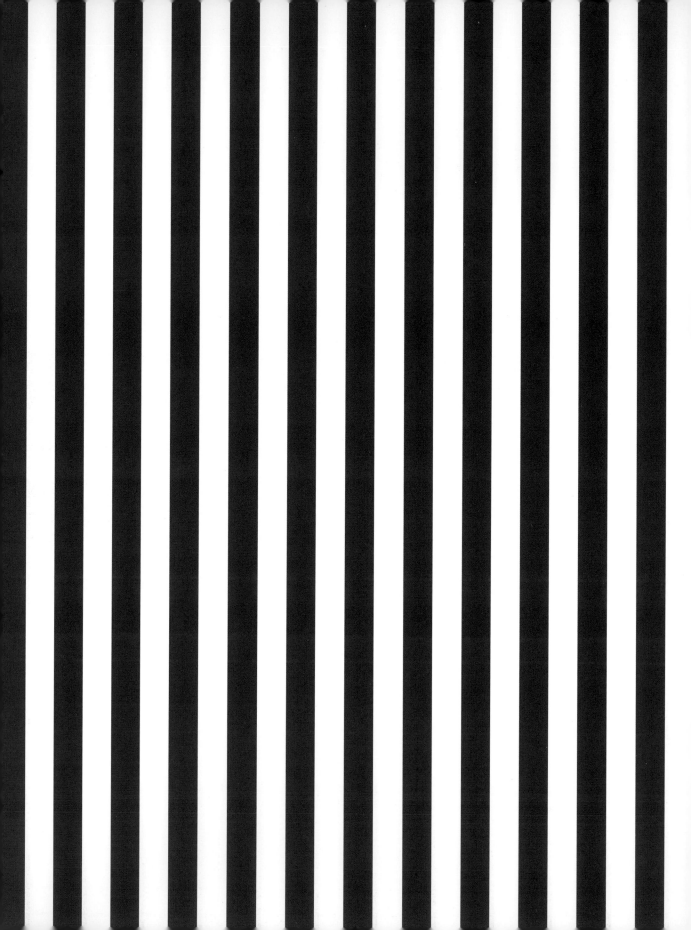

PASTA AND NOODLES

Providing plenty of energy and low in fat, Italian pasta and Asian noodles are easy to cook and a real stand-by in most people's kitchens. The easy-to-follow techniques in this chapter show you how to make your own fresh pasta – rolling, cutting, stuffing and shaping it – as well as then how to cook pasta and noodles. The recipe section is packed with delicious ideas from the simplest Fusilli with chilli and tomatoes, Penne with smoked salmon and Quick and easy carbonara to more complex dishes such as Mixed mushroom cannelloni, Classic lasagne, Chilli beef noodle salad and Salmon laksa curry.

MAKING FRESH PASTA

Although you can buy very good-quality fresh pasta, it's easy and fun to make at home. And although a pasta machine will make quick work of rolling and cutting, you can do it all by hand.

Making pasta by hand

To make pasta for 3–4 servings, you will need 300–400g (11–14oz) flour (see Cook's Tips), 4 medium eggs, beaten, 1 tbsp extra-virgin olive oil.

1 Sieve 300g (11oz) of the flour on to a clean worksurface. Make a well in the centre, then add the eggs and oil. Draw in the flour until the mixture resembles breadcrumbs.

2 When the flour and eggs are combined, knead the dough for 5–10 minutes until dry, smooth and elastic. Wrap in clingfilm and leave to rest for 1 hour.

3 Dust the dough and worksurface with flour and roll out until you can see the worksurface through it.

4 Hang the pasta over a rolling pin and leave to dry until it no longer feels damp, then cut (see opposite).

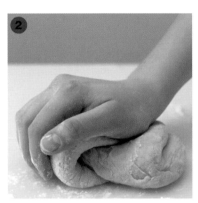

Using a pasta machine

1 Make the pasta dough as above and rest for 1 hour. Cut the dough into small pieces that will fit through the machine's rollers. Dust with flour. Set the rollers as wide apart as they will go, then feed the dough through. Repeat two or three times, folding the dough into three after each roll.

2 Narrow the rollers and repeat. Continue until the pasta is of the right thickness, then cut as required.

Cutting pasta with a knife

1 Lay the sheet of dough on a floured worksurface and dust lightly with flour. Lift one edge and fold it over, then keep folding to make a long, flat cigar-shape.

2 Cut the dough into strips of the required width. Unfold and leave them to dry on a clean teatowel for a few minutes before cooking.

Filling ravioli

1 Lay a sheet of dough over a ravioli tray and gently press into the indentations. Place teaspoonfuls of filling into the hollows. Be particularly careful not to overfill the ravioli as the filling may leak out during cooking.

2 Lay a second sheet of pasta on top of the first.

3 Using a circular cutter, cut a row between the lumps of filling in one direction, then cut in the other direction to make squares. Press the edges to seal the dough.

4 Separate the ravioli, dust very lightly with flour, and cover with a clean teatowel until needed. This will help prevent the ravioli drying out while you are preparing more of them.

Making shaped pasta

1 Roll out just one sheet of dough at a time. If you roll out more than one sheet at a time, the others might start drying out while you are cutting and filling the first.

2 Trim one edge to make a straight line, then cut a strip from the straight edge to the width of the pasta you want to make. Cut into pieces no bigger than 5cm (2in) square.

3 Place a teaspoonful of filling at the centre of one square, then fold over to make a triangle. Do not overfill.

4 Fold the topmost corner of the triangle down, then fold the other two edges over to leave a hollow space in the middle of the pasta. Press the two folded corners together firmly. Repeat with the remaining pasta and filling.

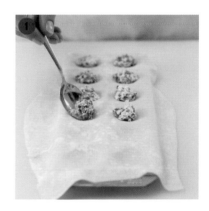

COOKING PASTA

This simple task has attracted a number of mistaken ideas, such as adding oil to the water, rinsing the pasta after cooking and adding salt only at a certain point. The basics couldn't be simpler.

Cooking dried pasta

1 Heat the water with about 1 tsp salt per 100g (3½oz) of pasta. Cover the pan to speed up boiling.

2 When the water has reached a rolling boil, put in all the pasta.

3 Stir well for 30 seconds, to keep the pasta from sticking either to itself or the pan. Once boiling, set the timer for 2 minutes less than the recommended cooking time on the pack and cook uncovered.

4 Check the pasta when the timer goes off, then every 60 seconds until it is cooked al dente: tender with a little bite at the centre. Scoop out a cup of cooking water (it may be useful for loosening up a thick sauce).

5 Drain the pasta well in a colander. Transfer to a serving bowl, and toss immediately with your chosen sauce.

> ### PERFECT PASTA
> - Use about 1 litre (1¾ pints) of water per 100g (3½oz) of pasta.
> - Rinse the pasta only if you are going to cool it for serving as salad, then dry well and toss with oil.
> - If a recipe calls for cooking the pasta with the sauce after it has boiled, undercook the pasta slightly when boiling it.

Cooking fresh pasta

Fresh pasta is cooked in the same way as dried, but for a shorter time.

1 Bring the water to the boil.

2 Add the pasta to the boiling water all at once and stir well. Set the timer for 2 minutes and keep testing every 30 seconds until the pasta is cooked al dente: tender but with a little bite in the centre.

> ### FILLED PASTA
> This is the only type of pasta that needs oil in the cooking water – the oil reduces friction, which could tear the wrappers and allow the filling to come out. Use 1 tbsp for a large pan of water.

COOKING ASIAN-STYLE NOODLES

Asian wheat or egg noodles are similar to pasta in both what they are made of and how they are cooked, while rice and cellophane noodles require different preparation.

Wheat noodles

These are the sturdiest and most versatile of Asian noodles and are particularly good for stir-fries.

1 Bring a pan of water to the boil and put the noodles in.

2 Agitate the noodles using chopsticks or a fork to separate them (this is especially important if they're dried noodles in a block). This can take a minute or even more.

3 Continue boiling until the noodles are cooked al dente: tender but with a little bite in the centre.

4 Drain well and then rinse in cold water and toss with a little oil if you are not using them immediately.

PERFECT NOODLES

- If you plan to re-cook the noodles after the initial boiling or soaking – for example, in a stir-fry – it's best to undercook them slightly.
- When cooking noodles sold as a block or nest, use a pair of forks or chopsticks to untangle the strands from the moment they go into the water.

Rice noodles

There are different ways of preparing these no-cook noodles, some calling for warm-water soaking and others for hot-water soaking. In both cases, the procedure is the same.

1 Cover the noodles with water and soak until they are al dente: tender but with a little bite in the centre. Drain well and toss with a little oil if you are not using them immediately.

QUANTITIES

- Use 50–75g (2–3oz) uncooked noodles per person.
- Dried egg noodles are often packed in layers. As a general rule, allow one layer per person for a main dish.

FUSILLI WITH CHILLI AND TOMATOES

Serves 4
Preparation 10 minutes
Cooking time 15 minutes
Techniques see also cooking pasta (page 272), preparing chillies (page 189), crushing garlic (page 183), chopping herbs (page 436)

350g (12oz) fusilli or other short pasta
4 tbsp olive oil
1 large red chilli, seeded and finely chopped
1 garlic clove, crushed
500g (1lb 2oz) cherry tomatoes
2 tbsp freshly chopped basil
50g (2oz) Parmesan shavings
salt and ground black pepper

1 Cook the pasta in a large pan of boiling salted water according to the pack instructions. Drain.
2 Meanwhile, heat the oil in a large frying pan. Add the chilli and garlic and cook for 30 seconds. Add the tomatoes, season and cook over a high heat for 3 minutes or until the skins begin to split.
3 Add the chopped basil and drained pasta and toss together. Sprinkle the Parmesan shavings over and serve.

COOK'S TIP
The easiest way to make Parmesan shavings is by using a vegetable peeler. Hold the piece of cheese in one hand and pare off wafer-thin strips of cheese using the peeler.

NUTRITION PER SERVING
479 cals | 17g fat (4g sats) | 69g carbs | 0.4g salt

SPAGHETTI BOLOGNESE

Serves 6
Preparation 15 minutes
Cooking time 40 minutes
Techniques see also cooking pasta (page 272), preparing chillies (page 189), preparing vegetables (pages 182–194), mincing meat (page 147)

500g (1lb 2oz) dried spaghetti
50g (2oz) freshly grated Parmesan

For the Bolognese sauce
2 tbsp olive oil
1 onion, finely chopped
2 garlic cloves, crushed
450g (1lb) extra-lean minced beef
2 tbsp sun-dried tomato paste
300ml (½ pint) red wine
400g can chopped tomatoes
125g (4oz) chestnut mushrooms, sliced
2 tbsp Worcestershire sauce
salt and ground black pepper

1 To make the Bolognese sauce, heat the olive oil in a large pan. Add the onion and fry over a medium heat for 10 minutes or until softened and golden. Add the garlic and cook for 1 minute.
2 Add the minced beef and brown evenly, using a wooden spoon to break up the pieces. Stir in the tomato paste and the red wine, cover and bring to the boil. Add the tomatoes, mushrooms and Worcestershire sauce, and season well with salt and pepper. Bring back to the boil, reduce the heat and simmer for 20 minutes.
3 Cook the spaghetti in a large pan of boiling salted water according to the pack instructions until al dente. Drain the pasta well, then return to the pan. Add the Bolognese sauce and toss to mix together. Check the seasoning.
4 Divide among warmed plates and sprinkle with the Parmesan to serve.

TRY SOMETHING DIFFERENT
Add 125g (4oz) chopped rinded smoked streaky bacon with the mince, brown, then stir in 200g (7oz) chopped chicken livers. Cook for 3 minutes before adding the tomato paste, then continue as above.

NUTRITION PER SERVING
510 cals | 12g fat (4g sats) | 67g carbs | 1.5g salt

PENNE WITH SMOKED SALMON

Serves 4
Preparation 5 minutes
Cooking time 12–15 minutes
Techniques see also cooking pasta (page 272), chopping herbs (page 436)

350g (12oz) penne
200ml carton half-fat crème fraîche
140g pack smoked salmon, roughly chopped
20g pack dill, finely chopped
salt and ground black pepper
lemon wedges to serve (optional)

1 Bring a large pan of water to the boil. Add the pasta, bring back to the boil and cook for 12 minutes or according to the instructions on the pack.
2 Meanwhile, put the crème fraîche into a large bowl. Add the smoked salmon and dill. Season well and mix together. Gently stir through the drained penne and serve immediately with lemon wedges, if you like, to squeeze over.

NUTRITION PER SERVING
432 cals | 11g fat (6g sats) | 67g carbs | 1.7g salt

QUICK AND EASY CARBONARA

Serves 4
Preparation 5 minutes
Cooking time 10 minutes
Techniques see also cooking pasta (page 272), separating eggs (page 54), chopping herbs (page 436)

350g (12oz) tagliatelle
150g (5oz) smoked bacon, chopped
1 tbsp olive oil
2 large egg yolks
140ml (4½fl oz) double cream
50g (2oz) freshly grated Parmesan
2 tbsp chopped parsley

1 Bring a large pan of water to the boil. Add the pasta, bring back to the boil and cook for 4 minutes or according to the instructions on the pack.
2 Meanwhile, fry the bacon in the oil for 4–5 minutes. Add to the drained pasta and keep hot.
3 Put the egg yolks in a bowl and add the cream. Whisk together. Add to the pasta with the Parmesan and parsley. Toss well.

NUTRITION PER SERVING
671 cals | 37g fat (18g sats) | 66g carbs | 1.8g salt

CHILLI BOLOGNESE

Serves 4
Preparation 15 minutes
Cooking time 26–38 minutes
Techniques see also preparing vegetables (pages 182–194), mincing meat (page 147), cooking pasta (page 272), chopping herbs (page 436)

1 tbsp olive oil
1 large onion, finely chopped
½ large red chilli, seeded and thinly sliced
450g (1lb) minced beef or lamb
125g (4oz) smoked bacon lardons
3 roasted red peppers, drained and finely chopped
400g can chopped tomatoes
125ml (4fl oz) red wine
300g (11oz) spaghetti
25g (1oz) freshly grated Cheddar or Gruyère cheese
2 tbsp freshly chopped flat-leafed parsley (optional)
salt and ground black pepper

1 Heat the oil in a large pan over a medium heat. Add the onion and chilli and fry for 5–10 minutes until soft and golden. Add the beef or lamb and lardons and stir over the heat for 5–7 minutes until well browned.
2 Stir in the red pepper, tomatoes and wine. Season, bring to the boil, then reduce the heat and simmer over a low heat for 15–20 minutes.
3 Meanwhile, cook the spaghetti according to the pack instructions, then drain.
4 Just before serving, stir the grated cheese, parsley, if using, and the sauce into the spaghetti.

NUTRITION PER SERVING
761 cals | 33g fat (13g sats) | 74g carbs | 1.4g salt

CLASSIC LASAGNE

Serves 6
Preparation 45 minutes
Cooking time about 1 hour
Techniques see also preparing vegetables (pages 182–194)

butter to grease
350g (12oz) fresh lasagne, or 225g (8oz) 'no need to
    pre-cook' dried lasagne (12–15 sheets – if using
    'no need to pre-cook' dried lasagne, add a little extra
    stock or water to the sauce)
3 tbsp freshly grated Parmesan

For the Bolognese sauce
2 tbsp olive oil
1 onion, finely chopped
2 garlic cloves, crushed
450g (1lb) extra-lean minced beef
2 tbsp sun-dried tomato paste
300ml (½ pint) red wine
400g can chopped tomatoes
125g (4oz) chestnut mushrooms, sliced
2 tbsp Worcestershire sauce
salt and ground black pepper

For the béchamel sauce
300ml (½ pint) semi-skimmed milk
1 onion slice
6 peppercorns
1 each mace blade and bay leaf
15g (½oz) butter
15g (½oz) plain flour
freshly grated nutmeg
salt and ground black pepper

1 To make the Bolognese sauce, heat the oil and fry the onion for 10 minutes until softened. Add the garlic and cook for 1 minute. Add the beef and brown evenly. Stir in the tomato paste and wine, cover and bring to the boil. Add the tomatoes, mushrooms and Worcestershire sauce. Season well. Bring back to the boil, then reduce the heat and simmer for 20 minutes.
2 To make the béchamel sauce, pour the milk into a pan. Add the onion, peppercorns, mace and bay leaf. Bring almost to the boil, then remove from the heat, cover and leave for 20 minutes. Strain. Melt the butter in a pan, stir in the flour and cook, stirring, for 1 minute until cooked but not coloured. Remove from the heat and gradually pour in the milk, whisking constantly. Season with nutmeg, salt and pepper. Return to the heat and cook, stirring, until the sauce is thickened and smooth. Simmer gently for 2 minutes.

3 Preheat the oven to 180°C (160°C fan oven) mark 4. Spoon one-third of the Bolognese sauce over the base of a greased 2.3 litre (4 pint) ovenproof dish. Cover with a layer of lasagne sheets, then a layer of béchamel. Repeat these layers twice more, finishing with a layer of béchamel. Sprinkle the Parmesan over the top and stand the dish on a baking sheet. Cook for 45 minutes or until well browned and bubbling.

NUTRITION PER SERVING
326 cals | 13g fat (6g sats) | 37g carbs | 0.5g salt

MACARONI CHEESE

Serves 4
Preparation 10 minutes
Cooking time 15 minutes
Techniques see also making breadcrumbs (page 318)

225g (8oz) short-cut macaroni
50g (2oz) butter
50g (2oz) plain flour
900ml (1½ pints) milk
½ tsp grated nutmeg or mustard powder
225g (8oz) mature Cheddar cheese, grated
3 tbsp fresh white or wholemeal breadcrumbs
salt and ground black pepper

1 Cook the macaroni in a large pan of salted boiling water, according to the pack instructions, until al dente.
2 Meanwhile, melt the butter in a pan, stir in the flour and cook, stirring, for 1 minute. Remove from the heat and gradually stir in the milk. Bring to the boil and cook, stirring, until the sauce thickens. Remove from the heat. Season with salt and pepper, and add the nutmeg or mustard.
3 Drain the macaroni and add to the sauce, together with three-quarters of the cheese. Mix well, then turn into an ovenproof dish.
4 Preheat the grill to high. Sprinkle the breadcrumbs and remaining cheese over the macaroni. Put under the grill for 2–3 minutes until golden brown on top and bubbling. Serve immediately.

NUTRITION PER SERVING
680 cals | 34g fat (21g sats) | 67g carbs | 2g salt Ⓥ

THAI CHICKEN AND NOODLE SOUP

Serves 4

Preparation Time 20 minutes

Cooking Time about 30 minutes

Techniques see also preparing fresh ginger and galangal (page 437), making stock (page 36), preparing vegetables (pages 182–194), making coconut milk (page 231) peeling prawns (page 87)

vegetable oil to shallow- or deep-fry
225g (8oz) firm tofu, patted dry and cut into 1cm (½in) cubes
2.5cm (1in) piece fresh root ginger, peeled and finely chopped
2.5cm (1in) piece fresh or dried galangal, peeled and thinly sliced (optional, see Cook's Tip)
1–2 garlic cloves, crushed
2 lemongrass stalks, halved lengthways and bruised
1 tsp chilli powder
½ tsp ground turmeric
275g (10oz) cooked chicken, skinned and cut into bite-size pieces
175g (6oz) cauliflower, broken into small florets and any thick stems thinly sliced
1 large carrot, cut into matchsticks
600ml (1 pint) coconut milk
600ml (1 pint) chicken or vegetable stock, or water
a few green beans, trimmed and halved
125g (4oz) fine or medium egg noodles
125g (4oz) peeled prawns (optional)
3 spring onions, thinly sliced
75g (3oz) beansprouts
2 tbsp soy sauce

1 Heat the oil in a wok or deep-fryer to 180°C (test by frying a small cube of bread; it should brown in 40 seconds). Fry the tofu, in batches, for about 1 minute or until golden brown all over. Drain on kitchen paper.

2 Heat 2 tbsp oil in a large pan. Add the ginger, galangal, if using, garlic, lemongrass, chilli powder, turmeric and chicken. Cook, stirring for 2 minutes.

3 Add the cauliflower, carrot, coconut milk and stock or water. Bring to the boil, stirring all the time. Reduce the heat and simmer for 10 minutes. Add the beans and simmer for 5 minutes.

4 Meanwhile, bring a large pan of water to the boil and cook the noodles for about 4 minutes or according to the pack instructions. Drain the noodles and add them to the soup with the prawns, if using, the tofu, spring onions, beansprouts and soy sauce. Simmer gently for 5 minutes or until heated through. Serve immediately.

COOK'S TIP
Dried galangal, similar in flavour to fresh root ginger, needs to be soaked for 30 minutes before using. It's used chopped or grated in many Thai, Indonesian and Malay dishes.

NUTRITION PER SERVING
384 cals | 15g fat (3g sats) | 36g carbs | 2g salt

CHILLI BEEF NOODLE SALAD

Serves 4

Preparation 15 minutes, plus soaking

Techniques see also preparing rice noodles (page 273), preparing chillies (page 189), crushing garlic (page 183), preparing fresh gingers (page 437)

150g (5oz) dried rice noodles
juice of 1 lime
1 lemongrass stalk, outside leaves discarded, finely chopped
1 red chilli, seeded and chopped
2 tsp finely chopped fresh root ginger
2 tsp caster sugar
2 garlic cloves, crushed
1 tbsp Thai fish sauce
3 tbsp extra-virgin olive oil
50g (2oz) rocket (wild if possible)
125g (4oz) sliced cold roast beef
125g (4oz) sunblush tomatoes, chopped (these are partly
    dried and not as dehydrated as sun-dried)
salt and ground black pepper

1 Put the noodles in a large bowl and pour boiling water over to cover. Put to one side for 15 minutes.
2 Meanwhile, in a small bowl, whisk together the lime juice, lemongrass, chilli, ginger, sugar, garlic, fish sauce and oil. Season.
3 While they are still warm, drain the noodles well, put in a large bowl and toss with the dressing. Leave to cool.
4 Just before serving, toss the rocket leaves, sliced beef and chopped tomatoes through the noodles.

NUTRITION PER SERVING
290 cals | 12g fat (2g sats) | 36g carbs | 0.8 salt

SALMON LAKSA CURRY

Serves 4
Preparation 15 minutes
Cooking time 22 minutes
Techniques see also preparing onions (page 182), making coconut milk (page 231), making stock (page 36), preparing rice noodles (page 273), chopping herbs (page 436)

1 tbsp olive oil
1 onion, finely sliced
3 tbsp laksa paste
200ml (7fl oz) coconut milk
900ml (1½ pints) hot vegetable stock
200g (7oz) baby corn, halved lengthways
600g (1lb 5oz) piece skinless salmon fillet,
    cut into 1cm (½in) slices
225g pack baby leaf spinach, washed
250g pack medium rice noodles
salt and ground black pepper

To garnish
2 spring onions, sliced diagonally
2 tbsp freshly chopped coriander
2 limes, cut into halves

1 Heat the oil in a large pan. Add the onion and fry over a medium heat for 10 minutes, stirring, until golden. Add the laksa paste and cook for 2 minutes.
2 Add the coconut milk, stock and baby corn and season. Bring to the boil, reduce the heat and simmer for 5 minutes.
3 Add the salmon slices and spinach, stirring to immerse them in the liquid. Cook for 4 minutes or until the fish is opaque to the centre.
4 Meanwhile, put the noodles in a large bowl, pour boiling water over and soak for 30 seconds. Drain, then stir into the curry. Pour into bowls and garnish with the onions, coriander and lime. Serve immediately.

NUTRITION PER SERVING
607 cals | 24g fat (4g sats) | 59g carbs | 2.6g salt

THAI NOODLES WITH PRAWNS

Serves 4

Preparation time 10 minutes

Cooking time 5 minutes

Techniques see also preparing wheat noodles (page 273), preparing onions (page 182), preparing chillies (page 189), making coconut milk (page 231), preparing prawns (page 87), chopping herbs (page 436)

4–6 tsp Thai red curry paste
175g (6oz) medium egg noodles (wholewheat if possible)
2 small red onions, chopped
1 lemongrass stalk, trimmed and sliced
1 Thai red chilli, seeded and finely chopped
300ml sachet low-fat coconut milk
400g (14oz) raw tiger prawns, peeled
4 tbsp freshly chopped coriander
salt and ground black pepper
torn coriander to garnish

1 Put 2 litres (3½ pints) boiling water into a large pan, add the curry paste, noodles, onions, lemongrass, chilli and coconut milk. Bring to the boil, then add the prawns and chopped coriander. Reduce the heat and simmer for 2–3 minutes until the prawns turn pink. Season to taste.
2 Serve in large bowls sprinkled with the torn coriander.

COOK'S TIP
Don't overcook this dish, or the noodles will taste soggy and the prawns will be tough.

NUTRITION PER SERVING
343 cals | 11g fat (2g sats) | 40g carbs | 1g salt

PORK AND NOODLE STIR-FRY

Serves 4

Preparation 10 minutes

Cooking time 7–8 minutes

Techniques see also preparing fresh ginger (page 437), preparing vegetables (pages 182–194), sprouting beans (page 253), preparing rice noodles (page 273)

1 tbsp sesame oil
5cm (2in) piece fresh root ginger, peeled and grated
2 tbsp soy sauce
1 tbsp fish sauce
½ red chilli, finely chopped
450g (1lb) stir-fry pork strips
2 red peppers, halved, seeded and roughly chopped
250g (9oz) baby corn, halved lengthways
200g (7oz) sugarsnap peas, halved
300g (11oz) beansprouts
250g pack rice noodles

1 Put the oil into a large bowl. Add the ginger, soy sauce, fish sauce, chilli and pork strips. Mix well and leave to marinate for 10 minutes.

2 Heat a large wok until hot. Lift the pork out of the marinade with a slotted spoon and add to the pan. Stir-fry over a high heat for 5 minutes. Add the red peppers, corn, sugarsnap peas, beansprouts and remaining marinade and stir-fry for a further 2–3 minutes until the pork is cooked.

3 Meanwhile, bring a large pan of water to the boil and cook the noodles according to the pack instructions.

4 Drain the noodles, tip into the wok and toss together, then serve immediately.

NUTRITION PER SERVING
509 cals | 9g fat (2g sats) | 69g carbs | 3.4g salt

PASTRY

Crisp pastries, tempting pies and luscious tarts are some of the most
enticing treats to come out of the home kitchen. The easy-to-follow
techniques section in this chapter provides an invaluable guide to making
all the basic types of pastry, lining tart and pie tins, baking blind, and
topping, sealing and finishing pies. There are also essential cook's tips, plus
advice on making and using choux and filo pastries. The recipe section
utilises these basic skills in a collection of fabulous sweet and savoury
pies and tarts including Steak and kidney pie, Salmon and asparagus pie,
Goat's cheese parcels, Almond Bakewell tarts, Cinnamon custard tart,
Sausage rolls and Easy pear and toffee tarte tatin.

MAKING PASTRY

Shortcrust, sweet pastry, puff and flaky pastry are the four most frequently used pastries and are delicious when home made. Shortcrust is the most simple and quick to prepare.

Shortcrust pastry
Used for tarts and pies.

To make 125g (4oz) pastry, you will need 125g (4oz) plain flour, pinch of salt, 50g (2oz) unsalted butter, cut into small pieces, 1 medium egg yolk.

1 Sift the flour and salt into a bowl and add the butter. Using the fingertips or a pastry cutter, rub or cut the butter into the flour until the mixture resembles fine breadcrumbs.

2 Using a fork, mix in the egg yolk and 1½ tsp water until the mixture holds together; add a little more water if necessary. Knead lightly to form a firm dough.

3 Gather the dough in your hands and lightly knead.

4 Form the pastry into a ball, wrap tightly in clingfilm and chill for at least 1 hour before using. (This allows the pastry to 'relax' and prevents shrinkage when it is baked.)

Sweet shortcrust pastry

Used for sweet tarts and pies.

To make 125g (4oz) pastry, you will need 125g (4oz) plain flour, pinch of salt, 50g (2oz) unsalted butter, cut into pieces, 2 medium egg yolks, 50g (2oz) caster sugar.

1 Make as for shortcrust pastry above, adding the sugar with the egg yolks at step 2.

Using a food processor

1 You can make shortcrust or sweet shortcrust using a food processor. Put the dry ingredients into the food processor and pulse quickly to mix. Cut the butter into small pieces and add. Process until the mixture resembles breadcrumbs – do not over-process.

2 Add the egg yolk(s) and a little water if necessary, and pulse until the mixture just comes together. Continue as step 4 for shortcrust.

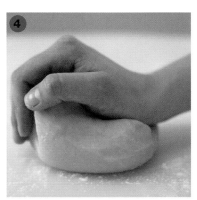

Puff pastry

If you can, make this a day ahead.

To make 450g (1lb) pastry, you will need 450g (1lb) strong white bread flour, pinch of salt, 450g (1lb) butter, chilled, 1 tbsp lemon juice.

1 Sift the flour and salt into a bowl. Dice 50g (2oz) butter. Flatten the rest into a 2cm (¾in) thick slab. Rub the diced butter into the flour. Using a knife, stir in the lemon juice and about 300ml (½ pint) cold water to make a soft elastic dough. Knead on a lightly floured surface until smooth. Cut a cross through half the depth.

2 Open out the 'flaps'. Roll out the dough, keeping the centre four times as thick as the flaps.

3 Put the slab of butter in the centre and fold the flaps over it. Gently roll out to make a rectangle measuring 40.5 × 20.5cm (16 × 8in).

4 Mark off three equal sections from top to bottom. Fold the bottom third of the pastry up over the middle and the top third down. Wrap in clingfilm and chill for 30 minutes (or freeze for 5–10 minutes).

5 Repeat the rolling, folding, resting and turning four more times, ensuring the folded edges are to the sides each time. Chill for at least 30 minutes before baking.

Rough puff pastry

Rough puff doesn't rise as much as puff pastry but is quicker to make. To make 225g (8oz), you will need 225g (8oz) plain flour, pinch of salt, 175g (6oz) butter, 1 tsp lemon juice.

1 Sift the flour and salt into a bowl. Cut the butter into 2cm (¾in) cubes and add to the flour. Mix lightly to coat the butter with flour. Using a knife, stir in the lemon juice and 100ml (3½fl oz) water to make a soft elastic dough.

2 Turn out the dough on to a lightly floured worksurface and knead until smooth. Roll out to a rectangle 30.5 × 10cm (12 × 4in). Mark off three equal sections from top to bottom. Fold the bottom third over the middle and the top third down. Press the edges with a rolling pin to seal. Wrap in clingfilm and chill for 30 minutes (or freeze for 5–10 minutes).

3 Repeat the rolling, folding, resting and turning five more times, ensuring the folded edges are to the sides. Chill for 30 minutes before baking.

QUANTITIES

Tart tins vary in depth, which affects the quantity of pastry needed. The following quantities are approximate.

Tart tin size	Pastry
18cm (7in)	125g (4oz)
20cm (8in)	175g (6oz)
23cm (9in)	200g (7oz)
25cm (10in)	225g (8oz)

USING PASTRY

A light touch and a little care with rolling and lifting your prepared dough will ensure your pastry case or pie crust is crisp and perfect. It's worth taking your time for the best results.

Lining tart and pie tins

1 Working carefully, roll out the chilled dough on a floured worksurface to make a sheet at least 5cm (2in) larger than the tart tin or pie dish. Roll the dough on to the rolling pin, then unroll it on to the tin, covering it completely with an even overhang all round. Don't stretch the dough.

2 Lift the hanging dough with one hand while you press it gently but firmly into the base and sides of the tin. Don't stretch the dough while you're pressing it down.

3 For a tart case, roll the rolling pin over the tin and remove the excess dough for later use. For a pie dish ensure the pastry covers the lip of the dish.

4 Push the dough into and up the sides of the tin or dish, so that the dough rises a little over the edge.

Baking blind

Cooking the pastry before filling gives a crisp result.

1 Preheat the oven according to the recipe. Prick the pastry base with a fork. Cover with foil or greaseproof paper 8cm (3¼in) larger than the tin.

2 Spread baking beans on top. Bake for 15 minutes. Remove the foil or paper and beans and bake for 5–10 minutes until light golden.

Topping

Covered pies need a lid of equal thickness to the base.

1 Roll out the pastry on a floured worksurface to about 2.5cm (1in) larger than the baking tin or dish. Roll on to the rolling pin, then unroll over the pie with an even overhang.

2 Using a small knife, cut off the overhang just outside the rim.

Sealing

1 Using your thumb and index finger, pinch the base and top of the pastry dough all the way round the rim. You don't need to squeeze hard, just firmly enough to stick them together. If the pie has no base, just press the top down on the rim of the tin or dish.

2 Use a fork to make decorative fluting marks on the rim.

Finishing

1 If you want to make decorations for the pie using leftover pastry, cut them out using pastry cutters and put them in place, using a little water to stick them to the pastry.

2 Brush the top of the pastry with beaten egg if you wish. Cut two slits in the top of the pie using a small, sharp knife to let the steam escape during baking.

USING CHOUX

This soft pastry is usually spooned or piped and is excellent for making cream-filled buns, profiteroles and savouries. It contains a lot of water so it puffs up beautifully and is wonderfully light and airy.

Choux buns

To make eight choux buns, you will need 65g (2½oz) plain flour, 50g (2oz) butter, cubed, 150ml (¼ pint) sparkling water, 1 tbsp golden caster sugar, 2 medium eggs, beaten.

1 Sift the flour on to a sheet of greaseproof paper. Melt the butter, water and sugar in a heavy-based pan and bring to the boil. Turn off the heat and tip in the flour all at once.

2 Beat thoroughly with a wooden spoon until the mixture forms a smooth ball in the centre of the pan. Turn the ball out into a bowl and leave to cool for 15 minutes. Preheat the oven to 220°C (200°C fan oven) mark 7.

3 Gradually beat in the eggs, adding a little at a time, and whisk until the mixture is shiny.

4 Sprinkle water on to a non-stick baking sheet and put the mixture on it in eight large spoonfuls. Make sure they aren't too close together. Bake for 30 minutes until the buns are risen and golden brown. Turn off the oven.

5 Pierce a small hole in each bun so that air can escape, then return the sheet to the oven for 15 minutes. Cool on a wire rack.

PERFECT CHOUX

- Before you start, have all the ingredients carefully measured and in place.
- Tip in all the flour at once, then leave the mixture to cool before beating in the eggs gradually.
- Use a dampened baking sheet (the steam will help the pastry to rise), and don't open the oven door for the first 20 minutes of baking, as the cold air will make the pastry sink.

CRÈME PÂTISSIÈRE

Pour 300ml (½ pint) milk into a pan. Slowly bring to the boil, take off the heat and leave for 10 minutes. Whisk 3 egg yolks with 50g (2oz) golden caster sugar until thick. Whisk in 2 tbsp plain flour and 2 tbsp cornflour until smooth. Whisk in the milk. Strain back into the pan. Slowly bring to the boil, whisking constantly. Cook, stirring, for 2–3 minutes until thickened and smooth. Pour into a bowl and stir in 1 tsp vanilla extract. Cover with wet greaseproof paper. Leave to cool. Makes 450ml (¾ pint).

USING FILO

Making filo pastry is time-consuming, but ready-made filo is an excellent alternative. The delicate sheets of pastry are usually brushed with butter, then layered and filled to create crisp, golden treats.

Baklava

To serve six to eight, you will need 175g (6oz) shelled unsalted pistachio nuts, 125g (4oz) pinenuts, 1 tsp ground cinnamon, ½ tsp ground cloves, pinch of freshly grated nutmeg, 2 tbsp caster sugar, 225g (8oz) filo pastry, 75g (3oz) unsalted butter, melted. For the syrup: 2 cardamom pods, bruised, grated zest and juice of ½ lemon, 225g (8oz) clear honey, 2 tbsp rosewater (optional).

1 Whiz the nuts and spices in a food processor until coarsely ground. Add the sugar. Preheat the oven to 170°C (150°C fan oven) mark 3.

2 Grease an 18 × 25.5cm (7 × 10in) baking tin. Brush a sheet of filo with butter and press it into the tin.

3 Repeat with half the filo sheets.

4 Scatter the nut mixture on top of the pastry sheets, then top with more buttered filo until all is used.

5 Cut the pastry in a diamond pattern, cutting down to the base of the tin. Drizzle over any remaining butter. Bake for 30 minutes. Increase the heat to 220°C (200°C fan oven) mark 7 and bake for 15 minutes until the top is crisp and golden.

6 Meanwhile, put the cardamom, lemon and honey in a pan and add 150ml (¼ pint) water. Bring to the boil, the reduce the heat and simmer for 5 minutes. Strain and stir in the rosewater, if using. Drizzle with half the syrup. Leave to cool, cut into diamonds and drizzle over the rest.

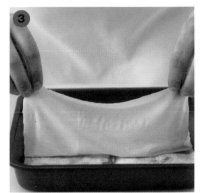

COOK'S TIPS

- Filo pastry is often sold frozen; if you plan to put it into the freezer at home, get it home quickly so that it doesn't defrost.
- Defrost it completely before you start to work with it, otherwise it can crack or crumble. The best way to do this is to leave it to thaw overnight in the fridge.
- As you work, cover the unused sheets with a clean damp teatowel, to prevent them from drying out.

STEAK AND KIDNEY PIE

Serves 6
Preparation 40 minutes, plus cooling
Cooking time about 1½ hours
Techniques see also preparing onions (page 182)

700g (1½lb) stewing steak, cubed and seasoned
2 tbsp plain flour, plus extra to dust
3 tbsp vegetable oil
25g (1oz) butter
1 small onion, finely chopped
175g (6oz) ox kidney, cut into small pieces
150g (5oz) flat mushrooms, cut into large chunks
small pinch of cayenne pepper
1 tsp anchovy essence
350g (12oz) puff pastry, thawed if frozen
1 large egg, beaten with a pinch of salt, to glaze
salt and ground black pepper

1 Preheat the oven to 170°C (150°C fan oven) mark 3.
Toss half the steak with half the flour. Heat the oil in a
flameproof, non-stick casserole and add the butter. Fry the
steak in batches until brown, remove and put to one side.
Repeat with the remaining steak. Add the onion and cook
gently until soft. Return the steak to the casserole with
200ml (7fl oz) water, the kidney, mushrooms, cayenne and
anchovy essence. Bring to the boil, the reduce the heat,
cover and simmer for 5 minutes. Transfer to the oven and
cook for 1 hour or until tender. The sauce should be syrupy.
If not, transfer the casserole to the hob, uncover, bring to
the boil and bubble for 5 minutes to reduce the liquid.
Leave to cool.
2 Preheat the oven to 200°C (180°C fan oven) mark 6.
Put the steak and kidney mixture into a 900ml (1½ pint)
pie dish. Pile it high to support the pastry.
3 Roll out the pastry on a lightly floured worksurface to
5mm (¼in) thick. Cut off four to six strips, 1cm (½in) wide.
Dampen the edge of the dish with cold water. Press the
pastry strips on to the edge. Dampen the pastry rim and
lay the sheet of pastry on top. Press the surfaces together,
trim the edge and press down with the back of a knife to
seal. Brush the pastry with the glaze and score with the
back of a knife. Put the pie dish on a baking sheet and cook
for 30 minutes or until the pastry is golden brown and the
filling is hot to the centre.

FREEZING TIP

Complete the recipe but do not glaze or bake. Wrap the
uncooked pie and freeze.
To use Thaw at cool room temperature overnight. Glaze
the pastry and add 5–10 minutes to the cooking time,
covering the pie with foil if the top starts to turn too
brown.

NUTRITION PER SERVING
565 cals | 36g fat (8g sats) | 26g carbs | 0.9g salt

LEEK AND HAM GALETTE

Serves 4
Preparation 30 minutes, plus cooling
Cooking time 40 minutes
Techniques see also making pastry (page 288)

25g (1oz) butter, plus extra to grease
350g (12oz) medium leeks, trimmed and cut into
    2cm (¾in) thick slices
25g (1oz) plain flour, plus extra to dust
50ml (2fl oz) milk
1 tbsp freshly chopped marjoram
50g (2oz) Beaufort or Gruyère cheese, cubed,
    plus 2 tbsp, grated
150g pack good-quality cooked sliced ham,
    thickly shredded
225g pack chilled puff pastry
½ medium egg, beaten with a pinch of salt
salt and ground black pepper

1 Preheat the oven to 220°C (200°C fan oven) mark 7.
Grease a baking sheet. Cook the leeks in boiling salted
water for 2–3 minutes until just beginning to soften.
Drain, keeping the cooking liquid to one side. Plunge the
leeks into cold water, drain and dry well on kitchen paper.
2 Melt the butter in a pan, take off the heat and mix in the
flour to form a smooth paste. Mix in 225ml (8fl oz) leek
water and the milk, stirring until smooth. Bring to the boil,
reduce the heat and simmer for 1–2 minutes, cover and
cool for 20 minutes or until cold. Add the marjoram, leeks,
cubed cheese and ham, and season.
3 Roll out the pastry on a lightly floured surface to a
30.5 × 33cm (12 × 13in) rectangle. Cut into two rectangles,
one 15 × 30.5cm (6 × 12in) and the other 18 × 30.5cm
(7 × 12in). Put the smaller piece on to the baking sheet.
Spoon on the ham mixture, leaving a 2cm (¾in) pastry
border all the way around. Brush the border with beaten
egg. Cover the filling with the larger pastry rectangle and
press the edges together. Cut slashes in the top of the
pastry to prevent the filling seeping out. Crimp the edges
of the pastry to seal, then cover and freeze for 20 minutes
or until firm.
4 Remove from the freezer, brush again with the beaten
egg, make a good-sized steam hole in the centre and
sprinkle with the grated cheese. Bake for 20–30 minutes
until brown and crisp.

FREEZING TIP

At step 3, line 8, cover in clingfilm and freeze on the baking
tray. When firm, remove from the baking tray. Wrap in
baking parchment, and then in clingfilm.
To use Thaw for 3 hours at cool room temperature on
baking parchment. Put a flat baking tray in the oven to
preheat to 220°C (200°C fan oven) mark 7 and complete
step 3 of the recipe. Put the galette on the hot tray (this
will keep the pastry base crisp) and bake for 40 minutes.

NUTRITION PER SERVING
395 cals | 25g fat (6g sats) | 29g carbs | 2g salt

SAUSAGE ROLLS

Serves 28
Preparation 25 minutes
Cooking time 30 minutes
Techniques see also making pastry (page 288)

450g (1lb) puff pastry, thawed if frozen
flour to dust
450g (1lb) pork sausagemeat
milk to brush
beaten egg to glaze

1 Preheat the oven to 220°C (200°C fan oven) mark 7.
Roll out half of the puff pastry on a lightly floured surface
to a 40.5 × 20.5cm (16 × 8in) rectangle; cut lengthways
into two strips.
2 Divide the sausagemeat into four, dust with flour and
form two portions into rolls, the length of the pastry. Lay a
sausagemeat roll on each strip of pastry. Brush the pastry
edges with a little milk, fold one side of the pastry over
and press the long edges together to seal. Repeat with
the remaining pastry and sausagemeat. Trim the ends.
3 Brush the pastry with egg to glaze and cut each roll into
5cm (2in) lengths. Make two or three slits in the top of
each one.
4 Transfer to a baking sheet and cook for 15 minutes.
Reduce the oven temperature to 180°C (160°C fan oven)
mark 4 and cook for a further 15 minutes. Transfer to a
wire rack. Serve hot or cold.

VARIATION
Add 1 hot red chilli, seeded and finely chopped, 1 tbsp
freshly grated ginger and a handful of chopped fresh
coriander leaves to the pork sausagemeat

NUTRITION PER SERVING
119 cals | 9g fat (2g sats) | 8g carbs | 0.4g salt

CHICKEN AND ARTICHOKE PIE

Serves 4
Preparation 20 minutes
Cooking time 45 minutes
Techniques see also using filo pastry (page 293)

3 skinless chicken breasts, about 350g (12oz)
150ml (¼ pint) dry white wine
225g (8oz) reduced-fat soft cheese with garlic and herbs
400g can artichoke hearts in water
4 sheets filo pastry, about 40g (1½oz), thawed if frozen
olive oil
1 tsp sesame seeds
salt and ground black pepper
fresh thyme to garnish (optional)

1 Preheat the oven to 200°C (180°C fan oven) mark 6. Put the chicken and wine in a pan and bring to the boil, then reduce the heat, cover and simmer for 10 minutes. Put the chicken to one side. Add the cheese to the wine and mix until smooth. Bring to the boil, then reduce the heat and simmer until thickened.
2 Cut the chicken into bite-size pieces. Drain and quarter the artichokes and add to the sauce with the chicken. Season and mix well.
3 Put the mixture in a shallow ovenproof dish. Brush the pastry lightly with oil, scrunch slightly and put on top of the chicken. Sprinkle with sesame seeds.
4 Cook for 30–35 minutes until crisp. Serve garnished with thyme, if you like.

VARIATION
Replace the artichoke hearts with 225g (8oz) brown-cap mushrooms, cooked in a little water with seasoning and lemon juice.

NUTRITION PER SERVING
241 cals | 9g fat (5g sats) | 7g carbs | 0.2g salt

SALMON AND ASPARAGUS PIE

Serves 6–8
Preparation 40 minutes, plus chilling
Cooking time 1 hour 10 minutes, plus cooling
Techniques see also making pastry (pages 288–289)

275g (10oz) plain flour, plus extra to dust
200g (7oz) chilled butter, cubed
1 large egg, beaten, plus 1 large egg, beaten, to glaze

For the filling
2 large eggs and 2 large yolks, beaten
200ml (7fl oz) crème fraîche
3 tbsp freshly chopped dill
25g (1oz) butter
200g (7oz) button mushrooms, sliced
150g (5oz) thick asparagus tips
450g (1lb) fresh salmon fillet, cut into wide strips,
    11.5cm (4½in) long
salt and ground black pepper

1 Whiz the flour, butter and salt in a food processor until
they resemble breadcrumbs. Add one egg and 2 tbsp cold
water and pulse until the mixture just comes together.
Knead lightly. Cut off one-third, wrap both pieces and chill
for 30 minutes.

2 Preheat the oven to 200°C (180°C fan oven) mark 6.
Roll out the larger piece to a 28cm (11in) round. Use to
line a 20.5cm (8in), 5cm (2in) deep, loose-based tin and
prick the base with a fork. Line with greaseproof paper
and baking beans and put on a baking sheet. Bake for
25 minutes. Remove paper and beans, brush the pastry
with beaten egg and cook for 5–10 minutes until the
pastry is almost cooked. Cool.

3 To make the filling, combine the whole eggs, crème
fraîche and dill and season. Melt the butter and fry the
mushrooms for 1–2 minutes. Season and cool. Add the
asparagus to boiling water, bring back to the boil, then drain.
Refresh in iced water. Arrange half the fish in the pie case.
Arrange the vegetables on top. Finish with fish and pour
over the crème fraîche mixture to within 1cm (½in) of
the top. Brush the rim with beaten egg. Cut the remaining
pastry into a 25.5cm (10in) round, place on top and seal
the edges. Brush with egg. Make a steam hole. Put the
baking tray in the oven to heat. Bake the pie on the tray for
40 minutes or until golden and the filling is cooked. Cool in
the tin.

COOK'S TIPS

➥ To check the pie is cooked, insert a skewer in
the centre for 30 seconds – it should feel hot
when you pull it out.

➥ Cool the pie in the tin for 1 hour to serve
warm, or 3 hours to serve at room temperature.

NUTRITION PER SERVING FOR 6
782 cals | 59g fat (32g sats) | 37g carbs | 0.8g salt

NUTRITION PER SERVING FOR 8
587 cals | 45g fat (24g sats) | 28g carbs | 0.6g salt

QUICHE LORRAINE

Serves 8
Preparation 35 minutes, plus chilling
Cooking time 1 hour
Techniques see also making pastry (pages 288–289), preparing onions (page 182)

Shortcrust Pastry (see page 288) made with 200g (7oz) plain flour, a pinch of salt, 100g (3½oz) chilled butter and 1 large egg

For the filling
5 large eggs
225g (8oz) unsmoked streaky bacon, rind removed
40g (1½oz) butter
125g (4oz) shallots, onions or spring onions, finely chopped
400g (14oz) crème fraîche
100g (3½oz) Gruyère cheese, grated
salt and ground black pepper
crispy bacon and fried spring onions to garnish

1 Preheat the oven to 200°C (180°C fan oven) mark 6. Roll out the pastry thinly and use to line a 23cm (9in), 3cm (1¼in) deep, loose-based tart tin. Prick the base and bake blind (see page 290).
2 Meanwhile, lightly whisk the eggs for the filling. Use a little to brush the inside of the pastry case and return it to the oven for 5 minutes to seal any cracks. Reduce the oven temperature to 190°C (170°C fan oven) mark 5.
3 Cut the bacon into 5mm (¼in) strips. Put the bacon in a pan of cold water and bring to the boil. Drain, refresh under cold water and dry on kitchen paper.
4 Melt the butter in a frying pan. Add the shallots or onions and cook for 1 minute. Add the bacon and cook, stirring, until brown.
5 Mix the eggs with the crème fraîche and Gruyère cheese and season. Put the bacon mixture in the pastry case and spoon the crème fraîche mixture on top (see Cook's Tip). Cook for 30–35 minutes until golden and just set. Cool for 10 minutes before serving. Garnish with bacon and fried spring onions.

COOK'S TIP
Fill the pastry case as full as possible. You may find you have a little mixture left, as flan tins vary in size.

NUTRITION PER SERVING
595 cals | 50g fat (29g sats) | 22g carbs | 1.5g salt

GOAT'S CHEESE PARCELS

Serves 6, makes 12
Preparation 45 minutes, plus chilling
Cooking time 10 minutes, plus cooling
Techniques see also preparing vegetables (pages 182–194)

125g (4oz) fresh spinach leaves
2 tbsp sunflower oil
1 onion, finely chopped
1 large garlic clove, chopped
250g (9oz) soft goat's cheese
270g pack filo pastry, thawed if frozen
50g (2oz) butter, melted
sesame seeds to sprinkle
salt and ground black pepper
rocket to garnish

1 Plunge the spinach into a pan of boiling water, bring back to the boil and bubble for 1 minute, then drain and run it under very cold water. Once cold, squeeze out all the excess liquid and chop finely. Put to one side.
2 Heat the oil in a pan. Add the onion and garlic and cook until translucent, then leave to cool. Combine the spinach, onion mixture and goat's cheese in a bowl and season generously with salt and pepper.
3 Cut the filo pastry into twenty-four 12.5cm (5in) squares. Brush one square with melted butter, cover with a second square and brush with more melted butter. Put to one side and cover with a damp teatowel to prevent drying out. Repeat with the remaining squares, to make 12 sets.
4 Put a dessertspoonful of the filling in the centre of each square and join up the corners to form a square parcel. Brush the pastry with a little more butter, sprinkle with sesame seeds and chill for 20 minutes. Meanwhile, preheat the oven to 220°C (200°C fan oven) mark 7.
5 Bake for about 5 minutes or until the pastry is crisp and brown at the edges. Arrange on serving plates and garnish with rocket.

NUTRITION PER SERVING
345 cals | 22g fat (12g sats) | 26g carbs | 0.8g salt

TREACLE TART

Cuts into 6 slices
Preparation 25 minutes, plus chilling
Cooking time 45–50 minutes, plus cooling
Techniques see also making pastry (page 288), making breadcrumbs (page 318), zesting citrus fruits (page 217)

Sweet Shortcrust Pastry (see page 288), made with 225g (8oz) plain flour, 150g (5oz) unsalted butter, 15g (½oz) golden caster sugar and 1 medium egg yolk
plain flour to dust

For the filling
700g (1½lb) golden syrup
175g (6oz) fresh white breadcrumbs
grated zest of 3 lemons
2 medium eggs, lightly beaten

1 Preheat the oven to 180°C (160°C fan oven) mark 4. Roll out the pastry on a lightly floured surface and use to line a 25.5cm (10in), 4cm (1½in) deep, loose-based fluted tart tin. Prick the base all over with a fork and chill for 30 minutes.
2 To make the filling, heat the syrup in a pan over a low heat until thinner in consistency. Remove from the heat and mix in the breadcrumbs and lemon zest. Stir in the beaten eggs.
3 Pour the filling into the pastry case and bake in the oven for 45–50 minutes until the filling is lightly set and golden. Leave to cool slightly. Serve warm.

TRY SOMETHING DIFFERENT
For the pastry, replace half the plain flour with wholemeal flour. For the filling, use fresh wholemeal breadcrumbs instead of white.

NUTRITION PER SERVING
486 cals | 15g fat (8g sats) | 88g carbs | 1.1g salt **V**

CINNAMON CUSTARD TART

Serves 8
Preparation 50 minutes, plus chilling and standing
Cooking time 1½ hours
Techniques see also preparing exotic fruits (page 220)

250g (9oz) plain flour, plus extra to dust
100g (3½oz) butter
100g (3½oz) icing sugar
4 large eggs
450ml (¾ pint) milk
285ml (9½fl oz) double cream
1 vanilla pod, split
1 cinnamon stick, crumbled
275g (10oz) caster sugar
1 mango, 1 small pineapple, 2 clementines and 125g (4oz)
 kumquats to serve

1 Pulse the flour, butter and icing sugar in a food processor until the mixture forms fine crumbs. (Alternatively, rub the fat into the flour by hand or using a pastry cutter, then stir in the icing sugar.) Beat one egg and add to the flour mixture with 1 tbsp water. Process (or stir) until the crumbs make a dough. Wrap in clingfilm and chill for 30 minutes.
2 Use the pastry to line a 23cm (9in) loose-based tart tin. Prick the base and line with greaseproof paper and baking beans. Chill for 30 minutes. Preheat the oven to 200°C (180°C fan oven) mark 6. Put on a baking tray and bake for 15 minutes. Remove the paper and beans and cook for 10–15 minutes until the base is cooked. Lightly whisk the remaining eggs. Use 1 tbsp egg to brush over the pastry. Return to the oven for 2 minutes. Reduce the temperature to 150°C (130°C fan oven) mark 2.
3 Bring the milk, cream, vanilla and cinnamon slowly to the boil. Leave to infuse for 20 minutes. Mix the whisked eggs with 150g (5oz) caster sugar. Stir the milk into the egg mixture, strain into a jug and pour into the tart. Cook for 40–50 minutes until the filling has just set. Turn the oven off and leave the tart in the oven for 15 minutes. Remove and cool in the tin for 20–30 minutes. Transfer to a wire rack to cool.
4 Make the caramelised fruit (see Finishing Touches). Cut the tart into portions and spoon the fruit over the top to serve.

FINISHING TOUCHES
To decorate, cut the fruits into thick slices and arrange on two non-stick baking sheets. Put the remaining caster sugar in a small, heavy-based pan. Cook over a low heat until the sugar begins to dissolve, then turn up the heat and cook to a pale caramel. Cool a little and drizzle over the fruit. Leave to set. (The caramel will stay brittle for 1–2 hours.)

NUTRITION PER SERVING
664 cals | 34g fat (20g sats) | 87g carbs | 0.4g salt

LEMON MERINGUE PIE

Serves 8
Preparation 20 minutes, plus chilling
Cooking time about 40 minutes, plus cooling
Techniques see also zesting citrus fruits (page 217)

1 quantity of Pâte Sucrée (see Cook's Tip)
flour to dust
pared rind and juice of 2–3 lemons
65g (2½oz) cornflour
50–75g (2–3oz) caster sugar
2 medium egg yolks

For the meringue
3 medium egg whites
175g (6oz) caster sugar

1 Roll out the pastry on a lightly floured worksurface until large enough to line a 23cm (9in) loose-bottomed fluted quiche tin. Prick the base all over and chill for 30 minutes.
2 Meanwhile, put the lemon rind and 600ml (1 pint) water into a pan. Bring to the boil, then remove from the heat and leave to cool for 30 minutes. Preheat the oven to 190°C (170°C fan) mark 5.
3 Bake the pastry blind (see page 290). Cool in the tin on a wire rack.
4 Remove the lemon rind from the water and discard. Stir in the lemon juice. In a separate bowl, blend the cornflour with a little lemon water to make a smooth paste. Add back to the pan and combine. Bring to the boil, then reduce the heat and cook, stirring constantly, until thickened. Remove from the heat. Stir in the sugar to taste, then beat in the egg yolks. Pour the lemon filling into the cooled pastry case.
5 Whisk the egg whites in a large grease-free bowl until stiff. Gradually whisk in the sugar until stiff and glossy. Spoon the meringue over the filling and rough up the top to form peaks. Bake in the oven for 5–10 minutes until very lightly browned. Leave to cool before serving.

COOK'S TIP

Pâte sucrée Sift 100g (3½oz) plain flour and a pinch of salt into a bowl. Tip on to a worksurface and make a well in the middle. Put 50g (2oz) softened butter, 2 medium egg yolks and 50g (2oz) caster sugar into the well. Using your fingertips, pinch and work the sugar, butter and egg yolks together until well blended. Gradually work in the flour to bring the pastry together. Knead lightly until smooth, then wrap in clingfilm and chill for 30 minutes. Makes 100g (3½oz) pastry.

NUTRITION PER SERVING
289 cals | 8g fat (4g sats) | 53g carbs | 0.4g salt

CLASSIC APPLE PIE

Serves 6
Preparation 20 minutes
Cooking time 35–40 minutes
Techniques see also preparing apples (page 216), making pastry (page 288)

900g (2lb) cooking apples, peeled, cored and sliced
50g (2oz) sugar
flour to dust
225g shortcrust pastry, made with 225g (8oz) flour
caster sugar to dust

1 Preheat the oven to 190°C (170°C fan oven) mark 7.
2 Layer the apples and sugar in a 1.1 litre (2 pint) pie dish. Sprinkle with 1 tbsp water.
3 Roll out the pastry on a lightly floured worksurface to a circle 2.5cm (1in) larger than the pie dish. Cut off a strip, dampen the rim of the dish and press on the strip. Dampen the strip and cover with the pastry, pressing the edges together well. Decorate the edge of the pastry (see page 291) and make a slit in the centre.
4 Bake for 35–40 minutes, until the pastry is lightly browned. Sprinkle with caster sugar before serving.

NUTRITION PER SERVING
268 cals | 11g fat (4g sats) | 43g carbs | 0.4g salt

ALMOND BAKEWELL TARTS

Makes 6
Preparation 25 minutes, plus chilling
Cooking time 50 minutes, plus cooling
Techniques see also making pastry (page 288)

For the sweet pastry
200g (7oz) plain flour, plus extra to dust
a pinch of salt
100g (3½ oz) unsalted butter, at room temperature cut into pieces
3 large egg yolks
75g (3oz) caster sugar
½ tsp vanilla extract

For the filling
125g (4oz) unsalted butter, softened
125g (4oz) caster sugar
3 large eggs
125g (4oz) ground almonds
2–3 drops almond extract
6 tbsp redcurrant jelly

For the crumble topping
25g (1oz) unsalted butter
75g (3oz) plain flour
25g (1oz) caster sugar
Plum Sauce (see Cook's Tip) to serve

1 To make the pastry, sift the flour and salt into a mound on a clean surface. Make a large well in the centre and add the butter, egg yolks, sugar and vanilla extract. Using the fingertips of one hand, work the sugar, butter and egg yolks together until well blended. Gradually work in all the flour to bind the mixture together. Knead the dough gently on a lightly floured surface until smooth, then wrap in clingfilm and chill for at least 30 minutes before rolling out.
2 Roll out the pastry thinly on a lightly floured surface and line six 10cm (4in), 3cm (1¼in) deep tartlet tins. Chill for 30 minutes. Preheat the oven to 190°C (170°C fan oven) mark 5.
3 Bake the tartlet cases blind (see page 290). Remove from the oven and leave to cool.
4 To make the filling, beat the butter and sugar together until light and fluffy. Gradually beat in 2 eggs, then beat in the remaining egg with one-third of the ground almonds. Fold in the remaining almonds and the almond extract.
5 Melt the redcurrant jelly in a small pan and brush over the inside of each pastry case. Spoon in the almond filling. Put the tarts on a baking sheet and bake for 20–25 minutes until golden and just firm. Leave in the tins for 10 minutes, then unmould on to a wire rack and leave to cool completely.

6 To make the crumble topping, rub the butter into the flour and add the sugar. Spread evenly on a baking sheet and grill until golden. Cool, then sprinkle over the tarts. Decorate with plums (see Cook's Tip) and serve with Plum Sauce.

COOK'S TIP
Plum Sauce Put 450g (1lb) halved and stoned ripe plums, 50–75g (2–3oz) soft brown sugar and 150ml (¼ pint) sweet white wine into a pan with 150ml (¼ pint) water. Bring to the boil, then reduce the heat and simmer until tender. Remove 3 plums to decorate; thickly slice and put to one side. Cook the remaining plums for about 15 minutes until very soft. Put into a food processor and whiz until smooth. Sieve, if you like, adding more sugar to taste. Leave to cool.

NUTRITION PER SERVING
931 cals | 52g fat (24g sats) | 104g carbs | 0.8g salt

EASY PEAR AND TOFFEE TARTE TATIN

Serves 6
Preparation 15 minutes
Cooking time 25–30 minutes, plus cooling
Techniques see also making dulce de leche (page 373), making puff pastry (page 289), making vanilla ice cream (page 394)

4 small rosy pears
8 tbsp dulce de leche toffee sauce
225g (8oz) sheet ready-rolled puff pastry
flour to dust
thick cream or vanilla ice cream to serve

1 Preheat the oven to 200°C (180°C fan oven) mark 6. Quarter the pears – no need to peel them – and cut out the cores. Put into a large non-stick frying pan and add the toffee sauce. Cook over a medium heat for 5 minutes or until the pears are well coated and the sauce has turned a slightly darker shade of golden brown.
2 Tip the pears and the sauce into a 20.5cm (8in) round non-stick sandwich or tart tin. Arrange the pears skin side down in a circle and leave to cool for 10 minutes.
3 Unroll the puff pastry, rolling it out wider on a floured surface, if necessary. Lay it over the pears and press down on to the edge of the tin. Trim off any excess pastry. Prick the pastry all over and bake the tart for 20–25 minutes until the pastry is well risen and golden.
4 Leave the tart to cool for 5 minutes. To turn out, hold a large serving plate or baking sheet over the tart, turn over and give a quick shake to loosen. Lift off the tin. Serve the tart immediately, cut into thick wedges, with cream or vanilla ice cream.

NUTRITION PER SERVING
294 cals | 12g fat (2g sats) | 46g carbs | 0.5g salt **V**

JAM ROLY-POLY

Serves 4
Preparation 25 minutes
Cooking time 1 hour
Techniques see also making vanilla custard (page 28)

butter to grease
6 tbsp jam
a little milk
Fresh Vanilla Custard (see page 28) to serve

For the suet crust pastry
175g (6oz) self-raising flour, plus extra to dust
¼ tsp salt
100g (3½oz) shredded suet

1 Preheat the oven to 180°C (160°C fan oven) mark 4.
Grease a piece of foil 23 × 33cm (9 × 13in).
2 To make the pastry, sift the flour and salt into a bowl,
added the shredded suet and stir to mix. Using a round-
bladed knife, mix in enough cold water to make a soft
dough – you will need about 100ml (3½fl oz). If the
dough seems too dry, add a little extra liquid. Knead very
lightly until smooth.
3 Roll out the suet crust pastry on a lightly floured
worksurface to a rectangle about 23 × 28cm (9 × 11in).
Spread the jam on the pastry, leaving 5mm (¼in) clear
along each edge. Brush the edges with milk and roll up the
pastry evenly, starting from one short side.
4 Put the roll on the greased foil and wrap the foil around
it loosely, to allow for expansion, but seal the edges well.
Put a rack in a roasting tin. Fill with 2.5cm (1in) boiling
water, making sure it does not come higher than the rack.
Put the foil-covered roll on the rack. Cover the whole tray
tightly with foil to make sure no steam escapes. Steam for
1 hour. Remove from the foil and serve with custard.

NUTRITION PER SERVING
449 cals | 22g fat (13g sats) | 62g carbs | 0.7g salt

SWEET AND SAVOURY BREADS

Very little beats the smell of freshly baked bread. This chapter provides you with all the know-how you will ever need to get baking – from how to make the simplest white and brown loaves to using a bread machine and making other classic loaves such as sourdough, soda bread and flatbread. Then there are topped breads such as pizza and focaccia. The chapter is packed with advice on basic bread-making ingredients, including yeast, plus troubleshooting tips and hints on achieving perfect results every time. There's also a section on using bread as an ingredient, including making breadcrumbs, bruschetta, wraps and sandwiches. The recipe section includes more complex loaves and bread recipes including Black olive bread, Walnut and garlic bread, Warm cornbread, Marbled chocolate teabread, Kugelhopf, Tuna melt pizza and Bread and butter pudding.

BREAD BASICS

Baking bread is one of the greatest pleasures of the kitchen, and one of the simplest. Simple loaves provide the foundation for further experimentation, so they are the best place to start with bread-making.

White farmhouse loaf

You will need 700g (1lb 9oz) strong plain white flour, 1 tbsp salt, 1 tsp golden caster sugar, 1½ tsp fast-action (easy-blend) dried yeast, a little vegetable oil.

1 Sift the flour into a large bowl and stir in the salt, sugar and yeast. Make a well in the middle and stir in 450ml (¾ pint) warm water to make a soft sticky dough, adding a little extra water if necessary.

2 Knead thoroughly for 10 minutes until the dough is smooth and elastic, then shape into a ball and put into an oiled bowl.

3 Cover and leave to rise for 1–2 hours until doubled in size.

4 Knock back the dough for 2–3 minutes on a lightly floured surface, by pressing down with your knuckles to expel any air. Shape into a large oval loaf and transfer to a floured baking sheet. Cover loosely with lightly oiled clingfilm and leave to prove (rise) for a further 30 minutes.

5 Preheat the oven to 230°C (210°C fan) mark 8. Slash the top of the loaf with a very sharp knife, dust with flour and bake for 15 minutes.

6 Reduce the heat to 200°C (180°C fan) mark 6 and bake for a further 15–20 minutes until the bread is risen and sounds hollow when tapped underneath. Cool on a wire rack.

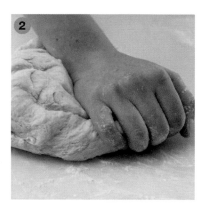

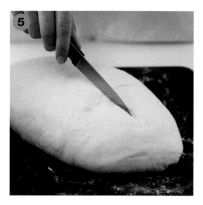

MAKING BREAD

Yeast Fresh yeast is activated when blended with warm liquid. Dried yeast needs sugar to activate it (no sugar is needed if using milk): blend the yeast with a little of the water plus sugar (or milk) and leave for 15 minutes to froth. Fast-action (easy-blend) dried yeast is sprinkled directly into the flour and the liquid added afterwards. As a rough guide, for 700g (1lb 9oz) flour use 15g (½oz) fresh yeast, 1 tbsp dried yeast or a 7g sachet (2 tsp) fast-action dried yeast.

Liquid This needs to be slightly warm to the fingertips. Milk gives bread a softer texture than water.
Flour Use strong white or wholemeal flour, or Granary flour.
Salt This controls fermentation, strengthens the gluten, which gives the bread its texture, and adds flavour.
Fats Some recipes use fat for flavour and to improve keeping quality.

SHAPING LOAVES

The shape and size of bread can be varied almost endlessly after the first rise. After the second rising, the dough is ready to bake. Understanding the basics will ensure success.

Simple rolls

1 After knocking back, cut the dough into even pieces, each about 40g (1½oz). Roll each piece with the palm of your hand on a lightly floured worksurface to make a ball.

2 Place on a greased baking sheet, seam side down, and press down slightly. Cover with clingfilm and leave to prove for 30 minutes before baking.

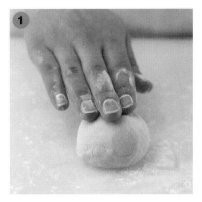

Long loaves

1 After knocking back, cut the dough into pieces, each weighing about 200g (7oz). Roll one piece until it is about 40.5cm (16in) long. Transfer to a baking sheet, seam side down. Repeat with remaining pieces.

2 Cover with oiled clingfilm and leave to prove (rise) for 30 minutes. Slash 3–4 times before baking.

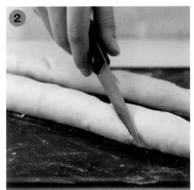

PERFECT BAKING

- Make sure shaped dough has risen sufficiently – usually to double.
- Always oil or flour the loaf tin or baking sheet, to prevent it sticking.
- Make sure the oven is at the correct temperature before baking.
- Bake on a preheated ceramic baking stone (from good kitchen shops) if possible, even if the bread is in a loaf tin. The heat of the stone will give the bread a crisp base.

TROUBLESHOOTING

The loaf hasn't risen enough:
- Not enough liquid was added.
- The yeast was not fresh.
- The dough was left to prove (rise) for too long causing it to collapse during baking.

The loaf is too dense in texture:
- The dough was not allowed to rise.
- Not enough, or too little, liquid.
- Dough not kneaded long enough.

COOLING

If baked bread is left for too long either in the loaf tin or on the baking sheet, steam will gather and, as a result, the underneath will start to become soggy. To prevent this, always remove the loaf immediately and put it on a wire rack. Then leave it to cool completely before slicing, as you like.

USING A BREAD MACHINE

Bread machines are now becoming extremely popular as a way for busy people to enjoy home-baked bread. As well as baking loaves, the machine can make doughs for all kinds of shaped breads.

Mixed grain loaf

You will need 1 tsp fast-action (easy-blend) dried yeast, 300g (11oz) strong white bread flour, 100g (3½oz) strong wholemeal bread flour, 50g (2oz) bulgur wheat, 25g (1oz) millet grain, 2 tbsp linseed, 2 tbsp porridge oats or wheat flakes, plus extra to sprinkle, 1½ tsp salt, 1 tbsp golden caster sugar, 25g (1oz) butter, 350ml (12fl oz) water.

1 Put the ingredients in the bread bucket following the guidelines in the manufacturer's manual. (Most machines specify adding the liquid(s) first followed by the dry ingredients and yeast.

2 Fit the bucket into the bread machine and set to the programme recommended in the manual for a large multigrain loaf with the crust of choice. Press start and leave the bread to mix and rise.

3 Before baking, brush the top of the risen bread dough with water and sprinkle with oats or wheat flakes.

4 After baking, remove the loaf from the bread machine as soon as it is cooked and place on a wire rack to cool.

WHICH MACHINE?

Bread machines knead, prove and bake, but models vary. Most will bake different sizes of loaf as well as different breads, and some have a special 'beep' function to tell you when to add other ingredients during the dough cycle. Most machines allow you to select your preferred crust colour, and some have a timer so that you can set the machine to bake bread ready for a selected time, such as first thing in the morning.

PERFECT MACHINE-BAKED BREAD

➴ Always follow the bread machine instructions carefully; it is essential that the ingredients go into the machine in the order stated, as the yeast must not come into contact with the liquid until the machine begins to mix.

➴ Measure out all the ingredients carefully, as exact quantities are essential for a perfect loaf.

➴ Avoid lifting the lid during the rising and baking cycles as this may cause the loaf to sink.

➴ The loaf is best removed from the machine as soon as it is baked, otherwise it will become soggy.

➴ Use recipes that have been designed for bread machine use only, as conventional bread recipes use different quantities of ingredients and are not converted easily.

MAKING CLASSIC BREADS

There are numerous classic breads – from a simple brown loaf made with wholemeal flour and distinctive-tasting sourdough to unleavened flatbreads and unyeasted soda breads and scones.

Brown loaf

You will need 300g (11oz) strong white bread flour, 200g (7oz) strong wholemeal flour, 15g (½oz) fresh yeast or 1 tsp dried yeast, 2 tsp salt.

1 Sift flours into a bowl and make a well in centre. Pour in 325ml (11fl oz) water. Sprinkle over the yeast and mix in a little of the flour to make a batter. Sprinkle salt over the dry flour, so that it doesn't come into contact with the yeast. Cover and leave for 20 minutes.

2 Mix to make soft dough. Knead for 10 minutes until smooth and elastic. Shape into a ball and place in a lightly oiled bowl. Cover and leave for ¾–1½ hours until doubled in size.

3 Punch the dough to knock back on a lightly floured surface by pressing with your knuckles to expel the air.

4 Knead for 2–3 minutes, then shape and put in a greased 900g (2lb) loaf tin

or on a lightly floured baking sheet. Cover, and leave to rise for ¾–1½ hours until doubled.

5 Preheat the oven to 200°C (180°C fan oven) mark 6. Bake for 50 minutes–1 hour if using a loaf tin, or 45–50 minutes on baking sheet.

6 Tap the base of the loaf: it should sound hollow. Cool on a wire rack.

Sourdough

Old-fashioned sourdough has a close texture and a deliciously tangy flavour. You can adapt a basic bread recipe to make sourdough bread. Simply use 125ml (4fl oz) of the starter (see below) in place of each 15g (½oz) fresh yeast or 1 tsp dried yeast called for in a recipe.

1 For the starter, you will need 15g (½oz) fresh yeast or 1 tsp dried yeast, 450ml (¾ pint) water, about 225g (8oz) strong white bread flour.

2 Mix the ingredients to a thick, pourable batter. Then cover the bowl with a clean damp cloth and leave at room temperature for between three and five days. During this time, the starter will ferment and, as a result, it will take on the distinctive and sought-after sourdough flavour that characterises this bread, which is what it is all about.

COOK'S TIP

Sourdough starter keeps well but must be 'refreshed'. Keep the starter covered in the refrigerator and whisk in a handful of flour and a small cup of water every day – this provides fresh nutrients for the yeast and aids its leavening properties.

Soda bread

You will need 350g (12oz) plain wholemeal flour, 125g (4oz) coarse oatmeal, 2 tsp bicarbonate of soda, 1 tsp salt, 300ml (½ pint) buttermilk, 1 tsp clear honey, 2–3 tbsp milk, plus extra to brush.

1 Preheat the oven to 200°C (180°C fan oven) mark 6. Combine the dry ingredients in a bowl and make a well in the middle.

2 Gradually beat in the buttermilk, honey and just enough milk to form a soft dough. Knead for 5 minutes or until smooth.

3 Shape into a 20.5cm (8in) round and place on a lightly oiled baking sheet. Cut a cross on top. Brush with milk and bake for 30–35 minutes until slightly risen; it should sound hollow when tapped on its base.

Spicy griddled flatbread

You will need 300g (11oz) strong white bread flour, 175g (6oz) gram flour, 1 tsp salt, 2 tsp dried yeast, 2 tsp ground cumin, ½ tsp golden caster sugar.

1 Mix the flours together in a large bowl, then stir in the remaining ingredients. Make a well in the middle and gradually work in 250–300ml (9fl oz–½ pint) water to make a soft dough.

2 Knead the dough for about 10 minutes or until it becomes smooth and slightly elastic. Transfer to an oiled bowl, cover, and leave to rise for 1–1½ hours until doubled in size.

3 Punch the dough to knock it back and divide into 12 equal pieces. Roll out each piece to make a small oval, about 7.5 × 15cm (3 × 6in), and put on well-floured baking sheets.

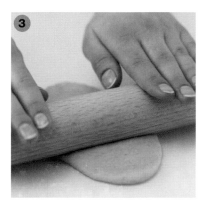

4 Spray the breads lightly with water, cover loosely, and leave to rise for another 15 minutes.

5 Preheat a lightly oiled flat griddle, or the grill, and cook the breads, a few at a time, until they're puffed up and golden (1–2 minutes). Turn and cook the underside for another 30–60 seconds. Cover and keep warm while you cook the remaining breads. Eat as soon as possible.

COOK'S TIPS

- If grilling the breads, position the rack about 10cm (4in) from the heat so that they have room to puff up.
- If you need to speed things up, use a food processor for step 1.

Enriched breads

An enriched dough contains more fat, and often milk and sugar or honey. A typical recipe would have 50g 2oz) butter rubbed into every 225g (8oz) flour, plus 1 egg and 100ml (3½fl oz) milk.

1 Mix the ingredients in normal way.

2 Knead and shape, then bake and cool in the usual way.

Scones

To make eight scones, you will need 225g (8oz) self-raising flour, pinch of salt, 75g (3oz) butter at room temperature, cut into small pieces, 40g (1½oz) golden caster sugar, 1 large egg, 4–10 tbsp buttermilk or soured milk (milk with lemon juice).

1 Preheat the oven to 220°C (200°C fan oven) mark 7. Sift the flour and salt into a bowl. Add the butter and rub it in until the mixture looks like breadcrumbs. Stir in the sugar.

2 Put the egg in a jug and beat in 2 tbsp of the buttermilk or soured milk. Make a well in centre of the flour mixture and pour in the egg mixture. Using a round-bladed knife, gradually stir in. Bring the dough together with your hands – it should be soft but not sticky; if too dry, add a drop more liquid. Shape the dough into a ball and pat into a round.

3 Flour the worksurface and rolling pin, and roll out the dough to 2.5cm (1in) thick. Dip a 5cm (2in) cutter in flour, and cut out 8 rounds.

4 Arrange the scones on a floured baking sheet. Lightly brush with milk and dust with flour.

5 Bake at the top of the oven for 10–12 minutes until well risen and golden. Leave to cool on wire rack for 5 minutes.

VARIATIONS

Wholemeal scones Replace half the white flour with wholemeal flour. Add a little extra milk if needed.
Cheese and herb scones Sift 1 tsp mustard powder with the dry ingredients. Stir in 50g (2oz) finely grated Cheddar cheese, then add the milk. After glazing, sprinkle the tops with a little extra cheese.

MAKING PIZZA AND FOCACCIA

Whereas pizza has a rich topping, focaccia's topping is much lighter. The dough takes only about 10 minutes to make and needs just one rise, so it can be ready to use within an hour.

Pizza

For one pizza, you will need 225g (8oz) strong white bread flour, 7g sachet fast-action (easy-blend) dried yeast, ½ tsp salt, 4 tbsp extra-virgin olive oil, cornmeal or flour, to sprinkle.

1 Sift the flour into a large bowl, stir in the yeast and salt and make a well in the centre. Pour 150ml (¼ pint) water into the well with 1 tbsp of the oil. Use your fingertips or a large spoon to stir together.

2 Turn on to a lightly floured surface and knead for 5 minutes or until the dough is smooth. It should be quite soft. Lightly oil the mixing bowl, put in the dough and turn it over to coat in the remaining oil. Cover with oiled clingfilm or a clean teatowel. Put in a warm, draught-free place to rise for 45 minutes or until doubled in size.

3 Preheat the oven to 240°C (220°C fan oven) mark 9. Quickly punch the dough to knock it back, then roll it out into a circle or rectangle about 1cm (½in) thick.

4 Sprinkle a baking sheet fairly generously with cornmeal or plain flour. Roll the dough over the rolling pin and lift it on to the baking sheet, then unroll and spread with sauce.

5 Add your choice of toppings (see right) and bake for 20–25 minutes until the rim is crusty and the topping is bubbling.

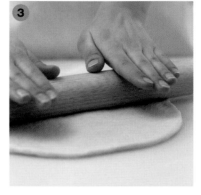

PERFECT PIZZAS

- Pizza should not be a heavy dish so add toppings with a light hand.
- If you can't get good mozzarella, use another cheese instead – Taleggio, Fontina, or even just good Cheddar all work well.
- A ceramic baking stone (from good kitchen shops) is extremely useful for cooking pizza, to help cook the pizza evenly and give crunchiness to the base. (Put the stone into the oven before preheating.)

TOPPINGS

Scatter one or two of the following on top of a basic cheese and tomato topping:
- Pancetta bits or slices of prosciutto
- Rocket leaves
- Dried chilli flakes
- Capers
- Sliced sun-dried tomatoes
- Pepperoni slices
- Roasted peppers
- Artichoke hearts, drained and quartered
- Sliced mushrooms.

Focaccia

A very popular Italian bread, focaccia scores highly as a tasty comfort food. It is made from pizza dough, pressed into a roughly rectangular shape, a little thicker than pizza, and then topped with salt, extra-virgin olive oil and your choice of herbs.

You will need 1 quantity of pizza dough, 2 tbsp extra-virgin olive oil, a small handful of fresh herbs (basil, rosemary, flat-leafed parsley or thyme), roughly torn, 2 tsp coarse sea salt.

1 Roll the pizza dough into a rectangle about 2.5cm (1in) thick. Place it in a shallow baking tin or on a baking sheet, and leave to rise for 30 minutes.

2 Preheat the oven to 200°C (180°C fan oven) mark 6.

3 Dimple the surface of the bread by gently pressing a finger into the dough at regular intervals.

4 Drizzle the oil all over the top of the bread.

5 Scatter on your chosen herbs, then sprinkle with sea salt.

6 Bake for 30–35 minutes until the bread is well risen and golden brown in colour.

SEASONINGS

These should be scattered on with a light hand. Remember, they are a seasoning, not a main ingredient:
- Garlic, finely chopped
- Onions, thinly sliced
- Shallots, finely chopped
- Cracked black pepper
- Olives, roughly chopped
- Anchovies, finely chopped
- Dried herbs, such as oregano
- Sun-dried tomatoes, chopped
- Capers, finely chopped.

COOKING WITH BREAD

Bread is delicious eaten on its own, but it's also invaluable as an ingredient – whether processed into breadcrumbs, toasted and turned into bruschetta, made into wraps or sandwiches, or used in salads.

Fresh breadcrumbs

Used for stuffings or as a topping, these are best made just before using.

1 Cut off the crusts and discard. Chop the bread roughly.

2 Working in batches, put handfuls of bread in a food processor or blender and whiz until it becomes fine crumbs. Use as soon as possible or freeze for up to one month.

DRIED CRUMBS

Used for coating fish, meat and poultry before frying, dried breadcrumbs can be made from stale bread or from slices of bread dried in the oven at 200°C (180°C fan oven) mark 6 for 5–10 minutes. Break into pieces and whiz in the food processor.

Garlic bruschetta

To make six, you will need 3 garlic cloves, 6 thick slices bread, 5 tbsp virgin olive oil.

1 Heat a griddle until hot. Peel the garlic and bruise, then halve and rub on both sides of the bread.

2 Brush both sides of the bread with oil. Put on the griddle, press down and cook until golden brown.

Simple chicken wrap

Wraps are best made with a finely chopped filling so that the wrapper can fold around it easily.

You will need 1 tsp salt, 1 tsp ground black pepper, 2 cooked chicken breasts, finely chopped, 1 carrot, grated, 1 avocado, chopped, a small handful of rocket leaves, the juice of ½ lemon, 3 tbsp mayonnaise, 4 soft tortillas.

1 Put the salt and pepper in a bowl, then add the chicken, carrot, avocado and rocket and mix well.

2 In a separate bowl, combine the lemon juice and mayonnaise, then spread it over the tortillas. Divide the chicken mixture evenly between them and roll up tightly. Serve whole, or cut in half.

Tuscan bread salad

You will need 6–8 thick slices of country-style bread, about 250g (9oz) total weight, 3–4 large ripe tomatoes, 1 small or ½ large cucumber, 1 medium red onion, a small handful of fresh basil leaves, torn, home-made dressing made with 3 tbsp red wine vinegar and 6 tbsp extra-virgin olive oil, salt and ground black pepper.

1 Cut or tear the bread into pieces and put into a large bowl. Slice the vegetables into pieces a little smaller than the bread and add to the bowl with the basil.

2 Whisk the dressing, then pour about 7 tbsp of this over the salad.

3 Toss well, then leave to stand for 30 minutes–2 hours, depending on the freshness of the bread, tossing from time to time. Taste the salad, adjust the seasoning and serve.

SALT AND PEPPER ROLLS

Makes 16
Preparation 40 minutes, plus rising
Cooking time 30–35 minutes
Techniques see also bread basics (page 310)

675g (1½lb) strong white bread flour, plus extra to dust
7g sachet fast-action dried yeast
1 tsp sea salt flakes, plus extra to sprinkle
1 tsp each red and green peppercorns
2 tbsp olive oil, plus extra to grease
1 medium egg, beaten, to glaze

1 Sift the flour into a large warmed bowl. Stir in the yeast.
Crush the salt and peppercorns in a pestle and mortar and
stir into the flour. Make a well in the centre of the flour,
then pour in the oil and enough water – about 500ml
(almost 1 pint) – to make a soft dough. (Alternatively,
if using an electric hand mixer, put the flour, yeast, salt,
peppercorns, oil and water in the bowl and knead to
a soft dough with a dough hook.)
2 Put the dough in an oiled bowl, cover with oiled clingfilm
and leave in a warm place until doubled in size.
3 Knead the dough on a floured board for about 5 minutes.
Again, put in an oiled bowl, cover with oiled clingfilm and
leave in a warm place until doubled in size.
4 Punch the dough to knock back, then knead for 1 minute.
Divide into 16 pieces and shape into rolls. Put on greased
baking sheets, spaced well apart, cover with oiled clingfilm
and leave for 30 minutes or until spongy. Preheat the oven
to 220°C (200°C fan oven) mark 7.
5 Brush the rolls with egg, sprinkle with a little salt and
bake for 30–35 minutes until golden.

FREEZING TIP
At step 5, bake for 25 minutes. Cool and freeze.
To use Warm in the oven at 200°C (180°C fan oven)
mark 6 or thaw for 1 hour and warm at the same
temperature for 4–5 minutes.

NUTRITION PER ROLL
157 cals | 2g fat (trace sats) | 33g carbs | 0.3g salt **V**

BLACK OLIVE BREAD

Makes 2 loaves
Preparation 40 minutes, plus rising
Cooking time 30–35 minutes
Techniques see also cooling and troubleshooting (page 311)

2 tsp traditional dried yeast
500g (1lb 2oz) strong white bread flour, plus extra to dust
2 tsp coarse salt, plus extra to sprinkle
6 tbsp extra-virgin olive oil, plus extra to grease
100g (3½oz) black olives, pitted and chopped

1 Put 150ml (¼ pint) hand-hot water into a jug, stir in
the yeast and leave for 10 minutes or until foamy.
2 Put the flour into a bowl or in a food processor, then add
the salt, yeast mix, 200ml (7fl oz) warm water and 2 tbsp oil
to the bowl and use a dough hook to mix. Continue mixing
for 2–3 minutes to make a soft smooth dough. Put the
dough in a lightly oiled bowl, then cover with oiled clingfilm
and a teatowel. Leave in a warm place for 45 minutes or
until doubled in size. Punch the dough to knock out the air,
then knead on a lightly floured worksurface for 1 minute.
Add the olives and knead until combined.
3 Divide in half, shape into rectangles and put into two
greased tins, each around 15 × 25.5 × 4 cm (6 × 10 ×
1½in). Cover with clingfilm and leave in a warm place for
1 hour or until the dough is puffy. Preheat the oven to
200°C (180°C fan oven) mark 6.
4 Press your finger into the dough 12 times, drizzle over
2 tbsp oil and sprinkle with salt. Bake for 30–35 minutes
until golden. Drizzle with the remaining oil and cover with
a cloth for a softer crust. Cut into slices and serve warm.

FREEZING TIP
Wrap and freeze after sprinkling with salt at step 4.
To use Bake the dough from frozen at 200°C (180°C fan
oven) mark 6 for 35–40 minutes until cooked through.

NUTRITION PER LOAF
601 cals | 21g fat (3g sats) | 16g carbs | 0.7g salt **V**

WALNUT AND GARLIC BREAD

Serves 8
Preparation 20 minutes, plus rising
Cooking time 1 hour 50 minutes
Techniques see also preparing garlic (page 183)

oil to grease
500g (1lb 2oz) strong white bread flour with kibbled grains
    of rye and wheat, plus extra to dust
7g sachet fast-action dried yeast
2 tsp salt
2 tbsp malt extract
50g (2oz) butter, softened
3 garlic cloves, crushed
100g (3½oz) walnut pieces
1 tbsp milk

1 Lightly grease a 20.5cm (8in) springform tin. Put the
flour, yeast and salt into the bowl of a freestanding mixer
with a dough hook attachment. Add 300ml (½ pint)
lukewarm water and 1 tbsp malt extract, then mix to a
pliable dough. Increase the speed and machine-knead for
5 minutes.
2 Lightly dust a worksurface with flour, turn out the dough
and roll into a rectangle measuring about 40.5 × 28cm (16
× 11in). Mix together the butter and garlic and spread over
the dough. Scatter the walnuts over and, starting at the long
edge, roll up into a sausage. Cut into eight slices and put in
the tin. Cover with lightly oiled clingfilm and leave to rise in
a warm place for 45 minutes or until doubled in size.
Preheat the oven to 220°C (200°C fan oven) mark 7 and
put a baking sheet in to heat.
3 Remove the clingfilm, cover the bread with foil and put
on the hot baking sheet. Bake for 20 minutes. Reduce the
oven temperature to 200°C (180°C fan oven) mark 6 and
bake for 1 hour 10 minutes.
4 Mix the milk with the remaining malt extract and brush
the glaze over the bread. Bake, uncovered, for 5 minutes or
until golden brown. Leave in the tin to cool slightly, then
remove and serve warm.

FREEZING TIP
At step 3 turn the oven down to 200°C (180°C fan oven)
mark 6 and continue to bake for a further 40 minutes.
Remove from the oven and cool in the tin. Freeze for up to
one month.
To use from frozen, cover with foil, put on a hot baking
sheet and bake at 220°C (200°C fan oven) mark 7 for
45 minutes. Continue with the recipe.

NUTRITION PER SERVING
359 cals | 15g fat (4g sats) | 52g carbs | 1.3g salt

WARM CORNBREAD

Serves 8
Preparation 10 minutes
Cooking time 25–30 minutes, plus resting
Techniques see also making bread (page 310)

oil to grease
125g (4oz) plain flour
175g (6oz) polenta or cornmeal
1 tbsp baking powder
1 tbsp caster sugar
½ tsp salt
285ml (9½fl oz) buttermilk, or equal quantities of natural
    yogurt and milk, mixed together
2 medium eggs
4 tbsp extra-virgin olive oil

1 Preheat the oven to 200°C (180°C fan oven) mark 6.
Generously grease a 20.5cm (8in) square shallow tin.
2 Put the flour into a large bowl, then add the polenta
or cornmeal, baking powder, sugar and salt. Make a well in
the centre and pour in the buttermilk or yogurt and milk
mixture. Add the eggs and oil, then stir together until
evenly mixed.
3 Pour into the tin, then bake for 25–30 minutes until firm
to the touch. Double check by plunging a skewer into the
centre – if it comes out clean, the cornbread is done.
4 Leave the cornbread to rest in the tin for 5 minutes,
then turn out and cut into chunky triangles. Serve warm
with butter.

NUTRITION PER SERVING
229 cals | 8g fat (1g sats) | 32g carbs | 1.3g salt **V**

MARBLED CHOCOLATE TEABREAD

Cuts into about 10 slices
Preparation 15 minutes
Cooking time 1¼–1½ hours, plus cooling
Techniques see also zesting citrus fruits (page 217), melting chocolate (page 366)

225g (8oz) butter, plus extra for greasing
225g (8oz) caster sugar
4 medium eggs, beaten
225g (8oz) self-raising flour
finely grated zest of 1 large orange
1 tbsp orange juice
a few drops orange flower water (optional)
75g (3oz) plain chocolate
1 tbsp cocoa powder, sifted

1 Preheat the oven to 180°C (160°C fan oven) mark 4. Grease a 900ml (2 pint) loaf tin and line the base and sides with greaseproof paper.
2 Cream the butter and sugar together until pale and fluffy, then gradually beat in the eggs, beating well after each addition. Fold in the flour.
3 Transfer half the mixture to another bowl and beat in the orange zest, juice and orange flower water, if using.
4 Break the chocolate into pieces, put into a small bowl and place over a pan of simmering water, making sure the base of the bowl doesn't touch the water. Stir until the chocolate melts. Stir into the remaining cake mixture with the cocoa powder.
5 Put alternate spoonfuls of the two mixtures into the prepared tin. Use a knife to swirl through the mixture to make a marbled effect, then level the surface.
6 Bake in the oven for 1¼–1½ hours until well risen and firm to the touch. Turn out on to a wire rack to cool. Serve cut in slices.

NUTRITION PER SLICE
406 cals | 24g fat (14g sats) | 46g carbs | 0.1g salt Ⓥ

CHEESE AND WALNUT LOAF

Makes 1 large loaf
Preparation 25 minutes, plus rising
Cooking time 45 minutes, plus cooling
Techniques see also bread basics (page 310), chopping nuts (page 228), chopping herbs (page 436)

oil to grease
15g (½oz) fresh yeast or 1½ tsp dried and a pinch of sugar
450g (1lb) strong wholemeal flour, plus extra to dust
1 tsp salt
½ tsp paprika
1½ tsp mustard powder
175g (6oz) Cheddar cheese, grated
125g (4oz) walnut pieces, finely chopped
3 tbsp chopped fresh mixed herbs
or 1 tsp dried herbs

1 Grease a 900g (2lb) loaf tin. Blend the fresh yeast with 300ml (½ pint) warm water. If using dried yeast, sprinkle it into 300ml (½ pint) warm water with the sugar and leave in a warm place for 15 minutes or until frothy.
2 Put the flour, salt, paprika, mustard powder, 125g (4oz) of the cheese, the walnuts and herbs into a large bowl and mix together. Make a well in the centre, then pour in the yeast liquid. Mix together to make a smooth dough that leaves the sides of the bowl clean.
3 Turn the dough out on to a lightly floured worksurface and knead well for about 10 minutes or until smooth and elastic. Put into a clean bowl, cover with a clean teatowel and leave in a warm place for about 1 hour or until doubled in size.
4 Turn the dough out on to a floured worksurface and knead lightly. Shape the dough to fit the prepared tin. Cover and leave in a warm place for 30 minutes or until the dough rises almost to the top of the tin. Preheat the oven to 190°C (170°C fan oven) mark 5.
5 Sprinkle the dough with the remaining cheese and bake for 45 minutes or until well risen and the loaf sounds hollow when tapped underneath. Turn out on to a wire rack to cool.

NUTRITION PER SLICE
176 cals | 9g fat (3g sats) | 18g carbs | 0.5g salt **V**

KUGELHOPF

Serves 12
Preparation 45 minutes, plus overnight chilling and rising
Cooking time 50–55 minutes
Techniques see also zesting citrus fruits (page 217), toasting nuts (page 228)

200g (7oz) raisins, black seedless if possible
3 tbsp light rum
2 tsp fast-action dried yeast
300g (11oz) plain white flour, plus extra to dust
4 large eggs
100ml (3½fl oz) milk
225g (8oz) unsalted butter, softened, plus extra to grease
75g (3oz) caster sugar
pinch of salt
zest of 1 lemon
100g (3½oz) split blanched almonds, lightly toasted
icing sugar to dust
whole glacé fruits, nuts and silver or gold dragées
    to decorate

1 Combine the raisins and rum, cover and soak overnight. Put the yeast and flour in a food mixer. Lightly whisk the eggs and milk then, with the machine running on a slow speed, pour in the egg mixture and mix for 10 minutes or until the dough is very smooth, shiny and elastic. In another bowl, beat the butter, caster sugar, salt and lemon zest then, with the mixer running, add to the dough, a spoonful at a time, until evenly incorporated. Turn the mixture into a large lightly floured bowl. Cover with clingfilm and chill overnight.
2 Generously grease a 2 litre (3½ pint) Kugelhopf ring mould. Press one-third of the almonds on to the sides of the mould. Chill. Roughly chop the remaining almonds. Mix by hand into the dough with the raisins and rum, then put in the mould, cover and leave for 3 hours in a warm place until it feels spongy and has risen to within 2cm (¾in) of the top of the mould.
3 Preheat the oven to 200°C (180°C fan oven) mark 6. Bake on a shelf below the centre of the oven for 10 minutes. Cover with greaseproof paper, reduce the temperature to 190°C (170°C fan oven) mark 5 and bake for 40–45 minutes until the Kugelhopf sounds hollow when you tap the mould. Cool in the tin for 15 minutes. Turn on to a wire rack to cool completely. Decorate and serve dusted with icing sugar.

COOK'S TIP
This cake is made with yeast, so it's best eaten within two days or it will go stale. If you have any left over, wrap and freeze in slices – it's tasty toasted or used for making bread and butter pudding.

NUTRITION PER SERVING
382 cals | 22g fat (11g sats) | 39g carbs | 0.4g salt

BREAD AND BUTTER PUDDING

Serves 4
Preparation 10 minutes, plus soaking
Cooking time 30-40 minutes

50g (2oz) butter, softened, plus extra to grease
275g (10oz) white farmhouse bread, cut into 1cm (½in)
    slices, crusts removed
50g (2oz) raisins or sultanas
3 medium eggs
450ml (¾ pint) milk
3 tbsp golden icing sugar, plus extra to dust

1 Lightly grease four 300ml (½ pint) gratin dishes or one
1.1 litre (2 pint) ovenproof dish. Butter the bread, then cut
into quarters to make triangles. Arrange the bread in the
dish(es) and sprinkle with the raisins.
2 Beat the eggs, milk and sugar in a bowl. Pour the mixture
over the bread and leave to soak for 10 minutes. Preheat
the oven to 180°C (160°C fan oven) mark 4.
3 Put the pudding(s) in the oven and bake for 30–40
minutes. Dust with icing sugar to serve.

NUTRITION PER SERVING
450 cals | 13g fat (5g sats) | 70g carbs | 1.1g salt **V**

TUNA MELT PIZZA

Serves 4
Preparation 10 minutes
Cooking time 10–12 minutes
Techniques see also making pizza (page 316)

2 large pizza bases
4 tbsp sun-dried tomato pesto
2 × 185g cans tuna, drained
50g can anchovies, drained and chopped
125g (4oz) grated mature Cheddar cheese
rocket to serve

1 Preheat the oven to 220°C (200°C fan oven) mark 7.
Take the pizza bases and spread each base with 2 tbsp
sun-dried tomato pesto. Top each with half the tuna, half
the anchovies and half the grated cheese.
2 Put on to a baking sheet and cook for 10–12 minutes
until the cheese has melted. Sprinkle with rocket to serve.

COOK'S TIP
You can make your own pizza base from scratch
following the technique on page 316, or buy ready-
made bases from the supermarket. You can buy fresh
ones, vacuum-packed ones or packet mixes that you
mix, knead and roll out yourself.

NUTRITION PER SERVING
607 cals | 33g fat (10g sats) | 51g carbs | 3.1g salt

MUFFINS

Makes about 12
Preparation 20 minutes, plus rising
Cooking time 15 minutes per batch
Techniques see also bread basics (page 310)

15g (½oz) fresh yeast or 1½ tsp dried yeast
300ml (½ pint) warm milk
450g (1lb) strong white flour, plus extra to dust
1 tsp salt
1 tsp plain flour
1 tsp semolina

1 Dissolve the yeast in the milk. If using dried yeast,
sprinkle over the milk and leave in a warm place for
15 minutes or until frothy.
2 Sift the strong white flour and salt together, then make
a well in the centre. Pour the yeast liquid into the well,
draw in the flour and mix to a smooth dough.
3 Knead the dough on a lightly floured worksurface for
about 10 minutes or until smooth and elastic. Put in a clean
bowl, cover with a teatowel and leave in a warm place for
about 1 hour or until doubled in size.
4 Using a lightly floured rolling pin, roll out the dough on
a lightly floured surface to about 0.5–1cm (¼–½in) thick.
Leave to rest, covered with a teatowel, for 5 minutes.
Using a 7.5cm (3in) plain cutter, cut into rounds.
5 Put the muffins on a well-floured baking sheet. Mix
together the plain flour and the semolina and use to dust
the tops. Cover with a teatowel and leave in a warm place
until doubled in size.
6 Grease a griddle or heavy frying pan and heat over
a medium heat until a cube of bread turns brown in
20 seconds.
7 Cook the muffins on the griddle or frying pan for
about 7 minutes each side or until golden brown.

NUTRITION PER MUFFIN
142 cals | 1g fat (trace sats) | 30g carbs | 0.5g salt **V**

CAKES, COOKIES, BISCUITS AND TRAYBAKES

Learn the secrets of successful home baking with the easy-to-follow, step-by-step guide to preparation and cooking techniques – from lining tins and making cake and cookie mixtures, to baking, filling and decorating. This chapter is packed with tips for success including testing cakes for doneness, cooling cakes and cookies and troubleshooting tips. The recipe collection is full of wonderful treats for children and adults alike including Rich fruit cake, Apple madeleines, The ultimate chocolate brownie, Chocolate and hazelnut biscotti, Somerset apple cake, St Clements cupcakes, Carrot cake and Traditional flapjacks.

LINING TINS

Always line your cake tin with greaseproof paper – this will help to stop the cake sticking to the sides of the tin or burning. Lightly grease the tin first to help keep the paper in place.

Square tin

1 Cut out a square of greaseproof paper slightly smaller than the base of the tin. Cut four strips about 2cm (¾in) wider than the depth of the tin and fold up one of the longest edges of each strip by 1cm (½in).

2 Lightly grease the tin with butter, making sure it is coated on all sides and in the corners.

3 Cut one strip to the length of the side of the tin and press into place in one corner and then along the length of the strip with the narrow folded section sitting on the base. Continue, cutting to fit into the corners, to cover all four sides.

4 Lay the square on the base of the tin, then grease the paper, taking care not to move the side strips.

Round tin

1 Put the tin on a sheet of greaseproof paper and draw a circle around its circumference. Cut out the circle just inside the drawn line.

2 Cut a strip or strips about 2cm (¾in) wider than the depth of the tin and fold up one long edge of each strip by 1cm (½in). Make cuts, about 2.5cm (1in) apart, through the folded edge of the strip(s) up to the fold line.

3 Lightly grease the tin with butter, making sure it is completely coated.

4 Press the strip(s) on to the sides of the tin so that the snipped edge sits on the base.

5 Lay the circle in the bottom of the tin and grease the paper

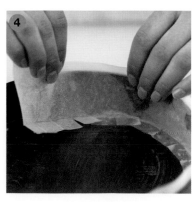

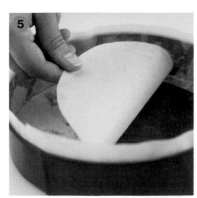

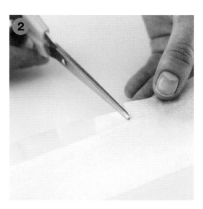

Swiss roll tin

Use this method for a Swiss roll or any other shallow baking tin.

1 Lightly grease the tin with butter, making sure it is completely coated.

2 Cut a piece of baking parchment into a rectangle 7.5cm (3in) wider and longer than the tin. Press it into the tin and cut at the corners, then fold to fit neatly. Grease all over.

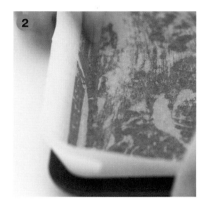

PERFECT LINING

→ Use greaseproof paper for all cakes and baking parchment for roulades and meringues.

→ Apply the butter with a small piece of greaseproof paper. Don't thickly grease the tin, as this would 'fry' the edges of the cake.

Loaf tin

1 Lightly grease the tin with butter, making sure it is completely coated.

2 Cut out a sheet of greaseproof paper to the same length as the base and wide enough to cover both the base and the long sides. Press it into position, making sure that it sits snugly in the corners.

3 Now cut another sheet to the same width as the base and long enough to cover both the base and the ends of the tin. Press into place. Grease the paper all over.

LINERS

Reusable, non-stick, silicone baking mats and liners are widely available and, as there is no need to grease them, they reduce the fat in your baking. Look out also for silicone muffin trays and cupcake moulds.

MAKING CAKES

A wide variety of cakes can be prepared using just three basic techniques: creaming, all-in-one and whisking. These straightforward basic recipes can be adapted in several ways.

Creamed sponge

A classic Victoria sponge can be used to make many cakes, including chocolate or fruit.

You will need 175g (6oz) softened butter, 175g (6oz) caster sugar, 3 medium eggs, 175g (6oz) self-raising flour, 150g (5oz) mascarpone, 4 tbsp raspberry jam, icing sugar to dust.

1 Preheat the oven to 180°C (160°C fan oven) mark 4. Grease and line the base of two 18cm (7in) sandwich tins with greaseproof paper.

2 Put the butter and sugar in a bowl and beat with an electric whisk or wooden spoon until pale, soft and creamy.

3 Beat the eggs and gradually add to butter and sugar mixture, beating well until the mixture is thick and of dropping consistency. (If you like, add a spoonful of flour while adding the eggs to prevent curdling.)

4 Gently fold in the flour using a large metal spoon or spatula, then divide the mixture between the two tins and level the surface. Bake for 25–30 minutes until golden and firm to the touch. Cool slightly in the tins, then turn out on to a wire rack to cool completely.

5 When the cakes are cold, spread one with mascarpone and then the jam. Place the other cake on top and lightly press together. Put on a serving plate and dust lightly with sifted icing sugar.

Testing sponges

1 Gently press the centre of the sponge. It should feel springy. If it's a whisked cake, it should be just shrinking away from the sides of the tin.

2 If you have to put it back into the oven, close the door gently so that the vibrations don't cause the cake to sink in the centre.

COOLING CAKES

- Sponge cakes should be taken out of their tins soon after baking. Invert on to a wire rack lined with sugar-dusted baking parchment.
- Leave fruit cakes to cool in the tin for 15 minutes before turning out.
- Leave rich fruit cakes to cool completely before turning out; there is a risk of breaking otherwise.

Whisked Genoese sponge

For this coffee cake, you will need 1 tbsp instant espresso granules, 50g (2oz) butter, 4 large eggs, 125g (4oz) golden caster sugar, 125g (4oz) sifted plain flour. For the filling, you will need 1 tbsp instant coffee, 250g (9oz) mascarpone, 125g (4oz) sifted golden icing sugar, plus extra to dust.

1 Preheat the oven to 190°C (170°C fan oven) mark 5. Line two 18cm (7in) sandwich tins. Dissolve the coffee in 2 tsp boiling water.

2 Melt the butter in a small pan. Put the eggs and sugar in a large bowl set over a pan of simmering water. Whisk for about 5 minutes with an electric hand mixer until creamy and pale and the mixture leaves a trail when you lift the whisk.

3 Gently fold half the flour into the mixture. Mix the coffee into the butter and pour half around the edge of the mixture, then fold in the remaining flour, coffee and butter.

4 Pour into the tins and bake for 25 minutes or until risen, firm to the touch and shrinking away from the

sides of the tin. Turn on to wire racks, remove the paper and leave to cool.

5 To make the filling, dissolve the coffee in 1 tbsp boiling water and beat with the mascarpone and sugar until smooth. Spread over one sponge, top with the other and dust with icing sugar.

All-in-one cherry cakes

To make 12 cupcakes, you will need 175g (6oz) butter, softened, 175g (6oz) golden caster sugar, 3 medium eggs, 175g (6oz) self-raising flour, sifted, pinch of baking powder, 75g (3oz) dried sour cherries, 2 tbsp milk.

1 Preheat the oven to 190°C (170°C fan oven) mark 5. Line a muffin tin with 12 muffin cases. Put the butter, sugar, eggs, flour and baking powder in a large bowl or mixer.

2 Mix slowly to start, then increase the speed slightly until well combined. Fold the cherries into the mixture with the milk. Spoon into the paper cases and bake for 15–20 minutes

until golden, risen and springy to the touch. Leave to cool on a wire rack. Ice with buttercream (see page 342).

Marbled cake

You will need 175g (6oz) butter, softened, 175g (6oz) golden caster sugar, 3 medium eggs, 125g (4oz) self-raising flour, 50g (2oz) ground almonds, 1 tsp baking powder, finely grated zest of 1 orange, 1 tbsp brandy, 4 tbsp cocoa powder, sifted.

1 Preheat the oven to 190°C (fan oven 170°C) mark 5. Line a 900g (2lb) loaf tin.

2 Cream the butter and sugar until pale, then beat in the eggs, one at a time. Sift the flour, almonds and baking powder over and fold in. Stir in the orange zest and brandy.

3 Divide the mixture between two bowls and stir the cocoa into one. Spoon the mixtures into the tin in two layers, then drag a skewer through. Bake for 45 minutes.

Fruity tea cake

You will need 75g (3oz) dried figs, 75g (3oz) stoned prunes, 150ml (¼ pint) hot Earl Grey tea, 200g (7oz) sultanas, 150g (5oz) dark muscovado sugar, 2 medium eggs, 225g (8oz) self-raising flour, 2 tsp ground mixed spice, vegetable oil to grease.

1 Chop the figs and prunes, then soak in the tea with the sultanas for 30 minutes.

2 Beat the sugar and eggs until creamy, then mix in the flour, spice, soaked fruit and tea.

3 Preheat oven to 190°C (fan oven 170°C) mark 5. Grease 900g (2lb) loaf tin and line with greaseproof paper. Pour in the mixture and bake for 1 hour or until a skewer inserted in the centre comes out clean. Cool on a wire rack. Serve sliced, with butter.

Testing fruit cakes

1 To test if a fruit cake is cooked, insert a skewer into the centre of the cake, leave for a few moments, then pull it out. If it comes away clean, the cake is ready.

2 If any mixture sticks to the skewer, the cake is not quite done so put the cake back in the oven for a few more minutes, then test again with a clean skewer.

TROUBLESHOOTING

A dense texture may be due to too little raising agent, or adding the eggs too quickly.
A peaked, cracked top appears if the oven is too hot or the cake is too near the top of the oven; the tin is too small; or too much raising agent was used.

MAKING ROULADES

A roulade is made from a very light cake mixture and does not contain flour. It remains very soft when baked, and can therefore be easily rolled around a layer of filling such as jam and cream.

Chocolate cherry roll

To serve eight, you will need 4 tbsp cocoa powder, 150ml (¼ pint) milk, 5 medium eggs, separated, 125g (4oz) golden caster sugar, 400g can pitted cherries, 1–2 tbsp cherry jam, sifted icing sugar to dust.

1 Preheat the oven to 180°C (160°C fan oven) mark 4 and line a 30.5 × 20.5cm (12 × 8in) Swiss roll tin with baking parchment.

2 Mix the cocoa with 3 tbsp milk in a bowl, then heat the remaining milk in a pan or in the microwave until almost boiling. Pour over the cocoa, stirring, then cool for 10 minutes.

3 Meanwhile, separate the eggs. Whisk the egg whites until soft peaks form. In another bowl, whisk the yolks with the sugar until pale and thick, then gradually whisk in the cooled milk.

4 Fold in the egg whites, spoon the mixture into the tin and level. Bake for 25 minutes until just firm.

5 Turn out on to a board lined with baking parchment and peel off the lining paper. Cover with a damp teatowel.

6 Drain the cherries and chop. Spread the jam over the roulade and top with the chopped fruit.

7 Very carefully, roll up from the shortest end. Dust with cocoa and icing sugar and serve in slices.

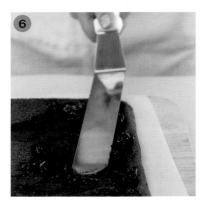

VARIATION

You can add whipped cream to a roulade, but you will need to cool the roulade first. To do this, turn out the roulade on to baking parchment. Do not remove the lining paper but roll the roulade around it while still warm. Leave to cool, unroll and peel off the paper. Spread with cream, and jam if you wish, and re-roll.

MAKING CUPCAKES AND MUFFINS

Cupcakes and muffins are two members of the same family: individual cakes, usually based on a mixture made with self-raising flour, baked in bun tins or muffin pans so that it rises and sets to an airy texture.

Vanilla cupcakes

To make 12 cupcakes, you will need 125g (4oz) softened butter; 125g (4oz) golden caster sugar; 2 medium eggs, 125g (4oz) self-raising flour; 1 tbsp vanilla extract, 200g (7oz) white chocolate.

1 Preheat the oven to 190°C (170°C fan oven) mark 5. Line a bun tin or muffin pan with 12 paper cases.

2 Beat the butter, sugar, eggs, flour and vanilla until smooth and creamy. Half-fill the muffin cases with the mixture and bake for 15–20 minutes until pale golden, risen and springy to the touch. Transfer to a wire rack to cool.

3 When the cupcakes are cool, melt the chocolate (see page 366). Spoon over the cakes and leave to set.

Banana and pecan muffins

To make 12 muffins, you will need 275g (10oz) self-raising flour; 1 tbsp bicarbonate of soda, 1 tsp salt, 3 very ripe, large bananas, about 450g (1lb), peeled and mashed, 125g (4oz) golden caster sugar, 1 large egg, 50ml (2fl oz) milk, 75g (3oz) melted butter, 50g (2oz) chopped roasted pecans.

1 Preheat the oven to 180°C (160°C fan oven) mark 4. Line a muffin pan with 12 paper cases. Sift together the flour, bicarbonate of soda and salt. Put to one side.

2 Combine the bananas, sugar, egg and milk, then pour the melted butter in and mix well. Add to the flour mixture with the nuts, stirring quickly and gently with just a few strokes.

3 Half-fill the muffin cases.

4 Bake for 20 minutes until golden and risen. Cool on a wire rack.

PERFECT MUFFINS

The secret to really light, fluffy muffins is a light hand.
- Be sure to sift the flour.
- Stir the mixture as little as possible; it's ok if it looks a little lumpy.
- Overmixing will give tough, chewy results.

MAKING CHEESECAKES

There are many ways to make this perennial favourite, which can be baked or simply chilled and set with gelatine. When baking cheeesecakes, watch the temperature – too high a heat can cause the top to crack.

Lemon cheesecake

You will need 125g (4oz) unsalted butter, 250g (9oz) digestive biscuits, 1 large lemon, 2 medium eggs, 500g (1lb 2oz) full-fat cream cheese, 140ml (4½fl oz) soured cream, 175g (6oz) golden caster sugar, 1½ tsp vanilla extract, 1 tsp cornflour, 50g (2oz) sultanas.

1 Grease base and sides of a 23cm (9in) springform tin. Melt the butter in a large pan. Chop the biscuits in a food processor, or put in a plastic bag and bash with a rolling pin. Stir into the butter, tip into tin and press down using back of a spoon. Chill for 1 hour.

2 Preheat the oven to 180°C (fan 160°C) mark 4. Grate the lemon zest into a large bowl and set aside. Halve the lemon, set aside 3 thin slices, and squeeze juice into bowl with zest.

3 Add the eggs, cream cheese, soured cream, sugar, vanilla and cornflour to the bowl. Using an electric mixer, whisk until smooth. Fold in the sultanas.

4 Pour the mixture into the tin and tap on the worksurface to level it out.

5 Bake for 30 minutes, then arrange the lemon slices on top and bake for 20–25 minutes until just set but still a little wobbly in the centre. Turn off the oven, leave the door ajar and allow to cool for at least 2 hours.

6 Chill. Remove from fridge 30 minutes before serving in slices.

CHILLED CHEESECAKE

An uncooked cheesecake is usually set with gelatine and made with a mixture of cream cheese and perhaps some cottage cheese flavoured with lemon zest. The mixture is poured on to a biscuit crumb base (usually made with crushed biscuits mixed with melted butter) that has been pressed into a flan tin then chilled until firm. The whole cheesecake is then chilled to set. Fresh fruit or a fruit coulis can be added as a topping.

COVERING CAKES

There are lots of options for covering cakes, depending on the finish you require. Marzipan, followed by a layer of ready-to-roll icing (sugar paste) is popular, as is buttercream or apricot glaze.

Marzipan

A versatile and attractive cake topping, marzipan can be used in a number of ways. Home-made marzipan has a good flavour and is not difficult to make.

To make 450g (1lb) marzipan, you will need 225g (8oz) ground almonds, 125g (4oz) golden caster sugar, 125g (4oz) sifted golden icing sugar, 1 large egg, 2 tsp lemon juice, 1 tsp sherry, 1–2 drops vanilla extract.

1 Put the ground almonds and sugars into a bowl and stir to combine. In another bowl, whisk together the remaining ingredients, then add to the dry ingredients.

2 Stir well to mix, pounding gently to release some of the oil from the almonds. Knead with your hands until smooth, then cover until ready to use.

> ### APRICOT GLAZE
>
> To make 450g (1lb), you will need 450g (1lb) apricot jam, 2 tbsp water. Put the jam and water into a saucepan and heat gently, stirring occasionally, until melted. Boil the jam rapidly for 1 minute, then strain through a sieve. Using a wooden spoon, rub through as much fruit as possible. Discard the skins left in the sieve. Pour the glaze into a clean, hot jar, then seal with a clean lid and cool. Store in the fridge for up to two months.

Covering a cake with marzipan

Once you have marzipanned the cake, you need to allow time for it to dry, for at least 12 hours and up to 2 days, before covering with icing. Home-made marzipan takes a little longer to dry out than the ready-made variety.

1 Trim the top of the cake level if necessary, then turn the cake over to give a flat surface to work on. Place on the cake board, which should be at least 5cm (2in) larger than the cake. Brush the cake with warmed apricot glaze.

2 Dust the worksurface with sifted icing sugar. Roll out half the marzipan to fit the top of the cake. Lift the marzipan on top of the cake and smooth over, neatening the edges.

3 Cut a piece of string the same height as the cake with the marzipan topping, and another to fit around the diameter of the cake. Roll out the remaining marzipan and, using the string as a guide, trim it to size. Roll up the marzipan strip loosely. Place one end against the side of the cake and

unroll the marzipan around the cake to cover it. Use a palette knife to smooth over the sides and joins. Leave the cake in a cool, dry place to dry out for at least 24 hours before covering with ready-to-roll icing. Leave to dry for at least two days before applying royal icing.

Covering a cake with ready-to-roll icing (sugar paste)

Ready-to-roll icing is pliable and can be used to cover cakes or moulded into decorative shapes. Blocks of ready-to-roll icing (sugar paste) are available in a variety of colours from supermarkets and specialist cake decorating shops.

A 450g (1lb) pack will cover an 18cm (7in) cake. Wrap any unused icing in clingfilm to stop it drying out and store in a cool, dry place.

1 Dust the worksurface and rolling pin with sifted icing sugar. Knead the icing until pliable, then roll out into a round or square 5–7.5cm (2–3in) larger than the cake all round. Lift the icing on top of the cake and allow it to drape over the edges.

2 Dust your hands with sifted icing sugar and press the icing on to the sides of the cake, easing it down to the board.

3 Using a sharp knife, trim off the excess icing at the base to neaten. Reserve the trimmings to make decorations if required.

4 Using your fingers dusted with a little sifted icing sugar, gently rub the surface in a circular movement to buff the icing and make it smooth.

Covering a cake with royal icing or buttercream

Buttercream can be spread directly on to the cake; if you are using royal icing, first cover the cake with apricot glaze (see opposite).

1 Stir royal icing or buttercream just before using, to make sure it is easy to spread.

2 Put the cake on a plate or cake board and use a palette knife to spread the icing evenly over the cake.

ICINGS

Royal

Royal icing can be bought in packs from supermarkets. Simply add water or egg white to use. To make 450g (1lb), enough to cover the top and sides of a 20cm (8in) cake, you will need 2 medium egg whites, ¼ tsp lemon juice, 450g (1lb) icing sugar, sifted, 1 tsp glycerine.

1 Put the egg whites and lemon juice into a clean bowl. Stir to break up the egg whites. Add sufficient icing sugar to mix to the consistency of unwhipped cream. Continue mixing and adding small quantities of icing sugar until the desired consistency is reached, mixing well and gently beating after each addition. The icing should be smooth, glossy and light, almost like a cold meringue in texture, but not aerated. Do not add the icing sugar too quickly or it will produce a dull heavy icing. Stir in the glycerine until well blended. (Alternatively, for large quantities of royal icing, use a food mixer on the lowest speed, following the same instructions as before.)

2 Allow the icing to settle before using it; cover the surface with a piece of damp clingfilm and seal well, excluding all the air.

3 Stir the icing thoroughly before use to disperse any air bubbles, then adjust the consistency if necessary by adding more sifted icing sugar.

Buttercream

To cover the top of a 20.5cm (8in) cake, you will need: 75g (3oz) unsalted butter, 175g (6oz) icing sugar, sifted, a few drops of vanilla extract, 1–2 tbsp milk.

1 Soften the butter in a mixing bowl, then beat until light and fluffy.

2 Gradually stir in the remaining ingredients and beat until smooth.

Glacé

To make 225g (8oz), enough to cover 18 fairy cakes, you will need 225g (8oz) icing sugar, few drops of vanilla or almond flavouring (optional), 2–3 tbsp boiling water, food colouring (optional).

1 Sift the icing sugar into a bowl. Add a few drops of flavouring, if you like.

2 Using a wooden spoon, gradually stir in enough water until the mixture is the consistency of thick cream. Beat until white and smooth and the icing is thick enough to coat the back of the spoon. Add colouring, if you like, and use immediately.

VARIATIONS

Citrus Replace the vanilla with a little grated orange, lemon or lime zest, and use some of the fruit's juice in place of the milk.
Chocolate Blend 1 tbsp cocoa powder with 2 tbsp boiling water. Cool, then add to the mixture in place of the milk.
Colour For a strong colour, use food colouring paste; liquid colouring gives a paler effect (see Cook's Tip below).

VARIATIONS

Orange or lemon Replace the water with strained orange or lemon juice.
Chocolate Sift 2 tsp cocoa powder with the icing sugar.
Colour Add a few drops of liquid food colouring, or use food colouring paste for a stronger colour if you prefer.

COOK'S TIP

Food colourings are available in liquid, paste or powder form. Add minute amounts with the tip of a cocktail stick until the desired colour is achieved.

FILLING AND TOPPING CAKES

To make sponge cakes even tastier, they can be split and filled with jam, cream or buttercream. Icings complete a special-occasion cake and are especially good when covering home-made marzipan.

Splitting and filling a cake

1 Leave the cake to cool completely before splitting. Use a knife with a shallow thin blade such as a bread knife, a ham knife, or a carving knife. Cut a notch from top to bottom on one side so you will know where to line the pieces up.

2 Cut midway between top and bottom, about 30% of the way through the cake. Turn the cake while cutting, taking care to keep the blade parallel with the base, until you have cut all the way around.

3 Cut through the central core and lift off the top of the cake.

4 Warm the filling slightly to make it easier to spread, then spread on top of the base, stopping 1cm (½in) from the edge.

5 Add the top layer of cake.

Easiest icing

To cover a 20.5cm (8in) marzipan-covered cake, you will need 3 medium egg whites, 2 tbsp lemon juice, 2 tsp glycerine, 675g (1½lb) icing sugar, sifted.

1 Put the egg whites in a large bowl and whisk until frothy. There should be just a layer of bubbles across the top. Add the lemon juice, glycerine and 2 tbsp of icing sugar and whisk until smooth.

2 Whisk in the rest of the sugar, a little at a time, until the mixture is smooth and thick, forming soft peaks.

3 Using a palette knife, smooth half the icing over the top and sides of the cake, then repeat using the remaining icing to cover. Run the knife around the sides to neaten, then use the tip to make peaks all over the top. Leave to dry in a cool place for at least 48 hours.

SHORTCUT CAKE

Lay one or two family-sized loaf cakes (available from supermarkets) next to each other on a cake board, depending on the size of the finished cake required. Cover with a thin layer of bought vanilla or chocolate buttercream-style icing, then cover with ready-to-roll icing and decorate with edible decorations. Or, cover with a thicker layer of buttercream and omit the ready-to-roll icing.

MAKING BISCUITS

Each recipe in this section covers one of the main techniques in biscuit making: creamed, the all-in-one method, rolled, refrigerator biscuits, whisked, melted, moulded and piped.

Creamed choc-oat cookies

Biscuits using this creaming method firm up when cooled.

To make 18 cookies, you will need 125g (4oz) white chocolate, 125g (4oz) plain chocolate, 125g (4oz) unsalted butter, softened, 125g (4oz) caster sugar, 1 medium egg, 1 tsp vanilla extract, 125g (4oz) porridge oats, 150g (5oz) plain flour, ½ tsp baking powder.

1 Preheat the oven to 180°C (160°C fan oven) mark 4 and lightly grease two baking sheets. Using a sharp knife, chop the white and plain chocolate into small chunks, no larger than 1cm (½in).

2 Cream the butter and sugar together in a bowl until pale. Add the egg, vanilla and oats. Sift in the flour and baking powder and mix until evenly combined. Stir in the chocolate chunks.

3 Place dessertspoonfuls of the mixture on to the baking sheets, spacing them apart to allow room for spreading. Flatten each one slightly with the back of a fork.

4 Bake for 12–15 minutes until risen and turning golden. Leave on the baking sheets for 5 minutes, then transfer to a wire rack to cool completely. Store in an airtight tin for up to one week.

All-in-one peanut cookies

Softened butter is essential for making all-in-one cookies.

To make 30 cookies, you will need 125g (4oz) butter, softened, 150g (5oz) caster sugar, 1 medium egg, 150g (5oz) plain white flour, ½ tsp baking powder, pinch of salt, 125g (4oz) crunchy peanut butter, 175g (6oz) raisins.

1 Preheat the oven to 190°C (170°C fan oven) mark 5 and lightly grease two baking sheets.

2 Put all the ingredients except the raisins into a bowl and beat together until well blended. Stir in the raisins.

3 Spoon large teaspoonfuls of the mixture on to the baking sheets, spacing them apart to leave room for spreading.

4 Bake for 15 minutes or until golden brown around the edges. Leave to cool slightly before lifting on to a wire rack to cool completely.

Rolled vanilla biscuits

The quickest and easiest way to make biscuits of consistent thickness is by rolling and then cutting using a biscuit cutter. The dough must be firm enough to roll to a thickness of 3mm (⅛in).

You will need 175g (6oz) softened unsalted butter, 200g (7oz) golden caster sugar, 350g (12oz) plain flour, 1 medium egg, 2 tsp vanilla bean paste, 2 tbsp golden icing sugar.

1 Preheat the oven to 200°C (180°C fan oven) mark 6. Put the butter, sugar, flour, egg and vanilla bean paste into a food processor and whiz to combine. Alternatively, cream the butter and sugar, and then stir in the flour, egg and vanilla bean paste.

2 Put the dough on a large sheet of baking parchment. Press the dough gently but firmly with the palm of your hand to flatten it slightly, then put another sheet of baking parchment on top – this will prevent the dough from sticking.

3 Use a rolling pin to roll out the dough to 3mm (⅛in) thick, and then remove the top sheet of baking parchment.

4 Using 6.5cm (2½in) cutters, stamp out biscuits, leaving a 3mm (⅛in) gap between each one.

5 Peel off the trimmings around the shapes, then slide the baking parchment and biscuits on to a flat baking sheet.

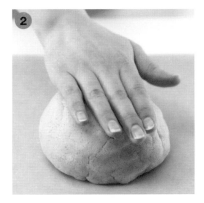

6 Re-roll the trimmings between two new sheets of baking parchment, then stamp out shapes as before and slide on to another baking sheet.

7 Bake the biscuits for 10–12 minutes until pale golden. Cool for a few minutes, then transfer to a wire rack to cool completely.

8 Dust the biscuits with sifted icing sugar. Store in an airtight container for up to five days.

Chocolate refrigerator roll

There is no baking required for refrigerator biscuits.

To make 14 slices, you will need 75g (3oz) digestive biscuits, 50g (2oz) flaked almonds, lightly toasted, 50g (2oz) ready-to-eat dried apricots, finely chopped, 1 piece preserved stem ginger in syrup, drained and finely chopped, 75g (3oz) white chocolate, roughly chopped, 175g (6oz) plain chocolate, in pieces, 65g (2½oz) unsalted butter, 50g (2oz) white chocolate, melted, to decorate.

1   Break the biscuits into chunky pieces and mix with the almonds, apricots, ginger and white chocolate.

2   Melt the plain chocolate with the butter in a heatproof bowl over a pan of gently simmering water, stirring occasionally, until smooth. Remove from the heat and leave until cool, but not beginning to set.

3   Pour the chocolate on to the biscuit mixture and stir gently to mix.

4   Spoon on to greaseproof paper and wrap this around the mixture, making a sausage about 20.5cm (8in) long. Chill for 1–2 hours until firm.

5   Cut the roll into 1cm (½in) slices.

6   Place on a clean sheet of greaseproof paper. Using a teaspoon, drizzle lines of melted white chocolate over the slices to decorate. Chill until ready to serve.

COOK'S TIP

Always make sure that the melted chocolate is quite cool before you mix it with the other ingredients, or the white chocolate will melt.

Melted ginger biscuits

Some biscuits using the melted method are soft, others brittle.

To make 24 biscuits, you will need 125g (4oz) golden syrup, 50g (2oz) butter, 50g (2oz) dark muscovado sugar, grated zest of 1 orange, 2 tbsp orange juice, 175g (6oz) self-raising flour, 1 tsp ground ginger.

1 Preheat the oven to 180°C (160°C fan oven) mark 4 and lightly grease two large baking sheets.

2 Put the syrup, butter, sugar, orange zest and juice in a pan and heat gently until melted. Mix. Leave the mixture to cool slightly, then sift in the flour with the ginger. Mix well until smooth.

3 Space spoonfuls well apart on baking sheets, to allow for spreading. Bake for 12 minutes or until golden brown. Leave for 1 minute, then transfer to a wire rack to cool.

Almond macaroons

To make 22 biscuits, you will need 2 medium egg whites, 125g (4oz) caster sugar, 125g (4oz) ground almonds, ¼ tsp almond extract, 22 blanched almonds,

1 Preheat the oven to 180°C (160°C fan oven) mark 4. Line two baking sheets with baking parchment.

2 Whisk the egg whites in a spotlessly clean, grease-free bowl until stiff peaks form. Gradually whisk in the sugar a little at a time, until thick and glossy. Gently stir in the ground almonds and almond extract.

3 Spoon teaspoonfuls of the mixture on to the prepared baking sheets, spacing them slightly apart. Press an almond into the centre of each one and bake in the oven for 12–15 minutes until just golden and firm to the touch.

4 Leave on the baking sheets for 10 minutes, then transfer to wire racks and leave to cool completely. On cooling, these biscuits have a soft, chewy centre; they harden up after a few days. Store in airtight containers for up to one week.

Chocolate chip cookies

The mixture for moulded biscuits is fairly soft but firm enough to shape into balls. It needs to be handled lightly and gently.

To make about 15 cookies, you will need 75g (3oz) softened butter, 75g (3oz) granulated sugar, 75g (3oz) soft light brown sugar, 1 tsp vanilla extract, 1 egg, beaten, 175g (6oz) self-raising flour, pinch of salt, 125g (4oz) chocolate drops, 75g (3oz) macadamia nuts, roughly chopped.

1 Preheat the oven to 180°C (160°C fan oven) mark 4 and grease two baking sheets. Cream the butter until soft, then beat in the sugars and vanilla extract. Mix in the egg.

2 Sift the flour and salt into a bowl. Fold into the creamed mixture. Add the chocolate drops and 50g (2oz) macadamia nuts. Stir together until thoroughly combined.

3 Roll the mixture into about 15 balls and arrange on the prepared baking sheets, leaving space for the cookies to spread.

4 Flatten lightly with a wet fork. Sprinkle the remaining nuts on top, pressing them down lightly.

5 Bake for 10 minutes, or until golden. Leave to cool on wire racks. Eat warm.

Viennese fingers

To make 20 fingers, you will need 125g (4oz) softened butter, 25g (1oz) icing sugar, 25g (1oz) plain chocolate, 125g (4oz) plain flour, ¼ tsp baking powder, 1 tbsp drinking chocolate, a few drops of vanilla extract, 50g (2oz) plain, milk or white chocolate, melted, to decorate.

1 Preheat the oven to 190°C (170°C fan oven) mark 5 and grease two baking sheets. Beat the butter and icing sugar until creamy.

2 Melt the plain chocolate in a bowl set over a pan of hot water. Cool for 10 minutes, then beat into the creamed mixture. Sift in the flour, baking powder and drinking chocolate. Fold in, then add the vanilla. Spoon into a piping bag with a star-shaped nozzle and pipe finger shapes about 7.5cm (3in) long on to baking sheets.

3 Bake for 15–20 minutes until golden. Cool on wire rack, then dip in melted chocolate and leave to set.

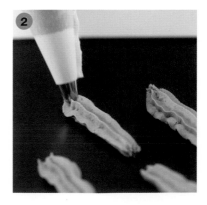

Muesli bars

Some of the simplest biscuits to make are traybakes, which are cooked in one piece and then cut into bars. The mixtures often contain fruit, nuts and sometimes oats.

To make 12 bars, you will need 175g (6oz) unsalted butter, cut into pieces, 150g (5oz) light muscovado sugar, 2 tbsp golden syrup, 375g (13oz) porridge oats, 100g (3½oz) ready-to-eat dried papaya, roughly chopped, 50g (2oz) sultanas, 50g (2oz) pecan nuts, roughly chopped, 25g (1oz) pinenuts, 25g (1oz) pumpkin seeds, 1 tbsp plain flour, 1 tsp ground cinnamon.

1 Preheat the oven to 180°C (160°C fan oven) mark 4. Melt the butter, sugar and golden syrup together in a heavy-based pan over a low heat.

2 Meanwhile, put the oats, dried fruit, nuts, seeds, flour and cinnamon into a large bowl and stir to mix. Pour in the melted mixture and mix together until combined.

3 Spoon the mixture into a 30.5 × 20.5cm (12 × 8in) non-stick baking tin and press down into the corners.

4 Bake for 25–30 minutes or until golden. Press the mixture down again if necessary, then use a palette knife to mark into 12 bars.

5 Leave to cool completely. Use a palette knife to lift the bars out of the tin and store in an airtight container.

PERFECT TRAYBAKES

- Be careful not to overcook traybakes. They are ready when they are golden brown, but will not be set firm when they come out of the oven.
- Some traybakes (such as flapjacks) are soft mixtures when hot and firm up when cold (especially when made with golden syrup or honey), so it is essential to mark the cooked bake into squares or bars while hot. Leave to cool completely in the baking tray before turning out of the tin.
- Remove carefully, using a spatula or palette knife, as some bakes can be a little crumbly.
- Some traybakes have a more 'cakey' mixture (containing a larger amount of flour and some eggs) and can be made with two different layers of mixture or an iced topping. These bakes are usually allowed to cool before they are cut into squares.

DECORATING AND FILLING BISCUITS

The simplest way to decorate a biscuit, and one of the best, is to dust it with icing sugar, but you can take other options for more elaborate effects and these are worth the effort.

Unbaked biscuits

A simple decoration for a plain biscuit is to add a glacé cherry or a whole nut, such as an almond, or a half-walnut on the raw biscuit dough before it is cooked.

1 Just press your chosen decoration very gently into the surface. This technique is suitable for firmer biscuit and cookie mixtures, such as moulded and rolled biscuits.

KID'S COOKIES

Small children can have fun decorating cut-out shapes from a rolled cookie mixture. Coloured sweets look pretty, but for a healthier option, try using nuts, seeds and dried fruit, such as raisins.

Icing biscuits

1 Mix 125g (4oz) icing sugar with a little water, or lemon or orange juice, until it is smooth and runny.

2 To drizzle, spoon thin trails of icing over the cooled biscuits.

3 To spread, make the icing a little thicker. If making the biscuits for children they can be decorated with brightly coloured sweets.

Filling biscuits

1 Cream filling To sandwich about 18 biscuits, cream 50g (2oz) butter until soft then beat in 75g (3oz) sifted icing sugar. Mix well and soften by adding a few drops of orange juice or vanilla extract until the mixture is of a firm, spreadable consistency. Spread the mixture on to the flat side of a biscuit and gently press a second biscuit on top to make a sandwich.

2 Chocolate filling Cream 50g (2oz) butter until soft then add 75g (3oz) icing sugar and 2 tsp cocoa powder. Mix well and add a few drops of milk to soften if necessary. (Makes enough to fill 18 biscuits.)

3 Toffee filling Spread dulce de leche over one biscuit and top with another. Roll the edges in desiccated coconut if you like.

Decorating with chocolate

1 Drizzling chocolate Melt some chocolate (see page 366) and drizzle over cooled biscuits. If you like, use a dark chocolate, leave it to set and then drizzle white or milk chocolate over the top. Alternatively, spoon melted chocolate into a piping bag with a narrow nozzle and pipe lines on to the biscuit. Leave to cool, then pipe a contrasting colour over the top.

2 Dipped chocolate Biscuits can be dipped in melted chocolate once they are cooked and completely cooled. To do this, dip half the biscuit into melted chocolate and rest it on the edge of a wire rack, so that the chocolate-covered area hangs over the edge while the chocolate cools and firms up.

COOKIE TROUBLESHOOTING

Although very simple in their composition, biscuits can be surprisingly prone to baking problems because they cook so quickly. It's as well to be aware of the possible problems and to know what can cause them. Following a few key points should minimise most of the risks and potential pitfalls.

— Use a shiny-based baking sheet; a darker-coloured sheet will absorb a greater amount of heat and can therefore burn the undersides of the biscuits.

— Don't overcrowd the biscuits on the baking sheet or in the oven – air needs to circulate all around them. If you are baking more than one sheet, make sure they are on shelves at least 20.5cm (8in) apart.

— Turn the baking sheet(s) around once or twice during baking. Most ovens get hotter in some places than in others, and this can cause uneven cooking.

— If you are cooking more than one sheet, be prepared to have them bake at different speeds. Watch them closely for uneven cooking.

— Start testing biscuits slightly before you expect them to be cooked. And watch them very closely during the final minutes, as they can go from perfect to overcooked in a matter of only a few seconds.

— Like cakes, biscuits must be transfered to a wire rack while they are still hot. The hot baking sheet will continue to cook them, and steam will build up underneath, which can make the bases soggy. As soon as they are cooked, lift the biscuits from the baking sheet and transfer to a wire rack to cool. Some biscuits, however (particularly those made with syrup), need to be left on the baking sheet to firm up a little before they are transferred to a rack.

— Put the biscuits on a fairly fine-meshed rack if at all possible.

— If possible, raise the rack by putting it on supports so that it is at least a few centimetres higher than the worksurface it's resting on: the more air circulating underneath, the crisper the bases will be.

— If the biscuits are tough or dry, the dough may have been overworked or too much flour may have been added.

— Biscuits that spread too much during baking contain too much butter or sugar, or the mixture may have been overbeaten.

— A cake-like texture indicates that too much flour was used or the biscuits were baked at too high a temperature.

RICH FRUIT CAKE

1 Grease and line the cake tin for the size of cake you wish to make (see opposite), using a double thickness of greaseproof paper. Tie a double band of brown paper round the outside of the tin.

2 Prepare the ingredients for the appropriate size of cake. Wash and dry all the fruit, if necessary, chopping any over-large pieces, and mix well together in a large bowl. Add the flaked almonds. Sift the flour and spices into another bowl with a pinch of salt.

3 Put the butter, sugar and lemon zest into a bowl and cream together until pale and fluffy. Add the beaten eggs gradually, beating well.

4 Gradually fold the flour lightly into the mixture with a metal spoon, then fold in the brandy. Finally, fold in the fruit and nuts.

5 Turn the mixture into the prepared tin, spreading it evenly and making sure there are no air pockets. Make a hollow in the centre to ensure an even surface when cooked.

6 Stand the tin on newspaper or brown paper in the oven. Bake at 150°C (130°C fan) mark 2 for the time in the chart until a skewer inserted in the centre comes out clean. Cover with greaseproof paper after about 1½ hours.

7 When cooked, leave the cake to cool in the tin before turning out on to a wire rack. Prick the top all over with a fine skewer and slowly pour 2–3 tbsp brandy over it.

8 Wrap the cake in a double thickness of greaseproof paper and place in an airtight tin, or wrap with foil and store in a cool place.

> ### COOK'S TIP
>
> If you are making a tiered cake, it is most important for the final overall result to choose the sizes of the tiers carefully, avoiding a combination that would look too heavy. Good proportions for a three-tier cake are 30, 23 and 15cm (12, 9 and 6in).

QUANTITIES AND SIZES FOR RICH FRUIT CAKES

To make a formal cake for a birthday, wedding or anniversary, the following chart will show you the amount of ingredients required to fill the chosen cake tin or tins, whether round or square.

Note: When baking large cakes, 25cm (10in) and upwards, it is advisable to reduce the oven heat to 130°C (110°C fan) mark 1 after two-thirds of the cooking time.

The amounts of almond paste quoted in this chart will give a thin covering. The quantities of Royal Icing should be enough for two coats. If using ready-to-roll fondant icing, use the quantities suggested for Royal Icing as a rough guide.

Size 1
Square tin: 12cm (5in)
Round tin: 15cm (6in)
Cooking time (approx.): 2½–3 hours
Weight when cooked: 1.1kg (2½lb)
225g (8oz) currants, 125g (4oz) each sultanas and raisins, 50g (2oz) glacé cherries, 25g (1oz) each mixed peel and flaked almonds, a little lemon zest, 175g (6oz) plain flour, 4 tsp each mixed spice and cinnamon, 150g (5oz) each softened butter and soft brown sugar, 2½ medium eggs, beaten, 1 tbsp brandy.
Almond paste: 350g (12oz)
Royal icing: 450g (1lb)

Size 2
Square tin: 15cm (6in)
Round tin: 18cm (7in)
Cooking time (approx.): 3 hours
Weight when cooked: 1.6kg (3¼lb)
350g (12oz) currants, 125g (4oz) each sultanas and raisins, 75g (3oz) glacé cherries, 50g (2oz) each mixed peel and flaked almonds, a little lemon zest, 200g (7oz) plain flour, ½ tsp each mixed spice and cinnamon, 175g (6oz) softened butter and soft brown sugar, 3 medium eggs, beaten, 1 tbsp brandy.
Almond paste: 450g (1lb)
Almond paste: 550g (1¼lb)

Size 3
Square tin: 20cm (8in)
Round tin: 23cm (9in)
Cooking time (approx.): 4 hours
Weight when cooked: 2.7kg (6lb)
625g (1lb 6oz) currants, 225g (8oz) each sultanas and raisins, 175g (6oz) glacé cherries, 125g (4oz) each mixed peel and flaked almonds, zest of ¼ lemon, 400g (14oz) plain flour, 1 tsp each cinnamon and mixed spice, 350g (12oz) softened butter and soft brown sugar, 6 medium eggs, beaten, 2 tbsp brandy.
Almond paste: 800g (1¾lb)
Almond paste: 900g (2lb)

Size 4
Square tin: 23cm (9in)
Round tin: 25cm (10in)
Cooking time (approx.): 6 hours
Weight when cooked: 4kg (9lb)
775g (1lb 12oz) currants, 375g (13oz) each sultanas and raisins, 250g (9oz) glacé cherries, 150g (5oz) each mixed peel and flaked almonds, zest of ¼ lemon, 600g (1lb 5oz) plain flour, 1 tsp each mixed spice and cinnamon, 500g (1lb 2oz) each softened butter and soft brown sugar, 9 medium eggs, beaten, 2–3 tbsp brandy.
Almond paste: 900g (2lb)
Almond paste: 1kg (2¼lb)

Size 5
Square tin: 28cm (11in)
Round tin: 30cm (12in)
Cooking time (approx.): 8 hours
Weight when cooked: 6.7kg (14¾lb)
1.5kg (3lb 2oz) currants, 525g (1lb 3oz) each sultanas and raisins, 350g (12oz) glacé cherries, 250g (9oz) each mixed peel and flaked almonds, zest of ½ lemon, 825g (1lb 13oz) plain flour, 2½ tsp each mixed spice and cinnamon, 800g (1lb 12oz) each softened butter and soft brown sugar, 14 medium eggs, beaten, 4 tbsp brandy.
Almond paste: 1.1kg (2½lb)
Almond paste: 1.4kg (3lb)

Size 6
Square tin: 30cm (12in)
Round tin: 33cm (13in)
Cooking time (approx): 8½ hours
Weight when cooked: 7.7kg (17lb)
1.7kg (3lb 12oz) currants, 625g (1lb 6oz) each sultanas and raisins, 425g (15oz) glacé cherries, 275g (10oz) each mixed peel and flaked almonds, zest of 1 lemon, 1kg (2lb 6oz) plain flour, 2½ tsp each mixed spice and cinnamon, 950g (2lb 2oz) each softened butter and soft brown sugar, 17 medium eggs, beaten, 6 tbsp brandy.
Almond paste: 1.4kg (3lb)
Almond paste: 1.6kg (3½lb)

SOMERSET APPLE CAKE

Cuts into about 10 slices
Preparation 20 minutes
Cooking time 1½ hours, plus cooling
Techniques see also preparing apples (page 216), lining tins (page 332)

125g (4oz) butter, plus extra to grease
175g (6oz) dark soft brown sugar
2 medium eggs, beaten
225g (8oz) plain wholemeal flour
1 tsp ground mixed spice
1 tsp ground cinnamon
2 tsp baking powder
450g (1lb) cooking apples, peeled, cored and chopped
3–4 tbsp milk
1 tbsp clear honey
1 tbsp light demerara sugar

1 Preheat the oven to 170°C (150°C fan oven) mark 3. Grease a deep 18cm (7in) round cake tin and line with greaseproof paper.
2 Cream the butter and soft brown sugar together until pale and fluffy. Add the eggs a little at a time, beating well after each addition. Add the flour, spices and baking powder and mix well. Fold in the apples and enough milk to give a soft dropping consistency.
3 Turn the mixture into the prepared tin and bake for 1½ hours or until well risen and firm to the touch. Turn out on to a wire rack to cool.
4 When the cake is cold, brush with the honey and sprinkle with the demerara sugar to decorate.

NUTRITION PER SERVING
248 cals | 10g fat (6g sats) | 38g carbs | 0.5g salt **V**

ST CLEMENTS CUPCAKES

Makes 9
Preparation 40 minutes
Cooking time 15–18 minutes, plus cooling and setting
Techniques see also making cupcakes (page 338), zesting citrus fruits (page 217)

1 small orange (about 200g/7oz)
175g (6oz) self-raising flour, sifted
100g (3½oz) caster sugar
100ml (3½fl oz) milk
1 medium egg, beaten
50g (2oz) unsalted butter, melted
1 tsp baking powder
zest of 1 large lemon

To decorate
400g (14oz) royal icing sugar, sifted
juice and zest of 1 small orange
sugar star sprinkles
edible glitter (optional)

1 Preheat the oven to 190°C (170°C fan oven), mark 5. Line two 6–hole muffin tins with 9 paper muffin cases.
2 Grate the zest from the orange into a large bowl and put to one side. Cut the top and bottom off the orange and stand it upright on a board. Using a serrated knife, cut away the pith in a downward motion. Roughly chop the orange flesh, discarding any pips. Put the chopped orange into a food processor and whiz until puréed.
3 Transfer the orange purée into the bowl with the zest. Add the flour, caster sugar, milk, egg, melted butter, baking powder and lemon zest. Stir with a spatula until just combined. Divide the mixture equally between the paper cases and bake for 15–18 minutes until golden and risen. Leave to cool in the tin for 5 minutes, then transfer to a wire rack and leave to go cold.
4 For the decoration, put the icing sugar, orange juice and zest into a bowl and whisk for 5 minutes until soft peaks form. Spoon a little over the top of each cake to flood the top, then sprinkle on the stars. Stand the cakes upright on the wire rack, or place back in the tins, and leave to set. Dust with edible glitter, if you like, when set.

NUTRITION PER SERVING
325 cals | 6g fat (4g sats) | 70g carbs | 0.2g salt

TOFFEE CHEESECAKE

Serves 10
Preparation 15 minutes, plus chilling
Cooking time 45 minutes–1 hour, plus cooling

300g pack digestive biscuits, broken
125g (4oz) butter, melted

For the filling
450g (1lb) curd cheese
140ml (4½fl oz) double cream
juice of ½ lemon
3 medium eggs, beaten
50g (2oz) golden caster sugar
6 tbsp dulce de leche toffee sauce, plus extra to drizzle

1 Preheat the oven to 200°C (180°C fan oven) gas mark 6. To make the crust, put the biscuits into a food processor and grind until fine. (Alternatively, put them in a plastic bag and crush with a rolling pin. Transfer to a bowl.) Add the butter and blend briefly, or stir in, to combine. Press the mixture evenly into the base and up the sides of a 20.5cm (8in) springform cake tin. Chill in the fridge.
2 To make the filling, put the curd cheese and cream in a food processor or blender and blend until smooth. Add the lemon juice, eggs, sugar and toffee sauce, then blend again until smooth. Pour into the chilled biscuit case and bake for 10 minutes. Reduce the oven temperature to 180°C (160°C fan oven) mark 4, then bake for 45 minutes or until set and golden brown.
3 Turn off the oven, leave the door ajar and let the cheesecake cool. When completely cool, chill to firm up the crust.
4 Remove the cheesecake from the tin by running a knife around the edge. Open the tin carefully, then use a palette knife to ease the cheesecake out. Cut into wedges, put on a serving plate, then drizzle with toffee sauce.

COOK'S TIP
To slice the cheesecake easily, use a sharp knife dipped into a jug of boiling water and then wiped dry.

NUTRITION PER SERVING
379 cals | 24g fat (13g sats) | 34g carbs | 1.1g salt

APPLE MADELEINES

Makes 24
Preparation 15 minutes
Cooking time 8–10 minutes
Techniques see also preparing apples (page 216)

150g (5oz) unsalted butter, melted and cooled,
    plus extra to grease
3 large eggs
150g (5oz) caster sugar
1 tsp vanilla extract
150g (5oz) plain flour, sifted
½ tsp baking powder
2 apples such as Cox's, peeled, cored and finely chopped
icing sugar to dust

1 Preheat the oven to 200°C (180°C fan oven) mark 6.
Grease the Madeleine tins. Using an electric whisk, beat the
eggs and caster sugar together until thick (this should take
about 8 minutes), then add the vanilla extract. Quickly but
gently, fold in the flour, baking powder and apples followed
by the melted butter, making sure the butter doesn't settle
at the bottom of the bowl.
2 Spoon the mixture into the Madeleine tins. Bake for
8–10 minutes until golden, then remove from the tins and
cool on wire racks. Dust with icing sugar before serving.

GET AHEAD
You can make these madeleines up to two days ahead.
Complete the recipe, then cool, cover and store in an
airtight container.

NUTRITION PER SERVING
106 cals | 6g fat (4g sats) | 13g carbs | 0.1g salt

CHOCOLATE AND HAZELNUT BISCOTTI

Makes about 20
Preparation 10 minutes
Cooking time 40 minutes
Techniques see also cookie troubleshooting (page 351)

125g (4oz) plain flour, sifted, plus extra to dust
75g (3oz) golden caster sugar
¼ tsp baking powder
pinch of ground cinnamon
pinch of salt
1 large egg, beaten
1 tbsp milk
¼ tsp vanilla extract
25g (1oz) hazelnuts
25g (1oz) plain chocolate chips

1 Preheat the oven to 200°C (180°C fan oven) mark 6.
Put the flour into a large bowl. Stir in the sugar, baking
powder and salt. Make a well in the centre and stir in the
beaten eggs, milk, vanilla extract, hazelnuts and chocolate
chips with a fork to form a sticky dough.
2 On a lightly floured worksurface, gently knead the
mixture into a ball. Roll into a 28cm (11in) sausage shape.
Put on a baking sheet and flatten slightly. Bake for 20–25
minutes or until pale golden.
3 Reduce the oven temperature to 150°C (130°C fan
oven) mark 2. Put the biscotti log on to a chopping board
and slice diagonally with a bread knife at 1cm (½in)
intervals. Arrange the slices on the baking sheet and put
back in the oven for 15 minutes or until golden and dry.
Transfer to a wire rack to cool. To enjoy Italian-style, dunk
into coffee or dessert wine.

FINISHING TOUCHES
To make as gifts, divide the biscuits among four large
squares of cellophane, then draw up the edges and tie
with ribbon. Label the packages with storage information
and an eat-by date.

NUTRITION PER SERVING
50 cals | 1g fat (trace sats) | 9g carbs | 0g salt

TRADITIONAL FLAPJACKS

Makes 12 squares
Preparation 10 minutes
Cooking time 25 minutes, plus cooling
Techniques see also zesting citrus fruits (page 217)

200g (7oz) butter, plus extra to grease
150g (5oz) demerara sugar
4 tbsp golden syrup
1 tsp ground cinnamon
finely grated zest of ½–1 orange
400g (14oz) jumbo oats
100g (3½oz) raisins or sultanas

1 Preheat the oven to 190°C (170°C fan oven) mark 5.
Grease a 20.5cm (8in) square baking tin and line with
baking parchment.
2 Melt the butter in a large pan. Add the sugar, syrup,
cinnamon and orange zest and heat gently until the sugar
dissolves.
3 Remove the pan from the heat and stir in the oats and
raisins or sultanas. Press the mixture into the prepared tin
and bake for 17–20 minutes until lightly golden. Cool
before cutting into squares. Store the flapjacks in an airtight
container for up to three days.

NUTRITION PER SERVING
354 cals | 17g fat (9g sats) | 50g carbs | 0.4g salt **V**

THE ULTIMATE CHOCOLATE BROWNIE

Makes 16
Preparation 15 minutes
Cooking time 1 hour 20 minutes, plus cooling
Techniques see also which chocolate to choose? (page 367), chopping nuts (page 228), lining tins (page 332), melting chocolate (page 366)

200g (7oz) salted butter, plus extra
to grease
400g (14oz) good-quality plain chocolate
225g (8oz) light muscovado sugar
1 tsp vanilla extract
150g (5oz) pecan nuts, roughly chopped
25g (1oz) cocoa powder, sifted
75g (3oz) self-raising flour, sifted
3 large eggs, beaten
sifted cocoa powder to dust

1 Preheat the oven to 170°C (150°C fan oven) mark 3. Grease and baseline a 20.5cm (8in) square, 5cm (2in) deep baking tin with non-stick baking parchment. Put the butter and chocolate in a heatproof bowl over a pan of gently simmering water and stir until melted. Remove from the heat and stir in the sugar, vanilla extract, pecan nuts, cocoa, flour and eggs.
2 Turn the mixture into the prepared tin and level the surface with the back of a spoon. Bake for about 1 hour 15 minutes or until set to the centre on the surface but still soft underneath.
3 Leave to cool in the tin for 2 hours. Turn out, dust with sifted cocoa powder and cut into squares. Eat cold or serve warm with ice cream.

COOK'S TIP
The secret to really moist, squidgy brownies is all in the timing. A few minutes too long in the oven will produce a dry texture, so be careful not to bake them for too long.

NUTRITION PER SERVING
257 cals | 11g fat (6g sats) | 38g carbs | 0.2g salt **V**

CARROT CAKE

Cuts into 12 slices
Preparation 15 minutes
Cooking time 40 minutes, plus cooling
Techniques see also preparing roots and tubers (page 193) page 367), lining tins (page 332)

250ml (9fl oz) sunflower oil, plus extra to grease
225g (8oz) light muscovado sugar
3 large eggs
225g (8oz) self-raising flour
large pinch of salt
½ tsp each ground mixed spice, ground nutmeg
and ground cinnamon
250g (9oz) carrots, peeled and coarsely grated

For the frosting
50g (2oz) butter, preferably unsalted, at room temperature
225g pack cream cheese
25g (1oz) golden icing sugar
½ tsp vanilla extract
8 pecan halves, roughly chopped

1 Preheat the oven to 180°C (160°C fan oven) mark 4. Grease two 18cm (7in) sandwich tins and base-line with greaseproof paper.
2 Using a hand-held electric whisk, whisk the oil and muscovado sugar together to combine, then whisk in the eggs, one at a time.
3 Sift the flour, salt and spices together over the mixture, then gently fold in, using a large metal spoon. Tip the carrots into the bowl and fold in.
4 Divide the cake mixture between the prepared tins and bake for 30–40 minutes until golden and a skewer inserted into the centre comes out clean. Remove from the oven and leave in the tins for 10 minutes, then turn out on to a wire rack and leave to cool completely.
5 To make the frosting, beat the butter and cream cheese together in a bowl until light and fluffy. Sift in the icing sugar, add the vanilla extract and beat well until smooth. Spread one-third of the frosting over one cake and sandwich together with the other cake. Spread the remaining frosting on top and sprinkle with the pecan halves.

TO STORE
Store in an airtight container. Eat within two days. Alternatively, the cake will keep for up to one week in an airtight container if it is stored before the frosting is applied.

NUTRITION PER SERVING
383 cals | 32g fat (10g sats) | 24g carbs | 0.3g salt Ⓥ

SCOTTISH OATCAKES

Makes about 12
Preparation 10 minutes
Cooking time 10 minutes
Techniques see also making biscuits (page 344)

225g (8oz) fine or medium oatmeal, plus extra to dust
a pinch of salt
a pinch of bicarbonate of soda
15g (½oz) lard
butter to serve

1 Put the oatmeal, salt and bicarbonate of soda into a large bowl.
2 Gently heat the lard and 150ml (¼ pint) water until the lard is melted, then quickly pour enough of it on to the dry ingredients to make a firm dough.
3 Roll out the dough on a worksurface sprinkled with oatmeal until about 3mm (⅛in) thick. Using a plain 7.5cm (3in) round cutter, cut out 12 rounds, re-rolling as necessary. Or, cut into triangles, if preferred.
4 Cook the oatcakes on a hot griddle, on one side only for about 5–8 minutes, until they curl and are firm. (Alternatively, place on a greased baking sheet and bake at 180°C (160°C fan oven) mark 4 for 15–20 minutes until crisp.) Eat spread with butter.

NUTRITION PER SERVING
46 cals | 2g fat (1g sats) | 6g carbs | 1.9g salt

SHORTBREAD

Makes 18
Preparation 20 minutes, plus chilling
Cooking time 15–20 minutes
Techniques see also cookie troubleshooting (page 351)

225g (8oz) butter, at room temperature
125g (4oz) golden caster sugar
225g (8oz) plain flour
125g (4oz) rice flour
a pinch of salt
golden or coloured granulated sugar to coat
caster sugar to sprinkle

1 Cream the butter and sugar together in a bowl until pale and fluffy. Sift the flours and salt together on to the creamed mixture and stir in, using a wooden spoon, until the mixture resembles breadcrumbs.
2 Gather the dough together with your hand and turn on to a clean worksurface. Knead very lightly until it forms a ball, then lightly roll into a sausage, about 5cm (2in) thick. Wrap in clingfilm and chill until firm.
3 Preheat the oven to 190°C (170°C fan oven) mark 5. Line two baking sheets with greaseproof paper. Remove the clingfilm and slice the dough into discs, 1cm (½in) thick. Pour some granulated sugar on to a plate and roll the edge of each disc in the sugar. Put the shortbread, cut side up, on the prepared baking sheets.
4 Bake the shortbread for 15–20 minutes, depending on thickness, until very pale golden. On removing from the oven, sprinkle with caster sugar. Leave on the baking sheets for 10 minutes, then transfer to a wire rack and leave to cool. Store in an airtight container for up to two weeks.

NUTRITION PER SERVING
190 cals | 10g fat (7g sats) | 23g carbs | 0.3g salt **V**

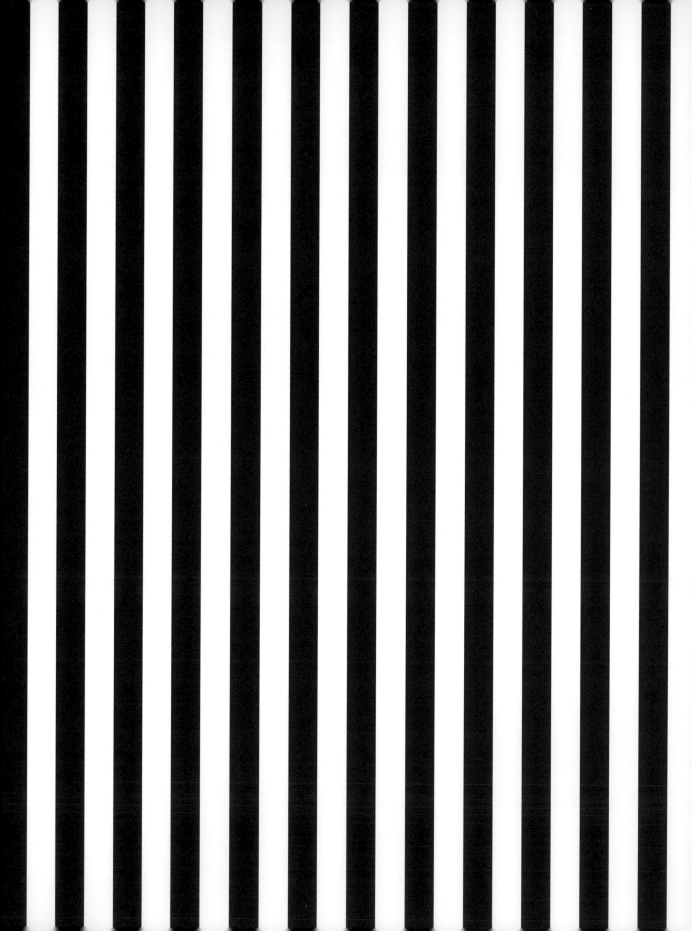

CHOCOLATE AND SUGAR

Chocolate is everyone's favourite – whether you're eating it on its own or turning it into an indulgent treat! This chapter guides you through all the basics, from melting chocolate to making chocolate decorations, dipping fruit and making sauces, plus there are invaluable tips on choosing the right chocolate for the job and ensuring perfect results. The recipe section builds on these skills with fabulous recipes including White chocolate mousse cake, Decadent chocolate cake, Nutty chocolate truffles, and Warm chocolate fondant.

Incredibly versatile, sugar can be heated and transformed into all kinds of sweet treats such as caramel, toffee, fudge and praline, which can be eaten on their own, or used in sweet recipes. This chapter provides a guide to all the basic techniques and the recipe section then puts these techniques into practice with indulgent recipes such as Cookies and cream fudge, Sticky banoffee pies, Brandy snaps, Strawberry brûlée and Sticky toffee puddings.

USING CHOCOLATE

Chocolate is delicious to eat, and is fabulous used with other ingredients in recipes. However, it has many other wonderful uses in the kitchen too, and can be turned into stunning decorations.

Melting

For cooking or making decorations, chocolate is usually melted first.

1 Break the chocolate into pieces and put in a heatproof bowl or in the top of a double boiler. Set over a pan of gently simmering water.

2 Heat very gently until the chocolate starts to melt, then stir regularly until completely melted.

COOK'S TIP
To melt chocolate in the microwave, break the chocolate into pieces and put in a microwave-proof bowl. Microwave at full power for 1 minute. Stir, then cook again for 30 seconds at a time until the chocolate is smooth and melted.

Shaving

This is the easiest decoration of all because it doesn't call for melting the chocolate.

1 Hold a chocolate bar upright on the work surface and shave pieces off the edge with a swivel peeler.

2 Alternatively, grate the chocolate, against a coarse or medium-coarse grater, to make very fine shavings.

Chocolate curls

1 Melt the chocolate, as above, and spread it out in a thin layer on a marble slab or clean worksurface. Leave to firm up.

2 Use a sharp, flat-ended blade (such as a pastry scraper or a very stiff spatula) to scrape through the chocolate at a 45-degree angle. The size of the curls will be determined by the width of the blade.

COOK'S TIPS
➤ When melting chocolate, use a gentle heat.
➤ Don't let water or steam touch the chocolate or it will 'seize' – become hard and unworkable. If it has seized, you can try saving it by stirring in a few drops of flavourless vegetable oil.

Chocolate leaves

1 Wash and dry some rose or bay leaves for coating. Spread slightly cooled melted chocolate in a thin, even layer over the shiny side of the leaf. Spread it right out to the edge using a paintbrush, but wipe off any chocolate that drips over the edge.

2 Leave to cool completely. Then, working very gently and carefully, peel the leaf off the chocolate.

Chocolate wafers

1 You can make flat or curved wafers in any shape you like. Cut a piece of greaseproof paper to the required width.

2 Brush the paper evenly with melted chocolate and leave until the chocolate has almost set.

3 Using a knife, cut the chocolate (while still on the paper) into pieces of the desired size and shape (straight or curved, square or triangular, narrow or wide). You can also cut out chocolate shapes using small cutters.

4 Leave to cool and harden completely, either on the work surface (for flat wafers) or draped over a rolling pin (for curled).

5 Carefully peel the wafers off the paper, handling them as little as possible, and store in the fridge for up to 24 hours.

WHICH CHOCOLATE TO CHOOSE?

The type of chocolate you choose will have a dramatic effect on the end product. For the best results, buy chocolate that has a high proportion of cocoa solids, preferably at least 70 per cent. Most supermarkets stock a selection. Chocolate with a high percentage of cocoa solids has a rich flavour and is perfect for sauces, ganache (see page 369), most sweets, cakes and desserts. At the top end of the scale, couverture chocolate is the one preferred by chefs for confectionery work and gives an intense chocolate flavour that is probably best reserved for special mousses and gâteaux. It is available in milk, plain and white varieties from specialist chocolate shops. For most purposes, a good-quality chocolate with a high proportion of cocoa solids will usually give great results.

Chocolate moulds

You can make almost any hollow container – such as an espresso cup or petit four case – into a mould.

1 Pour the melted chocolate into the mould, turning it to coat it evenly, and then pour out the excess. Chill until set.

2 Repeat the process until you have achieved the required thickness that you want (see Cook's Tips). Leave to set, and then turn out, remembering to handle very gently.

3 Alternatively, you can use a small paintbrush to layer the chocolate. Simply dip the brush – scrupulously clean, of course – into the melted chocolate and paint the inside of the mould with it. Chill until set, then repeat layering with chocolate until you have achieved the thickness required for your particular purpose.

COOK'S TIPS

- Your mould should not have any awkward curves or angles, or you will not be able to release the chocolate from the mould. A simple bowl or straight-sided shape is best.
- The larger the mould, the thicker the chocolate layer should be. For something small like a teacup, the thickness can be just a few coatings of chocolate; while for larger moulds, it should be around 6mm (¼ inch).
- Make sure that your mould is spotlessly clean, completely dry and free of lint or fibres (if you have dried it with a teatowel).

Piping

1 Draw your designs on a sheet of white paper, then lay a sheet of greaseproof paper on top.

2 Take a piping cone or piping bag fitted with a fine nozzle and fill with melted chocolate.

3 Using light, even pressure, pipe chocolate on to the paper following the outline of the drawing. Leave to set, then carefully remove the piped lines using a fine-bladed knife.

Chocolate-dipped fruit

1 Melt the chocolate in a bowl set over a pan of hot water. Lay a sheet of greaseproof paper on the worksurface next to the hob.

2 Ensure the fruit is dry. If using whole fruit such as strawberries, hold them by the stem and dip into the chocolate. Allow excess to drain off. Leave to cool on the greaseproof paper, then chill.

3 If using pieces of fruit or dried fruit, hold them individually with tongs or tweezers and dip in the chocolate. (You can do this faster by putting a handful of fruits on a skimmer or slotted spoon and dipping them together.) Allow the excess to drain, then put on greaseproof paper. Leave to cool and chill until needed (for a maximum of one day).

Chocolate sauce

1 Chop the best-quality dark chocolate (with a minimum of 70 per cent cocoa solids) and put it into a saucepan with 50ml (2fl oz) water per 100g (3½oz) chocolate.

2 Heat slowly, allowing the chocolate to melt, then stir until the sauce is smooth. To liven up this simple chocolate sauce, see the variations below right.

GANACHE

This topping is made from good-quality chocolate mixed with cream and butter. Increasing the ratio of cream to chocolate will make the ganache lighter, and sometimes the butter is left out so that the ganache won't be too rich. The recipe on page 382 (step 2 of Nutty Chocolate Truffles) is very versatile.

VARIATIONS

These are all suitable for a sauce made with 200g (7oz) chocolate:
- **Milk or single cream** Substituted in whole or in part for the water.
- **Coffee** Stir in a teaspoon of instant coffee or a shot of espresso when melting the chocolate.
- **Spices** Add a pinch of ground cinnamon, crushed cardamom seeds or freshly grated nutmeg to the melting chocolate.
- **Vanilla extract** Stir in ¼ tsp vanilla when melting the chocolate.
- **Rum, whisky or cognac** Stir in about 1 tsp alcohol when melting the chocolate.
- **Butter** Stir in 25g (1oz) towards the end of heating.

WORKING WITH SUGAR

Sugar is a wonderfully versatile ingredient. When heated it can be transformed entirely – into crisp caramel and praline, chewy toffee, creamy fudge and delicate spun sugar, to name but a few.

Dry caramel

Use to make decorations. They can be made up to 24 hours in advance and stored in an airtight container.

1 Line a baking sheet with oiled greaseproof paper. Put 200g (7oz) caster sugar in a heavy-based pan with 4 tbsp water. Heat gently until the sugar dissolves.

2 Bring to the boil, then cook until it turns a medium caramel colour. Dip the base of the pan in cold water. Use immediately before the caramel begins to harden.

3 For caramel flowers, with a fork make abstract shapes 4cm (1½in) in diameter on oiled greaseproof paper.

4 For caramel cages, lightly oil the back of a ladle. Drizzle caramel threads in a crisscross pattern, finishing with thread around the rim.

COOK'S TIPS

- Once the syrup starts to colour, watch it closely – the colour can deepen rapidly, and very dark caramel tastes bitter.
- Have a pan of cold water ready to dip the base of the pan into to stop the caramel cooking further.

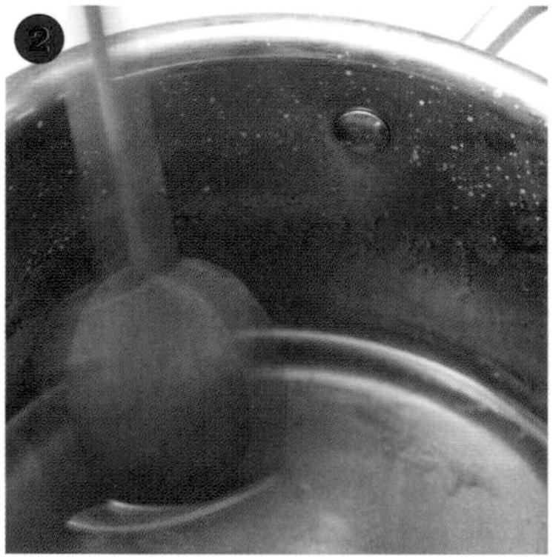

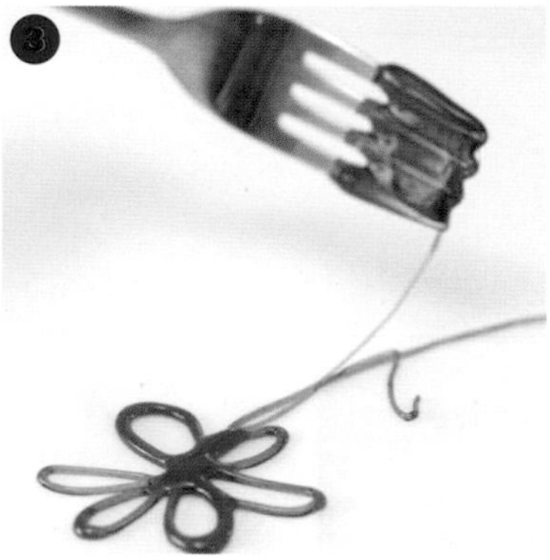

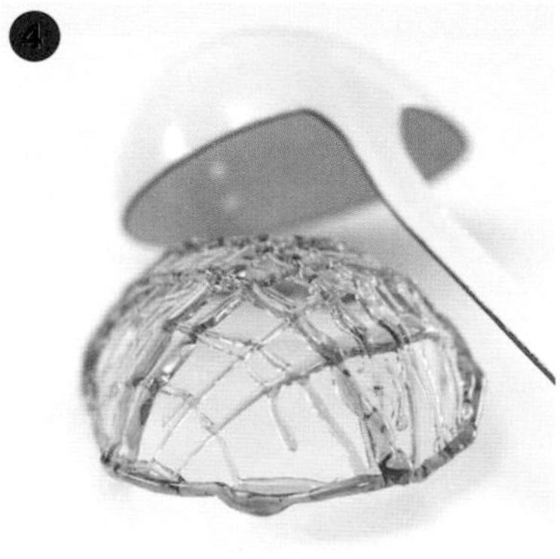

Wet caramel

A good sauce to use with fruit such as oranges, peaches and pineapple.

1 Put 200g (7oz) sugar in a heavy pan with 150ml (¼ pint) water. Heat gently to dissolve. Bring to the boil and cook until a medium caramel colour.

2 Remove from the heat, stand away and pour in 150ml (¼ pint) water. Heat and stir to dissolve, then cool.

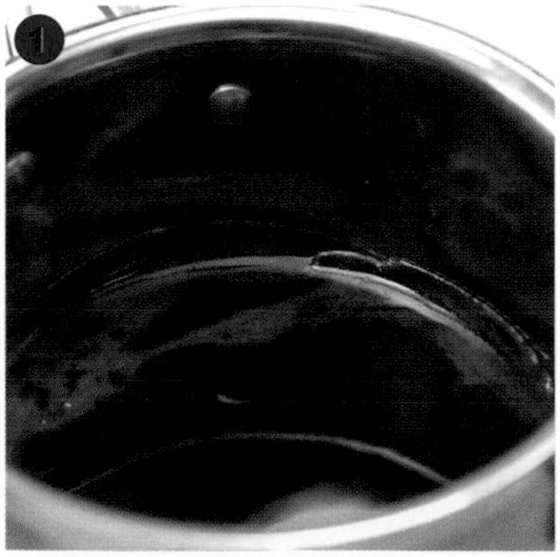

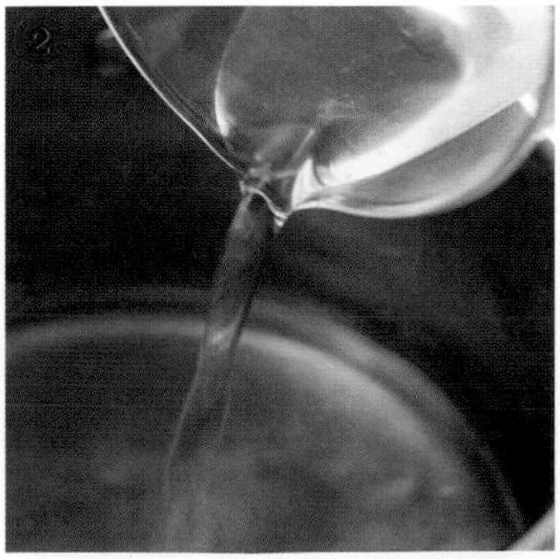

Sugar syrup

Perfect for dressing up a simple fruit salad or drizzling over a plain sponge. Serve the syrup plain or add a flavouring (see Flavourings, right).

You will need 275g (10oz) granulated sugar.

1 Put the sugar in a pan with 600ml (1 pint) cold water. Put the pan over a low heat and heat gently until the sugar has completely dissolved.

2 Bring the mixture to the boil and cook for 2–5 minutes.

3 Leave the syrup to cool and use immediately or store in a clean jar in the fridge for up to one week.

FLAVOURINGS

- Add the thinly pared zest of 1 lemon or ½ orange to the sugar and water in step 1.
- For a boozy sugar syrup, add 1–2 tbsp brandy or rum at the end of step 2.

Spun sugar

One of the most attractive sugar decorations, spun sugar is made from a light caramel syrup spun into a nest of hair-thin threads. The only equipment you need is a pair of forks, a rolling pin and sheets of paper to catch any drips of syrup that fall to the floor while you work.

1 Put the sugar and water in a heavy-based pan, using 4 tbsp water per 200g (7oz) sugar. Heat gently until the sugar dissolves.

2 Turn the heat up to high and bring to the boil. Continue to boil the syrup until it turns a light caramel colour. Dip the bottom of the pan in cold water to cool it, then leave to cool for 5 minutes.

3 Meanwhile, spread sheets of paper over the floor or table where you will be working.

4 Dip two or more forks, held in one hand, into the caramel. Flick them back and forth over a rolling pin held over the paper in your other hand, so that wispy threads fall over the pin.

5 When the rolling pin is full, carefully slide the threads off and gently form them into a ball or keep them as straight threads. Use immediately to decorate desserts.

Vanilla fudge

To make 50 pieces, you will need 450g (1lb) sugar, 113g carton clotted cream, 170g can evaporated milk, 50g (2oz) butter, 1 tsp vanilla extract.

1 Grease an 18cm (7in) square tin. Put the sugar, cream, milk and butter in a heavy-based pan. Heat gently, stirring, until the sugar has dissolved.

2 Boil for 30 minutes, stirring every 5 minutes, until light brown. Watch it does not burn! Plunge the base of the pan into cold water. Stir in the vanilla.

3 Beat with an electric whisk for about 5 minutes, scraping the sides, until thick.

4 Pour into the prepared tin, pressing the mixture into the corners.

5 Chill until firm, then cut into squares or bite-sized pieces.

Mixed nut praline

Used in ice creams and desserts.

To serve four, you will need 250g (9oz) golden caster sugar, 175g (6oz) mixed nuts, such as walnuts.

1 Put the sugar in a pan and warm over a gentle heat. Line a baking sheet with baking parchment and fill a bowl with very cold water.

2 Shake the pan gently to dissolve the sugar, keeping a close eye on it when it starts to colour.

3 When the sugar has turned a dark golden brown, pour in the nuts and stir once with a wooden spoon.

4 Dip the base of the pan into cold water to keep the praline from burning, then quickly pour the praline on to the parchment and spread out.

5 Cool for 20 minutes, then break into pieces with a rolling pin. For fine praline, crush in a food processor or coffee grinder.

Toffee

To make 500g (1lb 2oz) toffee, you will need 250g (9oz) butter, 250g (9oz) sugar.

1 Line a shallow roasting tin with oiled baking parchment. Put the butter and sugar in a heavy-based pan and cook gently to dissolve the sugar.

2 Turn the heat up to medium and continue cooking, stirring frequently, until the mixture is a deep brown. On a sugar thermometer it should give a reading of around 150°C (300°F). (Test by putting a little of the syrup into a cup of cold water; it should form thick threads that bend a little but then break up.)

3 Pour the mixture into the prepared roasting tin and smooth the top with a knife. Leave to set, then cut into squares or bite-sized pieces.

> ### NUTTY TOFFEE
>
> While the toffee is cooking, sprinkle the roasting tin with some coarsely chopped nuts, such as pecan nuts, almonds or walnuts. When the toffee is ready, pour it over the nuts and leave to set, as before. The mixture gives a really successful combination of flavours.

Caramel Sauce

To serve 6, you will need 50g (2oz) golden caster sugar, 150ml (¼ pint) double cream

1 Melt the sugar in a small heavy-based pan over a low heat until liquid and golden in colour. Increase the heat to medium and cook to a rich, dark caramel.

2 Immediately take off the heat and pour in the cream in a slow steady stream, taking care, as the hot caramel will cause the cream to boil up in the pan.

3 Stir over a gentle heat until the caramel has melted and the sauce is smooth. Serve hot or cold.

> ### COOK'S TIP
>
> Serve poured over ice cream or steamed or baked puddings.

CHOCOLATE AND CHERRY GATEAU

Serves 12
Preparation 1 hour, plus marinating and chilling
Cooking time 45 minutes
Techniques see also pitting cherries (page 218), toasting nuts (page 228), separating eggs (page 54), lining tins (page 332), making chocolate curls (page 366)

350g (12oz) cherries, pitted (or 400g can pitted cherries, drained), plus extra fresh cherries to decorate
3 tbsp dark rum
50g (2oz) almonds, toasted
50g (2oz) plain flour, sifted
350g (12oz) plain chocolate (70 per cent cocoa solids, if possible)
3 large eggs, separated
125g (4oz) butter, softened, plus extra to grease
125g (4oz) caster sugar
450ml (¾ pint) double cream
chocolate curls and cocoa powder to decorate
single cream to serve (optional)

1 Put the cherries in a bowl with 2 tbsp rum. Cover and soak for at least 6 hours.
2 Whiz the almonds and flour in a food processor until finely ground. Preheat the oven to 180°C (160°C fan oven) mark 4. Grease and baseline a 23cm (9in) diameter deep cake tin.
3 Melt 140g (4½oz) chocolate with 3 tbsp water in a bowl over a pan of gently simmering water. Remove from the heat, add the remaining rum and the egg yolks and beat until smooth. Beat the butter and sugar together until light and fluffy. Stir in the chocolate mixture and fold in the flour and almonds. Whisk the egg whites until soft peaks form, then fold into the chocolate mixture. Pour into the tin and bake for 30–35 minutes until a skewer comes out clean with a few crumbs on it. Cool in the tin for 10 minutes, then turn out on to a wire rack to cool.
4 Roughly chop the remaining chocolate. Bring the cream to the boil, pour over the chocolate, leave for 5 minutes, then stir until melted. Leave to cool, then, using an electric whisk, beat the mixture until thick and lighter in colour. Clean the cake tin and return the cake to the tin. Spoon the cherries and any juice over the cake. Spread the chocolate cream on top, smooth the surface, cover and chill for at least 2 hours. Decorate with chocolate curls, dust with cocoa and serve with cherries and cream, if you like.

FREEZING TIP
Complete step 2, but don't decorate the cake, then pack and freeze.
To use Thaw overnight at cool room temperature. Complete the recipe.

NUTRITION PER SERVING
537 cals | 41g fat (23g sats) | 38g carbs | 0.2g salt

WHITE CHOCOLATE MOUSSE CAKE

Serves 10
Preparation 30 minutes, plus overnight freezing
Cooking time 20–30 minutes
Techniques see also melting chocolate (page 366), zesting citrus fruits (page 217)

vegetable oil to grease
450g (1lb) white chocolate
285ml (9½fl oz) double cream
finely grated zest of 1 large orange
2 tsp orange liqueur, such as Grand Marnier
300ml (½ pint) full-fat Greek yogurt

1 Lightly oil a shallow 20cm (8in) round cake tin and line with baking parchment.
2 Break the chocolate into pieces and put into a large bowl with half the cream. Bring a large pan of water to the boil, remove from the heat and sit the bowl of chocolate and cream on top, making sure the base of the bowl doesn't touch the water. Leave for 20–30 minutes until the chocolate has melted. Don't stir; just leave it to melt.
3 Meanwhile, put the orange zest and liqueur into a small bowl. Leave to soak. Whip the remaining cream until it just holds its shape.
4 Remove the bowl of melted chocolate from the pan and beat in the yogurt. Fold in the cream with the zest and liqueur mix.
5 Spoon the mixture into the prepared tin, cover with clingfilm and freeze overnight or for up to one month. One hour before serving, transfer from the freezer to the fridge. Unwrap and put on a serving plate.

COOK'S TIP

If you like, you can decorate the mousse with a few halved strawberries, some blueberries and a handful of unsprayed rose petals, then dust with icing sugar.

NUTRITION PER SERVING
416 cals | 32g fat (19g sats) | 27g carbs | 0.2g salt

CHOCOLATE AMARETTI TART

Serves 8
Preparation 30 minutes, plus chilling
Cooking time 1½ hours, plus cooling
Techniques see also slivering nuts (page 229)

400g (14oz) pitted morello cherries (bottled or
    canned), drained
3 tbsp brandy, sloe gin or almond-flavoured liqueur
150g (5oz) butter, softened
50g (2oz) icing sugar, plus extra to dust
1 small egg, beaten
225g (8oz) plain white flour, plus extra to dust

For the filling
100g (3½oz) plain chocolate
125g (4oz) butter, softened
125g (4oz) caster sugar
3 large eggs, beaten
125g (4oz) ground almonds
25g (1oz) self-raising flour
50g (2oz) amaretti biscuits, crushed
75g (3oz) slivered or flaked almonds

1 Put the cherries in a bowl with the brandy, gin or liqueur
and leave for 30 minutes. Put the butter, icing sugar and egg
in a food processor and whiz until almost smooth. Add the
flour and whiz until the mixture begins to form a dough.
(Alternatively, rub the fat into the flour by hand or using a
pastry cutter and stir in the icing sugar and egg.) Lightly
knead the pastry on a floured worksurface, then wrap and
chill for 30 minutes. Roll out the pastry on a lightly floured
worksurface and line a 24cm (9½in) fluted loose-based flan
tin. Chill for 20 minutes. Preheat the oven to 200°C (180°C
fan oven) mark 6. Line the pastry base with greaseproof
paper and baking beans and cook for 15 minutes. Remove
the weighted paper and put back in the oven for a further
5 minutes. Reduce the oven temperature to 150°C (130°C
fan oven) mark 2.
2 For the filling, put the chocolate in a heatproof bowl
over a pan of gently simmering water. Stir until melted and
smooth. Cool. In a bowl, beat the butter with the sugar until
pale and fluffy. Gradually beat in the eggs alternately with
the almonds and flour. Fold in the chocolate and amaretti
biscuits. Spoon one-third of the mixture over the base of
the pastry case. Spoon the cherries over. Spread the
remaining filling mixture to cover the cherries. Sprinkle on
the almonds and bake for about 1 hour. The tart will have
a thin top crust but be soft underneath. Cool in the tin
for 10–15 minutes, then unmould, dust with icing sugar
and serve.

FREEZING TIP
Complete the recipe up to baking the cake at step 2, then
cool, wrap and freeze.
To use Thaw at cool room temperature overnight. Warm
through as above and dust with icing sugar before serving.

NUTRITION PER SERVING
777 cals | 50g fat (22g sats) | 71g carbs | 0.7g salt **V**

DECADENT CHOCOLATE CAKE

Serves 12

Preparation 30 minutes

Cooking time 1½ hours, plus cooling

Techniques see also separating eggs (page 54), making breadcrumbs (page 318), lining tins (page 332), melting chocolate (page 366), whisking egg whites (page 54), testing sponges (page 334), cooling cakes (page 334)

225g (8oz) unsalted butter, softened, plus extra to grease
300g (11oz) plain chocolate, broken into pieces
225g (8oz) golden caster sugar
225g (8oz) ground almonds
8 large eggs, separated
125g (4oz) fresh brown breadcrumbs
4 tbsp apricot jam (optional)
single cream to serve

For the ganache
175g (6oz) plain chocolate, broken into pieces
75g (3oz) butter, softened
4 tbsp double cream

1 Preheat the oven to 180°C (160°C fan oven) mark 4. Grease and line a 23cm (9in) springform cake tin. Melt the chocolate in a heatproof bowl over a pan of gently simmering water. Remove from the heat. Put the butter and sugar into a large bowl and beat until light and creamy. Add the almonds, egg yolks and breadcrumbs. Beat well until thoroughly mixed. Slowly add the chocolate and carefully stir it in. Do not over-mix as the chocolate may seize up. Put the egg whites into a clean grease-free bowl and whisk until stiff peaks form. Add half the whites to the chocolate mixture and fold in lightly using a large metal spoon. Carefully fold in the remainder. Pour into the tin and level the surface. Bake for 1 hour 20 minutes or until the cake is firm to the touch and a skewer inserted into the centre comes out clean. Cool in the tin for 5 minutes, then transfer to a rack for 2–3 hours to cool completely.

2 Put the jam, if using, into a pan and melt over a low heat. Brush the jam over the top and sides of the cooled cake.

3 Melt the chocolate, butter and cream in a heatproof bowl over a pan of gently simmering water. Stir just once until smooth. Either raise the cake off the worksurface on the upturned tin or put it (still on the rack) on to a tray to catch the drips. Pour the ganache over the centre and tip the cake to let it run down the sides evenly, or spread it with a palette knife. Serve with cream.

NUTRITION PER SERVING
687 cals | 49g fat (23g sats) | 54g carbs | 0.7g salt **V**

CHOCOLATE-CHUNK BREAD PUDDING

Serves 6
Preparation 20 minutes, plus chilling
Cooking time 55 minutes–1 hour 15 minutes
Techniques see also chopping nuts (page 228)

200g (7oz) baguette
100g (3½oz) milk chocolate, roughly chopped
500g carton fresh vanilla custard
150ml (¼ pint) milk
1 large egg, beaten
1 tbsp demerara sugar
50g (2oz) walnuts, finely chopped
50g (2oz) plain or milk chocolate, in chunks
icing sugar to dust
single cream to serve (optional)

1 Roughly chop the baguette and put it into a large bowl.
Put the milk chocolate in a pan with the custard and milk
over a low heat. Stir gently until the chocolate has melted.
Beat in the egg.
2 Pour the chocolate mixture over the bread, stir well to
coat, then cover and chill for at least 4 hours.
3 Preheat the oven to 180°C (160°C fan oven) mark 4.
Grease a 1.4 litre (2½ pint), 7.5cm (3in) deep ovenproof
dish. Spoon the soaked bread into the prepared dish and
bake for 30–40 minutes.
4 Sprinkle the surface with the demerara sugar, walnuts
and chocolate chunks. Return to the oven to cook for
20–30 minutes until lightly set. Dust with icing sugar.
Serve the pudding warm, with single cream, if you like.

NUTRITION PER SERVING
390 cals | 17g fat (6g sats) | 51g carbs | 0.7g salt

WARM CHOCOLATE FONDANT

Serves 6
Preparation 10 minutes
Cooking time about 25 minutes
Techniques see also separating eggs (page 54), melting chocolate (page 366), making vanilla ice cream (page 394)

3 whole medium eggs, plus 3 egg yolks
50g (2oz) golden caster sugar
175g (6oz) plain chocolate
150g (5oz) unsalted butter
50g (2oz) plain flour, sifted
6 chocolate truffles
good-quality vanilla ice cream to serve

1 Preheat the oven to 200°C (180°C fan oven) mark 6. Put the eggs, egg yolks and sugar into a large bowl and beat with an electric whisk for 8–10 minutes until light and fluffy. You can do this by hand but it will take a little longer.
2 Melt the chocolate and butter in a heatproof bowl over a pan of gently simmering water, taking care not to let the bowl touch the water.
3 Gently fold the flour into the egg mixture. Stir a spoonful of egg mixture into the melted chocolate, then gently fold the chocolate mixture into the remaining egg mixture.
4 Put a large spoonful of mixture into each of six 200ml (7fl oz) ramekins. Put a chocolate truffle into the centre of each, taking care not to push it down. Divide the remainder of the mixture among the ramekins to cover the truffle. Each ramekin should be about three-quarters full.
5 Bake for 10–12 minutes until the top is firm and starting to rise and crack. Serve with ice cream.

COOK'S TIP
Be sure to choose a good-quality chocolate with minimum 70 per cent cocoa solids. It will give the rich, intense chocolate flavour that you need in these indulgent fondants.

NUTRITION PER SERVING
502 cals | 37g fat (21g sats) | 39g carbs | 0.5g salt

WHITE CHOCOLATE MOUSSE

Serves 6
Preparation 15 minutes, plus chilling
Cooking time 15 minutes
Techniques see also separating eggs (page 54), melting chocolate (page 366), whisking egg whites (page 54)

100ml (3½fl oz) full-fat milk
1 cinnamon stick
250g (9oz) good-quality white chocolate
285ml (9½fl oz) double cream
3 large egg whites
50g (2oz) plain chocolate
a little cocoa powder and ground cinnamon to decorate

1 Put the milk and cinnamon stick in a small pan and warm over a medium heat until the milk is almost boiling. Take the pan off the heat and put to one side.
2 Melt the white chocolate in a heatproof bowl over a pan of gently simmering water. Take the bowl off the pan and leave to cool a little.
3 Strain the warm milk on to the melted chocolate and stir together until completely smooth. Leave to cool for 10 minutes.
4 Whip the cream in a bowl until it just begins to hold its shape – it should still be a bit floppy. Whisk the egg whites until soft peaks form. Fold the whipped cream into the chocolate mixture with a large metal spoon, then carefully fold in the egg whites. Spoon the mixture into six small bowls or glasses – each measuring about 150ml (¼ pint) – and chill for 4 hours or overnight.
5 Pull a vegetable peeler across the edge of the plain chocolate to make rough curls. Sprinkle over the mousse. Dust with cocoa powder and a pinch of cinnamon.

GET AHEAD
Make up to the end of step 4 up to one day ahead. Cover and chill until needed.
To use Complete the recipe.

NUTRITION PER SERVING
515 cals | 41g fat (25g sats) | 31g carbs | 0.2g salt Ⓥ

FLORENTINES

Makes 18
Preparation 15 minutes
Cooking time 8–10 minutes, plus cooling
Techniques see also lining tins (page 332), melting chocolate (page 366)

65g (2½oz) unsalted butter, plus extra to grease
50g (2oz) golden caster sugar
2 tbsp double cream
25g (1oz) sunflower seeds
20g (¾oz) chopped mixed candied peel
20g (¾oz) sultanas
25g (1oz) natural glacé cherries, roughly chopped
40g (1½oz) flaked almonds, lightly crushed
15g (½oz) plain flour
125g (4oz) plain chocolate (at least 70% cocoa solids),
     broken into pieces

1 Preheat the oven to 180°C (160°C fan oven) mark 4. Lightly grease two large baking sheets. Melt the butter in a small, heavy-based pan. Add the sugar and heat gently until dissolved, then bring to the boil. Remove from the heat and stir in the cream, sunflower seeds, peel, sultanas, cherries, almonds and flour. Mix until evenly combined. Put heaped teaspoonfuls on to the baking sheets, spacing well apart to allow for spreading.
2 Bake one sheet at a time, for 6–8 minutes, until the biscuits have spread considerably and the edges are golden brown. Using a large, plain, metal biscuit cutter, push the edges into the centre to create neat rounds. Bake for a further 2 minutes or until deep golden. Leave on the baking sheet for 2 minutes, then transfer to a wire rack to cool completely.
3 Melt the chocolate in a heatproof bowl over a pan of gently simmering water, stirring occasionally. Spread on the underside of each Florentine and mark wavy lines with a fork. Put, chocolate side up, on a sheet of baking parchment until set.

COOK'S TIP
Store the Florentines in an airtight container; they will keep for up to two weeks.

NUTRITION PER SLICE
115 cals | 8g fat (4g sats) | 11g carbs | 0.1g salt

NUTTY CHOCOLATE TRUFFLES

Makes about 30
Preparation 15–20 minutes
Cooking time 12 minutes, plus 1–2 hours chilling
Techniques see also melting chocolate (page 366)

100g pack hazelnuts
200g (7oz) plain chocolate (minimum 50 per cent
   cocoa solids), broken into pieces
25g (1oz) butter
140ml (4½fl oz) double cream
3 tbsp cocoa powder, sifted
3 tbsp golden icing sugar, sifted

1 Put the hazelnuts into a frying pan and heat gently
for 3–4 minutes, shaking the pan occasionally, to toast all
over. Put 30 nuts into a bowl and leave to cool. Whiz the
remaining nuts in a food processor until finely chopped.
Put the chopped nuts into a shallow dish.
2 Melt the chocolate in a heatproof bowl over a pan of
gently simmering water, taking care not to let the bowl
touch the water. In a separate pan, melt the butter and
cream together. Bring just to the boil, then remove from
the heat. Carefully stir into the chocolate. Whisk until cool
and thick, then chill for 1–2 hours.
3 Put the cocoa powder and icing sugar into separate
shallow dishes. Scoop up a teaspoonful of truffle mix and
push a hazelnut into the centre. Working quickly, shape into
a ball, then roll in cocoa powder, icing sugar or chopped
nuts. Repeat with remaining mix, then chill.

GET AHEAD
Store in an airtight container in the refrigerator for up to
two weeks.

NUTRITION PER SERVING
96 cals | 8g fat (4g sats) | 6g carbs | 0.1g salt

STEAMED SYRUP SPONGE PUDDINGS

Serves 4
Preparation 20 minutes
Cooking time 35 minutes or 1½ hours
Techniques see also vanilla (page 438)

125g (4oz) butter, softened, plus extra to grease
3 tbsp golden syrup
125g (4oz) golden caster sugar
few drops of vanilla extract
2 medium eggs, beaten
175g (6oz) self-raising flour, sifted
about 3 tbsp milk
custard or cream to serve

1 Half-fill a steamer or large pan with water and put it on to boil. Grease four 300ml (½ pint) basins or a 900ml (1½ pint) pudding basin and spoon the golden syrup into the bottom.
2 In a bowl, cream the butter and sugar together until pale and fluffy. Stir in the vanilla extract. Add the eggs, a little at a time, beating well after each addition.
3 Using a metal spoon, fold in half the flour, then fold in the rest with enough milk to give a dropping consistency. Spoon the mixture into the prepared pudding basin(s).
4 Cover with greased and pleated greaseproof paper and foil and secure with string. Steam for 35 minutes for individual puddings or 1½ hours for one large pudding, checking the water level from time to time and topping up with boiling water as necessary. Turn out on to warmed plates and serve with custard or cream.

VARIATIONS
Steamed jam sponge puddings Put 4 tbsp raspberry or blackberry jam into the bottom of the basins instead of the syrup.
Steamed chocolate sponge puddings Omit the golden syrup. Blend 4 tbsp cocoa powder with 2 tbsp hot water, then gradually beat into the creamed mixture before adding the eggs.

NUTRITION PER SERVING
580 cals | 29g fat (17g sats) | 76g carbs | 0.7g salt

STICKY TOFFEE PUDDINGS

Serves 4
Preparation 20 minutes
Cooking time 25–30 minutes, plus resting
Techniques see also making vanilla custard (page 28)

1 tbsp golden syrup
1 tbsp black treacle
150g (5oz) butter, softened
25g (1oz) pecan nuts or walnuts
75g (3oz) self-raising flour
125g (4oz) caster sugar
2 large eggs, beaten
custard or cream to serve

1 Preheat the oven to 180°C (160°C fan oven) mark 4. Put the syrup, treacle and 25g (1oz) butter into a bowl and beat until smooth. Divide the mixture among four 150ml (¼ pint) timbales or ramekins and put to one side.
2 Finely process the nuts in a food processor. Put the nuts in a bowl, sift in the flour and mix together well.
3 Put the remaining butter and the sugar into a food processor and blend briefly. (Alternatively, use an electric hand mixer.) Add the beaten eggs and the flour mixture and blend or mix again for 30 seconds.
4 Spoon the sponge mixture into the timbales or ramekins, covering the syrup mixture on the bottom. Bake for 25–30 minutes until risen and golden.
5 Remove the puddings from the oven and leave to rest for 5 minutes, then unmould on to warmed serving plates. Serve immediately with custard or cream.

NUTRITION PER SERVING
565 cals | 38g fat (21g sats) | 53g carbs | 0.9g salt **V**

STRAWBERRY BRÛLÉE

Serves 4
Preparation 15 minutes
Cooking time 5 minutes, plus cooling or chilling
Techniques see also preparing berries (page 219)

250g (9oz) strawberries, washed, hulled and sliced
2 tsp golden icing sugar
1 vanilla pod
400ml (14fl oz) Greek yogurt
100g (3½oz) golden caster sugar

1 Arrange the strawberries in the base of four ramekins and sprinkle with icing sugar.
2 Scrape the seeds from the vanilla pod and stir into the yogurt, then spread the mixture evenly over the fruit.
3 Preheat the grill to high. Sprinkle the caster sugar evenly over the top of the yogurt until it's well covered.
4 Put the ramekins on to a baking sheet or into the grill pan and grill until the sugar turns dark brown and caramelises. Cool for 15 minutes or until the caramel is cool enough to eat, or chill in the fridge for up to 2 hours before serving.

VARIATIONS
Use raspberries or blueberries in place of the strawberries.

NUTRITION PER SERVING
240 cals | 10g fat (5g sats) | 35g carbs | 0.2g salt Ⓥ

STICKY BANOFFEE PIES

Serves 6
Preparation 15 minutes
Techniques see also shaving chocolate (page 366)

150g (5oz) digestive biscuits
75g (3oz) unsalted butter, melted, plus butter to grease
1 tsp ground ginger (optional)
450g (1lb) dulce de leche toffee sauce
4 medium-sized bananas, peeled, sliced and tossed in the
    juice of 1 lemon
285ml (9½fl oz) double cream, softly whipped
plain chocolate shavings

1 Put the biscuits in a food processor and whiz to a crumb. (Alternatively, put them in a plastic bag and crush with a rolling pin. Transfer to a bowl.) Add the melted butter and ginger and process, or stir well, for 1 minute to combine.

2 Grease six 10cm (4in) rings or tartlet tins and line with greaseproof paper. Press the biscuit mixture into each ring. Divide the toffee sauce equally among the rings and top with the bananas. Pipe or spoon on the cream, sprinkle with chocolate shavings and chill. Remove from the rings or tins to serve.

FINISHING TOUCHES

Finish the banoffee pies with any kind of chocolate decorations you like. Grated chocolate, chocolate shavings and curls all look good. Check out the techniques on page 366.

NUTRITION PER SERVING
827 cals | 55g fat (32g sats) | 84g carbs | 1.2g salt **V**

BRANDY SNAPS

Makes about 12
Preparation 10 minutes
Cooking time 12 minutes, plus cooling
Techniques see also zesting citrus fruits (page 217)

50g (2oz) butter, plus extra to grease
50g (2oz) caster sugar
2 tbsp golden syrup
50g (2oz) plain flour
½ tsp ground ginger
1 tsp brandy
finely grated zest of ½ lemon
150ml (¼ pint) double cream

1 Preheat the oven to 180°C (160°C fan oven) mark 4. Line two or three large baking sheets with baking parchment.
2 Gently heat the butter, sugar and syrup in a pan until the butter has melted and the sugar has dissolved. Remove from the heat.
3 Sift the flour and ginger together, then stir into the melted mixture with the brandy and lemon zest.
4 Drop teaspoons of the mixture on to the prepared baking sheets, leaving 10cm (4in) between each one. Bake for 7 minutes or until cooked.
5 Using a palette knife, quickly remove from the baking sheets and roll each one around the buttered handle of a wooden spoon. Leave on the handles until set, then gently twist to remove. Cool on a wire rack.
6 If the biscuits set before they have been shaped, return them to the oven for a few minutes to soften. Store in an airtight container until required.
7 Just before serving, whip the cream until it just holds its shape. Spoon into a piping bag fitted with a star nozzle and pipe cream into the brandy snaps. Serve immediately.

NUTRITION PER BISCUIT
132 cals | 10g fat (6g sats) | 10g carbs | 0.1g salt Ⓥ

ALMOND TOFFEE MERINGUES

Serves 4
Preparation 35 minutes
Cooking time 22–25 minutes, plus overnight cooling
Techniques see also separating eggs (page 54), slivering nuts (page 229), stoning fruits (page 218), making meringues (pages 60–1)

oil to grease
25g (1oz) light muscovado sugar
100g (3½oz) egg whites (about 3 medium eggs)
225g (8oz) caster sugar
25g (1oz) flaked almonds
lightly whipped cream to serve

For the marinated summer fruit
125ml (4fl oz) crème de cassis
juice of 1 orange
2 tbsp redcurrant jelly
200g (7oz) raspberries
4 nectarines, halved, stoned and sliced

1 To make the marinated fruit, put the crème de cassis, orange juice and redcurrant jelly in a small pan. Heat gently to melt, then bubble for 2–3 minutes until syrupy. Pour into a large bowl to cool. Add the raspberries and nectarines and stir gently. Cover and chill.
2 Preheat the oven to 170°C (150°C fan oven) mark 3 and preheat the grill. Lightly oil a baking sheet and sprinkle over the muscovado sugar. Grill for 2–3 minutes until the sugar begins to bubble and caramelise. Cool for about 15 minutes, then break the sugar into a food processor and whiz to a coarse powder.
3 Put the egg whites and caster sugar in a large clean bowl over a pan of gently simmering water. Stir until the sugar has dissolved and the egg white is warm, about 10 minutes. Remove from the heat and place on a teatowel. Beat with an electric whisk for at least 15 minutes or until cold and glossy and standing in stiff shiny peaks when the whisk is lifted. Cover two baking sheets with non-stick baking parchment. Fold half the powdered sugar into the meringue mixture. Spoon four oval mounds on to the baking sheets, leaving plenty of space between each. Sprinkle with flaked almonds and the remaining powdered sugar. Bake for 20 minutes, then turn off the heat and leave in the oven to dry out overnight. Serve with the marinated fruit and lightly whipped cream.

COOK'S TIP
• Make sure the bowl does not touch the hot water while you make the meringues.
• The flavour of the marinated fruit will be even better if you chill it overnight. (If the syrup thickens during chilling, stir in 1–2 tbsp orange juice.)

NUTRITION PER SERVING
458 cals | 4g fat (trace sats) | 95g carbs | 0.2g salt

CARAMELISED ORANGE TRIFLE

Serves 16
Preparation 45 minutes, plus chilling
Cooking time 5 minutes
Techniques see also preparing citrus fruit (page 217), making spun sugar (page 371)

125g (4oz) light muscovado sugar
2 × 135g packs orange jelly, broken into cubes
100ml (3½fl oz) brandy
10 oranges, peeled and all pith removed
150g pack ratafia biscuits
4 tbsp sweet sherry
500g carton fresh custard sauce
284ml carton double cream
2 × 250g cartons mascarpone cheese
¼ tsp vanilla extract
125g (4oz) granulated sugar

1 Put the muscovado sugar in a large heavy-based pan. Add 100ml (3½fl oz) water. Dissolve the sugar over a low heat. Increase the heat and cook for 5 minutes or until the sugar is syrupy and thick. Remove from the heat and add 450ml (¾ pint) boiling water (the sugar will splutter). Add the jelly and stir until dissolved. Add the brandy and put to one side.
2 Slice the orange flesh into rounds, putting any juice to one side. Add the juice – about 125ml (4fl oz) – to the jelly. Cool. Tip the ratafia biscuits into the base of a 3.5 litre (6¼ pint) bowl and drizzle with sherry. Arrange the orange rounds on top, then pour the jelly over. Chill for 4 hours until set. Pour the custard over the top and smooth over. Put the cream, mascarpone and vanilla extract in a bowl and combine with an electric hand mixer. Spoon three-quarters of the mixture on to the custard. Smooth the surface. Put the remainder in a piping bag and pipe 10 swirls around the edge. Chill.
3 Line a large baking sheet with baking parchment. Half-fill the sink with cold water. Heat the granulated sugar in a heavy-based pan until dissolved. Increase the heat and cook to a golden caramel, then plunge the base of the pan into the sink. Dip in a fork and pick up the caramel, then flick it back and forth over the parchment to form fine strands. Put the sugar strands on top of the trifle.

FINISHING TOUCHES

For an alternative, try sprinkling with silver dragees, toasted flaked almonds or grated chocolate (page 366) instead.

NUTRITION PER SERVING
358 cals | 15g fat (9g sats) | 48g carbs | 0.1g salt

CARAMEL CUSTARD SQUARES

Serves 4
Preparation 20 minutes
Cooking time 30 minutes, plus cooling
Techniques see also separating eggs (page 54), lining a loaf tin (page 333), making caramel (page 370)

vegetable oil to grease
50g (2oz) white granulated sugar
75g (3oz) golden caster sugar
1 tsp vanilla extract
6 large egg yolks

1 Preheat the oven to 170°C (150°C fan oven) mark 3. Lightly oil a 450g (1lb) loaf tin and line the base with baking parchment.

2 Put the granulated sugar into a small pan and heat gently until dissolved. Bring to the boil and cook for 2–3 minutes, tilting the pan but not stirring until the syrup turns a golden caramel. Pour into the prepared tin. Put the caster sugar into a pan with 75ml (2½fl oz) cold water and the vanilla extract. Heat gently until the sugar has dissolved. Increase the heat and boil for 3 minutes or until syrupy. Cool for 5 minutes.

3 Put the egg yolks into a large bowl and gradually stir in the cooled sugar syrup with a wooden spoon. Strain through a metal sieve into the loaf tin on to the caramel. Pour 2.5cm (1in) boiling water into a roasting tin, then rest a wire rack on top. Sit the loaf tin on the rack and cover the whole roasting tin with foil. Bake for 25 minutes until just firm and a skewer inserted into the centre comes out clean. Cool and chill.

4 To serve, dip the base of the tin into a shallow dish of boiling water for 10 seconds. Run a sharp knife around the custard to loosen, then upturn on to a serving dish – there may be some caramel left in the tin but don't worry. Cut into eight squares and put in petits fours cases.

COOK'S TIP
Serve these sweet squares with a coffee after dinner.

NUTRITION PER SERVING
210 cals | 8g fat (2g sats) | 31g carbs | 0g salt **V**

COOKIES AND CREAM FUDGE

Makes 36 pieces
Preparation 10 minutes
Cooking time 15 minutes
Techniques see also toasting nuts (page 228), vanilla fudge (page 372)

sunflower oil to grease
125g (4oz) unsalted butter
200ml (7fl oz) evaporated milk
450g (1lb) golden caster sugar
1 tsp vanilla extract
75g (3oz) plain chocolate, chopped
25g (1oz) hazelnuts, toasted and roughly chopped
6 Oreo cookies or bourbon biscuits, roughly chopped

1 Lightly grease a 450g (1lb) loaf tin with a little oil.
2 Put the butter, evaporated milk, sugar, vanilla extract and 50ml (2fl oz) water in a large heavy-based pan, set over a low heat, and stir until the butter has melted and the sugar dissolved. Increase the heat to a gentle boil and cook for about 10 minutes, stirring all the time, until the fudge forms a soft ball when half a teaspoonful is dropped into a cup of cold water. Remove the pan from the heat and, working quickly, divide the fudge mixture between two bowls. Add the chocolate to one of the bowls and allow it to melt into the fudge. Stir the mixture gently until smooth.
3 Pour half the chocolate fudge into the tin and smooth the surface, then scatter over half the hazelnuts and half the biscuits.
4 Pour the vanilla fudge into the tin on top of the nuts and biscuits, then top with the remaining nuts and biscuits.
5 Finish with a final layer of the chocolate fudge and leave to cool. Cover with clingfilm and leave in the fridge overnight to set firm. Once the fudge has set, remove it from the loaf tin and cut into slices, then chop up each slice to serve.

FINISHING TOUCHES
To make a gift, wrap piles of the fudge in clear cellophane and tie with a pretty ribbon, then attach a label to each parcel with an eat-by date and a note that the fudge should be stored in the fridge.

NUTRITION PER SERVING
81 cals | 2g fat (1g sats) | 17g carbs | 0.1g salt **V**

ICE CREAMS, SORBETS AND ICED DESSERTS

Rich and creamy, fresh and fruity or sweet and indulgent, ice creams and iced desserts are easy to make yourself. With easy-to-follow step-by-step instructions, the techniques section guides you through the basics of making ice creams and sorbets – in a machine and by hand – as well as parfaits and ice cream bombes, and shows you the secrets of layering and rippling. The recipe collection builds on these skills with stunning desserts including Frozen yogurt sorbet, Spicy ginger ice cream, Iced lemon meringue, Cranberry Christmas bombe and Italian ice cream cake.

MAKING ICE CREAM

Good ice cream needs a smooth, creamy texture. Using an ice-cream maker is the best way to achieve it, but freezing and breaking up the ice crystals by hand works well, too.

Vanilla ice cream

To serve four to six, you will need 300ml (½ pint) milk, I vanilla pod, split lengthways, 3 medium egg yolks, 75g (3oz) golden caster sugar, 300ml (½ pint) double cream.

1 Put the milk and vanilla in a pan. Heat slowly until almost boiling. Cool for 20 minutes and remove the vanilla. In a large bowl, whisk the egg yolks and sugar until thick and creamy. Gradually whisk in the milk, then strain back into the pan.

2 Cook over a low heat, stirring, until thick enough to coat the back of the spoon. (Do not boil.) Pour into a chilled bowl and leave to cool.

3 Whisk the cream into the custard.

4 Pour into an ice-cream maker and freeze or churn according to the manufacturer's instructions.

VARIATIONS

- **Fruit ice cream** Sweeten 300ml (½ pint) fruit purée (such as rhubarb, gooseberry, raspberry or strawberry) to taste, then stir into the cooked custard and churn.
- **Chocolate ice cream** Omit the vanilla and add 125g (4oz) dark chocolate to the milk. Heat gently until melted, then bring almost to the boil and proceed as above.
- **Coffee ice cream** Omit the vanilla and add 150ml (¼ pint) cooled strong coffee to the cooked custard.

Making by hand

1 If possible, set the freezer to fast freeze I hour ahead. Pour the ice-cream mixture into a shallow freezer-proof container, cover and freeze until it's partially frozen.

2 Spoon into a bowl and mash with a fork to break up the ice crystals. Return to the container and freeze for another 2 hours.

3 Repeat and freeze for another 3 hours.

LAYERING, SHAPING AND RIPPLING

Freshly made ice cream is soft enough to shape into moulds, layer and ripple for a more elegant presentation. You can buy a bombe or ice-cream mould, or just use a bowl or loaf tin.

Layering

1 For a layered effect, make two or more flavoured ice creams of distinct colours. While the first ice cream is still soft, pack it into a mould lined with clingfilm. Freeze until firm, then layer the second ice cream on top and freeze until firm.

2 Continue in the same way with the remaining flavour(s) and serve cut into slices.

Ice cream bombes

1 First make two flavours of ice cream. While the first ice cream is still soft, press it against the sides and base of a large mould or bowl, making a hollow in the centre. Freeze until firm.

2 Fill the hollow with the soft second ice cream and cover with clingfilm. Freeze until firm, then unmould and serve in slices.

Rippling and marbling

1 Make vanilla ice cream and churn in an ice-cream maker (or make by hand) until thick, but soft. Spoon a layer into a freezerproof container, then drizzle with fruit purée. Top with more ice cream and purée.

2 Pass a skewer or knife through the mixture until the marbled/rippled effect is achieved.

MAKING PARFAITS

Ice-cream parfait is a kind of frozen, sweet mousse, which doesn't require an ice-cream maker.
The mixture can be frozen as it is, with no need for churning.

Pistachio parfait

To serve six, you will need 75g (3oz)
shelled pistachio nuts, plus extra to
decorate, oil to grease, 200ml (7fl oz)
double cream, 4 large egg whites,
75g (3oz) icing sugar, 2 tbsp orange-
flavoured liqueur, such as Grand
Marnier, 75g (3oz) white chocolate.

1 Toast the pistachios in a dry frying
pan and chop finely. Lightly oil and line
six 150ml (¼ pint) ramekins with
greaseproof paper. Sprinkle lightly
with 25g (1oz) nuts. Cut six strips of
greaseproof paper, each 5 × 25.5cm
(2 × 10in), and lightly oil one side of
each strip. Sprinkle with 25g (1oz)
nuts and line each ramekin with a
strip, nut side inwards.

2 Lightly whip the cream.

3 Whisk the egg whites until just soft,
then whisk in the icing sugar.

4 Fold the remaining nuts into the
egg whites with the liqueur and
whipped cream. Do not over-mix.

5 Divide the mixture between the
ramekins and freeze overnight.

6 Melt chocolate in a bowl over
hot water. Cut six strips of baking
parchment measuring 5 × 25.5cm
(2 × 10in), and spread each one with
chocolate. Leave to firm up slightly.
Unmould the parfaits and remove
the lining papers. Lift the chocolate-
covered strips and wrap each one
around a parfait, with the chocolate
side inside. Freeze for 30 minutes.
To serve, remove the paper strips.

COOK'S TIPS

→ For a much simpler dessert,
you could omit the chocolate
and just make the recipe up
to step 5, then unmould the
parfaits and serve.

→ To decorate, use 75g white
chocolate and make
chocolate curls following the
instructions on page 366.

MAKING SORBET

Sorbets have a fine, smooth texture and are most frequently fruit-flavoured. Fruits vary in sweetness, so taste the mixture before freezing. Remove the sorbet from the freezer 20 minutes before serving.

Simple orange sorbet

To serve six, you will need the zest of 3 oranges and the juice of 6 oranges, about 600ml (1 pint), 200g (7oz) granulated sugar, 1 tbsp orange flower water, 1 medium egg white.

1 Put the orange zest and sugar in a pan with 300ml (½ pint) water. Bring slowly to the boil, stirring. Simmer for 5 minutes, leave to cool for 2 minutes, then strain and cool completely.

2 Strain the orange juice into the syrup and add the orange flower water. Chill for 30 minutes.

3 Using an ice-cream maker, follow the manufacturer's instructions but remove the sorbet halfway through.

4 Whisk the egg white, add to the bowl, and continue churning until the sorbet is firm enough to scoop.

GRANITAS

Granita is an Italian water ice with larger crystals than a sorbet. It isn't churned but is broken up with a fork, which makes it more like a frozen fruit slush. Quick to melt, it must be served and eaten quickly and makes a wonderful refresher in summer. Fruit-flavoured, granitas are frequently also popularly flavoured with coffee.

Making by hand

1 Pour the mixture into a shallow container, cover and freeze for about 3 hours, until partially frozen to a slushy consistency. Beat the sorbet with a whisk or fork until smooth.

2 Whisk the egg white and fold into the mixture, then return to the freezer and freeze until firm enough to scoop, 2–4 hours.

LEMON SORBET

Serves 4
Preparation 10 minutes, plus chilling and freezing
Cooking time 15 minutes
Techniques see also separating eggs (page 54), zesting citrus fruits (page 217)

3 juicy lemons
125g (4oz) golden caster sugar
1 large egg white

1 Finely pare the lemon zest, using a zester, then squeeze the juice. Put the zest into a pan with the sugar and 350ml (12fl oz) water and heat gently until the sugar has dissolved. Increase the heat and boil for 10 minutes. Leave to cool.
2 Stir the lemon juice into the cooled sugar syrup. Cover and chill in the fridge for 30 minutes.
3 Strain the syrup through a fine sieve into a bowl. In another bowl, beat the egg white until just frothy, then whisk into the lemon mixture.
4 For best results, freeze in an ice-cream maker. Otherwise, pour into a shallow freezerproof container and freeze until almost frozen; mash well with a fork and freeze until solid. Transfer the sorbet to the fridge 30 minutes before serving to soften slightly.

TRY SOMETHING DIFFERENT
Orange Sorbet Replace two of the lemons with oranges.
Lime Sorbet Replace two of the lemons with four limes.
Mango Sorbet Make the sugar syrup as directed, but using the zest of 1 lime instead of the lemons. Blend the flesh of two ripe mangos with the juice of the lime until smooth and then stir in the cooled sugar syrup. Complete the recipe from step 4.

NUTRITION PER SERVING
130 cals | 0g fat (0g sats) | 33g carbs | trace salt

FROZEN YOGURT SORBET

Serves 8
Preparation 15 minutes, plus freezing
Techniques see also separating eggs (page 54)

450g (1lb) thawed frozen mixed fruit, plus extra to serve
100g (3½oz) clear honey
3 medium egg whites
450g (1lb) low-fat natural Greek yogurt

1 Line a 750ml (1¼ pint) loaf tin with clingfilm. Whiz the thawed frozen mixed fruit in a food processor or blender to make a purée. Sieve into a bowl, pressing all the juice through with the back of a spoon. Stir the honey into the juice.
2 Whisk the egg whites in a clean grease-free bowl until soft peaks form, then fold into the fruit with the yogurt. Pour the mixture into the prepared tin and freeze for 4 hours. Stir to break up the ice crystals, then freeze again for 4 hours. Stir again, then freeze for a further 4 hours or until firm.
3 Transfer to the fridge for 20 minutes, then turn out of the tin and remove the clingfilm. Slice and serve with a spoonful of thawed frozen berries.

COOK'S TIP
Use any selection of frozen mixed berries that you like. Summer berries and forest fruits work well.

NUTRITION PER SERVING
120 cals | 6g fat (3g sats) | 14g carbs | 0.2g salt

SPICY GINGER ICE CREAM

Serves 8
Preparation 30 minutes, plus chilling and freezing
Cooking time 5 minutes, plus cooling
Techniques see also separating eggs (page 54), rippling ice cream (page 395)

575ml (19½fl oz) double cream
125g (4oz) golden caster sugar, plus 1 tbsp
4 medium eggs, separated
2 tsp ground ginger
4 pieces stem ginger, roughly chopped
brandy snaps to serve

For the sauce
50g (2oz) unsalted butter
50g (2oz) golden caster sugar
2 tbsp whisky
2 tbsp ginger syrup (from the jar of stem ginger)

1 Whip the cream until just thickened. Leave to chill. Whisk the 125g (4oz) caster sugar with the egg yolks until pale and creamy.
2 Beat the egg whites in a clean grease-free bowl until stiff. Beat in the 1 tbsp caster sugar.
3 Fold the cream into the egg yolk and sugar mixture with the ground ginger, then quickly fold in the beaten egg whites. Pour into a freezerproof container and freeze for 4 hours.
4 To make the sauce, put the butter, sugar, whisky and ginger syrup in a pan and heat gently. Bring to the boil, reduce the heat and simmer for 5 minutes or until thick. Leave to cool.
5 Fold the stem ginger through the ice cream and drizzle the sauce over. Stir once or twice to create a ripple effect and continue to freeze for 4 hours or overnight. Serve with brandy snaps.

NUTRITION PER SERVING
541 cals | 46g fat (28g sats) | 27g carbs | 0.2g salt Ⓥ

INSTANT BANANA ICE CREAM

Serves 4
Preparation 5 minutes, plus freezing
Techniques see also vanilla (page 438)

6 ripe bananas, about 700g (1lb 9oz), peeled, cut into thin
 slices and frozen (see Cook's Tips)
1–2 tbsp virtually fat-free fromage frais
1–2 tbsp orange juice
1 tsp vanilla extract
splash of rum or Cointreau (optional)
a few drops of lime juice to taste

1 Leave the frozen bananas to stand at room temperature
for 2–3 minutes. Put the still frozen pieces into a food
processor or blender with 1 tbsp fromage frais, 1 tbsp
orange juice, the vanilla extract and the liqueur, if you like.
2 Whiz until smooth, scraping down the sides of the
bowl and adding more fromage frais and orange juice as
necessary to give a creamy consistency. Add lime juice to
taste and serve at once or turn into a freezer container
and freeze for up to one month.

COOK'S TIPS
To freeze bananas, peel and slice them thinly, then put
the banana slices on a large non-stick baking tray and
put into the freezer for 30 minutes or until frozen.
Transfer to a plastic bag and store in the freezer
until needed.

Cheat's Raspberry Ice cream
Put six ramekins or freezerproof glasses into the freezer
to chill. Put 300g (11oz) frozen raspberries (don't allow
them to thaw first) into a food processor with 5–6 tbsp
golden icing sugar. Whiz for 3–4 seconds until the
raspberries look like large crumbs. Add 300ml (½ pint)
extra-thick double cream and whiz again for 10 seconds.
Spoon into the ice-cold dishes and serve immediately, or
spoon into a small freezerproof container and freeze for
20–30 minutes. Serve with summer fruit or wafers, if you
like. Depending on the sweetness of the raspberries, you
may need to add a little more icing sugar – taste the
mixture before you spoon the ice cream into
the dishes.

NUTRITION PER SERVING
178 cals | 1g fat (0g sats) | 42g carbs | 0.3g salt

CINNAMON AND NUTMEG ICE CREAM

Serves 8
Preparation 10 minutes, plus freezing
Cooking time 5 minutes
Techniques see also making ice cream by hand (page 394)

½ tsp ground cinnamon, plus extra to dust
½ tsp freshly grated nutmeg
50g (2oz) golden caster sugar
140ml (4½fl oz) double cream
250g (9oz) mascarpone cheese
400g carton fresh custard

1 Put the cinnamon, nutmeg, sugar and cream in a small pan, bring slowly to the boil, then put to one side to cool.
2 Put the mascarpone in a large bowl and beat until smooth. Stir in the custard and the cooled spiced cream. Pour the mixture into a shallow freezerproof container and freeze for 2–3 hours.
3 Whisk to break up the ice crystals and freeze for a further 2–3 hours before serving, dusted with cinnamon.

COOK'S TIP
The ice cream will keep in the freezer
for up to one month.

NUTRITION PER SERVING
221 cals | 15g fat (9g sats) | 16g carbs | 0.1g salt

PISTACHIO AND DATE ICE CREAMS

Serves 6
Preparation 15 minutes, plus freezing
Techniques see also making ice cream by hand (page 394)

100g (3½oz) shelled pistachio nuts
218g can condensed milk
300ml (½ pint) double cream
1 tbsp orange flower water
125g (4oz) Medjool dates, stoned and roughly chopped
3 pomegranates

1 Keep 15g (½oz) pistachio nuts to one side and put the rest in a food processor. Add the condensed milk and whiz for 1–2 minutes to roughly chop the nuts and flavour the milk.
2 Pour the cream into a bowl and whip until soft peaks form. Stir in the chopped pistachios and condensed milk, orange flower water and dates.
3 Line six 150ml (¼ pint) dariole moulds or clean yogurt pots with clingfilm, leaving some clingfilm hanging over the edges. Spoon in the cream mixture and freeze for at least 5 hours.
4 Cut the pomegranates in half, scoop out the seeds and discard any pith. Push the seeds through a sieve to extract the juice. Put the juice in a pan and bring to the boil, then reduce the heat and simmer for 8 minutes until reduced to a syrup. Leave to cool, put in a small airtight container and chill until needed.
5 To serve, ease the ice cream out of the moulds and remove the clingfilm. Cut each in half vertically and arrange on plates. Chop the remaining pistachios and sprinkle them over, then drizzle over some pomegranate sauce.

TRY SOMETHING DIFFERENT
Replace the pistachios with hazelnuts and the dates with dried cherries.

NUTRITION PER SERVING
516 cals | 38g fat (19g sats) | 38g carbs | 0.4g salt **V**

CHILLED BLACKBERRY SNOW

Serves 6
Preparation 30 minutes, plus freezing
Techniques see also separating eggs (page 54), whisking egg whites (page 54)

450g (1lb) blackberries, fresh or frozen, thawed
2 medium egg whites
50g (2oz) caster sugar
300ml (½ pint) double cream

1 Rub the blackberries through a nylon sieve. Pour the purée into a rigid container and freeze for about 2 hours or until mushy.
2 Whisk the egg whites until stiff, then gradually add the sugar, whisking until the mixture stands in soft peaks. Whip the cream until it just holds its shape.
3 Remove the frozen blackberry purée from the freezer and mash to break down the large ice crystals, being careful not to break it down completely.
4 Fold the cream and egg whites together, then quickly fold in the semi-frozen blackberry purée to form a 'swirled' effect. Spoon into tall glasses and serve immediately.

NUTRITION PER SERVING
303 cals | 27g fat (17g sats) | 13g carbs | 0.1g salt **V**

ICED LEMON MERINGUE

Serves 8
Preparation 30 minutes, plus drying
Cooking time 1 hour 35 minutes
Techniques see also separating eggs (page 54), slivering nuts (page 229), zesting citrus fruits (page 217), freezing fruit (page 445), whisking egg whites (page 54), making meringues (pages 60–61), toasting nuts (page 228)

4 large egg whites, at room temperature
1 tsp lemon juice
100g (3½oz) golden caster sugar
100g (3½oz) light muscovado sugar
1 tbsp cornflour, sifted
½ tsp almond extract
25g (1oz) flaked almonds

For the lemon filling
2 tbsp cornflour, sifted
4 large egg yolks
100g (3½oz) golden caster sugar
zest and juice of 1 lemon
zest and juice of 1 lime
125ml (4fl oz) milk
285ml (9½fl oz) double cream

For the raspberry coulis
200g (7oz) frozen raspberries
1 tbsp golden icing sugar

1 Preheat the oven to 140°C (120°C fan oven) mark 1. Draw three 25.5 × 10cm (10 × 4in) rectangles on baking parchment. Cut around each, leaving a 10cm (4in) border. Turn over and put on a baking sheet. Whisk the egg whites to soft peaks. Add the lemon juice and whisk until stiff. Whisk in the sugars, 1 tbsp at a time, until glossy and soft peaks form. Beat in 1 tbsp boiling water, then fold in the cornflour and almond extract. Divide among the rectangles and lift into peaks. Put 1 tbsp almonds to one side and sprinkle the rest over the meringues. Bake for 20 minutes, reduce the oven temperature to 110°C (90°C fan oven) mark ¼ and bake for 1¼ hours. Turn off the oven and leave for 30 minutes–1 hour to dry.
2 To make the filling, mix the cornflour with 1 tbsp water, then stir in the egg yolks, sugar, citrus zest and juice. Bring the milk to the boil, stir in the cornflour and stir over a gentle heat until thick. Tip into a bowl, cover with wet greaseproof paper and cool. Whip the cream to soft peaks, then fold into the filling. Sandwich the meringues with the filling. Put on a baking sheet and open freeze until firm. Wrap and refreeze.

3 Reserve eight raspberries and gently heat the remainder with the icing sugar and 1 tbsp water for 5 minutes. Cool, then sieve. To serve, transfer the meringue to the fridge for 5 minutes. Toast the reserved almonds, sprinkle over the top with the reserved frozen raspberries and serve in slices with the coulis.

NUTRITION PER SERVING
420 cals | 24g fat (13g sats) | 49g carbs | 0.1g salt

MANGO ICE CREAM TERRINE

Serves 8
Preparation 20–25 minutes, plus overnight freezing
Techniques see also preparing mangoes (page 220), layering ice cream (page 395)

vegetable oil to grease
2 small mangoes, peeled and chopped
2 medium eggs
125g (4oz) golden caster sugar
285ml (9½fl oz) double cream, whipped
1½ tsp Malibu
4 ratafia biscuits, roughly crushed

1 Lightly oil a 900g (2lb) loaf tin, then line with clingfilm, leaving enough to hang over the edges and smoothing any creases.
2 Whiz the mangoes in a food processor or blender until smooth. Set aside. Put the eggs and sugar into a large bowl. Using an electric hand whisk, mix together until thick – this should take 5 minutes.
3 Add the whipped cream to the mixture and fold together with a large metal spoon. Fold in three-quarters of the puréed mango and the Malibu. Spoon the remaining mango purée into the lined tin to cover the base, then pour in the ice cream mixture. Cover with the overhanging clingfilm and freeze overnight or for up to one month.
4 Remove the ice cream from the freezer 5 minutes before serving. Unwrap the clingfilm. Turn out on to a serving dish, cover with the biscuits, slice and serve.

NUTRITION PER SERVING
306 cals | 21g fat (13g sats) | 26g carbs | 0.1g salt **V**

CRANBERRY CHRISTMAS BOMBE

Serves 8–10
Preparation 30 minutes, plus chilling and freezing
Cooking time 15 minutes
Techniques see also separating eggs (page 54), whisking egg whites (page 54), making ice cream bombes (page 395)

125g (4oz) granulated sugar
300ml (½ pint) cranberry juice
225g (8oz) each cranberries and raspberries, fresh or frozen
2 large egg whites
75g (3oz) caster sugar
groundnut oil to grease
500ml tub good-quality vanilla ice cream

For the sugared redcurrants
a few sprigs of redcurrants
1 large egg white, lightly beaten
a little caster sugar

1 Put the granulated sugar and cranberry juice in a pan and heat gently until the sugar has dissolved. Bring to the boil, then add the cranberries. Reduce the heat, cover and simmer for 15 minutes until very soft. Leave to cool. Blend with the raspberries in a food processor or blender, press through a nylon sieve, then chill. Whisk the egg whites until soft peaks form. Whisk in the sugar a spoonful at a time until stiff and glossy. Fold into the fruit purée. Pour into an ice-cream maker and churn until stiff.

2 Meanwhile, lightly grease a 1.4 litre (2½ pint) pudding basin with a little oil, then put a disc of foil in the base. Put in the freezer for 30 minutes. Spoon the sorbet into the basin (reserving 3–4 tbsp), creating a hollow in the centre, and return to the freezer. Leave the ice cream at room temperature for 10 minutes. Spoon the ice cream into the centre of the sorbet and press down well. Spread the reserved sorbet on top. Freeze for 4 hours or until firm.

3 To make the sugared redcurrants, dip the sprigs in the beaten egg white, then in the sugar. Allow to harden on a baking sheet lined with greaseproof paper. To unmould the bombe, dip the basin in hot water for 10 seconds, then loosen the edges with a round-bladed knife, invert on to a plate, shake firmly and remove the foil. Decorate with redcurrants, then use a warm knife to cut the bombe into wedges.

NUTRITION PER SERVING FOR 8
236 cals | 6g fat (4g sats) | 44g carbs | 0.1g salt **V**

NUTRITION PER SERVING FOR 10
189 cals | 5g fat (3g sats) | 35g carbs | 0.1g salt **V**

ITALIAN ICE CREAM CAKE

Serves 10
Preparation 40 minutes, plus freezing
Techniques see also pitting cherries (page 218), separating eggs (page 54), chopping nuts (page 228)

400g (14oz) fresh cherries, pitted and quartered
4 tbsp amaretto liqueur
10 tbsp crème de cacao liqueur
200g (7oz) Savoiardi biscuits or sponge fingers
5 medium egg yolks
150g (5oz) golden caster sugar
450ml (¾ pint) double cream, lightly whipped
1 tbsp vanilla extract
75g (3oz) pistachio nuts or hazelnuts, roughly
    chopped in a food processor
75g (3oz) plain chocolate, roughly chopped in
    a food processor
2–3 tbsp cocoa powder
2–3 tbsp golden icing sugar

1 Put the cherries and amaretto in a bowl, stir, cover with clingfilm and put to one side. Pour the crème de cacao into a shallow dish and take out a large chopping board. Quickly dip a sponge finger into the liqueur – on one side only, so that it doesn't go soggy and fall apart – then put on to the board and cut in half lengthways to separate the sugary side from the base. Repeat with each biscuit.
2 Double line a 24 × 4cm (9½ × 1½in) round tin with clingfilm. Arrange the sugar-coated sponge finger halves, sugar side down, on the base of the tin. Drizzle with any remaining crème de cacao.
3 Put the yolks and caster sugar into a bowl and whisk until pale, light and fluffy. Fold in the cream, vanilla extract, nuts, chocolate and cherries, plus any remaining amaretto. Spoon on top of the sponge fingers in the tin and cover with the remaining sponge finger halves, cut side down. Cover with clingfilm and freeze for at least 5 hours.
4 To serve, upturn the cake on to a serving plate and remove the clingfilm. Sift cocoa and icing sugar over the cake and cut into wedges. Leave at room temperature for 20 minutes if the weather is warm, 40 minutes at cool room temperature, or 1 hour in the fridge, to allow the cherries to thaw and the ice cream to become moussey.

FINISHING TOUCHES

Use the tin to cut a circle of greaseproof paper, then fold to make eight triangles. Cut these out and put four on the cake and dust with cocoa powder. Remove the triangles. Cover the cocoa with four triangles and dust with icing sugar.

NUTRITION PER SERVING
522 cals | 33g fat (15g sats) | 46g carbs | 0.2g salt

ICED RASPBERRY SOUFFLÉS

Serves 8
Preparation 1¼ hours, plus chilling and freezing
Techniques see also separating eggs (page 54), melting chocolate and making chocolate curls (page 366)

juice of 1 orange
juice of 1 lemon
700g (1lb 9oz) raspberries
225g (8oz) caster sugar
450ml (¾ pint) double cream
2 large egg whites
400g (14oz) plain chocolate
350g (12oz) mixed berries, such as redcurrants, blueberries and blackberries

1 Wrap eight 100ml (3½fl oz) glasses with non-stick baking parchment, 6.5 × 25.5cm (2½ × 10in), to form a collar above the rim. Put 2 tbsp each of the citrus juices in a food processor or blender with the raspberries and sugar. Process until smooth, then sieve. Set aside 150ml (¼ pint), then cover and chill. Put the remaining sauce in a large bowl. Whip the cream until it just holds its shape, then fold the cream into the sauce. Whisk the egg whites until soft peaks form. Fold into the raspberry cream and spoon into the prepared glasses and freeze overnight.
2 Cut eight strips of non-stick baking parchment. Melt 225g (8oz) chocolate in a heatproof bowl over a pan of gently simmering water. Cool slightly, then brush over the parchment strips to cover completely. Remove the soufflés from the freezer and peel off the parchment. Carefully wrap the chocolate-covered strips around the tops of the soufflés and return to the freezer for 5 minutes. Peel the baking parchment away from the chocolate and return the soufflés to the freezer.
3 Melt the remaining chocolate as before, then spread it over a marble slab or worksurface. When it has just set, push the blade of a knife at a 25-degree angle across the chocolate to form the curls. Put the soufflés in the fridge for 20 minutes before serving. Serve decorated with mixed berries, chocolate curls and the reserved sauce.

COOK'S TIPS
- Don't over-whip the cream, as the acidity of the raspberries will help to thicken it – aim for a soft dropping consistency.
- If the chocolate doesn't form curls easily and breaks up, it has set too much. Melt it again and reuse.
- To make one large soufflé, line the outside of a 1.3 litre (2¼ pint) soufflé dish with a collar of non-stick baking parchment, deep enough to come about 5cm (2in) above the rim of the dish. Omit the chocolate collar (step 2) and don't turn the soufflé out of its dish for serving.

NUTRITION PER SERVING
683 cals | 45g fat (27g sats) | 69g carbs | 0.1g salt

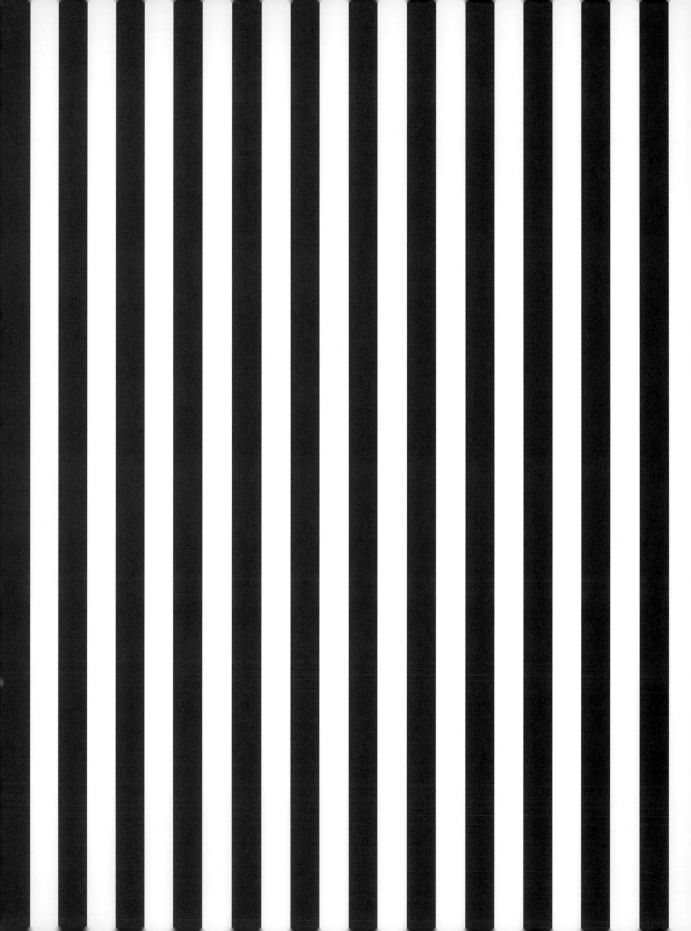

PRESERVES

Very little beats a storecupboard full of home-made jams, jellies, marmalades, chutneys, pickles, relishes and other delicious preserves. Follow the step-by-step techniques to learn how to sterilise jars, test for a set and pot preserves, as well as how to make all the basic types of preserve. There are invaluable cook's tips to ensure perfect results plus advice on avoiding the pitfalls, as well as a handy table showing the pectin content and setting properties of different fruits. The recipe collection includes recipes for every type of preserve so try your hand at making Strawberry and redcurrant jam, Quick marmalade, Spiced clementines in brandy, Plum chutney, Sweetcorn relish, Sweet and sour figs or The ultimate barbecue sauce, to name but a few.

PREPARING JARS

A completely sterile jar is essential for making preserves to ensure the jam, jelly, chutney, relish or pickle keeps properly and does not become mouldy. There are various ways of sterilising jars.

Sterilising methods

Prepare the jars in advance so that they are ready to fill.

1 Thoroughly wash new and used jars (soak them in hot water first if necessary to remove old labels).

2 **Oven method** Preheat the oven to 140°C (120°C fan oven) gas 1. Put the jars on a clean baking sheet or roasting tin in the oven for 10–15 minutes or until completely dry.

3 **Microwave method** First ensure there are no metal parts on the jars. Quarter fill the jars with water and arrange in a circle in the microwave. Bring to the boil on full power. Remove the jars with oven gloves, pour out the water and invert on to a clean teatowel or some kitchen paper.

4 **Dishwasher method** Run the upturned jars through a hot dishwasher cycle.

FOOD SAFETY

When making jams and preserves in larger quantities that are likely to take longer to finish, sterilising is essential to ensure that there is no bacteria in the jar that might later cause the preserve to become mouldy.

PACKING PRESERVES

Everything you need to cover, seal and label preserves can be bought in small cellophane packs. These will usually contain wax discs to cover the jam, cellophane to go over the top of the jar, and elastic bands to secure it. Use metal lids on top of this, which can still be covered attractively with paper or fabric, if you want an extra seal.

LABELLING

A sticky white label is the best way of guaranteeing that you know what's inside your jars. Write the preserve and date with a pen. When the jars have been filled, sealed and are completely cool, stick on the label, then store in a cool dry place.

POTTING PRESERVES

Correct potting of your home-made preserves, by sealing the surface and making the jars airtight, will ensure that they keep well. Label each jar so that you know when it was made.

Filling and covering

All preserves should go into their storage jars as soon as they have been made, and then be sealed quickly. Cut rounds of greaseproof or waxed paper to fit exactly the diameter of the rim of your preserving jars.

1 When the preserve has reached setting point (see below), leave it to cool for a few minutes while you get the jars ready.

2 Pour the preserve into the jars using a jam funnel, filling them to within 5mm (¼in) of the rim.

3 Put a piece of wax paper (wax side down) on top of the preserve.

4 Wet a cellophane disc and put on the top of the jar, then secure with a rubber band.

> ### SCREW-TOP LIDS
>
> If you want to use lids to cover your jars, sterilise them with the jars. Fill the jars to within 1cm (½in) of the rim, and then proceed from step 3. Use the screw-top lids instead of the cellophane discs at step 4. The end result will be a little more professional-looking, but some people prefer the home-made look.

Testing for a set

There are three methods for doing this:

1 Thermometer test Dip a sugar thermometer or an instant-read thermometer into the centre of the pan shortly before the cooking time is complete. Keep it away from the base and sides of the pan, and leave it for a few moments. Jams and jellies set when the temperature reaches 105°C (220°F). If you have to take a second reading, wash the probe before using it again.

2 Saucer test Put two or three saucers in the freezer to chill. When the preserve is nearly ready, take the pan off the heat and spoon a blob of preserve on to a plate and chill for a few minutes. When the preserve has cooled, push the surface with your finger. If the surface wrinkles and doesn't break to reveal liquid jam, it is set.

3 Flake test Using a large wooden spoon, lift a little of the jam out of the pan. Let it cool slightly, then tip the spoon so that the jam drops back into the pan. If setting point has been reached, it will run together along the edge of the spoon and form flakes that will break off.

MAKING JAMS

You can use a special preserving pan, but a large stainless steel pan with a thick base will do.
It should have a capacity of at least 9 litres (15¾ pints).

Summer jam

To make 3.2kg (7lb) jam, you will need
900g (2lb) prepared summer fruits
(raspberries, blackcurrants, loganberries,
blackberries or blueberries), 900g
(2lb) granulated or preserving sugar,
2 lemons, pinch of salt.

1 Prepare the fruits and layer them,
being careful not to bruise them, with
the sugar in a non-metallic bowl. Halve
the lemons and strain their juice on to
the fruit and sugar. Then cover the
bowl and leave for at least 8 hours
until the sugar has dissolved.

2 Put the fruit and juices in a
preserving pan and bring slowly to
the boil. Boil as rapidly as possible,
without letting the jam boil over,
until setting point has been reached
(see page 413). Then add the salt
and cool slightly.

3 Pour into warm, sterilised jars (see
page 412). Seal and label, and store in
a cool dark place for up to one year.

PERFECT JAMS

- Just-ripe fruits have the highest level of pectin. Make sure they are in
  perfect condition and don't use over-ripe fruits.
- Don't wash the fruit unless absolutely necessary, as any water that
  remains will dilute the juice.
- Leave summer fruits whole but remove the stalks. Halve and stone
  apricots and plums.
- Apricots gel quickly, but for a better flavour cook to a deep terracotta.
- If making a jam containing whole strawberries or other pieces of fruit,
  leave to stand for 15 minutes before potting, to prevent the fruit rising.

MICROWAVE JAM

Put 700g (1lb 9oz) sugar, 700g
(1lb 9oz) prepared fruit and juice
of 2 lemons into a 2 litre (3½ pint)
microwave-proof bowl. Mix well.
Cook at full power for 12–16
minutes, stirring once or twice.
Test for a set (see page 413).
Leave to stand for 5 minutes, then
pot. Makes 900g (2lb). Best served
after two to three days.

PECTIN

Naturally found in fruit, pectin combines with sugar to make cooked fruits gel.
Low pectin fruits are usually cooked with high pectin fruits or with commercial
pectin, citric acid or tartaric acid to help them set.

Pectin content	Fruit
High	Cooking apples, crab apples, cranberries, citrus fruit, damsons, gooseberries, redcurrants, blackcurrants, some plums, quince.
Medium	Apricots, blackberries, dessert apples, greengages, loganberries, mulberries, raspberries, some plums.
Low	Bananas, cherries, figs, grapes, japonicas, marrows, medlars, melons, nectarines, peaches, pears, pineapples, rhubarb, strawberries.

MAKING MARMALADE

Orange marmalade is the best-known type of marmalade but you can also make it from other citrus fruits – or from a combination of two or more, such as lemon, grapefuit or lime.

Seville orange marmalade

To make 1.4kg (3lb) marmalade, you will need 450g (1lb) Seville oranges, 1 lemon, 900g (2lb) granulated sugar.

1 Wash the oranges and halve them. Squeeze out the juice and pips into a bowl. Squeeze the lemon into the same bowl and discard the peel. Collect the pips – plus any membranes that come away in squeezing – and tie them up in a piece of muslin.

2 Slice the orange peel thickly or thinly, as you prefer, and put it into a preserving pan with the fruit juices, muslin bag and 1.1 litres (2 pints) water. Simmer gently for about 2 hours or until the peel is really soft and the liquid has reduced by about half.

3 Remove the bag and squeeze it over the pan so that the juices run back. Add the sugar.

4 Heat gently and stir until the sugar has dissolved, then bring back to the boil and boil rapidly for about 15 minutes or until setting point has been reached (see page 413). Remove any scum from the surface with a slotted spoon.

5 Pour into warm, sterilised jars (see page 412). Seal and label, and store in a cool dark place for up to one year.

PERFECT MARMALADE

- Citrus peel gives marmalade its distinctive flavour and texture, but it is tough and needs lengthy cooking. Citrus fruits are high in pectin so marmalades tend to set well.
- Seville oranges are by far the best choice because of their tart flavour.
- Wash citrus fruits well to remove their waxy coating.
- The pith and pips of citrus fruit contain pectin, which makes the marmalade set. Collect all the pips and put them into a muslin bag to be cooked with the fruit and then discarded.
- Squeeze the citrus juice into the pan and slice the peel thinly or thickly according to your preference.
- Make sure the peel is very soft and tender before adding the sugar, as it will not soften any more once the sugar is added.

MAKING JELLIES

Clear fruit jellies made from summer berries, plums and currants make delicate preserves to serve with scones or to use in cake making and desserts.

Mixed berry jelly

The recipe here uses a mixture of fruits, but you can substitute others – or use just a single fruit.

To make 3.2kg (7lb) jelly, you will need 450g (1lb) redcurrants, 450g (1lb) raspberries, 450g (1lb) Morello or May Duke cherries, 450g (1lb) strawberries, 4 tbsp lemon juice, granulated sugar.

1 Put all the fruits in a preserving pan with the lemon juice and 600ml (1 pint) water. Simmer gently for about 1 hour, or until the fruit is really soft and pulpy. Stir from time to time to prevent sticking.

2 Tie a jelly bag or heavy cloth to the legs of an upturned stool, and place a large bowl on the underside of the seat. Spoon the pulp into the bag and leave to strain for at least 12 hours.

3 Discard the pulp remaining in the bag. Measure the extract by volume of juice and return it to a preserving pan. Add 450g (1lb) sugar for every 600ml (1 pint) of extract.

4 Heat gently, stirring, until the sugar has dissolved. Bring to the boil and boil rapidly for about 10 minutes or until setting point has been reached (see page 413). Remove any scum with a slotted spoon.

5 Leave to cool slightly, then pour into warm, sterilised jars (see page 412). Seal and label, and store in a cool dark place for up to two years.

PERFECT JELLIES

- Home-made jellies take longer to make than jams and marmalades because the fruit pulp needs to be left to strain in a jelly bag to ensure a clear juice. The fruit is not peeled, cored or stoned, as this will be discarded after straining, although you will need to roughly chop larger fruits such as apples or pears. After cooking the fruit is strained very slowly (overnight is best). Sugar is added to the fruit juice after the initial cooking.
- Choose fruits with a high level of pectin (see page 414).
- The fruit should be simmered very gently until tender; this can take from 30 minutes to 1½ hours.
- Scald the jelly bag in boiling water before adding the fruit for straining.
- The jelly should be bright and clear, so do not squeeze the jelly bag used for straining the juice, as this will make the jelly cloudy.

MAKING FRUIT CURDS AND CHEESES

Eggs are used for making fruit curds, and the ever-popular lemon curd is especially good when home-made. If you have a glut of home-grown stone fruits, a fruit cheese is well worth considering.

Lemon curd

To make 700g (1lb 9oz), you will need 4 lemons, 100g (3½oz) butter, 4 eggs, 350g (12oz) caster sugar.

1 Put the lemon zest and juice in a double boiler. Cut the butter into small pieces. Add the butter, eggs and sugar. Place over simmering water. Stir until the sugar dissolves and heat gently, without boiling, for 20 minutes. Strain into jars, cover and refrigerate.

VARIATIONS

Both lime and orange curd can be made in the same way. In place of the lemons, use:
- 5–8 limes depending on size.
- 2–3 oranges.

Damson cheese

To make 1.4kg (3lb), you will need 1.4kg (3lb) damsons or plums, sugar.

1 Wash the fruit and put into a pan. Cover with water and simmer gently for 15–20 minutes until the fruit is soft. As the fruit cooks, scoop out any stones that float to the surface.

2 Using a wooden spoon, press the fruit pulp through a nylon or stainless steel sieve into a large bowl. Measure the purée by volume and return it to the pan.

3 Add 350g (12oz) sugar for each 600ml (1 pint) of purée. Heat gently, stirring, until the sugar has dissolved, then bring to the boil and boil gently, stirring, for 30–40 minutes until the mixture is so thick that a spoon leaves a clean line when drawn along the bottom of the pan.

4 Pot and cover the cheese or, if you prefer, set in several dishes or moulds.

PERFECT CURDS AND CHEESES

- In fruit curd, the juice of the fruit is set using egg as the thickener. Because of the eggs, these differ from jams, jellies and marmalades in being unsuitable for long storage. Store in the fridge, and keep for no more than two weeks.
- Fruit cheeses are made with stone fruits, such as plums and damsons, and are a good thing to make if the fruits are plentiful and cheap, as you need a large quantity of fruit to make a purée.
- As with any dish containing eggs, heat control is vital. Don't let the bottom of the bowl touch the simmering water, and take it off the heat for a minute or so if it shows signs of coming to the boil.
- Make only as much as you can eat in two weeks.

MAKING BOTTLED FRUITS

Fruit preserved in this way can be steeped in water or, better still, in a full-flavoured syrup. Here, peaches are bottled in a sweet brandy syrup.

Brandied peaches

To make 450g (1lb), you will need 225g (8oz) sugar, 450g (1lb) fresh peaches, about 150ml (¼ pint) brandy or orange-flavoured liqueur.

1 Make a light syrup by dissolving 100g (3½oz) sugar in 300ml (½ pint) water. Skin the peaches by plunging them into boiling water, then gently peeling off the skins. Halve and remove the stones, then gently poach the fruit in the syrup for 4–5 minutes.

2 Remove the pan from the heat, drain the peaches, reserving the syrup, and leave to cool. Arrange the fruit in wide-necked sterilised jars (see page 412).

3 Add the remaining sugar to the syrup and dissolve it slowly. Bring it to the boil and boil to a temperature of 110°C, then leave to cool.

4 Measure the syrup and add an equal quantity of brandy or liqueur. Pour over the peaches and cover with the lids. Label and leave for two to three months before eating.

PERFECT BOTTLED FRUIT

- In this method of preserving, fruit is kept whole or halved and is surrounded by a boiled sugar syrup. It is essential to use fresh, ripe fruit of the best quality. Make sure the fruit is properly cleaned and prepared so that no stalks or stems remain.
- Bottling is appropriate for a wide variety of fruits, such as berries, rhubarb, apples, peaches and plums.
- It's best to use a sugar thermometer or an instant-read thermometer while making the syrup. If you don't have one, boiling the syrup for a minute or two should be enough to bring it to the correct temperature.

MAKING PICKLES

Vegetables pickled in a good, spicy vinegar go well with cold meats and savouries and none is more popular than pickled onions.

Pickled onions

To make 1.8kg (4lb), you will need 1.8kg (4lb) pickling onions, unpeeled and roots trimmed, 450g (1lb) salt, 1.1 litres (2 pints) spiced vinegar (see page 440).

1 Put the unpeeled onions into a large bowl. Dissolve half the salt in 2.3 litres (4 pints) water, pour it over the onions and leave for 12 hours.

2 Drain the onions, then carefully slit the skins and peel off. Put the onions in a bowl.

3 Cover the onions with a fresh brine made from the remaining salt and a further 2.3 litres (4 pints) water. Leave for 24–36 hours.

4 Drain the onions and rinse well, then pack into sterilised jars (see page 412) and cover with the spiced vinegar. It is worth noting that a 450g (1lb) jar will usually hold about 450g (1lb) of prepared vegetables. Cover and seal the jars, label and leave for three months before using.

PERFECT PICKLES

- Pickling uses vinegar to preserve fresh or lightly cooked vegetables and fruits, but first they have to be soaked in brine (salted water) to draw out their juices. A good-flavoured vinegar with herbs and spices is essential for the best taste, and the bottled pickles need to be left for at least one month before eating.
- Choose young, fresh vegetables and firm, ripe fruits for the best flavour and texture.
- Wash the vegetables well, removing any damaged parts, then peel and trim as required in the recipe.
- Vegetables such as onions are wet brined (submerged in a brine solution), whereas those containing large amounts of water are dry brined (layered with plenty of salt in a large bowl) to draw out excess water, which would dilute the flavour and reduce the storage time.

MAKING CHUTNEYS

Chutneys differ from other preserves in that they can be eaten soon after making them, if you like. But they can also be stored for long periods as long as they are bottled in sterilised containers.

Tomato and apple chutney

To make 3kg (6½lb), you will need 1.5kg (3lb 3½oz) cooking apples, 1kg (2lb 3½oz) tomatoes, chopped, 1.4kg (3lb) onions, finely chopped, 5cm (2in) piece fresh ginger, peeled and grated, 1½ tsp ground turmeric, 750ml (1¼ pints) distilled malt vinegar, 350g (12oz) sultanas, 375g (13oz) light brown soft sugar.

1 Peel, core and chop the apples and put in a large pan along with the rest of the ingredients. Bring to the boil then lower the heat and simmer for 1½ hours or until reduced and thick – there should be hardly any liquid left.

2 While still hot, pack into hot sterilised jars, cover with a waxed disc and seal. Label and leave to mature for at least a month.

Plum chutney

To make 3kg (6½lb), you will need 2kg (4½lb) plums, 2 cooking apples, 2 red onions, finely chopped, 600ml (1 pint) red wine vinegar, 600g (1lb 5oz) light muscovado sugar, 1 tsp cloves, 1 tsp salt, 1 tbsp mustard.

1 Halve, stone and roughly chop the plums. Peel, core and roughly chop the apples.

2 Put all the ingredients in a large pan and cook over a low heat, stirring until the sugar dissolves.

3 Bring to the boil, reduce the heat and simmer, uncovered, over a low heat for about 3 hours – until the mixture is thick and pulpy. There should be hardly any liquid left.

4 Cool and use the chutney immediately, or pack into six sterilised 300ml (½ pint) jars, and seal and label (see page 412).

PERFECT CHUTNEY

➝ When you make chutney for use immediately, always make extra for the storecupboard.
➝ The flavour of chutney improves with keeping.
➝ Use jars with plastic or coated-metal lids – vinegar corrodes metal so chutneys must be covered with airtight, vinegar-proof lids. Vinegar will also evaporate through jam pot discs and covers.

MANGO CHUTNEY

To make 225g (8oz), you will need the flesh of 1 large ripe mango (see page 220), 1 seeded fresh green chilli, juice of 1 lime, ¼ tsp cayenne pepper, ½ tsp salt. Put the mango into a bowl. Cut the chilli into fine rings and mix with the mango, lime juice cayenne pepper and salt. Chill for 1 hour before serving. It will keep for up to two days in the fridge.

MAKING REFRIGERATOR PRESERVES

Some preserves are designed to be kept for a matter of weeks rather than months.
The good thing is that they start to taste really good within only a day of making.

Marinated olives

These can be made with green or black olives, or both.

To make 1kg (2¼lb), you will need 750g (1lb 10oz) plain olives with the pits still in, a small pinch each of dried oregano and thyme, 2 bay leaves, 3 large garlic cloves, 1 small chilli, halved and seeded, 100ml (3½fl oz) red wine vinegar, 2 tbsp whole black peppercorns, 200ml (7fl oz) extra-virgin olive oil.

1 Peel the garlic and smash with a knife blade but leave whole.

2 Put all the ingredients in a glass bowl. Cover with a lid or clingfilm and chill in the fridge for at least a day, stirring occasionally.

3 Spoon into two jars and chill for two days before using, shaking now and then. Store for up to one month.

Chilli sauce

You can make this sauce hotter by leaving some or all of the seeds in the chillies, and vary the seasonings.

To make about 600ml (1 pint), you will need 100g (3½oz) fresh chillies, seeded and chopped, 50g (2oz) pinenuts, 15 garlic cloves, chopped, 1 small onion, chopped, 1 tsp ground cumin, 1 tsp ground coriander, ½ tsp paprika, ½ tsp dried oregano, 2 tbsp tomato paste, 300ml (½ pint) red wine vinegar, salt and ground black pepper.

1 Place the chopped chillies in the bowl of the blender with the rest of the ingredients.

2 Blend until smooth, then add 300ml (½ pint) water.

3 Pour into two or three clean glass bottles and chill in the fridge for up to two months.

COOK'S TIPS

→ Refrigerated preserves will keep better if they contain no animal products of any kind, including fat, meat or dairy products.
→ Although they are not destined for long storage, they will keep for longer in a sterilised jar or bottle (see page 412).

MAKING RELISHES

Relishes are a type of pickle, but whereas pickles can be either cooked or uncooked, relishes are always cooked.

Mustard relish

To make 1.4kg (3lb), you will need 225g (8oz) cauliflower, 100g (3½oz) tomatoes, 1 red and 1 green pepper, 175g (6oz) finely chopped cucumber, 175g (6oz) finely chopped onion, 225g (8oz) thickly sliced fresh gherkins, 25g (1oz) salt, 1 tbsp mustard seeds, 250g (9oz) sugar, 25g (1oz) plain flour, ½ tsp mustard powder, ½ tsp ground turmeric, 450ml (½ pint) malt vinegar.

1 Break the cauliflower into florets. Core and roughly chop the tomatoes. Seed and finely chop the peppers. Put all the vegetables in a large bowl. Dissolve the salt in 1.1 litres (2 pints) water and pour over the vegetables, then cover and leave overnight.

2 Drain the vegetables and rinse well. Blend the remaining ingredients except the vinegar in a large heavy pan, then gradually stir in the vinegar. Bring to the boil, stirring.

3 Add all the vegetables to the pan and bring to the boil.

4 Reduce the heat and simmer gently, uncovered, for 30 minutes or until all the vegetables are soft. Stir gently from time to time to prevent sticking.

5 Pour into warm, sterilised jars (see page 412). Seal, label when cold, and store in a cool dark place for up to one year.

COOK'S TIPS

- Don't be tempted to use less sugar than a recipe requires. The sugar is a preservative, and the relish may ferment if there isn't enough of it.
- Relishes, like chutneys, must be covered with airtight, vinegar-proof lids. Use jars with plastic or coated-metal lids.
- Add a slice of chilli pepper to the mixture at step 4 for a mild touch of heat.

VARIATIONS

Instead of making relish with a combination of vegetables, you can adapt this recipe to include just one or two. Use vegetables with a total weight comparable to that in the recipe. Other good vegetables to use include: sweetcorn, green tomatoes, French beans, courgettes, marrow, yellow squash, celery.

MAKING SAUCES

Preserved sauces are worth making when you can buy the main ingredient very fresh and of the highest quality, at a reasonable price. With tomatoes, this means making ketchup in summertime.

Tomato ketchup

To make 1.1 litres (2 pints), you will need 2.7kg (6lb) ripe tomatoes, 225g (8oz) sugar, 300ml (½ pint) spiced vinegar (page 440), 1 tbsp tarragon vinegar (optional), pinch of cayenne pepper, 1 tsp paprika, 1 tsp salt.

1 Slice the tomatoes and cook over a very low heat, stirring frequently, until they cook down to a pulp, about 45 minutes. Bring to the boil and cook rapidly, stirring frequently, until the pulp thickens.

2 Press the pulp through a nylon or stainless steel sieve, then return to the pan and stir in the remaining ingredients. Simmer gently until the mixture thickens.

3 Pour the ketchup into warm, sterilised bottles (see page 412). Seal and label, and store in a cool dark place for up to one year.

> ### COOK'S TIP
>
> As well as its use as a condiment, tomato ketchup can also be used to flavour sauces such as marie rose. It is a barely-kept secret that many professional chefs keep ketchup on hand for adding tomato flavour, extra spice, and a nicely balanced sweet-sour taste to sauces, stews and soups.

Tomato sauce

This contains no oil or butter, so stir some in just before serving.

To make 2.5kg (5½lb), you will need 2.7kg (6lb) ripe tomatoes, 3 finely chopped onions, 6 finely chopped garlic cloves, 150ml (¼ pint) sun-dried tomato paste, 1 tbsp freshly chopped oregano, salt and ground black pepper.

1 Skin, seed and quarter the tomatoes, then chop the flesh.

2 Put all the ingredients in a large pan and bring to the boil. Reduce the heat and simmer, uncovered, over a low heat for 25–30 minutes, stirring occasionally, until the sauce is thick and pulpy. Season to taste, and cook for a few minutes more.

3 Pour into warm, sterilised jars (see page 412). Seal and label, and store in a cool dark place for up to six months.

STRAWBERRY JAM

Makes about 1.8kg (4lb)
Preparation 10 minutes, plus standing
Cooking time about 10 minutes
Techniques see also sterilising jars (page 412), testing for a set (page 413), potting preserves (page 413), labelling (page 412)

900g (2lb) strawberries, hulled
1kg (2¼lb) 'sugar with pectin'
juice of ½ lemon

1 Put the strawberries into a preserving pan with the sugar and lemon juice. Heat gently, stirring until the sugar has dissolved.
2 Bring to the boil and boil steadily for 4 minutes or until setting point is reached (see page 413).
3 Remove the pan from the heat and remove any scum from the surface with a slotted spoon. Leave to stand for 15–20 minutes. Stir the jam gently, then pot and cover in the usual way.

NUTRITION PER TABLESPOON
35 cals | 0g fat (0g sats) | 9g carbs | trace salt

QUICK MARMALADE

Makes 4.5kg (10lb)
Preparation 25 minutes
Cooking time 1 hour 10 minutes
Techniques see also sterilising jars (page 412), testing for a set (page 413), potting preserves (page 413), labelling (page 412), making marmalade (page 415)

900g (2lb) Seville oranges, scrubbed and chopped, pips discarded
2kg (4½lb) preserving sugar

1 Whiz the chopped oranges briefly in a food processor or blender, then put in a preserving pan with 1.6 litres (2½ pints) water. Bring to the boil, reduce the heat and simmer for 1 hour.
2 Add the sugar and stir over a gentle heat until dissolved. Bubble rapidly for 4 minutes or until setting point has been reached (see page 413). Leave to cool for 5 minutes, stirring once or twice, then pot and seal. Label when cold and store the jars in a cool, dry place for up to six months.

COOK'S TIP
Seville oranges are the traditional marmalade orange due to their unique bitter flavour. They are only available and in season for a very short time – usually mid–late winter.

NUTRITION PER TEASPOON
9 cals | 0g fat (0g sats) | 2g carbs | 0g salt

CRANBERRY AND APPLE JELLY

Makes about 1.4kg (3lb)
Preparation 25 minutes, plus standing
Cooking time 1 hour 20 minutes
Techniques see also sterilising jars (page 412), testing for a set (page 413), potting preserves (page 413), labelling (page 412), making jellies (page 416)

1.4kg (3lb) cooking apples, washed
900g (2lb) cranberries, washed
granulated sugar

1   Remove any bruised or damaged portions from the apples, then roughly chop them without peeling or coring.
2   Put the apples and cranberries into a preserving pan with sufficient water to cover them, and simmer gently for 45 minutes–1 hour until the fruit is really soft and pulpy. Stir from time to time to prevent sticking.
3   Spoon the pulp into a jelly bag or cloth attached to the legs of an upturned stool, and leave to strain into a large bowl for at least 12 hours.
4   Discard the pulp remaining in the jelly bag. Measure the extract and return it to the preserving pan with 450g (1lb) sugar for each 600ml (1 pint) of extract. Bring slowly to the boil, stirring, until the sugar has dissolved, then boil rapidly for about 10 minutes or until setting point has been reached (see page 413).
5   Remove any scum with a slotted spoon, then pot and cover. Label when cold and store in a cool, dark place for up to six months..

COOK'S TIP
Don't be tempted to squeeze the jelly bag in an attempt to speed up the straining process.
It will result in a cloudy jelly

NUTRITION PER TEASPOON
10 cals | 0g fat (0g sats) | 2.7g carbs | 0g salt

SPICED CLEMENTINES IN BRANDY

Makes two 500ml (18fl oz) jars
Preparation 25 minutes
Cooking time 13 minutes
Techniques see also preparing fresh ginger (page 437), sterilising jars (page 412), potting preserves (page 413), labelling (page 412)

350g (12oz) caster sugar
14 kumquats, halved lengthways, seeds removed
5cm (2in) piece fresh root ginger, peeled and finely sliced
1 tsp allspice berries
8 clementines, peel and pith removed
6 fresh bay leaves
225ml (8fl oz) brandy

1 Put 175g (6oz) sugar with 300ml (½ pint) water in a wide pan and heat gently to dissolve the sugar. Add the kumquats, ginger and allspice. Bring to a simmer and poach with the lid on for 8 minutes or until softened.
2 Lift the kumquats and spices out of the pan with a slotted spoon and put to one side. Add the remaining sugar and dissolve, stirring, over a low heat. Increase the heat and boil uncovered for about 5 minutes or until the liquid measures about 250ml (9fl oz). Cool slightly.
3 Pierce the clementines all over with a skewer and arrange in sterilised jars with the kumquats, spices and bay leaves. Add the brandy to the syrup and pour over the fruit, making sure the fruit is submerged. Seal, label when cold and store in the fridge for up to 1 month.

NUTRITION PER JAR
999 cals | 0g fat (0g sats) | 197g carbs | 0g salt **V**

PLUM CHUTNEY

Makes six 300ml (½ pint) jars
preparation 20 minutes
Cooking time 3–3½ hours
Techniques see also stoning fruits (page 218), preparing apples
(page 216), sterilising jars (page 412), potting preserves (page 413),
making chutneys (page 420)

2kg (4½lb) plums, halved, stoned and roughly chopped
2 red onions, finely chopped
2 cooking apples, peeled, cored and roughly chopped
600ml (1 pint) red wine vinegar
600g (1lb 5oz) light muscovado sugar
1 tsp each cloves and salt
1 tbsp mustard seeds

1 Put all the ingredients in a large pan and cook over a
low heat, stirring until the sugar dissolves.
2 Bring to the boil, then reduce the heat and simmer,
uncovered, over a low heat for 3–3½ hours until the
mixture is thick and pulpy. There should be hardly any
liquid left.
3 Spoon the chutney into six 300ml (½ pint) jars, then
cover with a waxed disc and a larger circle of dampened
clear wrap. Secure around the rim with an elastic band.
Label when cold, and keep in a cool, dark place for one
month to mature. Store for up to six months.

NUTRITION PER TEASPOON
30 cals | 0g fat (0g sats) | 2g carbs | 0g salt Ⓥ

RHUBARB AND GINGER CHUTNEY

Makes about 1.6kg (3½lb)

Preparation 15 minutes, plus standing

Cooking time 1¼ hours

Techniques see also preparing onions (page 182), preparing fresh ginger (page 437), sterilising jars (page 412), potting preserves (page 413), labelling (page 412), making chutneys (page 420)

1kg (2¼lb) thick rhubarb stems, trimmed and cut into 5cm (2in) pieces

4 tsp salt

225g (8oz) red onions, cut into thick slices

700g (1lb 9oz) dark muscovado sugar

450ml (½ pint) white wine vinegar

25g (1oz) fresh root ginger, peeled and coarsely grated

¼ tsp ground allspice

125g (4oz) raisins

1 Put the rhubarb into a non-metallic bowl, mix with 1 tsp salt, then cover and leave in a cool place for 12 hours.

2 Drain and rinse the rhubarb, then put in a preserving pan with all the other ingredients except the raisins. Cook over a gentle heat until the sugar has dissolved, then increase the heat and bubble for 45 minutes–1 hour until well reduced and pulpy. Add the raisins and bubble for 5 minutes.

3 Pot the chutney hot or cool (not warm) into sterilised jars, then cover, and label the jars when cold. Store in a cool, dark place for up to six months.

COOK'S TIP

This spiced chutney is a useful preserve to have in the storecupboard and tastes especially good with mature cheeses and cold meats.

NUTRITION PER TEASPOON

10 cals | 0g fat (0g sats) | 3g carbs | 0.1g salt Ⓥ

SWEETCORN RELISH

Makes 2.3kg (5lb)
Preparation 25 minutes
Cooking time 40 minutes
Techniques see also preparing vegetables (pages 182–194), sterilising jars (page 412)

6 corn cobs, trimmed, and leaves and silk removed
½ small white cabbage, trimmed and roughly chopped
2 medium onions, skinned and halved
1½ red peppers, washed, seeded and quartered
2 tsp salt
2 tbsp plain flour
½ tsp ground turmeric
175g (6oz) sugar
2 tsp mustard powder
600ml (1 pint) distilled vinegar

1 Cook the corn cobs in boiling salted water for 3 minutes, then drain. Using a sharp knife, cut the corn from the cobs. Coarsely mince the cabbage, onions and red peppers and combine with the corn.
2 Blend together the salt, flour, turmeric, sugar and mustard powder in a preserving pan, then gradually stir in the vinegar. Heat gently, stirring, until the sugar has dissolved, then bring to the boil. Reduce the heat, add the vegetables and simmer for 25–30 minutes, stirring occasionally.
3 Spoon the relish into jars, cover and seal. Label when cold and store in a cool, dark place for up to three months.

NUTRITION PER TEASPOON
5 cals | trace fat (0g sats) | 1g carbs | 0g salt **V**

SWEET AND SOUR FIGS

Makes about 700g (1lb 9oz)
Serves 10
Preparation 20 minutes, plus overnight standing
Cooking time 15 minutes
Techniques see also preparing fresh ginger (page 437), zesting citrus fruits (page 217), sterilising jars (page 412)

450ml (½ pint) distilled malt vinegar
small piece of fresh root ginger, peeled and thinly sliced
3 allspice berries
6 black peppercorns
3 whole cloves
2 cinnamon sticks
pared zest of 1 lemon
2 tbsp honey
250g (9oz) sugar
700g (1lb 9oz) firm green figs, stalks trimmed

1 Put the vinegar in a large shallow pan with the ginger, allspice, peppercorns, cloves, cinnamon, lemon zest, honey and sugar. Heat gently, stirring, until the sugar has dissolved.
2 Bring to the boil, boil for 1 minute, then remove from the heat. Thickly slice the figs into the warm vinegar. Bring to the boil, then reduce the heat and simmer, uncovered, for 1 minute, gently pushing the fig slices under the vinegar. Carefully transfer the figs and vinegar to a large non-metallic bowl. Cover tightly with clingfilm and leave overnight.
3 Remove the fig slices from the vinegar with a slotted spoon. Tightly pack into clean preheated jars. Return the vinegar mixture to a clean pan and bring to the boil. Boil rapidly until reduced to 150ml (¼ pint).
4 Pour the hot vinegar into the jars. Cover and seal. Label when cold and store for at least one week before using.

COOK'S TIP
Serve these pickled figs with cheese or
cold roast meats.

NUTRITION PER SERVING
198 cals | 1g fat (0g sats) | 50g carbs | 0.1g salt

MIXED DILL PICKLE

Makes 1.5–2kg (3lb 5oz–4lb 8oz)
Preparation 30 minutes, plus standing
Cooking time 15 minutes
Techniques see also preparing vegetables (pages 182–194),
sterilising jars (page 412), making pickles (page 419)

1 cauliflower, about 550g (1¼lb), divided into small florets
175g (6oz) courgettes, cut into 5mm (¼in) diagonal slices
1 green pepper, about 225g (8oz), cut into 5mm (¼in) strips
175g (6oz) fine green beans, trimmed and halved
100g (3½oz) pickling or button onions, peeled with
    roots intact
1 cucumber, halved lengthways and sliced
225g (8oz) coarse salt
1.1–1.3 litres (2–2¼ pints) white wine vinegar
2 tbsp pickling spice
1 tbsp salt
100g (3½oz) sugar
2 garlic cloves
2 good stalks of fresh dill
1 tsp dried dill
2 stalks of tarragon

1 Put all the prepared vegetables in a large bowl. Cover
with the coarse salt. Mix, cover and leave in a cold place
for 24 hours.
2 Put the remaining ingredients in a preserving pan. Heat
gently to simmering point. Remove from the heat and leave
to cool completely.
3 Drain the vegetables, rinse well and drain again. Bring
two large pans of water to the boil. Add the vegetables
and bring back to the boil. Drain the vegetables and refresh
under cold water to stop the cooking process and preserve
the colour. Leave to drain well.
4 Pack the vegetables into preheated jars. Leave to stand
for 1 hour, then drain off the excess liquid. Pour the cooled
pickling vinegar over to cover completely. Cover and seal
the jars, then label. The pickle will darken a little on storing
but it will remain clear if stored in the fridge for up
to one month.

NUTRITION PER TABLESPOON WITHOUT LIQUID
13 cals | 0g fat (0g sats) | 2g carbs | 0.1g salt **V**

THE ULTIMATE BARBECUE SAUCE

Makes about 300ml (½ pint)
Preparation 5 minutes
Cooking time 15 minutes
Techniques see also preparing garlic (page 183), sterilising jars (page 412)

3 tbsp olive oil
3 garlic cloves, finely chopped
3 tbsp balsamic vinegar
4 tbsp dry sherry
3 tbsp sun-dried tomato paste or tomato purée
3 tbsp sweet chilli sauce
300ml (½ pint) passata
5 tbsp clear honey

1 Mix together the oil, garlic, vinegar, sherry, sun-dried tomato paste or tomato purée and chilli sauce.
2 Turn into a small pan and add the passata and honey. Bring to the boil, reduce the heat and simmer gently for 10–15 minutes or until thickened and glossy. Bottle in sterilised jars and store in the fridge for up to one month.

COOK'S TIP
Quick to make, this sauce goes well with chicken, pork, burgers or pork sausages.

NUTRITION PER TEASPOON
12 cals | 1g fat (0g sats) | 2g carbs | 0.1g salt

HERBS, SPICES AND FLAVOURINGS

Flavourings are an essential in every kitchen and will make the difference between a good dish and a really delicious one – and this chapter shows you how to make the most of them. As well as preparing fresh herbs and fresh and dried spices, the step-by-step techniques show you how to make flavoured vinegars that can be used in dressings and sauces, flavoured sugars that can be used in desserts and baking, and flavoured salts that can be used to add extra flavour to savoury dishes.

USING HERBS

Most herbs are the leaf of a flowering plant, and are usually sold with much of the stalk intact.
They have to be washed, trimmed and then chopped or torn into pieces suitable for your recipe.

Washing

1 Trim the roots and part of the stalks from the herbs. Immerse in cold water and shake briskly. Leave in the water for a few minutes.

2 Lift out of the water and put in a colander or sieve, then rinse again under the cold tap. Leave to drain for a few minutes, then dry thoroughly on kitchen paper or teatowels, or use a salad spinner.

Chopping

1 Trim the herbs by pinching off all but the smallest, most tender stalks. If the herb is one with a woody stalk, such as rosemary or thyme, it may be easier to remove the leaves by rubbing the whole bunch between your hands; the leaves should simply pull off the stems.

2 If you are chopping the leaves, gather them into a compact ball in one hand, keeping your fist around the ball (but being careful not to crush them).

3 Chop with a large knife, using a rocking motion and letting just a little of the ball out of your fingers at a time.

4 When the herbs are roughly chopped, continue chopping until the pieces are in small shreds or flakes.

> ### COOK'S TIP
>
> **Bouquet garni**
> A small bunch of herbs tied together with string, or placed inside a piece of muslin, are an essential flavouring for stocks, soups and stews. The herbs can vary but usually include parsley, thyme and a bay leaf; spices such as peppercorns and cloves may also be included. The bouquet garni is removed after cooking.

USING SPICES

The flavour of spices is most pronounced when they are first roasted and then ground for use in recipes. Fresh root ginger is one of the most frequently used wet spices and is easy to prepare.

Roasting spices

Whole spices are roasted in a dry frying pan to bring out their flavour.

1 Place a small frying pan over a high heat. When it's very hot, pour in the spices and cook until they take on a darker colour and just begin to pop and release their fragrance. Don't let them burn.

2 Remove to a bowl and cool.

GRINDING

The traditional method uses a mortar and pestle. The alternative, quicker method is to buy a hand-cranked spice mill or use a coffee grinder; if you use a coffee grinder, use it only for spices or they will flavour your coffee!

Preparing fresh spices

Ginger, galangal and turmeric are the most common fresh spices. They are prepared in the same way.

1 Grating Peel a large section of the spice with a vegetable peeler and cut off any soft brown spots.

2 Using a wooden or fine metal grater resting on a small plate or bowl, grate the spice. Discard any large fibres adhering to the pulp.

3 Chopping Cut slices off the spice and cut off the skin carefully and remove any soft brown spots. If you need very large quantities, you can peel a large section with a vegetable peeler before slicing.

4 Stack the slices and cut into shreds of the required thickness. To make dice, stack the shreds and cut to the required size.

5 Pressing If you need just the juice, cut thick slices off the ginger or galangal root and cut off the skin carefully, taking care to remove any soft brown spots under the skin. If you need very large quantities, you can peel a large section with a vegetable peeler. Cut the slices into chunks, and press them with a garlic press into a small bowl.

Vanilla

Available as whole pods and extract, vanilla, with its strong, heady aroma, is one of the most popular flavourings used in sweet cooking – either on its own, or paired with chocolate, coffee or fruits. Interestingly, vanilla is not sweet in itself; we think of it that way because it is used almost exclusively in sweet dishes. Vanilla flavouring (or essence) has a high proportion of artificial flavourings.

Vanilla extract

This is a dark brown, intensely flavoured liquid extracted from vanilla pods. It is quicker and more convenient to use than vanilla pods and can be stirred directly into mixtures and desserts. Vanilla extract is not itself a sweet flavouring and should always be combined with sugar, syrup or another sweetener. When buying, look for genuine vanilla extract.

Vanilla pods

Sticky black vanilla pods are the seed case of a type of climbing orchid native to Central America. The pod can be used to flavour sugar for cakes, biscuits and desserts (see page 441), or milk or cream for custards, sauces and ice creams. The whole pod can be split and the tiny seeds removed and used in custard or ice cream.

To flavour milk or cream Split the whole vanilla pod, then bring the liquid almost to the boil, add the pod and leave to infuse for about 15 minutes.

To extract seeds from a vanilla pod Split the vanilla pod lengthways and scrape the seeds into a pan. Don't discard the pod; put it in a jar of caster sugar to make delicious vanilla sugar, great for using in cakes and biscuits.

Vanilla custard

To serve eight, you will need 600ml (1 pint) full-fat milk, 1 vanilla pod or 1 tbsp vanilla extract, 6 large egg yolks, 2 tbsp golden caster sugar, 2 tbsp cornflour.

1 Put the milk into a pan. Split the vanilla pod and scrape the seeds into the pan, then drop in the pod. If using vanilla extract, pour it in. Bring to the boil, then turn off the heat and leave to cool for 5 minutes.

2 Put the egg yolks, sugar and cornflour into a bowl and whisk to blend. Remove the vanilla pod from the milk and gradually whisk the warm milk into the egg mixture.

3 Rinse out the pan. Pour the custard back in and heat gently, stirring constantly, for 2–3 minutes. The mixture should thicken enough to coat the back of a wooden spoon in a thin layer. Remove the pan from the heat.

SPICE PASTES AND MIXES

The spice pastes and mixes available in supermarkets tend to be generic blends of spices for the Western cook. Far better to create your own to suit exactly the dish you are going to cook.

Harissa Grill 2 red peppers until softened and charred (see page 189), cool, then skin, core and remove the seeds. Put 4 seeded and roughly chopped red chillies into a food processor with 6 peeled garlic cloves, 1 tbsp ground coriander and 1 tbsp caraway seeds. Process to a rough paste. Add the grilled peppers, 2 tsp salt and 4 tbsp olive oil and whiz until smooth. Put the harissa into a screw-topped jar, cover with a thin layer of olive oil and store in the fridge for up to two weeks.

Thai pastes

Red curry paste Using a small sharp knife, halve and seed 2 long, thin, fresh red chillies (see page 189) and 8 dried chillies, then roughly chop the chillies and 4 kaffir lime leaves. Peel a 2.5cm (1in) piece galangal, trim and discard any woody or shrivelled parts, then chop. Peel and chop 4 shallots and 4 garlic cloves. Peel off and discard any tough outer layers from 2 lemongrass stalks. Trim the ends, then chop. Put these prepared ingredients and 1 tsp each ground black pepper and ground turmeric along with 2 tbsp sunflower oil in a spice grinder or mortar. Grind or pound to form a smooth paste, adding a little water if necessary. Store the paste in a screw-topped jar for up to one month.

Green curry paste Using a small sharp knife, halve and seed 4 long, thin green chillies and 2–4 small green chillies, then roughly chop. Peel and chop 4 garlic cloves, a 2.5cm (1in) piece fresh root ginger and 1 lemongrass stalk. Chop 6 spring onions, 4 coriander roots and 1 tbsp chopped fresh coriander. Shred

4 kaffir lime leaves. Place all the ingredients in a spice grinder or mortar. Grind or pound to form a smooth paste, adding a little water if necessary. Store in a screw-topped jar for up to one month.

Indian pastes

Balti paste Put 1 tbsp each fennel seeds and ground allspice, 2–3 roughly chopped garlic cloves, a 1cm (½in) piece peeled and roughly chopped fresh root ginger, 50g (2oz) garam masala (see page 229), 25g (1oz) curry powder and 1 tsp salt into a food processor with 8 tbsp water and blend. Divide the paste into three equal portions, then freeze for up to three months.

Korma paste Put 3 tbsp ground cinnamon, the seeds from 36 green cardamom pods, 30 cloves, 18 bay leaves, 1 tbsp fennel seeds and 1 tsp salt into a food processor and blend to a powder. Tip the powder into a bowl and add 4 tbsp water, stirring well to make a paste. Divide the paste into three equal portions, then freeze for up to three months.

Madras paste Put 1 finely chopped small onion, a 2.5cm (1in) piece peeled and finely chopped fresh root ginger, 2 crushed garlic cloves, juice of ½ lemon, 1 tbsp each cumin seeds and coriander seeds, 1 tsp cayenne pepper, 2 tsp each ground turmeric and garam masala (see page 229) and 1 tsp salt into a food processor with 2 tbsp water and blend until smooth. Divide into three equal portions, then freeze for up to three months.

Tandoori paste Put 24 crushed garlic cloves, a 5cm (2in) piece peeled and chopped fresh root ginger, 3 tbsp each coriander seeds, cumin seeds, ground fenugreek and paprika, 3 seeded and chopped red chillies, 3 tsp English mustard, 2 tbsp tomato purée and 1 tsp salt into a food processor with 8 tbsp water and blend to a paste. Divide into three equal portions, then freeze for up to three months.

Spice mixes

Curry powder Put 1 tbsp each cumin and fenugreek seeds, ½ tsp mustard seeds, 1½ tsp each poppy seeds, black peppercorns and ground ginger, 4 tbsp coriander seeds, ½ tsp hot chilli powder and 2 tbsp ground turmeric into a food processor or grinder. Grind to a fine powder. Store in an airtight container and use within one month.

Five-spice powder Grind together 1 tbsp fennel seeds, 2 tsp Sichuan pepper and 8 star anise. Stir in ½ tsp ground cloves and 1 tbsp ground cinnamon. Store in an airtight container. Use within one month.

MAKING FLAVOURED VINEGARS

These are easy to make using tarragon, thyme or rosemary, and can be stored in a cool dark place for one month. Use sterilised storage bottles, wash all the ingredients well and dry before adding to the vinegar.

Herb vinegar

You will need 25g (1oz) fresh herbs, plus extra sprigs for bottling, 600ml (1 pint) red or white wine vinegar.

1 Put the herbs and vinegar in a pan and bring to the boil. Pour into a bowl, cover and leave overnight.

2 Strain through a muslin-lined sieve and bottle with herb sprigs. Store for one week before using.

Fruit vinegar

You will need 450g (1lb) raspberries and blackberries, plus extra for bottling, 600ml (1 pint) wine vinegar.

1 Break up fruit with back of spoon and add vinegar. Cover and leave to stand for 3 days, stirring now and then.

2 Strain through a muslin-lined sieve and bottle with extra fruits. Store for two weeks before using.

Spiced vinegar

Perfect for pickling. You will need 500ml (18fl oz) malt vinegar, 1 tbsp mace, 1 tbsp allspice berries, 1 tbsp cloves, 18cm (7in) cinnamon stick, 6 peppercorns, 4 dried red chillies, 1 small bay leaf.

1 Put all the ingredients in a pan and bring to the boil. Remove from the heat, cover and leave to infuse for about 2 hours.

2 Strain through a muslin-lined sieve to remove the herbs and spices.

3 Pour the vinegar into sterilised bottles or jars and seal tightly. The vinegar can be used immediately or stored until required.

MAKING FLAVOURED SUGAR AND SALT

Sugar or salt flavoured with spices or aromatics is a great way to add instant flavour to sweet or savoury dishes. They can be stored almost indefinitely in an airtight container in a dry place.

Flavoured sugars

These are perfect for using in cakes, biscuits and desserts.

1 Cinnamon sugar Mix 1 tbsp ground cinnamon with 200g (7oz) caster sugar.

2 Citrus sugar Mix 200g (7oz) caster sugar with 1 tbsp finely chopped orange, lemon or lime zest and store in an airtight container. Cover and leave for a few days before use.

3 Lavender sugar Mix 200g (7oz) caster sugar with 2 tbsp dried lavender flowers. Cover and leave to stand for one week before use.

4 Vanilla sugar Put a whole vanilla pod in an airtight container and pour in caster sugar to cover. Cover and leave to stand for at least one week before use.

Flavoured salt

1 Chilli salt Grind 2 tbsp dried chilli flakes to a coarse powder and mix with 4–6 tbsp fine salt.

2 Herb salt Grind 2 tbsp dried herbs to a coarse powder and mix with 4–6 tbsp fine salt.

3 Spicy salt Roast 2 tbsp whole spices (see page 437) and leave to cool, then grind to a fine powder in a mortar or spice grinder. Mix with 4–6 tbsp fine salt.

VARIATIONS

- **Spices:** black or white peppercorns, cardamom, coriander, cumin, fennel seeds, fenugreek, mustard seeds.
- **Herbs:** chervil, mixed herbs, marjoram, oregano, parsley, rosemary, sage, tarragon, thyme.

FREEZING AND DRYING

Keeping a well-stocked freezer can be a real boon to the home cook. This chapter provides invaluable advice on how to freeze everything from liquids such as stocks, soups and stews to solid foods such as meat, fish, poultry, fruit and vegetables. There are also essential hints on labelling and packing your freezer and safe storage times so you know how long you can keep food for. However, freezing isn't the only way to preserve foods and there are also techniques showing you how to dry fruits, vegetables and herbs, plus tips on reconstituting them for future use.

FREEZING STOCKS, SAUCES AND STEWS

Stocks, stews, sauces and soups can be frozen for up to four months. Liquid-based dishes are among the most straightforward to freeze. Make sure that the containers are not overfilled and that they are well sealed.

Freezing in tubs

1 Line a plastic container with a freezer bag and pour the food into the bag to leave a space of 2.5cm (1in) at the top to allow the food to expand as it freezes.

2 Cover tightly and freeze as quickly as possible. Once the food is frozen, you may remove from the container and store in the bag. Alternatively, store in the container.

FREEZING TIPS

- Use only suitable, food-approved containers with tight-fitting lids.
- Never put hot or warm food in the freezer.
- Leave space at the top of the container, as food expands when frozen.

Freezing stock

Frozen stock is very useful in the kitchen, but it can use up a lot of freezer space. Save valuable space in the freezer by concentrating the stock before freezing it. To use, simply reconstitute it to its full volume by adding water.

1 **Concentrating the stock** Put the clarified, degreased stock (see page 37) in a clean pan and bring to the boil. Bubble to reduce it to about 25 per cent of its volume.

2 Pour the stock into plastic containers, filling to leave a space of 2.5cm (1in) at the top.

3 Put the lid on tightly and freeze as quickly as possible.

Frozen stock cubes

1 Freeze the reduced stock in an ice cube tray, then put the frozen cubes in a sealable tub. You can take out as many cubes as you need and reseal the tub. If the cubes have a build-up of ice on the surface, just wash it off under the cold tap before adding the cube to the dish.

FREEZING FRUIT

Fruit can be frozen for up to six months. Although freezing affects the texture, it preserves the flavour wonderfully and the thawed fruit is perfect for use in cooking, purées, smoothies and fruit salads.

Sugaring

Most fruits can be frozen without cooking, but when defrosted they will soften because of cell damage from ice crystals. To minimise that damage, freeze fruit pieces dusted with sugar or in syrup. Because of the extra sugar, you should use this method only with fruit that you are planning to use in a sweet dish.

1 Wash the fruit gently and dry thoroughly on clean teatowels or kitchen paper. Prepare as required, then place on a baking sheet or shallow roasting tin, spacing them well apart.

2 Sprinkle on enough caster sugar to give all the pieces of fruit a generous, even coating.

3 Freeze until solid, then quickly transfer to a sealable container and return to the freezer.

Freezing in syrup

You will need 175g (6oz) sugar per 600ml (1 pint) of water.

1 Dissolve the sugar in the water over a low heat. Bring to the boil and boil for 2 minutes, then cool.

2 Wash and dry the fruit, and cut it up as needed. Put in a sealable container and pour the syrup over to cover. If any fruit protrudes, place a piece of greaseproof paper on top and press down, then freeze.

FREEZING VEGETABLES

Vegetables can be frozen for up to six months. Most must be cooked or part-cooked by blanching before freezing to reduce the activity of enzymes that would affect nutritional value and quality.

Blanching in water

1 Wash and prepare the vegetables and cut them into bite-sized pieces as appropriate.

2 Bring a pan of water to the boil using at least 6 litres (10½ pints) salted water per 450g (1lb) of vegetables. Have ready a large bowl of iced water.

3 Put the vegetables into the boiling water, bring quickly back to the boil, and cook as shown in the table below.

They should be hot all the way through and slightly tender, but not fully cooked.

4 Lift out with a slotted spoon and plunge into the iced water.

5 Dry thoroughly on kitchen paper and pack into containers. Freeze.

IN SEASON

Freeze vegetables when they're in season. They're cheap, in abundance and at their very best so it makes sense to preserve them now. If you grow your own – even better! Freeze them when they're freshly picked and their flavour is at its very best.

Blanching in steam

Ideal for most vegetables, especially those that might get waterlogged if cooked in water.

1 Wash and prepare the vegetables. Have ready a bowl of iced water.

2 Steam the vegetables for the time shown in the table, right. They should be hot all the way through and slightly tender, but not fully cooked. Plunge into the iced water. Dry, pack into containers and freeze.

BLANCHING TIMES

Times given are for blanching in boiling water. For blanching in steam add 2–4 minutes. Test regularly to avoid overcooking.

Vegetable	Preparation	Blanching time
Asparagus	stalk ends removed	2–4 minutes
Broad beans	shelled	2–3 minutes
Broccoli	woody stalks removed	3–5 minutes
Brussels sprouts	trimmed at the base	3–5 minutes
Cauliflower	broken into florets	3–5 minutes
French beans	topped and tailed	2–3 minutes
Runner beans	strings removed, sliced	2–3 minutes
Sweetcorn	whole ears, husked	4–6 minutes

FREEZING MEAT, POULTRY AND FISH

These all follow essentially similar procedures and principles. The most crucial point is to keep air out and avoiding 'freezer burn'. Follow the freezing times given below to ensure the food quality remains good.

Freezing in bags

1 Put the food in the bag, keeping it as flat as possible.

2 Squeeze all the air out so that the bag fits snugly around the food.

3 Tie the bag securely and freeze as quickly as possible.

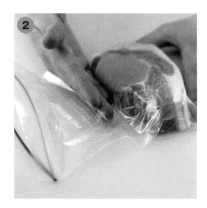

Tray freezing

1 Pieces of food can be frozen separately, then bagged together so you can use one piece at a time.

2 Put the pieces on a baking sheet, making sure that they don't touch each other. Freeze until solid.

3 Quickly transfer to a freezer bag, squeeze out the air and seal. Return to the freezer.

MAXIMUM FREEZING TIMES

Meat	Maximum time	Poultry	Maximum time
Mince (any meat)	3 months	Poultry, whole	1 year
Bacon	1 month	Poultry, pieces	9 months
Sausages	1 month		
Steak	6 months	**Fish**	**Maximum time**
Chops	4 months	White fish (such as cod, haddock, plaice)	6 months
Joints, lean	10 months	Oily fish (such as herring, mackerel)	2 months
Joints, fatty	4 months	Cooked fish	4 months
Offal	3 months	Smoked fish	2 months
Cooked meat	3 months	Shellfish	3 months

DRYING FRUIT, VEGETABLES AND HERBS

Herbs can be frozen for up to three months. It is a good way to preserve fresh summer herbs for use later in the year. Herbs are also great for drying, as are other foods, including fruit, mushrooms and tomatoes.

Drying fruit

You can dry fruit in the oven or in the open air if the weather is hot and dry. An electric dehydrator is very efficient but only useful if you're going to dry fruit regularly.

1 Prepare the fruit for drying (see right). Preheat the oven to its lowest possible setting.

2 Put in the fruit and leave the door ajar. Dry the fruit until it has lost 90 per cent of its weight. This can take up to 24 hours for large fruit, or 6–8 hours for slices.

3 Leave the fruit to cool, then pack into containers about two-thirds full and loosely cover. Leave for another seven days, shaking the container every day to distribute the remaining moisture evenly. Pack into airtight containers and keep for a maximum of 12 months.

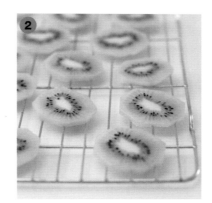

PREPARING FRUIT FOR DRYING

Enzymes in fruit cause it to discolour once cut. You can slow their activity by soaking the fruit in a bath of acidulated water. Squeeze the juice from 6–8 lemons and mix with an equal quantity of water; or stir 1 tsp citric acid (available in Asian and health-food shops) into 1 litre (1¾ pints) water; or make an ascorbic acid solution by crushing 4 × 500mg tablets of unflavoured vitamin C per 1 litre (1¾ pints) water.
Wash the fruit and prepare: apples, pineapples and bananas should be sliced about 5mm (¼in) thick, stone fruits halved and stoned, cherries stoned. Soak the fruit for 10 minutes, then drain on racks before drying.

Drying mushrooms

1 Put the unwashed mushrooms on a flat wire rack.

2 Dry in a warm, well-ventilated place for 1–2 days, turning occasionally.

3 When the mushrooms are dry, store in an airtight container for up to one year. To reconstitute, soak in warm water for 10–20 minutes until soft all over. Clean well before use.

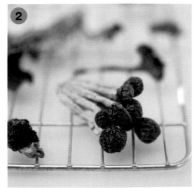

Drying tomatoes

1 Halve the tomatoes lengthways and remove the cores and seeds. Sprinkle with salt and place, cut side down, on a wire rack. Leave for 30 minutes.

2 Preheat the oven to its lowest setting. Dry the tomatoes for 10–12 hours until wrinkled and leathery. Store for up to six months in an airtight container.

RICH FLAVOUR

➜ Use plum or Roma tomatoes for the best results, as these have thick skin and a lower percentage of seed and jelly to flesh.

➜ Choose red, ripe summer tomatoes with a good flavour.

Drying herbs

1 To air-dry fresh herbs, tie them in small bunches and hang in a warm, well-ventilated place until dry.

2 To bag-dry herbs, tie the herbs in small bunches and cut holes in several brown paper bags. Put each bunch in a bag, leaf side down, and tie string around the stems. Hang in a warm, well-ventilated place until dry.

BAG DRYING

The following herbs are all prone to developing mould, so are best dried in a paper bag. Never try to dry them in a plastic bag.

➜ Basil
➜ Lemon balm
➜ Mint
➜ Tarragon

Herb ice cubes

Unlike drying, freezing preserves the flavour of herbs perfectly. However, it does affect their texture, which makes them suitable for cooking only, rather than garnishing. One of the easiest ways to freeze herbs is to freeze them in ice cubes. Simply add them to food and as it cooks, the ice cube will melt, releasing the herbs.

1 Wash the herbs, pat dry and chop finely. Put about 1 tsp in each compartment of an ice cube tray, then fill with water and freeze.

2 Pop the cubes out of the tray and put in plastic bags. Squeeze out the air, seal, label and return to the freezer. Use within three months.

FOOD STORAGE AND HYGIENE

Storing food properly and preparing food in a hygienic way is important to ensure that food remains as nutritious and flavourful as possible, and to reduce the risk of food poisoning. When you are preparing food, always follow these important guidelines:

- Wash your hands thoroughly before handling food and again between handling different types of food, such as raw and cooked meat and poultry. If you have any cuts or grazes on your hands, be sure to keep them covered with a waterproof plaster.

- Wash down worksurfaces regularly with a mild detergent solution or multi-surface cleaner.

- Use a dishwasher if available. Otherwise, wear rubber gloves for washing-up, so that the water temperature can be hotter than unprotected hands can bear. Change drying-up cloths and cleaning cloths regularly. Note that leaving dishes to drain is more hygienic than drying them with a teatowel.

- Keep raw and cooked foods separate, especially meat, fish and poultry. Wash kitchen utensils in between preparing raw and cooked foods. Never put cooked or ready-to-eat foods directly on to a surface which has just had raw fish, meat or poultry on it.

- Keep pets out of the kitchen if possible; or make sure they stay away from worksurfaces. Never allow animals on to worksurfaces.

Shopping

To ensure you buy the freshest produce possible, always choose fresh ingredients in prime condition from stores and markets that have a regular turnover of stock.

To ensure food safety, stick to the following guidelines:

- Make sure items are within their 'best before' or 'use by' date. (Foods with a longer shelf life have a 'best before' date; more perishable items have a 'use by' date.)

- When supermarket shopping, pack frozen and chilled items in an insulated cool bag at the check-out and put them into the freezer or fridge as soon as you get home.

- During warm weather in particular, buy perishable foods just before you return home. After you pack items at the supermarket check-out, sort them according to where you will store them when you get home – the fridge, freezer, storecupboard, vegetable, rack, fruit bowl, etc. This will make unpacking much easier – and quicker.

The storecupboard

Having a storecupboard well stocked with the basic essentials will save repeated visits to the shops to pick up missing items. Although storecupboard ingredients will generally last a long time, correct storage is important.

The following guidelines apply:

- Always check packaging for storage advice – even with familiar foods

because storage requirements may change if additives, sugar or salt have been reduced.

- Check storecupboard foods for their 'use by' date and do not use them if the date has passed.

- Keep all food cupboards scrupulously clean and make sure food containers and packets are properly sealed.

- Once opened, treat canned foods as though fresh. Always transfer the contents to a clean container, cover and keep in the fridge. Similarly, jars, sauce bottles and cartons should be kept chilled after opening. (Check the label for safe storage times after opening.)

- Transfer dry goods such as sugar, rice and pasta to moisture-proof containers. When supplies are used up, wash the container well and thoroughly dry before refilling with new supplies.

- Store oils in a dark cupboard away from any heat source as heat and light can make them turn rancid and affect their colour. For the same reason, buy olive oil in dark green bottles.

- Store vinegars in a cool place; they can turn bad in a warm environment.

- Store dried herbs, spices and flavourings in a cool, dark cupboard or in dark jars. Buy in small quantities as their flavour will not last indefinitely.

- Store flours and sugars in airtight containers.

Refrigerator storage

Fresh food needs to be kept in the cool temperature of the fridge to keep it in good condition and discourage the growth of harmful bacteria. Store day-to-day perishable items, such as opened jams and jellies, mayonnaise and bottled sauces, in the fridge along with eggs and dairy products, fruit juices, bacon, fresh and cooked meat (on separate shelves), and salads and vegetables (except potatoes which don't suit being stored in the cold).

A fridge should be kept at an operating temperature of 4–5°C. It is worth investing in a fridge thermometer to ensure the correct temperature is maintained.

To ensure your fridge is functioning effectively for safe food storage, follow these guidelines:

- Store cooked and raw foods on separate shelves to avoid bacterial cross-contamination, putting cooked foods on the top shelf. Ensure that all items are well wrapped.

- Never put hot food into the fridge as this will cause the internal temperature of the fridge to rise.

- Avoid overfilling, as this restricts the circulation of air and prevents the appliance from working properly.

- It can take some time for the fridge to return to the correct operating temperature once the door has been opened, so don't leave it open any longer than is necessary.

- Clean the fridge regularly, using a specially formulated germicidal 'refrigerator cleaners'. Alternatively, use a weak solution of bicarbonate of soda: 1 tbsp to 1 litre (1¾ pints) water.

- If your fridge doesn't have an automatic defrost facility, defrost it regularly.

MAXIMUM REFRIGERATOR STORAGE TIMES

For pre-packed foods, always adhere to the 'use-by' date on the packet. For other foods the following storage times should apply, providing the food is in prime condition when it goes into the fridge and that your fridge is in good working order:

Vegetables and fruit

salad leaves	2–3 days
green vegetables	3–4 days
soft fruit	1–2 days
hard and stone fruit	3–7 days

Dairy food

milk	4–5 days
cheese, soft	2–3 days
cheese, hard	1 week
eggs	1 week

Fish

fish	1 day
shellfish	1 day

Raw meat

joints	3 days
poultry	2 days
game	2 days
raw sliced meat	2 days
minced meat	1 day
offal	1 day
sausages	3 days
bacon	7 days

Cooked meat

joints	3 days
casseroles/stews	2 days
pies	2 days
sliced meat	2 days
ham	2 days
ham, vacuum-packed	1–2 weeks
(or according to the instructions on the pack)	

GLOSSARY OF COOKERY TERMS

Acidulated water Water to which lemon juice or vinegar has been added in which fruit or vegetables, such as pears or Jerusalem artichokes, are immersed to prevent discolouration.

Al dente Italian term commonly used to describe food, especially pasta and vegetables, which are cooked until tender but still firm to the bite.

Antipasto Italian selection of cold meats, fish, salads, etc., served as a starter.

Au gratin Describes a dish that has been coated with sauce, sprinkled with breadcrumbs or cheese and browned under the grill or in the oven. Low-sided gratin dishes are used.

Bain-marie Literally, a water bath, used to keep foods, such as delicate custards and sauces, at a constant low temperature during cooking. On the hob a double saucepan or bowl over a pan of simmering water is used; for oven cooking, the baking dish(es) is placed in a roasting tin containing enough hot water to come halfway up the sides.

Baking blind Pre-baking a pastry case before filling. The pastry case is lined with greaseproof paper and weighted down with dried beans or ceramic baking beans.

Baking powder A raising agent consisting of an acid, usually cream of tartar, and an alkali, such as bicarbonate of soda, which react to produce carbon dioxide. This expands during baking and makes cakes and breads rise.

Bard To cover the breast of game birds or poultry, or lean meat with fat to prevent the meat from drying out during roasting.

Baste To spoon the juices and melted fat over meat, poultry, game or vegetables during roasting to keep them moist. The term is also used to describe spooning over a marinade.

Beat To incorporate air into an ingredient or mixture by agitating it vigorously with a spoon, fork, whisk or electric mixer. The technique is also used to soften ingredients.

Béchamel Classic French white sauce, used as the basis for other sauces and savoury dishes.

Beurre manié Equal parts of flour and butter kneaded together to make a paste. Used to thicken soups, stews and casseroles. It is whisked into the hot liquid a little at a time at the end of cooking.

Bind To mix beaten egg or other liquid into a dry mixture to hold it together.

Blanch To immerse food briefly in fast-boiling water to loosen skins, such as peaches or tomatoes, or to remove bitterness, or to destroy enzymes and preserve the colour, flavour and texture of vegetables (especially prior to freezing).

Bone To remove the bones from meat, poultry, game or fish, so that it can be stuffed or rolled before cooking.

Bottle To preserve fruit, jams, pickles or other preserves in sterile glass jars.

Bouquet garni Small bunch of herbs — usually a mixture of parsley stems, thyme and a bay leaf — tied in muslin and used to flavour stocks, soups and stews.

Braise To cook meat, poultry, game or vegetables slowly in a small amount of liquid in a pan or casserole with a tight-fitting lid. The food is usually first browned in oil or fat.

Brochette Food cooked on a skewer.

Brûlée A French term, literally meaning 'burnt', used to refer to a dish with a crisp coating of caramelised sugar.

Butterfly To split a food, such as a large prawn or poussin, almost in half and open out flat, so that it will cook more quickly.

Calorie Strictly a kilocalorie, this is used in dietetics to measure the energy value of foods.

Canapé Small appetiser, served with drinks.

Candying Method of preserving fruit or peel by impregnating with sugar.

Caramelise To heat sugar or sugar syrup slowly until it is brown in colour; ie forms a caramel.

Carbonade Rich stew or braise of meat, which includes beer.

Casserole A dish with a tight-fitting lid used for slow-cooking meat, poultry and vegetables, now used to describe food cooked in this way.

Charcuterie French term for cooked pork products, including hams, sausages and terrines.

Chill To cool food in the fridge.

Chine To sever the rib bones from the backbone, close to the spine. This is done to meat joints, such as loin of pork or lamb, to make them easier to carve into chops after cooking.

Clarify To remove sediment or impurities from a liquid. Stock is clarified by heating with egg white, while butter is clarified by melting and skimming. Butter that has been clarified will withstand a higher frying temperature. To clarify butter, heat until melted and all bubbling stops. Remove from the heat and let stand until the sediment has sunk to the bottom, then gently pour off the fat, straining it through muslin to remove sediment.

Compote Fresh or dried fruit stewed in sugar syrup. Served hot or cold.

Concassé Diced fresh ingredient, used as a garnish. The term is most often applied to skinned, seeded tomatoes.

Consistency Term used to describe the texture of a mixture, eg firm, dropping or soft.

Coulis A smooth fruit or vegetable purée, thinned if necessary to a pouring consistency.

Court bouillon Aromatic cooking liquid containing wine, vinegar or lemon juice, used for poaching delicate fish, poultry or vegetables.

Cream To beat together fat and sugar until the mixture is pale and fluffy, and resembles whipped cream in texture and colour. The method is used in cakes and puddings that contain a high proportion of fat and require the incorporation of a lot of air.

Crêpe French term for a pancake.

Crimp To decorate the edge of a pie, tart or shortbread by pinching it at regular intervals to give a fluted effect.

Croquette Seasoned mixture of cooked potato and fish, meat, poultry or vegetables shaped into a small roll, coated with egg and breadcrumbs and shallow-fried.

Croûte Circle or other shaped piece of fried bread, typically used as a base for serving small game birds.

Croûtons Small pieces of fried or toasted bread, served with soups and salads.

Crudités Raw vegetables, usually cut into slices or sticks, typically served with a dipping sauce as an appetiser.

Crystallise To preserve fruit in a sugar syrup.

Curdle To cause sauces or creamed mixtures to separate once the egg is added, usually by overheating or over-beating.

Cure To preserve fish, meat or poultry by smoking, drying or salting.

Daube Braising meat and vegetables with stock, often with wine and herbs added.

Deglaze To heat stock, wine or other liquid with the cooking juices left in the pan after roasting or sautéeing, scraping and stirring vigorously to dissolve the sediment on the bottom of the pan.

Dégorge To draw out moisture from a food, eg salting aubergines to remove bitter juices.

Dice To cut food into small cubes.

Draw To remove the entrails from poultry or game.

Dredge To sprinkle food generously with flour, sugar, icing sugar, etc.

Dress To pluck, draw and truss poultry or game. The term is also used to describe tossing a salad in vinaigrette or other dressing.

Dry To preserve food such as fruit, pasta and pulses by dehydration.

Dust To sprinkle lightly with flour, cornflour, icing sugar, etc.

Emulsion A mixture of two liquids, which do not dissolve into one another, such as oil and vinegar. Vigorous shaking or heating will emulsify them, as for a vinaigrette.

En croûte Term used to describe food that is wrapped in pastry before cooking.

En papillote Term used to describe food that is baked in a greaseproof paper or baking parchment parcel and served from the paper.

Enzyme Organic substance in food that causes chemical changes. Enzymes are a complex group. Their action is usually halted during cooking.

Escalope Thin slice of meat, such as pork, veal or turkey, from the top of the leg, usually pan-fried.

Extract Concentrated flavouring, which is used in small quantities, eg yeast extract, vanilla extract.

Ferment Chemical change deliberately or accidentally brought about by fermenting agents, such as yeast or bacteria. Fermentation is utilised for making bread, yogurt, beer and wine.

Fillet Term used to describe boned breasts of birds, boned sides of fish, and the undercut of a loin of beef, lamb, pork or veal.

Flake To separate food, such as cooked fish, into natural pieces.

Flambé Flavouring a dish with alcohol, usually brandy or rum, which is then ignited so that the actual alcohol content is burned off.

Folding in Method of combining a whisked or creamed mixture with other ingredients by cutting and folding so that it retains its lightness. A large metal spoon or plastic-bladed spatula is used.

Frosting To coat leaves and flowers with a fine layer of sugar to use as a decoration. Also an American term for icing cakes.

Fry To cook food in hot fat or oil. There are various methods: shallow-frying in a little fat in a shallow pan; deep-frying where the food is totally immersed in oil; dry-frying in which fatty foods are cooked in a non-stick pan without extra fat; see also Stir-frying.

Galette Cooked savoury or sweet mixture shaped into a round.

Garnish A decoration, usually edible, such as parsley or lemon, which is used to enhance the appearance of a savoury dish.

Glaze A glossy coating given to sweet and savoury dishes to improve their appearance and sometimes flavour. Ingredients for glazes include beaten egg, egg white, milk and syrup.

Gluten A protein constituent of grains, such as wheat and rye, which develops when the flour is mixed with water to give the dough elasticity.

Grate To shred hard food, such as cheese and carrots, with a grater or food processor attachment.

Griddle A flat, heavy, metal plate used on the hob for cooking scones or for searing savoury ingredients.

Grind To reduce foods such as coffee beans, nuts and whole spices to small particles using a food mill, pestle and mortar, electric grinder or food processor.

Gut To clean out the entrails from fish.

Hang To suspend meat or game in a cool, dry place for a number of days to tenderise the flesh and develop flavour.

Hull To remove the stalk and calyx from soft fruits, such as strawberries.

Infuse To immerse flavourings, such as aromatic vegetables, herbs, spices and vanilla, in a liquid to impart flavour. Usually the infused liquid is brought to the boil, then left to stand for a while.

Julienne Fine 'matchstick' strips of vegetables or citrus zest, sometimes used as a garnish.

Knead To work dough by pummelling with the heel of the hand.

Knock back To knead a yeast dough for a second time after rising, to ensure an even texture.

Lard To insert small strips of fat or streaky bacon into the flesh of game birds and dry meat before cooking. A special larding needle is used.

Liaison A thickening or binding agent based on a combination of ingredients, such as flour and water, or oil and egg.

Macerate To soften and flavour raw or dried foods by soaking in a liquid, eg soaking fruit in alcohol.

Mandolin A flat wooden or metal frame with adjustable cutting blades for slicing vegetables.

Marinate To soak raw meat, poultry or game – usually in a mixture of oil, wine, vinegar and flavourings – to soften and impart flavour. The mixture, which is known as a marinade, may also be used to baste the food during cooking.

Medallion Small round piece of meat, usually beef or veal.

Mince To cut food into very fine pieces, using a mincer, food processor or knife.

Mocha Term which has come to mean a blend of chocolate and coffee.

Parboil To boil a vegetable or other food for part of its cooking time before finishing it by another method.

Pare To finely peel the skin or zest from vegetables or fruit.

Pâté A savoury mixture of finely chopped or minced meat, fish and/or vegetables, usually served as a starter with bread or toast.

Patty tin Tray of cup-shaped moulds for cooking small cakes and deep tartlets. Also called a bun tin.

Pectin A naturally occurring substance found in most varieties of fruit and some vegetables, which is necessary for setting jams and jellies. Commercial pectin and sugar with pectin are also available for preserve-making.

Pickle To preserve meat or vegetables in brine or vinegar.

Pith The bitter white skin under the thin zest of citrus fruit.

Pluck To remove the feathers from poultry and game birds.

Poach To cook food gently in liquid at simmering point; the surface should be just trembling.

Pot roast To cook meat in a covered pan with some fat and a little liquid.

Prove To leave bread dough to rise (usually for a second time) after shaping.

Purée To pound, sieve or liquidise vegetables, fish or fruit to a smooth pulp. Purées often form the basis for soups and sauces.

Reduce To fast-boil stock or other liquid in an uncovered pan to evaporate water and concentrate the flavour.

Refresh To cool hot vegetables very quickly by plunging into ice-cold water or holding under cold running water in order to stop the cooking process and preserve the colour.

Render To melt fat slowly to a liquid, either by heating meat trimmings, or to release the fat from fatty meat, such as duck or goose, during roasting.

Rennet An animal-derived enzyme used to coagulate milk in cheese-making. A vegetarian alternative is available.

Roast To cook meat by dry heat in the oven.

Roulade A soufflé or sponge mixture rolled around a savoury or sweet filling.

Roux A mixture of equal quantities of butter (or other fat) and flour cooked together to form the basis of many sauces.

Rub-in Method of incorporating fat into flour by rubbing between the fingertips, used when a short texture is required. Used for pastry, cakes, scones and biscuits.

Salsa Piquant sauce made from chopped fresh vegetables and sometimes fruit.

Sauté To cook food in a small quantity of fat over a high heat, shaking the pan constantly – usually in a sauté pan (a frying pan with straight sides and a wide base).

Scald To pour boiling water over food to clean it, or loosen skin, eg tomatoes. Used to describe heating milk to just below boiling point.

Score To cut parallel lines in the surface of food, such as fish (or the fat layer on meat), to improve its appearance or help it cook quickly.

Sear To brown meat quickly in a little hot fat before grilling or roasting.

Seasoned flour Flour mixed with a little salt and pepper, used for dusting meat, fish etc., before frying.

Shred To grate cheese or slice vegetables into very fine pieces or strips.

Sieve To press food through a perforated sieve to obtain a smooth texture.

Sift To shake dry ingredients through a sieve to remove lumps.

Simmer To keep a liquid just below boiling point.

Skim To remove froth, scum or fat from the surface of stock, gravy, stews, jam etc. Use either a skimmer, a spoon or kitchen paper.

Smoke To cure meat, poultry and fish by exposure to wood smoke.

Souse To pickle food, especially fish, in vinegar flavoured with spices.

Steam To cook food in steam, usually in a steamer over rapidly boiling water.

Steep To immerse food in warm or cold liquid to soften it, and sometimes to draw out strong flavours.

Sterilise To destroy bacteria in foods by heating.

Stew To cook food, such as tougher cuts of meat, in flavoured liquid which is kept at simmering point.

Stir-fry To cook small even-sized pieces of food rapidly in a little fat, tossing constantly over a high heat, usually in a wok.

Suet Hard fat of animal origin used in pastry and steamed puddings. A vegetarian alternative is readily available.

Sugar syrup A concentrated solution of sugar in water used to poach fruit and make sorbets, granitas, fruit juices, etc.

Sweat To cook chopped or sliced vegetables in a little fat without liquid in a covered pan over a low heat to soften.

Tepid The term used to describe temperature at approximately blood heat, ie 37°C (98.7°F).

Thermometer, Sugar/Fat Used for accurately checking the temperature of boiling sugar syrups, and fat for deep-frying respectively. Dual purpose thermometers are obtainable.

Truss To tie or skewer poultry or game into shape prior to roasting.

Unleavened Flat bread, such as pitta, made without a raising agent.

Vanilla sugar Sugar in which a vanilla pod has been stored to impart its flavour.

Whipping (whisking) Beating air rapidly into a mixture either with a manual or electric whisk. Whipping usually refers to cream.

Zest The thin coloured outer layer of citrus fruit, which can be removed in fine strips with a zester.

INDEX

P

paella 248
pancetta
    poussins with pancetta,
    artichoke and potato
    salad 133
pan-frying
    chicken 122
    eggs 57
    fish 83
    fruit 225
    meat and game 157
    potatoes 198
pancakes 63
pans 13
papaya 221
parchment paper 332
parfait, pistachio 396
Parma ham
    stuffed chicken breasts 128
parsley
    parsley sauce 21
    salsa verde 26
parsnips 193
    parsnip soup with cheese
    crisps 48
    roasted potatoes and
    parsnips 207
passion fruit 221
    lemon and passion fruit fool
    242
pasta 270–2
    chilli Bolognese 278
    classic lasagne 279
    cooking 272
    fusilli with chilli and tomatoes
    274
    lasagne 279
    macaroni cheese 280
    penne with smoked salmon
    276
    quick and easy carbonara
    277
    ravioli 271
    spaghetti Bolognese 275
    pasta machines 270
pastry 286–307
    baklava 293
    blind baking 290
    choux 292
    decorations 291
    filo 293, 297, 300
    goat's cheese parcels 300
    hot water crust 233
    leek and pea flan 71
    lining tins 290
    making 288–9
    nut and cranberry terrine
    233
    puff 289, 294–6, 306
    quiche lorraine 299
    rough puff 289

sausage rolls 296
sealing 291
shortcrust 288
sweet shortcrust 288
topping 291
treacle tart 301
using 290–1
see also pies, tarts
pâte sucrée 303
patisserie see biscuits, cakes,
    pastry, tarts
pavlova 62
peaches
    brandied peaches 418
    peeling 218
    summer gratin 240
peanut butter
    all-in-one peanut cookies
    344
pearl barley 250
pears 216
    drunken pears 237
    easy pear and toffee tarte
    tatin 306
    rhubarb and pear crumble
    235
peas 186
pecan nuts
    banana and pecan muffins
    338
    ultimate chocolate brownie
    360
pectin 414
peeling vegetables 191
penne with smoked salmon 276
peppers 189
    roasted stuffed peppers 212
pesto 23, 202
pheasant with cider and apples
    177
pickles
    mixed dill pickle 432
    pickled onions 419
pie tins 14
pies
    apple pie 304
    baked raspberry meringue
    pie 76
    chicken and artichoke pie
    297
    classic apple pie 304
    leek and ham galette 295
    lemon meringue pie 303
    old-fashioned fish pie 106
    salmon and asparagus pie
    298
    shepherd's pie 171
    steak and kidney pie 294
    sticky banoffee pies 386
    see also pastry, tarts
pilau
    spiced chicken pilau 255

pine nuts 293
pineapples 220
piping
    chocolate 368
    sauces 33
pistachio nuts
    baklava 293
    Italian ice cream cake 408
    pistachio and date ice cream
    403
    pistachio parfait 396
pizza 316
    ready-made bases 328
    toppings 316
    tuna melt pizza 328
plums
    American-style plum cobbler
    239
    plum chutney 420, 428
    sauce 305
poaching
    eggs 56
    fish 82
    fruit 224
    poultry 125
polenta 252
    cheesy polenta 163, 258
    warm cornbread 323
polypropylene chopping boards
    10
pomegranate 221
pork
    belly of pork with cider 173
    carving 161
    honey roast pork 172
    Italian meatballs 176
    pork and noodle stir-fry 285
    preparing 151–3
    roasting 161
    spicy pork and bean stew
    263
pot-roasting
    meat and game 157
    poultry 124
potatoes
    chips 198
    crushing 196
    cullen skink 49
    fish and chips 105
    frying 198
    mashing 196
    mussel and potato stew 104
    old-fashioned fish pie 106
    potato and chorizo tortilla
    58
    poussins with pancetta,
    artichoke and potato
    salad 133
    roasted potatoes and
    parsnips 207
    roasting 201
    vichyssoise with spinach

cream 43
    warm new potato salad
    202
pots and pans 13–14
potted prawns 101
potting preserves 413
poultry 110–39
    buying 112
    cooking 118–25
    freezing 113, 447
    marinades 125
    preparing 112–17
    roasting 118, 119
    storing 112
    see also chicken, duck, etc
poussins 112
    poussins with pancetta,
    artichoke and potato
    salad 133
praline, mixed nut 372
prawns 87
    potted prawns 101
    prawn and lemon risotto
    256
    special fried rice 262
    Thai green shellfish curry
    108
    Thai noodles with prawns
    284
preserves 410–33
    bottled fruits 418
    chutneys 420
    fruit curds and cheeses 417
    jams 414
    jellies 416
    marmalade 415
    pickles 419
    potting 413
    preparing jars 412
    refrigerator preserves 421
    relishes 422
    sauces 423
    testing for a set 413
pressure cookers 13
processors see food processors
prunes
    fruity tea cake 336
    guinea fowl with prunes 138
    lamb, prune and almond
    tagine 169
    rabbit casserole with prunes
    179
puddings
    almond toffee meringues
    388
    American-style plum cobbler
    239
    apples with butterscotch
    sauce 387
    baked apples 236
    baked orange custard 72
    baked raspberry meringue